Mark Twain
and
The Gilded Age

From The Theatre *(London), December 1, 1879*
Courtesy Mark Twain Home Board, Hannibal, Mo.

"There's millions in it!"
(John T. Raymond as Colonel Sellers)

Mark Twain

and

The Gilded Age

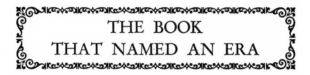

THE BOOK
THAT NAMED AN ERA

BRYANT MOREY FRENCH

SOUTHERN METHODIST UNIVERSITY PRESS : DALLAS

Published with the Assistance of a Grant
From the Ford Foundation
Under its Program for the Support of Publication
In the Humanities and Social Sciences

PRINTED IN THE UNITED STATES OF AMERICA
BY THE
SOUTHERN METHODIST UNIVERSITY PRINTING DEPARTMENT
AT DALLAS, TEXAS

To Greenie

who first told me of the
importance of Mark Twain

Acknowledgments

EVERY WORK worth its salt is in a very true sense a social product, and the author acts not only as an individual writer but as a scribe for the collective effort of many others. In this spirit, then, I make the following acknowledgments.

I am indebted to the trustees of the Mark Twain Estate for permission to quote from a number of unpublished manuscripts, letters, and notes of Samuel L. Clemens, and to Frederick Anderson, Editor of the Mark Twain Papers, for his unstinting cooperation in making these materials available to me and for his many helpful suggestions. I am likewise indebted to Harper & Row, Publishers, for permission to quote extensively from *The Writings of Mark Twain*, Author's National Edition.

I wish to express my gratitude to Helen Azhderian, Marion Schulman, and Robert Knutson of the Doheny Memorial Library, University of Southern California, for reference assistance far beyond the call of duty; to Donald Gallup, Curator of the Collection of American Literature, Yale University Library, for giving me generous access to the Willard S. Morse Collection and other files of Mark Twain manuscripts; and to Mrs. Marian Clarke, Curator of the Watkinson Library, Trinity College, Hartford, for granting equally generous access to the Warner Papers and that library's Clemens collection. Other institutions whose staffs deserve mention for their help are the Mark Twain Library and Memorial, Hartford; Mark Twain Home Board, Hannibal, Missouri; Kansas State Historical Society, Topeka; Bancroft Library, University of

California, Berkeley; Hartford Public Library; and Bibliothèque Nationale, Paris.

It is with a profound sense of scholarly fellowship that I wish to acknowledge the unreserved generosity of Hamlin Hill, of the University of New Mexico, in volunteering valuable information regarding *Gilded Age* manuscript and in exchanging data, interpretations, and evaluations. I wish to thank Drew B. Pallette, of the University of Arizona, and Eleazer Lecky and Arthur Kooker, of the University of Southern California, for their many helpful suggestions during the period of gestation and writing of the present volume; and Bruce R. McElderry, Jr., for his invaluable advice as an "elder statesman." I am grateful to L. R. Trilling for his critical reading of the book while yet in proof.

It gives me especial pleasure to thank Professor M. Mendelson, Writer's Union, Moscow, for the friendly and lively interview he granted me in March, 1959, and his subsequent intercultural exchange of correspondence.

Among the many other colleagues, librarians, curators, and officials who have given me assistance are Chester L. Davis, John D. Gordan, Margaret Hackett, Mrs. Horace B. Learned, Martha Nolan, Felix Pollak, David A. Randall, William H. Runge, Floyd C. Shoemaker, Maynard Smith, Mrs. Samuel C. Webster, John A. Winkler, Lyle H. Wright, and Emily Zeitlin. As a personal note I wish to express my heartfelt gratitude to Dorothe, Morey, Jeffery, Kristina, and Wayne for enduring with sweet patience the inordinate absorption of husband and father in the task here represented.

Last but far from least, I want to thank my wife, Ruth, for her enthusiastic and unfailing encouragement and for a superlative job of indexing.

B.M.F.

Los Angeles
May 5, 1965

Contents

Illustrations

xi

PART I

The Novel Is Born

CHAPTER I

The Expectant Father

"I CONSIDER IT one of the most astonishing novels that was ever written." So wrote Mark Twain to the American people in the columns of the New York *Daily Graphic*, April 17, 1873.[1] The novel was *The Gilded Age*, written by Twain in collaboration with Charles Dudley Warner, the manuscript of which they had just completed. A month later Clemens, accompanied by his wife, Olivia, and his fourteen-month-old daughter, Susy, left for England. He had planned the trip the previous year as a prolonged second visit to a country with which he had had as yet but short acquaintance; but a more practical purpose was also being served. Having run the risk of a legally invalid British copyright for his last book, *Roughing It*,[2] he had decided to take no chances with the new novel, which was to be published simultaneously in the United States and England, but be safely residing in London when the book was published; for in the days before the Berne Convention simultaneous publication of an American book in the United Kingdom did not assure protection without the physical presence of the author in a British residence on the publication date.[3] Clemens was under the impression that *The Gilded Age* was scheduled for early fall publication and his plans for the combined pleasure and business trip had been made accordingly.[4] This supposition, however, proved to be little more than a hope. As late as the end of September or the early part of October, Mrs. Clemens, writing home, reported, "There has not one sheet of Mr. Clemens's proof come yet."[5] At the suggestion of British friends Clemens made use of the extended

3

waiting period by lecturing in London in order to build not only a "larger but a more enviable reputation" before the book should appear.[6] After a few nights of lectures in mid-October, he sailed for home with his family on the twenty-first but immediately returned to London to continue the lecture series and read proofsheets.[7] His proofreading continued until the middle of December.[8] The book was finally published a few days before Christmas.[9]

The Gilded Age made its appearance in the United States in the midst of the financial crisis of 1873. Clemens, who had sailed from the United States during the initial panic in the American stock market[10] and must have read of the severe September crash and have witnessed the temporary London panic in November, was naturally fearful of the adverse effect of the business crisis upon sales.[11] Nevertheless, by the time he had returned from London, at the end of January, 1874, the book was in its third printing and twenty-six thousand copies had been sold.[12] In a letter to his recently acquired Scottish friend Dr. John Brown, author of the engaging dog story *Rab and His Friends,* dated from Hartford, February 28, he wrote:

> The fearful financial panic hit the book heavily, for we published it in the midst of it. But nevertheless in the 8 weeks that have now elapsed since the day we published, we have sold 40,000 copies; which gives £3,000 royalty to be divided between the authors.[13] This is really the largest two-months' sale which any American book has ever achieved (unless one excepts the cheaper editions of Uncle Tom's Cabin). The average price of our book is 16 shillings a copy—Uncle Tom was 2 shillings a copy. But for the panic our sale would have been doubled, I verily believe. I do not believe the sale will ultimately go over 100,000 copies.[14]

Considering the economic depression during which *The Gilded Age* was published,[15] initial sales were exceptionally good (as Clemens himself admits above). Within the first year, something over fifty thousand copies had been sold, and by the end of 1879 over fifty-six thousand.[16]

It may seem surprising in the light of mid-twentieth-century marketing procedure and shopping mores that a book published immediately before Christmas, when presumably the Christmas buying rush was practically over, should have achieved what were in that day record sales in so short a time. To effect comparable sales in the book business today—sales necessitating three printings in the first month—a novel such as *The Gilded Age* that is intended for the Christmas trade would have to be on display in the book-stores, with the accompaniment of advertising fanfare, by mid-October. The fact is that a large network of agents and their sales-men had for months been taking orders, placing advertisements in small-town newspapers in remote corners of the United States, and seeking out prospective customers among all classes of the popula-tion. For *The Gilded Age* was a subscription book, and subscrip-tion bookselling was in its heyday in America. Not only that, but Mark Twain's best-seller *The Innocents Abroad,* published a scant four years before, and his almost equally popular *Roughing It,* pub-lished only a year before, had both been subscription books and, together with Twain's widespread reputation as a lecturer and writer, had established a ready market in the canvassers' territories.

Subscription books, the traditional backbone of commercial book publishing enterprise, had been first sold, in North America, in the early Colonial period, and the development of subscription publishing in the English colonies and the post-Revolutionary United States had paralleled that in Great Britain and continental Europe. In the United States publishing by subscription had begun along two independent lines, underwriting in advance by patrons (the earlier form) and peddling from door to door after publica-tion. The latter practice, which had begun with the chapbook peddlers of the Colonial period, was, according to Frank Luther Mott, "eventually assimilated into the subscription projects because traveling agents became necessary to get the subscription pledges— and there was little difference between a book-agent selling books already printed and a solicitor selling books from a prospectus in advance of publication."[17] Subscription bookselling developed rapidly in the United States after the Civil War and employed an "army of book agents numbering many thousands who skirmished through every city, town and hamlet, armed with their prospec-tuses showing various styles of binding and containing persuasive testimonials to back up the carefully memorized sales arguments of the solicitors."[18]

For the most part, the peddling of subscription books did not interfere seriously with the retail bookstore trade, for there was a vast territory in the frontier United States only scantily served by retail book outlets, and the titles canvassed for were generally not available in bookstores.[19] "Gift books and sets of collected works of an author, text-books of an encyclopedic character, and children's publications were the regular stock-in-trade of subscription book-selling."[20] A kind of black market did, however, exist, and both the distributing agent and the individual canvasser employed by him would on occasion make extra commissions by selling subscription books at a discount to bookstores in violation of contracts with the publishers.[21]

The two forms of retailing were, nevertheless, competitive and mutually predatory, particularly when publishing houses chose to utilize both methods simultaneously. Publishers could not sell through bookstores without handicapping the sales of their own agents; conversely, booksellers complained when they could not carry on their shelves titles a demand for which had been created by the itinerant canvassers.[22] The fact that a number of publishers, in order to obtain the far larger market reached through canvassing, sold their books exclusively by the subscription method[23] made it difficult enough for the regular booksellers. The further fact that the works of some of the most popular living authors were sold *only* by this method heightened the booksellers' alarm. Mark Twain was one of these authors.[24]

Samuel Clemens was a convinced advocate of subscription book-selling for the right kind of book. Twelve years after *The Gilded Age* appeared he was to prove his point by his spectacular success in publishing, through his own firm, Webster and Company, the two-volume *Memoirs* of General Ulysses Grant, a high point in the annals of the book trade.[25] He realized, nevertheless, that "mighty few books" that can be classified "under the head of *literature* will sell by subscription."[26] A sampling of subscription book titles of the time picked at random bears this out: *Cuba, with Pen and Pencil*, the *Life of Barnum*, *Woman's Pilgrimage in the Holy Land*,

General McClellan's *Golden States, or West of the Rocky Mountains, Knots Untied* (a book by a New York detective), William H. Seward's *Voyage Around the World*.[27] Clemens' own virtually unclassifiable satire-travel books *The Innocents Abroad* and *Roughing It* had been sold only by subscription with notable success, as already mentioned. A novel, however, was something else again. There may be only slight exaggeration in William Dean Howells' statement that "no book of literary quality was made to go by subscription except Mr. Clemens's books."[28] In fact, the reviewer of *The Gilded Age* in the literary magazine *Old and New* commented:

> This curious book is a novel in more senses than one. It is a story; and it is, moreover, the first instance, so far as we know, of a story-book issued "by subscription." That this mode of publishing should be selected by businessmen for a novel is an interesting indication of the enormous extent to which reading is now practised in this country; for the subscription publishing-business, more than the "regular," must suit a widely-dispersed average of customers, and it is a very reading public indeed that buys novels. Except to readers, a novel is no great luxury.[29]

Clemens was well aware of the business risk involved. In a letter to the publisher on May 3, 1873, just a few days before he and Warner handed in the manuscript, he advises: ". . . think it all over—Sheldon & Co think we will make a serious and damaging mistake if we try to sell a novel by subscription."[30] Yet a little over a year later, Warner was writing to the poet and future novelist Helen Hunt, who had solicited advice: "There is no doubt . . . that 'by subscription' is the only way for the author to make any money. I will tell you. The copyright just to Clemens and myself . . . on 50000 Gilded Age has been eighteen thousand dollars. . . ."[31] Apparently impressed by Clemens' success in using this method, especially when in partnership with another author, John W. De Forest wrote to Clemens proposing that they gather together stories by each of them and issue a "conjoint volume by subscription."[32]

During the 1860's, or roughly from just before the Civil War until several years afterward, Hartford, Connecticut, was the publishing center of the United States. It was also one of the four principal subscription publishing centers, the other three being Philadelphia, Cincinnati, and Chicago.[33] According to D. P. O'Harra, "From 1861-68 about thirty subscription sets were published by 14 Hartford firms. These yielded a return of $5,000,000. About 10,000 book agents were used in selling 1,426,000 copies."[34] It was to Hartford that Clemens had moved in 1871, scarcely more than a year and a half after his marriage to Olivia Langdon, daughter of a wealthy coal merchant of Elmira, New York; and it was the offer of a Hartford subscription book publisher, Elisha Bliss, Jr., to publish *The Innocents Abroad* that had initially brought him to the city. During his courtship of Livy, as Olivia was called by her family and friends, Clemens had closed the contract with Bliss. The attractiveness of the city as a place of bourgeois residence that maintained a standard of living to which he felt his wife was entitled and to which he himself aspired,[35] and the stimulating company of the friends he had already made there, led Clemens to leave the home in Buffalo, New York, which his father-in-law had given as a marriage present, and his partnership in the *Buffalo Express*, the editorship of which he had found uncongenial, and to move into the charmed circle of Hartford's "Nook Farm" colony of writers and intellectuals, numbering among them Harriet Beecher Stowe, Charles Dudley Warner, the actor William Gillette, the militant woman's rights advocate Isabella Beecher Hooker, and the Reverend Joseph H. Twichell.

Besides Mark Twain's books, the American Publishing Company, of which Elisha Bliss, Jr., was the president and manager, at that time published, by subscription, the books of the then popular Albert D. Richardson, as well as such miscellaneous titles as H. S. Olcott's *People from Another World*, Edward King's *The Great South*, and Joel Tyler Headley's *History of the Rebellion*.[36] Even before publication of Twain's best-selling *Innocents Abroad*, the company had had a large success with the works of Richardson.[37] Clemens' confidence in the company was justified not alone by the sales record it made with his books in the early seventies;[38] in 1883, three years after he had ceased publishing with the firm, interpreting as dishonesty Elisha Bliss's astute profit-making, he wrote to his friend George W. Cable, "if I were going to advise you to issue through a Hartford house, I would say, every time, go to my former publishers, The American Publishing Company, 284 Asylum St. They swindled me out of huge sums of money in the old days, but they do know how to push a book; . . ."[39] The company had agents throughout the United States—in Boston, New York, Philadelphia, Syracuse, Cincinnati, Chicago, San Francisco— who were shipped books bearing their own imprint below that of the parent firm.[40] The canvassers, enticed from the ranks of "disabled Soldiers, aged and other Clergymen having leisure hours, Teachers and Students during vacation, &c., Invalids unable to endure hard physical labor, Young Men who wish to travel and gather knowledge and experience,"[41] and "Women who can devote time to the work, often . . . the best of canvassers,"[42] were given territories, books, and prospectuses and sent forth to solicit, from homes of the wealthy to tenements, from business offices to mine shafts, from parish houses to barrooms.[43]

Typical of the frontier environment in which Mark Twain had had his journalistic apprenticeship was Anton Roman, proprietor of A. Roman & Company, San Francisco agent for the American Publishing Company. Roman, a native of Bavaria, migrated in 1851 to Shasta, California, where he became a successful gold miner. Wandering into a bookstore one day, he was induced to buy a large stock of books, which he took back to Shasta to sell during the winter months. Liking bookselling better than mining, he went to San Francisco in 1859 and started a bookstore. Though in the eighties he became best known as the founder and publisher of the *Overland Monthly*, edited in its early years by Bret Harte, in 1874 he was busy distributing and selling books to the West Coast, not least of which was *The Gilded Age*.[44] The first copies, which had been promised for December 15, finally arrived in March and were added to the canvassers' stocks in a choice of cloth or leather bindings.[45] So insidious had been the conditioning of the speculative optimism of the postwar boom that, even amidst a narration of insults and discouragements, one of Roman's women canvassers referred in her memoir to Twain's book as "The Golden Age."[46]

Among the many occupations and trades satirized by Mark Twain in the course of his long career subscription book canvassing was not included. Indeed, Clemens was too thoroughly involved in subscription publishing to be able to afford the detachment requisite for satirizing it. As one student of Mark Twain has pointed out,

With one or two minor exceptions, all of Mark Twain's books for the first thirty years of his writing career were sold by subscription—at first by the American Publishing Company of Hartford, . . . later by Osgood of Boston, and finally by his own firm of Charles L. Webster and Company. Not until the firm of Harper and Brothers became his publisher in 1896 did he abandon this not altogether happy method of marketing his books, and even after that date he lapsed into the former method upon occasion . . . .[47]

Clemens was not inclined to bite the hand that fed him, at least directly. A writer in *Book News* in 1885 recognized this fact: "If Mark Twain did not find it expedient to adopt this peculiar method of selling his books, he would have a good opportunity for the exercise of his humor in picturing an agent's sales and attempts at sales."[48] When, as early as 1870, a reader of his "Memoranda" department in the *Galaxy* urged him not to ignore the traveling book agents, "especially the 'red-nosed chaps' who sell 'juveniles,' temperance tracts, and such like delectable fodder," he admitted that "such subscription canvassers, probably, are all this correspondent's fancy paints them"; then added, "None but those canvassers who sell compact concentrations of solid wisdom, like the work entitled 'The Innocents Abroad,' can really be said to be indispensable to the nation."[49]

In the United States a writer who published by the subscription method was distinctly at a disadvantage insofar as book reviews were concerned—for two reasons. One reason was that, because the typical subscription publisher's list was made up, as we have seen, largely of collected works, encyclopedic textbooks, juveniles, and gift books, the reviewers almost completely ignored the field. The other reason was that the subscription book, regardless of its individual merits, faced the actual antagonism of the literary reviewers, who were dependent upon the regular trade for their material and who consequently evinced their self-interest in snobbism. "Subscription books are in bad odor," said one Brahminical editor, "and cannot possibly circulate among the best classes of readers, owing to the general and not unfounded prejudice against them as a class."[50] "They are not *published*," wrote Professor S. S. Haldeman to the president of the American Book Trade Union, "and, as a consequence, they cannot be quoted, nor can they be reviewed in respectable periodicals."[51]

If any subscription writer could overcome this handicap it was Mark Twain. Both he and Warner were skilful at whetting their audience's appetite and uncommonly resourceful in soliciting notices. Their campaign had begun the moment the novel was finished. In his letter to the editor of the *Daily Graphic* the preceding April, Twain announced the forthcoming book as follows:

> During the last two months my next-door neighbor, Chas. Dudley Warner, has dropped his "Back-Log Studies," & he & I have written a bulky novel in partner-ship. He has worked up the fiction & I have hurled in the facts. I consider it one of the most astonishing novels that ever was written. Night after night I sit up reading it over & over again and crying. It will be published early in the fall, with plenty of pictures. Do you consider this an advertisement?—& if so, do you charge for such things, when a man is your friend & an orphan?[52]

Even earlier both Clemens and Warner had written Whitelaw Reid, editor of the *New-York Tribune,* proposing an announcement in that newspaper. From Hartford, on April 7, Warner wrote:

DEAR MR. REID:

> Maybe it's a great piece of presumption, but Mark and I are writing a novel, and can so nearly see the end of it that it is safe to speak of it. No one here, except our wives, knows anything of it. We conceived the design early in the winter, but were not able to get seriously at work on it till some time in January. . . .
> We hope to get it ready for the press before Clemens goes to England. . . .[53]

"It *is* an experiment," Reid replied. "Still it has been successful two or three times abroad, and you and Twain will make it successful if anybody can here. Besides it seems to me that you and he were well calculated to fit into and supplement each other's work. Good luck attend you both."[54] Clemens wrote in his own manner: "We want a mere mention, *now,* with either exceedingly complimentary additions, or pitiless abuse accompanied with profanity. We shall be down there within a fortnight. We think a pretty good deal of this novel I can tell you; even the paper it is written on cost eleven dollars."[55]

Reid turned the latter plea over to his colleague John Hay with the endorsement, "Dear Hay. Here's a chance for a rollicking bit of minion"; and Hay, the diplomat and poet, rollicked as follows in the *Tribune's* columns two days after the *Graphic* letter:

Beaumont and Fletcher may now retire as instances of genius working in double harness. Mark Twain and Charles Dudley Warner have written a novel in partnership! . . . The book deals with the salient features of our American life of to-day; and, as might easily be divined, is in the nature of a satire. It is known to contain all the profound philosophy, the sound learning, and geological truth which are found in "Innocents Abroad" and "Roughing It," and even more of the practical wisdom and agricultural suggestion than in "My Summer in a Garden." It is no holiday work. It deals with every aspect of modern society, and we are authorized to announce that the paper on which it is written cost eleven dollars.[56]

Alarmed over the possibly negative effect such flippancy of editorial comment might have upon the book's reception—flippancy was the prerogative of the humorist, not his critic—Clemens wrote immediately to Reid:

HARTFORD,
April 22nd, 1873.

MY DEAR REID:

. . . All right! You go ahead and give us that other notice. Bilious? I was more than bilious—I was *scared.* When a man starts out in a new role, the public always says he is a fool and won't succeed. So I wanted to make every knife cut that could *help* us succeed, anyway. Why of *course* The Tribune would make Hartford talk, and the rest of the country for that matter—else why would I be so solicitous about what The Tribune said? That is just the point. I want The Tribune to say it *right* and say it powerful—and then I will answer for the consequences. The consequence will be that all other papers will *follow suit*—which you know as well as I do. And then our game is made and our venture launched with a fair wind instead of a baffling one.

Yours,

CLEMENS.[57]

Meanwhile, apparently, Reid had sent Clemens a copy of another editorial notice (probably his own), and later the same day, after the mail had arrived, another note was dashed off.

HARTFORD,
April 22nd, 1873.

MY DEAR REID:

Now, *that* notice is bully! If any man is deceived by that he will be deceived in the happy direction, at any rate—and that is what we want. All right, now!

Yours,

MARK.[58]

This "bully" notice, which was published in the *Tribune* the next day, stated that the novel was "likely to prove the chief literary event of the season," then continued:

It is called "The Gilded Age"—a name which gives the best promise of the wealth of satire and observation which it is easy to expect from two such authors. It is an unusual and a courageous enterprise for two gentlemen who have already won honorable distinction in other walks of literature to venture upon untrodden paths with a work so ambitious and so important as this is likely to be. In one sense there is nothing to fear. An immense audience is already assured beforehand; and it is fair to conclude that writers who have displayed so much wit, insight and delicacy and fanciful observation in former works, will not be unprovided with the equipment which is necessary to successful fiction. The new novel will be eagerly looked for and enormously read, and we hazard little in predicting that it will contain as much food for thought as for laughter.[59]

(The "delicacy and fanciful observation" unquestionably refers to Warner.)[60]

Both items were quickly quoted by the *Chicago Tribune,* a newspaper which gave the forthcoming publication particularly generous publicity throughout the year.[61] This prepublication campaign, indeed, had notable results; when the book was actually issued many reviews began by speaking of the "long-talked-of new work," "this much-heralded book," "of which the public has heard and expected so much." The *Springfield* (Mass.) *Republican* said: "Scarcely any announcement of the season has aroused livelier anticipations than the promise of a book which should be the joint work of those favorite writers, Charles Dudley Warner and 'Mark Twain.' " The New York *World* remarked that "the 'Gilded Age' was looked for with the confident expectation that it would prove more amusing than 'My Summer in a Garden' or 'The Innocents Abroad' "; Theodore Tilton's *Golden Age* agreed that "there was at once a general interest, not unmixed with curiosity, to see the result of this strange experiment in literary work." According to the Boston *Saturday Evening Gazette,* few works had been looked for "with more of interest and curiosity . . . ."[62]

Not all of the campaign, however, went as satisfactorily. Warner asked E. C. Stedman to review the book in *Scribner's;* but after having read it through "with curious interest" this apostle of ideality found his head "in no clear & settled condition with respect to its qualities" and declined. "I beg you will believe in my loyalty," he wrote, "till I find some more feasible opportunity of showing it."[63] Stedman asked Richard Watson Gilder of *Scribner's* to find "some level-headed & sound-hearted fellow" to undertake the chore, and Gilder handed the proofsheets over to the journalist and western adventure writer Noah Brooks.[64] In the end, *Scribner's* ignored the book. So did *Harper's,* the *North American Review,* and the *Overland Monthly*. The *Nation* merely noted receipt of it in the semiannual index.[65]

Even Clemens' faithful friend William Dean Howells, editor of the *Atlantic,* who could usually be depended on to start the "sheep jumping in the right places," rather than write a review in which he could not with a clear conscience voice praise, chose to remain silent and eventually placed the novel without comment under "Other Publications."[66] "I will withold [*sic*] my public opinion altogether if you like," Howells wrote Warner, "and if on revision of the book, it does not strike me more favorably, I should prefer to do so; though I should be able to praise parts of it with heartiness and sincerity."[67]

In at least one instance, *The Gilded Age* was denied a review at the express wish of Clemens. Shortly after he and Warner had finished the novel, early in May, Edward H. House, who was visiting the Clemenses in Hartford, read it in manuscript, liked it, and "wanted to do it a favor." According to Clemens,

He proposed to review it in the New York Tribune before some other journal should get a chance to give it a start which might not be to its advantage. But the project failed. He said Whitelaw Reid abused him and charged him with bringing a dishonorable proposal from Warner and me. That seemed strange; indeed unaccountable, for there was nothing improper about . . . the proposition, and would not have been if it really had come from Warner and me. . . .[68]

Having "taken House's report at its face value," Clemens was furious. On shipboard en route to England he wrote Warner:

Ask House to tell you about Whitelaw Reid. He is a contemptible cur, and I want nothing more to do with him. I don't want the Tribune to have the book at all. Please tell Bliss *not to send a copy there under any circumstances.* If you feel at any time like explaining, you may tell Reid or anyone that I desired this.[69]

One of the most interesting and unexpected results of the co-authors' private promotion—certainly the most exasperating to Clemens—was the review in the newly founded tabloid the *Daily Graphic,* allegedly an unauthorized journalistic beat. This is the way Clemens described it thirty-three years later in his autobiography:

When Charles Dudley Warner and I were about to bring out *The Gilded Age,* the editor of the *Daily Graphic* persuaded me to let him have an advance copy, he giving me his word of honor that no notice of it should appear in his paper until after the *Atlantic Monthly* notice should have appeared. This reptile published a review of the book within three days afterward. I could not really complain, because he had only given me his word of honor as security. I ought to have required of him something substantial. I believe his notice did not deal mainly with the merit of the book, or the lack of it, but with my moral attitude toward the public. It was charged that I had used my reputation to play a swindle upon the public—that Mr. Warner had written as much as half of the book, and that I had used my name to float it and give it currency—a currency which it could not have acquired without my name—and that this conduct of mine was a grave fraud upon the people. The *Graphic* was not an authority upon any subject whatever. It had a sort of distinction in that it was the first and only illustrated daily newspaper that the world had seen; but it was without character, it was poorly and cheaply edited, its opinion of a book or of any other work of art was of no consequence. Everybody knew this, yet all the critics in America, one after the other, copied the *Graphic's* criticism, merely changing the phraseology, and left me under that charge of dishonest conduct. Even the great Chicago *Tribune*, the most important journal in the Middle West, was not able to invent anything fresh, but adopted the view of the humble *Daily Graphic*, dishonesty charge and all. . . .[70]

The *Daily Graphic* review actually appeared on December 23,[71] the probable publication date of the novel.[72] As the Boston *Transcript*, the *New York Herald*, and, presumably, other papers published reviews on December 22 and 23,[73] the *Graphic* notice can hardly be considered a beat. What angered Clemens and caused him in retrospect to single out the *Daily Graphic* for attack was the charge of "dishonest conduct" that constituted "a grave fraud upon the people," a charge that in Clemens' memory was associated with the *Graphic*.[74] In reality, the *Graphic* was guilty of no such offense. The closest it came to questioning Clemens' integrity was the facetious remark: "We are inclined to think that Mark Twain originally intended that the story should be made as incoherent and exasperating as possible, by way of a joke, but that he was finally overruled, . . ." Although the review was highly derogatory, its derogation was devoted almost exclusively to the "wonderful weakness" of the plot, the general lack of cohesiveness, and the coauthors' purportedly harmful influence upon one another's styles, literary criticisms shared by many of the reviewers.[75] If Clemens believed, as he seems to have, that the *Graphic* review was the first one out, it is quite understandable that to him the *Daily Graphic* rather than the *New-York Tribune* appeared to have started the sheep jumping—and in the wrong places.

Clemens' more serious charge that all the critics in America copied the *Graphic* in accusing him of duplicity deserves examination, for it bears directly upon consideration of the divided reception accorded *The Gilded Age*.[76] The "charge of dishonest conduct" originated not in the *Graphic* but in the *Chicago Tribune*. This influential newspaper, which as late as November had been publishing favorable press releases about the forthcoming novel, in its review dramatically reversed its stand. It declared that the authors had "wilfully degraded their craft, abused the people's trust, and provoked a stern condemnation."

It is not as if the book had been written by a pair of obscure writers. It then could be passed over in silence, in the certainty that it would obtain a circulation in accordance with its merits. But it comes indorsed with the names of two of the most popular authors of American humorous literature. The work which both had hitherto produced had been of such excellent quality as to secure the respect of the public, and the confidence that whatever either might present would be worthy of the giver and the receiver. Therefore, when the two have condescended to trifle with their honorable reputation and with the confidence of the public, indignation is justly excited and outspoken.

. . . When . . . a book so utterly bald, so puerile, so vicious even, as "The Gilded Age," appears with the signatures of Mark Twain and Charles Dudley Warner to give it a passport among respectable readers, wrath and disgust may rightfully inspire the critic to chastise them with[out] mercy.

It is not, as we have said, as if these writers were unknown and without influence . . . . Their names had become a sort of certificate of high character. It is a fraud to the reading public to append them to a trashy book like the mongrel before us. Stupidity can be forgiven, but deliberate deceit—never.

The anger of this reviewer was intensified by the apparent helplessness of the press in attempting to kill a book sold by subscription: "Moreover, it is not as if the work were to be deposited on the shelves of the booksellers, to be sold as called for. It is to be carried from door to door throughout the country, into the rural districts, where a voice of warning from the press usually does not penetrate . . . ."[77] As if this scathing attack were not enough, the *St. Louis Democrat* resorted to facetious ridicule. It asserted that able critics, after having carefully studied the work, had "decided that it bears no marks of the presence of the peculiar wit and wisdom which characterize either of these gifted men."

But the Secret is out. It is confidently asserted that the "Gilded Age" is a gigantic practical joke. It is declared that, wishing to test the credulity of the public, these two notorious wits had the book prepared by several obscure newspaper local reporters. The covenant was solemnly made that the joke was to be kept a profound secret till 300,000 copies of the work were sold. The whole story is probably a canard, but any one who, out of respect for the alleged authors, will read the book, will feel that the account is extremely probable.[78]

The known fact that Twain had been guilty of perpetrating hoaxes before lent plausibility to the assertion. The Boston *Literary World* added insult to injury:

We have read enough of the book to convince us that it is not worth reading and to fill us with wonder as to how a man of Mr. Warner's literary reputation could lend his name to such cheap and feeble stuff. . . . The book has a strong savor of lucre; it was evidently written to sell, and in the hope of gaining a liberal heap of that money, whose worship it purports to ridicule. It is not witty, or in any respect interesting; the only feature of it that we can conscientiously praise is the illustrations.[79]

To say, as some investigators have, that such outbursts resulted from the disappointment of reviewers at not finding the easily quotable "funny" book that they had anticipated as a joint production of two leading humorists, while it is not without some justification,[80] obscures the real reason. F. B. Perkins' penetrating review in *Old and New* reveals the sore spot the novel had touched.

The book is a story with a purpose as much as "The Pilgrim's Progress." It is written to expose speculators, lobbyists, and corrupt legislators. . . .

There is a great power in the book, and of an uncommon kind. It is a determined and bitter satire; but the satire is veiled by an absence of comment and moral explanation that reminds one of the passionless record manner of the story of Uriah the Hittite, and the criminal department generally of the Bible history. . . . [The reader's] first thought over this book, for instance, is most likely to be, "This is a repulsive and unfeeling record of monstrous infamies." It requires some mental philosophy, and of a practical kind too, to go on thus: "The writer tells this story as a matter-of-course and every-day story, in order to have me stop and ask if such things are really every-day matters of fact. And, truly, they are; and I don't like it, *and I will try to have a really good man represent me next election.*" Thus the story means, for its central meaning, "PURIFY THE SUFFRAGE."[81]

After all, the *Chicago Tribune* as an apologist for the corrupt Grant administration could hardly fail to condemn a book that even by implication attacked the administration's notorious abuses, and little more could be expected of the *St. Louis Democrat,* the great Republican paper of the West.[82]

Other reviewers less directly concerned in a political sense had their disappointment turned into sourness by the distasteful task of evaluating a serious and pointed social satire. And what exasperated Clemens was that instead of having the integrity and courage to face up to the challenge and criticize the book in a serious fashion and on its own terms they wriggled out of the corner in which they found themselves by making innuendoes. In his letter to Whitelaw Reid, Warner had said, "If there is any satire on the times in it, it won't be our fault, but the fault of the times."[83] Even the condemnatory reviews either tacitly or explicitly acknowledged the satire. The *Literary World,* for example, as part of its condemnation said:

The book is intended to be a satire on our national politics, with special reference to society and legislation at Washington. . . . We have no doubt that the descriptions here given of the methods by which legislation is expedited, by which senators are elected, and by which official opportunities are employed for private ends, are measurably accurate; but there is needed an agency of higher moral tone than this book, to remedy these evils, or even to lead the public to serious disapproval of them. Neither a buffoon nor a bumpkin can successfully lead a reform. . . .[84]

The leading religious newspaper, the *Independent,* remarked:

We took up "Mark Twain's" and Charles Dudley Warner's joint volume with quite too high anticipations, hoping that possibly we might find in it an American "Pickwick Papers." . . . The impression made— and this is our main objection to the book—is one of unrelieved venality and corruption. There is enough of this in Washington, no doubt; but to represent it as a general and pervading feature is terribly exaggerated. Unfortunately, the reader does not get the idea of strained and grotesque unreality which characterizes Mark Twain's other books; but that this is intended for a fair representation of congressional life, and he will learn from it that it is a disgrace to be a congressman and will learn to despise his country. We should blush to see this book republished in Europe. . . .[85]

Yet the novel had an almost equal proportion of defenders for the same reason for which it was attacked. The fact that it came to grips with contemporary political conditions in an unusually outspoken way provoked praise as well as blame. Perkins in his *Old and New* review summarized it by saying, "without any relative or qualifying expression, it is a book of real and high purpose, much graphic and portrait power, much knowledge of men and things, and uncommon swiftness and force of action."[86] The Boston *Transcript* said that it could "hardly fail to help on the reforming tendency in the politics of the day."[87] The *New York Herald* stated that "as a clever though rude satire upon certain customs and institutions, many of which deserve contempt and reprobation, it will scarcely be too highly praised."[88] *Appleton's Journal* similarly stated that Twain and Warner had "given most of the falsities of the time a sound thrashing that will be appreciated in quarters to which no one of the Olympian bolts of the thunderers in daily press and Sunday pulpit could ever penetrate."[89] Edward and George Cary Eggleston's *Hearth and Home* with simple honesty analyzed the process of mental readjustment that many of the novel's readers must have undergone:

It is sometimes very annoying to begin reading a book under the impression that it is an excellent thing of one sort, and discover that it is an excellent thing of quite a different kind. But such occurrences are not always annoying, by any means, and we have just had an experience of the kind which was one of unmixed pleasure. When we began the reading of *The Gilded Age, a story of to-day,* by Mark Twain and Charles Dudley Warner, we confidently expected a treat, and we were not disappointed, though the book turned out to be as unlike what we expected it to be as was possible. We imagined it an extremely funny exaggeration of life with here and there a touch of Mr. Warner's dainty humor, and thought the whole would prove an inimitable burlesque of the modern novel peculiarly rich in the characteristics of both its authors. We find it instead as genuine a novel as any, full of humor, with now and then a laughable exaggeration of character and life, but on the whole, rather a pathetic than a humorous production. . . .

The satire of the book is pungent enough to have grown on a red-pepper plant, and the accuracy of aim with which it is delivered is not excelled by that of a Wimbledon prize-winner. The story is full of purpose. . . . There is fun enough in the book to make the fortune of half a dozen novels, but clearly it was written not in fun but very much in earnest.[90]

A strong element in the appreciation accorded by the favorable reviews was the noticeable wincing of the reviewers under Twain's and Warner's unexpected lash or the uncomfortableness of their predicament in having to handle the novel in a sober fashion. The New York *World* called it "a severe, truthful, and painful satire." The Springfield (Mass.) *Union* said: "the thoughtful reader will rise from the perusal of 'The Gilded Age' in a mood rather depressed than exhilarated. It is about as amusing reading to Americans as the satires of Juvenal probably were to reflective Romans." Most outspoken of all, the *Cincinnati Daily Times* called it "a cruel, unflinching dissection of our moral and social condition . . . ."

The authors have missed no feature of our life that was capable of burlesquing. . . . coolly and deliberately as professors at the dissecting table they probe to the bottom every sore upon the body politic, and lay open to the public gaze every hidden rottenness. It is a cruel task, done without mercy; a sad, sad picture, and more grievous still because pity 'tis 'tis so nearly true. . . .[91]

As the above excerpts show, *The Gilded Age* aroused a considerable critical response in the United States both pro and con; it is significant that virtually no one was neutral. Indeed, the novel was more widely reviewed than any previous Twain volume or, for that matter, any of the following six.[92] It is apparent, moreover, that the reason lay not in the distribution of review copies[93]—it must be kept in mind that *The Gilded Age* was sold by subscription—not in the prominence of the coauthor Warner, as has sometimes been suggested,[94] nor in the careful solicitation of notices by both authors, but in the fact that it had a serious social import, clothed in clever satire.

Convinced though he was of the advantageousness of subscription publishing in the United States, with its vast hinterland of relatively isolated readers, Clemens was quite content to utilize the customary method of book publishing in England. So it was that the British edition of *The Gilded Age* was published by George Routledge and Sons on December 23 or 24, 1873, in three volumes, at £1 5s. 6d., and displayed on the shelves of the regular booksellers.[95] (Routledge, the publisher to whom Clemens had entrusted the British edition of *Roughing It* in order to discourage Hotten from pirating it,[96] had ironically enough been brought to the Court of Chancery for piracy shortly before that;[97] the company's relations with Clemens, however, appear to have been entirely honest.)[98] Writing to his close friend the Reverend "Joe" Twichell from London early in January, Clemens said, "I have read the *novel* here, and I like it"; then he added, "I have made no inquiries about it, though. My interest in a book ceases with the printing of it."[99] Natural though this assertion may seem, uttered as it was upon the surcease of the pangs of birth, it was no more than a fleeting sigh of relief, as was soon shown by his active interest in the judgments of the reviewers.

In England *The Gilded Age* did not have the handicap of subscription publication to overcome in order to reach the reviewers, but it did have the handicap of Twain's reputation as a popular humorist, especially among the more conservative journals.[100] His great success with his lectures in the Queen's Concert Rooms in Hanover Square, though it may have helped build sales interest in the book, hardly served to alter his reputation. Many organs of literary opinion, therefore, ignored him, as they continued to do for several years. Yet the very nature of the novel compelled attention just as much in England as in New England. There was a striking difference, however. The British reviews were almost unanimously unfavorable. In a letter to Warner, Stedman expressed the hope that the English would understand the book's satire and not assume that it was meant as a picture of "the *best* American life." "*The Gilded Age,* unfortunately, is the truth & nothing but the truth," he wrote, "but I hope they won't take it to be 'the whole truth.' "[101] The novel, however, not only seemed to confirm all the worst misgivings the English had long held about conditions in America but in their eyes demonstrated a typically American (or at least un-English) lack of reticence in exposing the seamy side.

The first English review that I have been able to find appeared in the London *Evening Standard* less than a week after the book had been published.

We do hope that we shall never hear any more about English libels upon America. From long before the publication of Boz's "American Notes" down to the days of "Martin Chuzzlewit" and of George Francis Train, the people of the United States have been in a chronic state of indignation respecting the pictures drawn of them and their state of society by independent Englishmen, who did not want to conciliate British Radicalism or to make money by a winter's lecturing through the Union. It has been pointed out more than once that no English picture was so altogether damaging to the American character as the limning of some of the native journalists and other authors. Here is a proof that there is no getting over. *The Gilded Age* . . . is one of those works which, in essence a satire of the bitterest kind, is in reality a hardly overdrawn picture of the condition of society in some of the states that obey the laws of the Washington Congress. It is a bitter pill for Americans to swallow, but the medicine is, in the judgment of its authors, a necessary one, and it is not for Britishers to disagree with them. . . . It is a work which . . . every one should read, and which, when read, must make the world wonder how the Americans could ever have objected to a single word in "Martin Chuzzlewit."[102]

The *Athenaeum*, leading weekly cultural journal, remarked with calculated understatement that it did not "quite like the spirit which brings to light all the '*linge sale*' of American speculation for the benefit of foreign readers." "It is true," it continued, "that the book appears to have been already published in America; but it might as well have been left to find its way to England, if its literary merits were sufficient . . . ."[103] The illustrated weekly the *Graphic* was far more explicit.

Messrs. Twain and Warner are both American citizens, and so can hardly be suspected of any wish wantonly to foul their own nest for the amusement of foreigners; but we are confident that if any Englishman had ventured on a picture of American manners and institutions half as highly coloured, he would at once have been loudly accused of the most rancorous spite and the grossest misinterpretation. To say nothing of the "lobbyings" and unblushing corruption in all the departments of State which play so large a part in the action of this story, the very description of the City of Washington would have been stigmatised as an outrageous libel. . . .[104]

The *Spectator's* reviewer declared that his first reaction was "one of satisfaction that the writers are not English."

Americans, as they read its bitter exposures of American folly and cupidity, will know that their satirists are still at least their countrymen, and that the book cannot be accepted as one proof more of the malignant persistence with which British writers misconceive and misrepresent Americans.[105]

It might well be asked, what was the particular quality of *The Gilded Age* that it should provoke such angry condemnation on the one hand yet win sincere applause on the other? An examination of the book's constituent elements and the sources from which they were drawn should furnish an answer to this question.

CHAPTER II

A Literary Burlesque

IT HAS BEEN a subject of speculation why Mark Twain and Charles Dudley Warner—both of them writers of humorous sketches yet widely divergent in their styles, neither of them experienced in fiction—came to collaborate on a novel. An apparently simple explanation is given in Albert Bigelow Paine's authorized biography of Twain. According to Paine, whose words have been accepted by most commentators with almost the reverence accorded gospel, the origin of the project was as follows:

It was a very simple matter, a perfectly natural development.

At the dinner-table one night, with the Warners present, criticisms of recent novels were offered, with the usual freedom and severity of dinner-table talk. The husbands were inclined to treat rather lightly the novels in which their wives were finding entertainment. The wives naturally retorted that the proper thing for the husbands to do was to furnish the American people with better ones. This was regarded in the nature of a challenge, and as such was accepted—mutually accepted: that is to say, in partnership. On the spur of the moment Clemens and Warner agreed that they would do a novel together, that they would begin it immediately. This is the whole story of the book's origin; so far, at least, as the collaboration is concerned. Clemens, in fact, had the beginning of a story in his mind, but had been unwilling to undertake an extended work of fiction alone. He welcomed only too eagerly, therefore, the proposition of joint authorship. His purpose was to write a tale around that lovable character of his youth, his mother's cousin, James Lampton —to let that gentle visionary stand as the central figure against a proper background. The idea appealed to Warner, and there was no delay in the beginning. . . .[1]

As far as the essential facts of the catalytic dinner-table episode are concerned, there is no need to question Paine's veracity. Obviously Clemens was satisfied with the version (though in later years his memory was not always reliable), and as will be shown there is much evidence that the story is substantially correct. There are, however, at least two other versions of the origin of the project that must be considered in order that the background of the episode may be filled in, for one cannot help being struck by the improbability of the spur-of-the-moment impulsiveness that Paine implies.

Charles Warren Stoddard, poet and man of letters, with whom Clemens had become friends in San Francisco and whose companionship he always relished,[2] relates how Clemens read parts of the novel to him in London when it was just published and had him guess at the authorship of each part. "The story," he goes on, "was written in this wise:"

> Mark and Charles Dudley Warner were walking to church one Sunday in Hartford. Said Warner: "Let us write a novel!" Mark wondered what in the world there was to write a novel about, but promised to think the matter over, and proceeded to do so. On the way home it was decided that Mark should begin and write till he got tired, and that there should be a gathering of the wives and Joe Twichell—the clerical chum—for the reading of the same. . . .[3]

The fact that Stoddard had this information presumably from Clemens' own mouth during their leisurely evenings together in the latter's London apartments barely a year after the actual event gives it strong credibility, particularly as it in no way controverts Paine's version but merely supplements it. Paine says that Clemens "had the beginning of a story in his mind"; when, according to Stoddard's version, he "promised to think the matter over, and proceeded to do so," the story that he already had in mind about his cousin James Lampton apparently suited the scheme, for on the way home it was decided that he should be the one to get the novel under way.

Another version, which suggestively parallels Stoddard's, is given by the Missouri biographers Wilfred R. Hollister and Harry Norman, who claim to have been furnished their information "al-

most entirely by members of the families and personal friends."[4]
According to them,

> It came about in this way: One day Clemens and Warner were returning
> from a walk in Hartford in which they had discussed the merits of the
> modern novel. "Warner," said Clemens, "let us write a burlesque on the
> modern novel." Mr. Warner was favorable to the proposition, and soon
> they were formulating plans for the production of the story. . . . (p. 55)

The wives of the authors are mentioned only to the extent that the
novel was to be submitted to them for criticism "when the manuscript was completed," condensed, and revised. The value of the
latter version is that it points up the important and logical fact that
Clemens and Warner were seriously concerned about the sterility
of the contemporary popular novel and not, as Paine implies,
smugly contemptuous of their wives' reading material. Olivia
Clemens is known to have been an intelligent and well-educated
woman with a perceptive taste. There is every reason to suppose
that Susan Warner was similarly a woman of intelligence and culture. The truth appears to be that both women were wholeheart-
edly supporting their writer-husbands' proposal to show up the
meretriciousness of contemporary fiction and that they were in
turn accorded their husbands' respect as exacting critics.

Whether Clemens or Warner (or both) stated that they could
write a better novel than the current popular fare and were chal-
lenged to do so by their wives or simply expressed their distaste and
were dared by their wives to write a better novel is of little importance.[5] There was obviously much talk about contemporary
fiction among the members of the Nook Farm circle and much
serious criticism of it. In the "Sixth Study" of Warner's *Backlog
Studies,* published in the June, 1872, issue of *Scribner's,* there is a
discussion among the *Backlog* characters of this very subject.
(Somewhat in the tradition of Holmes's *Breakfast-Table* papers,
the fireside conversations recorded in this series of informal essays
involve a stable set of characters representing real Nook Farm
persons, some of whom are easily identifiable.)[6] The subject is introduced as follows:

Herbert [unidentified] said he had been dipping into the recent novels written by women, here and there, with a view to noting the effect upon literature of this sudden and rather overwhelming accession to it. There was a good deal of talk about it evening after evening, off and on, and I can only undertake to set down fragments of it.

HERBERT. I should say that the distinguishing feature of the literature of this day is the prominence women have in its production. . . . to them we are indebted for the oceans of Sunday-school books, and they write the majority of the novels, the serial stories, and they mainly pour out the watery flood of tales in the weekly papers. . . .

The Mistress (Susan Warner) comes to the defense of women writers, citing George Eliot, Mrs. Gaskell, George Sand, and Mrs. Browning. Herbert replies that these are of course exceptions, then continues:

I refer to the great body of novels, which you would know by internal evidence were written by women. They are of two sorts:—the domestic story, entirely unidealized, and as flavorless as water-gruel; and the spiced novel, generally immoral in tendency, in which the social problems are handled, unhappy marriages, affinity and passional attraction, bigamy, and the violation of the seventh commandment. These subjects are treated in the rawest manner, without any settled ethics, with little discrimination of eternal right and wrong, and with very little sense of responsibility for what is set forth. Many of these novels are merely the blind outbursts of a nature impatient of restraint and the conventionalities of society, and are as chaotic as the untrained minds that produce them.

MANDEVILLE [unidentified]. Don't you think these novels fairly represent a social condition of unrest and upheaval?

HERBERT. Very likely; and they help to create and spread abroad the discontent they describe. Stories of bigamy (sometimes disguised by divorce), of unhappy marriages, where the injured wife, through an entire volume, is on the brink of falling into the arms of a sneaking lover, until death kindly removes the obstacle, and the two souls, who were born for each other but got separated in the cradle, melt and mingle into one in the last chapter, are not healthful reading for maids or mothers.

. . . .

OUR NEXT DOOR [NEIGHBOR] [Clemens]. We are living, we are dwelling, in a grand and awful time; I'm glad I don't write novels.

THE PARSON [Twichell]. So am I.

OUR NEXT DOOR. I tried a Sunday-school book once; but I made the good boy end in the poor-house, and the bad boy go to Congress; and the publisher said it would n't do, . . .[7]

From Scribner's Monthly, *January, 1874*
Charles Dudley Warner

Out of this immediate background sprang the partnership of
Clemens and Warner.

It must not be supposed, however, that concern about the contemporary novel was confined to Nook Farm. Had it been, there is little likelihood that *The Gilded Age* would have come into being or, having come into being, either have taken the particular shape it did or have caused much stir among the reading public. The Nook Farm circle served as one of the most articulate intellectual foci of a general affection. Dissatisfaction with the quality of contemporary American novels was being expressed in the leading organs of culture; and the conservative journals, which were seeking to maintain a high literary standard, deliberately, almost pointedly, ignored most popular fiction and drew a curtain of silence around it. But even while the *Atlantic*, the *Galaxy*, *Scribner's*, and *Harper's* were serializing such writers as John W. De Forest and William Dean Howells or, owing to a dearth of American writers who met their standards, importing Anthony Trollope, Charles Reade, and Dickens, a number of fiction weeklies with huge circulations, notably Robert Bonner's *New York Ledger*, Street and Smith's *New York Weekly*, and *Saturday Night*, were supplying a far greater audience with banal, sentimental, or sensational serialized novels, many of which were quickly published in book form.[8] These story papers did not cater to the masses, however; indeed, the large industrial proletariat of the late nineteenth century and the twentieth had barely begun to develop. The reading public for current fiction both serialized and in book form was to be found among middle-class groups—farmers, small tradesmen, skilled mechanics—and the lower bourgeoisie. These groupings comprised a very large audience, and it was principally the higher-income, more fully educated groups, among whom could be numbered the Clemenses and Warners, who had a basis of comparison with the finest contemporary writing.

Scarcely a year before Clemens and Warner began writing *The Gilded Age*, the management of the Boston Public Library named as the most popular authors of the day Mrs. E. D. E. N. Southworth, Caroline Lee Hentz, and Mary Jane Holmes.[9] These three novelists were representative of a large body of sentimental escapists, mostly women writers, including Susan Warner, Maria Cummins, Catherine Warfield, and Marion Harland, plus a few men, Timothy Shay Arthur, Sylvanus Cobb, and Emerson Bennett, most of whom had begun their careers in the "feminine fifties" or earlier and who performed much the same function for their times as the almost anonymous writers of radio and TV "soap operas" do for ours. The devoutly religious Mrs. Southworth, whose stock in trade was self-sacrifice, the evils of divorce, and the clinging-vine ideal of conduct and whose devices included dungeons, spectres, and buried treasure, wrote sixty bulky novels in her fifty-year literary life, most of them originally serialized in the *New York Ledger*. Mary Jane Holmes, "Queen of the Human Heart," increased the circulation of the *New York Weekly* by 50,000 with her story "Marian Grey." From the initial phenomenal success of Susan Warner's volume *Wide, Wide World* in 1850 on through the works of the one-man fiction mill Sylvanus Cobb, who manufactured 122 novels in thirty years, this deluge of mediocrity was administering its opiate to a country torn with civil strife and radically changing social relations.[10]

The only excuse that could be offered in defense of this bogus literature was that it was highly moral in tone and that its readers might well be putting their time to worse uses.[11] Even Walt Whitman in an article on "Sensation Stories" said that many of their readers "might do worse if debarred from the enjoyment of their favorite mental *pabulum*."[12] Occasionally, however, a critic broke the ostracizing silence. A reviewer in the *Atlantic* summed up Mrs. Southworth's output in one sentence: " 'The Fatal Marriage' is one of forty-three novels by this writer, every one of which is a separate astonishment."[13]

In this period there was considerable discussion of the possibilities for writing the "great American novel"; and using this topic as a point of departure the critic Thomas Sergeant Perry in the *North American Review* of October, 1872, set before his readers "some of the more obvious faults" of the currently popular novelists.[14] Ranging from the "weird visions of the Southern novelist[s]," those "thunder-storms in print," to the "innocently prattling stories" of *Harper's*, Perry proceeded to dissect the contemporary American novel. He lauded De Forest and Stowe for their American traits but berated most of the writers for being afraid of their heroes and heroines and for Anglicizing them. Discussing Frank Lee Benedict's novel *Miss Van Kortland*,[15] he stated:

> There was the general air of English country life barely disguised by American names. Congress was made exactly like Parliament. It was an English bottom sailing under American colors. . . . The reader could not help being reminded of the Yankees in Punch's caricatures, who would be arrested as suspicious characters in the backwoods of Maine, nor could their apt use of "old hoss" save them. . . .

He was particularly concerned about the fantastic stories of the southern novelists (such as Mrs. Southworth) who dealt "with the most tremendous manifestations of the power of love and jealousy, which combine to poison young lives and lead to the most heinous crimes." And he came to the conclusion that contemporary American society probably offered "nothing tempting to the writer, unless, indeed, to the satirist, who should turn to ridicule the shallowness, greedy pretence, and emptiness which he might see about him." Articles such as Perry's, infrequent though they were, are highly significant because they reveal the thinking of informed intellectuals, who, while they for the most part confined these judgments to private, personal discussions, could on occasion be stirred to utter them publicly.

In the post-Civil War years, northern capitalism was triumphantly following up its victory over southern slave manorialism by an unprecedented frontier exploitation accompanied by graft and corruption. Of the resultant disruption in human values there was an almost total absence of literary expression. Instead, a commercialized "pabulum" literature served as a vast emotional tranquilizer. Under such historical and literary conditions a reaction became inevitable, a resurgence of realism, a swing to a literature of actual contemporary life with an indigenous American base. The story of the rise of realism and its development into the naturalism and muckraking of the turn of the century is so well known that it hardly needs discussion here. In the years 1872-73, however, the weight of "pabulum" literature was in precarious equilibrium with that of creative restiveness and of quiet but strongly critical revulsion, and it needed but the push of a truthful and talented author to tip the balance and bring about the onset of critical realism. As always in history, there were numerous individuals both consciously and unconsciously attempting to tip that balance. That Twain, with the help of Warner, succeeded where others failed had its reasons also.

To begin with, Clemens, whether in private conversation, personal correspondence, or public print, was an outspoken foe of sentimentalism, sensationalism, and the literature of illusion in general. Writing in September, 1870, to his "Quaker City" excursion friend and mentor of earlier days, Mrs. Mary Mason ("Mother") Fairbanks, he lambasted the novel *Robert Falconer,* by the English mystic and idealist George MacDonald, which had recently been published in an American edition and had apparently been recommended to the Clemenses by Mrs. Fairbanks.

> Shargar was the only character in the book . . . who was *always* welcome, & of him the author gave us just as little as possible, & filled his empty pages with the added emptiness of that tiresome Ericson & his dismal "poetry"—hogwash, *I* call it.
> . . . what on earth the author lugged in that inanity, Miss Lindsay, for, goes clear beyond my comprehension. Page after page, & page after page about that ineffable doughnut . . . . Hang such [an author] a character!
> And Miss St. John— . . . when she concluded that the man she first loved was small potatoes & that that big booby of an Ericson was the man that completely filled her idea of masculine perfection I just wanted to send her a dose of salts with my compliments.
> Mind you, we are not through yet—two or three chapters still to read—& that idiot is still hunting for his father. . . .[16]

All this with interpolations by "Livy" such as "thats not correct," "how dreadful," and "scandalous," and a postscript by her beginning, "I would make erasures in this letter but it is a hopeless undertaking." This playful duel fought between husband and wife for "Mother" Fairbanks' benefit would seem to bear out Paine's implication of weakness in Olivia Clemens' taste were it not that not even writers of the stature of George Meredith, George Eliot, and Henry James were invulnerable to her husband's barbs.[17]

Fourteen years later, Clemens was to write an entertaining critique of S. Watson Royston's short romance *The Enemy Con-*

quered; or, Love Triumphant (1845), an extraordinary piece of turgid prose fiction called to his attention by George W. Cable.[18] His article, published as "A Cure for the Blues" in *The £1,000,000 Bank-Note, and Other Stories* (1893), indicates even more effectively than the diatribe against Scott's influence on southern sentimentalism in *Life on the Mississippi* his reaction to the southern novelists' thunderstorms in print.[19] He asserts that the author, whose identity he disguises under the pseudonym G. Ragsdale McClintock, "recognized only one kind of eloquence—the lurid, the tempestuous, the volcanic."

> The reader must not imagine that he is to find in it wisdom, brilliancy, fertility of invention, ingenuity of construction, excellence of form, purity of style, perfection of imagery, truth to nature, clearness of statement, humanly possible situations, humanly possible people, fluent narrative, connected sequence of events—or philosophy, or logic, or sense. No; the rich, deep, beguiling charm of the book lies in the total and miraculous *absence* from it of all these qualities . . . .

In the early days of his married life Clemens wrote a travesty of Elizabeth Stuart Phelps's tremendously popular novel of death and consolation, *The Gates Ajar* (1868), which he refrained from publishing at the time purportedly in deference to his wife's feelings of propriety, though the novel had already been attacked by Bret Harte in an *Overland* review.[20] After Mrs. Clemens' death he at length decided to publish it in a modified form in *Harper's* (December, 1907, and January, 1908) as the now well-known "Extract from Captain Stormfield's Visit to Heaven."[21] One has only to know that *The Gates Ajar* discussed a literal, tangible heaven ("a mean little ten-cent heaven about the size of Rhode Island")[22] and its inhabitants, occupations, and scenery to realize with what relish the agnostic Clemens must have warmed up to his ridicule and to appreciate the burlesque fun of "Captain Stormfield."[23]

The dime novels, those early paperback thrillers of lust, passion, murder, revenge, and mystery published in the thousands by Irwin P. Beadle & Co. and their competitors, which helped satisfy the appetite roused by the story weeklies and which provoked parents' protests of much the same nature as the present-day campaign against violent and brutal "comic" books, were never mentioned specifically by Clemens (possibly because some of his own sketches had appeared in *Beadle's Dime Book of Fun No. 3* and Beadle's *Dime Dialogues No. 10*).[24] But such pieces as his *Golden Era* review of the melodrama *Ingomar, the Barbarian*, which he describes in a slangy, cops-and-robbers vernacular; the co-operative novel serialized in the short-lived Virginia City "literary" paper *Weekly Occidental*, which he describes in *Roughing It* and in which the most typical episodes are purported to have been written by a collaborator who was consistently drunk when he wrote; and his own burlesque love story, "The Loves of Alonzo Fitz Clarence and Rosannah Ethelton," with its hyperbole, stilted dialogue, and ludicrous device of courtship and marriage by telephone, all show his familiarity with this type of literature and his love for ridiculing it.[25]

There is no question that Clemens was entirely familiar with contemporary writing and that he therefore spoke from firsthand knowledge whenever he criticized it. From his earliest youth he had been an omnivorous reader and a broad one. Though his record of his reading is relatively meager and scattered, he must have known, or known about, almost all the popular fiction of his time.[26] From the Hannibal days—when the typical parlor-table literature consisted of the "chaste and innocuous 'Godey's Lady's Book,'" subscription miscellanies "with their sappy inanities," and "two or three goody-goody works" such as he described later in *Life on the Mississippi*, and when it was a great event for him to discover a torn leaf from a history of Joan of Arc—up through his association with the self-educated Scotsman Macfarlane and his discovery of Scott's *Fortunes of Nigel* as a cub pilot, he kept reading constantly and industriously.[27] In 1876 he told Mrs. James T. Fields, wife of the Boston publisher, that, not having been able to have reading material " 'when I was hungry for it, I can only read the Encyclopedia nowadays.' Which is not true," she adds, "he reads everything."[28] Among the many periodicals he read were the *Atlantic Monthly, Godey's Lady's Book, Harper's Monthly Magazine, Harper's Weekly Magazine, New York Ledger,* and

Overland Monthly.[29] Along with Harriet Beecher Stowe, he was
a regular customer of Israel Witkower's bookshop in Hartford,
as he was of James Guild's bookshop in Washington whenever he
visited the capital.[30]

Three of the most voluminous and popular of the sensation
novelists whose work Clemens knew well were Sylvanus Cobb, Jr.,
Timothy Shay Arthur, and Emerson Bennett, all of whom wrote
for Bonner's *New York Ledger* and other story weeklies such as
The Flag of Our Union, Saturday Evening Post, Saturday Night,
and *New York Weekly*. He probably first made their acquaintance
when he was setting type for the *Ledger* in 1853.[31] In his *Galaxy*
"Memoranda" for November, 1870, writing to young aspirants to
literary fame, he said, ". . . if Sylvanus Cobb or T. S. Arthur had
submitted their maiden MSS. to you, you would have said, with
tears in your eyes, 'Now please don't write any more!' But you
see yourself how popular they are."[32] In *Roughing It* he compares
the language of James Fenimore Cooper's Indians to "such an
attempt to talk like a hunter or a mountaineer as a Broadway
clerk might make after eating an edition of Emerson Bennett's
works . . . ."[33] (Bennett was an imitator of Cooper.)[34] And in *The
Gilded Age* itself he writes of the typical railway hawker who
"hands you out a book of murders if you are fond of theology;
or . . . T. S. Arthur if you are fond of poetry."[35] Cobb, who was
called "decently sensational," always contrived to have vice pun-
ished and virtue rewarded; Arthur, author of the famous *Ten
Nights in a Bar-Room,* vividly condemned drinking, gambling,
and other vices; Bennett wrote of the woes of city life.[36]

In the light of the foregoing facts—the condition of contemporary literature, Clemens' knowledge of it, and his delight in
ridiculing it, a delight born of disgust—it is highly probable that
the Hollister-Norman version of the agreement between Clemens
and Warner that led to *The Gilded Age* is substantially valid.
Whether Clemens actually proposed to Warner in so many words
that they "write a burlesque on the modern novel" or whether this
account is an unconscious projection of effect into cause in retrospect can probably never be determined with certainty. The result,
however, was precisely that: a burlesque on the contemporary

popular novel; and the evidence shows without doubt that the burlesque was quite intentional.

The story of *The Gilded Age* begins in the hamlet of Obedstown in the district known as the "Knobs of East Tennessee," where "Squire" Hawkins and his family live. Si Hawkins, "Squire" by virtue of being postmaster of Obedstown, keeps the general store of the village of fifteen houses in a part of his own house. He has taken up seventy-five thousand acres of county land, worth at present less than three acres to the cent, but what with timber, grain, and the evidence of coal and of copper and iron ore in it promising to be worth a thousand dollars an acre someday and bring a fortune to his family and heirs. Meanwhile his family is poverty-stricken and the immediate outlook is hopeless; so he persuades his wife, Nancy, to heed a letter from his friend Eschol Sellers in Missouri begging him to move to the new frontier there and make a fresh start. Nancy consents, though with misgivings because Sellers has almost ruined their fortunes already in harebrained schemes in Virginia and Kentucky.

On the evening of the third day of their trek they come upon a cabin where a ten-year-old boy, Clay, has just become orphaned by the death of his mother from fever. With typical compassion and impracticality Squire Hawkins adopts Clay into his already overburdened family and travels on. They board a Mississippi steamboat to cover part of their journey. On the voyage their steamboat, the *Boreas,* becomes involved in a race with a rival boat, the *Amaranth.* Through overfiring, the *Amaranth* blows up, and the *Boreas* drops back to pick up wounded survivors and the dead. As a result of this episode the Hawkinses acquire another member of their household, the five-year-old Laura Van Brunt, orphaned by the disaster. Eventually they arrive at a tiny village on the Missouri shore, where they are greeted by the warmhearted, eccentric, visionary friend of Squire Hawkins, "Colonel" Eschol Sellers, and his large family. Hawkins joins Colonel Sellers in his latest speculation of raising mules for the southern market, a speculation which this time succeeds well, and he builds a two-story house and equips it with "store" furniture from St. Louis and decorated oilcloth window curtains. Through other shrewd speculations in produce and goods he prospers and his honorary title "Squire" becomes "Judge."

We skip ten years to find that little Laura (Van Brunt) Hawkins has become a beautiful and bewitching schoolgirl of seventeen. Judge Hawkins has had his ups and downs and has come near sacrificing the Tennessee Land when times have been hard, once for $1,500, another time for $3,000. At the moment, he is again facing poverty, and again a fortuitous stranger, representing an iron company, makes him an offer, this time for $10,000; but after considerable mental conflict Hawkins holds out for $30,000, the man vanishes, and Nancy once again is crestfallen. At this juncture young Washington Hawkins, a dreamy, impractically inventive lad of twenty-two, volunteers to go live with Colonel Sellers for a while to relieve the family burden until the Tennessee Land is sold. Emily Hawkins and Laura volunteer to go to St. Louis, the former to board on credit with a friend of the family, the latter to earn her own living. Clay comes home at the behest of Judge Hawkins, bringing with him savings of two hundred dollars from his own earnings, pays off his foster father's few small debts, bundles off Washington to Colonel Sellers in Hawkeye, Missouri, and goes back to his labors.

At Hawkeye Colonel Sellers fills Washington Hawkins' head with marvelous ideas for making both their fortunes, the most immediate of which is an Infallible Imperial Oriental Optic Liniment and Salvation for Sore Eyes, the formula for which he is working on and which will sell a million bottles in the United States and untold millions to the peoples of the Orient suffering from ophthalmia. These roseate visions, in all of which Washington firmly believes, are related to him in Sellers' house, barren of furniture, swarming with voluble little Sellerses, and chilled by a stove whose warm glow proves to be provided by a single candle within—a little invention of the Colonel's to prevent rheumatism. (Upon another occasion the Colonel entertains Washington with further marvels at a dinner consisting of clear, fresh water and a basin of raw turnips, the invaluably nourishing virtues of which are extolled by the resourceful Sellers.) Sellers secures Washington a job as clerk and bookkeeper to the local real estate promoter,

General Boswell, at whose house he is to board. Washington and General Boswell's daughter, Louise, promptly fall in love with one another. Before the eyewater has become a reality, Washington is summoned home because his father is critically ill. After a week of lingering illness Judge Hawkins dies, secure in the belief that the Tennessee Land will keep his family from penury.

The death of Si Hawkins is followed in a few days by that of a Major Lackland, formerly a man of note in the state but one who as congressman has sold his vote and been completely disgraced. The coroner's jury finds on his body certain memoranda that prove Laura is not the Hawkinses' own daughter, whereupon the local gossips get to work. Laura, distraught, ransacks the garret until she finds correspondence between Judge Hawkins and Major Lackland indicating that her real father suffered amnesia as a result of the steamboat explosion and after one or two reappearances disappeared for good. The gossips keep up their rumors and insinuations about Laura's questionable birth, rumors which no one can definitely dispel, with the result that she is ostracized even by her sweetheart.

At this point in the story a second set of characters is introduced. Philip Sterling and Harry Brierly are two young men out to make their fortunes in New York City, who live together in a Ninth Street boardinghouse. Philip, a Yale graduate, has been reading law and vainly trying to get an editorial job; his classmate Harry, who assumes the air of a man of affairs, has been talking of his connections and waiting for an opportunity of some kind to turn up. Finally, through Harry's uncle they secure positions with a party of engineers and surveyors being sent out to Missouri by New York capitalists to lay out a railroad. Arrived in St. Louis, they make the acquaintance of Colonel Sellers, who gets Harry interested in a land speculation that is an offshoot of the railroad they are surveying, the Salt Lick Pacific Extension. Sellers has persuaded the division engineer to route the railroad through the hamlet of Stone's Landing (to be named Napoleon) at the head of Goose Run (to be named the Columbus River), which he feels is a natural rail-water junction. While Philip, less impressionable than his friend, goes on ahead with the surveying party, Harry returns to Hawkeye with Colonel Sellers to prepare a petition to Congress for the improvement of the navigation of Columbus River.

Meanwhile in Philadelphia the young Quaker woman with whom Philip Sterling is in love, Ruth Bolton, has come home from a Quaker seminary impatient at its confining environment and announces to her family that she is going to study medicine. In spite of her parents' anxiety she enters the newly established Women's Medical College in the city and begins her exhausting studies.

In Hawkeye Harry Brierly meets and becomes fascinated with Laura Hawkins. In a flashback chapter we are told how during the Civil War Laura fell in love with a handsome Confederate officer, Colonel Selby, who enticed her into a false marriage and who abandoned her after revealing that he was already married. This experience has left her, still beautiful, with a cynical determination to make her way in the world by playing upon the susceptibilities of the now contemptible opposite sex. She skilfully manipulates Harry's fascination with her, much to Philip's sincere alarm, and it occurs to Harry that Laura would do a superb job of lobbying for the river improvement scheme at Washington. When Hawkeye is visited by Senator Abner Dilworthy, Colonel Sellers solicits his interest in the Columbus River project. The Senator, taken with Washington Hawkins' guilelessness and adaptability, hires him as his secretary and, taken with Laura's beauty and cleverness, invites her to visit his family during the winter session of Congress.

Finding a need for a more generalized cultural background before continuing medicine and being exhausted from close application to her special studies, Ruth Bolton decides to go away to school at a large coeducational New England seminary. Here she rooms with the family of a retired lawyer, Squire Montague, becomes good friends with his daughter Alice, and throws herself delightedly into the community life of the little college town of Fallkill. In midwinter, the railroad operations being temporarily suspended during the harsh weather, Philip and Harry come East, the one to try to secure a share in the railroad company's stock, the other to help procure a Congressional appropriation for the Columbus River project. While negotiations are pending, the two young men make a short visit to Fallkill, where Harry flirts and Philip becomes uneasy at seeing Ruth so apparently independent and far from pining for him.

In the national capital, Washington Hawkins learns the ins and outs of Congressional committees and is duly impressed with all he sees. He reports progress now and then in letters to Colonel Sellers back at Stone's Landing and at last is able to report passage of the bill which grants a $200,000 appropriation for the navigation project. Harry, who has been flitting around the capitol buttonholing congressmen and other influential personages, naïvely takes all the credit for the bill's passage and rushes back to Stone's Landing to take charge of engineering operations. After several weeks of dredging and digging have elapsed, the appropriation money still has not arrived, Harry's letters to the Columbus River Slackwater Navigation Company in New York remain unanswered, and his orders on the company to pay for wages and supplies are ignored. Colonel Sellers quells a mutiny of the workmen only by dividing all his savings among them and giving them lots in the proposed city of Napoleon. Harry goes to New York to find out what is the matter, while Sellers forgets his disappointment at the cessation of work on the project by dreaming wonderful dreams of the fortunes to be made in various land speculations along the route of the new railroad. New York headquarters finds no difficulty in explaining to Harry in detail not only how the $200,000 appropriation has been entirely consumed in necessary lobbying, vote-buying, and influencing the press, but that the company is at present $25,000 in debt. As the railroad creeps nearer, the little town of Hawkeye becomes panicky and subscribes such a large sum that the railroad company decides to forget Napoleon and follow the relatively straighter course through Hawkeye, whereupon the boom town of Stone's Landing suddenly fades into a ghost town and Colonel Sellers' hopes collapse. To cap the climax of misfortune, Washington Hawkins, who had written that he was about to accept $40,000 for the Tennessee Land, writes that he has held out for $150,000 and again a chance has been lost.

Meanwhile, Ruth's father, Eli Bolton, who has for years been a gullible listener to people in need of money and who is not averse to helping them attempt to enrich themselves, has become involved, through a Mr. Bigler, in a railroad speculation. He has been left holding a presently useless tract of land, in which it is rumored there may be coal, and he commissions Philip to explore the land for him. Philip, who has decided that the Salt Lick Pacific Extension is not a genuine venture but only an excuse for a Wall Street speculation, gladly accepts Mr. Bolton's offer. He feels a need to become a man worthy of Ruth's respect if he is to win her. He cannot understand her good-natured independence, which is no more than her own desire to prove herself as an individual before becoming a spouse. Alice Montague has secretly fallen in love with Philip, and Philip, piqued at Ruth's lack of attention, rather favors Alice for the moment. But when he breaks his arm in a theater fire scare, it is Ruth who with confident devotion and calmness assists the surgeon in dressing his wounds.

At the capital, Washington Hawkins has induced Senator Dilworthy to sell the Tennessee Land to the government as the site of an industrial university for Negroes, or "freedmen," as they are then called. The land's variety of growth and mineral resources make it an ideal location for the study of agriculture, husbandry, mining, and metallurgy. The Senator sends for Laura to groom her as a lobbyist for the necessary appropriation.

At this juncture we are introduced to postbellum Washington, its muddy streets, its *nouveau-riche*, pretentious society, its vulgar and costly lobbying. Laura quickly becomes a skilful lobbyist, combining lavish entertainment of committeemen with subtle coquetry, all the while keeping score of the votes she is winning for the Knobs Industrial University Bill. In her maneuvers she is guided by her mentor, Senator Dilworthy, who explains every move in hypocritical terms of devotion to the public good and benefaction to the "colored race." Her open flirtation, which marks her as one of the chief women lobbyists of the capitol, inspires a certain amount of gossip and infuriates Harry Brierly, who is hopelessly infatuated with her. When Colonel Selby, Laura's former lover and pretended husband, arrives with his wife and family and resumes

his extramarital relations with Laura, Harry, completely unaware
of Laura's past, becomes frantic. As soon as Philip gets out of him
the story of Laura's scandalous behavior with Colonel Selby, Philip
goes to Washington to find out what kind of a scrape his friend
has got himself into. He faces Laura bluntly with what he considers
her trifling with Harry and she tells him that Harry is a foolish
young flirt who had best stay away from her. Learning that Colonel
Selby is preparing to leave for Europe with his family, while all
along he has pretended to be ready to fly to the ends of the earth
with his paramour, Laura goes to his hotel and shoots him dead.
She is immediately apprehended along with her innocent "escort,"
Harry Brierly, and taken to the Tombs. Harry is released almost
at once but Laura remains in prison awaiting trial.

Before the murder, however, Laura has succeeded—through
blackmailing a senator whose speech she has ghost-written without
his knowledge—in securing a majority for the Knobs Industrial
University Bill. It is reported favorably out of committee and in
a suspenseful scene is carried by a two-thirds majority in the
House. The attack it has received in the newspapers as a swindle
designed to benefit the Hawkins family and their friends is considered by the experienced Senator Dilworthy a persecution very
helpful to their cause. When Congress convenes for the second
session in December, Colonel Sellers is worried about the prospects
of the bill in the Senate, for the repercussions of the trial of Laura
Hawkins, whose name is inextricably associated with the bill, may
well affect it adversely. Momentary relief comes with the successful
postponement of the trial. Senator Dilworthy and his faithful secretary Washington Hawkins through various statements and public appearances bring every moral and religious influence to bear
that they can in favor of the bill.

When the murder trial gets under way the defense, led by
the brilliant strategy of the famous criminal lawyer Mr. Braham,
succeeds in securing a jury suitably ignorant and illiterate for easy
manipulation, then proceeds to stage a moving and eloquent appeal
in behalf of the beautiful woman who has been victimized by men
and has in a moment of temporary insanity retaliated for her
injuries. While Colonel Sellers and Laura's brother wait with bated

breath in Washington for news of the trial and for the final reading of the bill in the Senate, a bombshell is dropped in the form of the sensational exposure of Senator Dilworthy's buying of votes for his re-election. When the Colonel and Washington rush to the capitol they find every senator with a newspaper extra in his hand. Needless to say, not a single vote is cast for the bill, and again the Sellers dream bubble bursts. There follows a Senate investigation into Senator Dilworthy's corruption, the result of which is that in the face of incontrovertible evidence and sworn testimony of vote-buying the Senate upholds its ancient dignity and exonerates Dilworthy by a verdict of no proof of bribery.

The strategy of Laura's counsel, Braham, in his plea for temporary insanity succeeds in winning a verdict of not guilty and Laura is freed amidst tumultuous public indignation. Approached by a lecture agent she attempts to make a public lecture on "The Revelations of a Woman's Life," but is hooted off the stage and hustled by a jeering crowd gathered outside the theater. She goes home crushed and dies of heart failure.

All this while Philip Sterling has been prospecting the Ilium coal field for Mr. Bolton with intermittent tantalizing indications of the presence of coal but with no actual success. Mr. Bolton is talked into lending his name as security to Bigler, who comes to him with another hard-luck story. He is neatly swindled by him and loses almost all he has, including his country home. Philip's work naturally has to cease, and he goes to visit the Montagues at Fallkill. Squire Montague, with the enthusiasm of complete ignorance, stakes Philip to a continuation of his prospecting; but after weeks more of fruitless effort Philip pays off his men—for he is too proud to ask Squire Montague for more money—and continues alone. Just as he is about to give up he strikes the vein of coal. Ironically enough, at this very moment he receives a telegram that Ruth is critically ill. He rushes to Philadelphia, where he finds her with a serious fever contracted during her work in the hospital. He stays by her bedside and imparts to her the strength to keep alive and return to health. We leave them happy in their love; and Alice Montague forever stifles in her own bosom the love that Philip will never know she had for him.

Clay Hawkins, who has years ago gone to Australia, reads the news of Laura's trouble and immediately embarks for the States, arriving in Hawkeye, Missouri, just in time to console his foster mother at Laura's death and to take upon himself the ordering of the household. Washington Hawkins, who has become prematurely old and white-haired, finally abandons hope in the Tennessee Land and, tearing up the latest tax bill on it, departs for Hawkeye and matrimony with Louise Boswell, accompanied by the ever rebounding and optimistic Colonel Sellers.

From this brief synopsis it can easily be seen that the principal ingredients of the sensation novel are present: disaster (in the steamboat explosion), unknown parentage, adoption, false marriage, murder, self-sacrificing devotion, and hovering between life and death. The steamboat explosion is used quite typically to precipitate the orphan Laura Van Brunt into the story. By the upper-class sound of her name at a time when Dutch-descended first families of New York were prominent in the news and by the reference to her real father (in the correspondence she unearths between her adopted father and Major Lackland) as a "handsome-featured aristocratic gentleman" (I, 116),[37] Laura obviously represents the missing heiress theme. The adopted son, Clay, conscious of his extraordinary obligation to Si and Nancy Hawkins, always steps in to right the family's misfortunes with a loyalty far above that of their natural children.[38] Laura's false marriage serves as the motivation for her murder of her seducer, Selby, and, while it also serves in part as motivation for her successful career as a woman lobbyist, is a stock device of the sensation novel. Similarly, Philip Sterling's dogged search after coal against seemingly hopeless odds and Ruth Bolton's struggle with death just as Philip's long-awaited success is at hand find their parallels throughout contemporary popular fiction. It is outside the scope of the present investigation to detail the similarities with other novels of the time or to trace these themes and devices in sensation fiction. For one thing, to try to find direct literary indebtedness to individual authors in an area of such overwhelming conformity and unconscious plagiarism would be fruitless and inconclusive; and for another, there are several excellent studies of the genre, such as

Mary Noel's *Villains Galore* (1954), Helen Waite Papashvily's *All the Happy Endings* (1956), and Fred Lewis Pattee's *The Feminine Fifties* (1940), to which the reader is referred.[39] Particularly revealing is Chapter XIV of Mary Noel's book, "Plot Conventions" (pp. 144-56).

DeLancey Ferguson, without mentioning the American dime novel or story weekly, finds the influence of the contemporary Victorian novel, stating that Clemens and Warner were writing "in the heyday of Wilkie Collins, Sheridan LeFanu, and Mrs. Henry Wood—the day of the Three-Decker, with its crew of Missing Heirs who had 'shipped as Able Bastards, till the Wicked Nurse confessed' " (p. 168). There is no question but what the Victorian sensation novel added its weight along with the native American brand. Novelists published by *Harper's Monthly* before 1885 included Dickens, Collins, and Reade, and *Frank Leslie's New Family Magazine* published serials largely by British writers, including Collins and Mrs. Henry Wood.[40] Joseph Sheridan Le Fanu apparently was not serialized in the United States, though he could be read in Dickens' *All the Year Round*.[41] In view of the far greater publication in the United States, both in magazines and in book form, of the American authors than the British, with the possible exception of Dickens, there is no need to look to the Victorians for Clemens' and Warner's inspiration; and to ignore the native product so well known by Clemens is to bypass the real point of departure. The correct conclusion to be drawn is that similar conditions gave rise to similar literature in England and the United States. The vogue of sensation fiction in England during the third quarter of the nineteenth century stemmed necessarily from the nature of the Victorian middle-class reading public, the status of popular publishing, and the tenets of British society. The *Quarterly Review* traced it to cheap magazines, railroad bookstalls, and libraries, the *Contemporary Review* to "widespread corruption in society."[42] British publishing enterprise had its own yellowbacks, *Penny Jupiters*, and "family story papers."

Most commentators on *The Gilded Age* have assumed that its melodramatic, sensational elements were the result of Twain's ignorance of the art of fiction and his journalistic upbringing and

Warner's lack of originality and consequent reliance on the hackneyed. According to Ferguson, "these cavilers at the contemporary popular novel, when they began to plan one of their own, were wholly unable to free their minds from the stock pattern of stock Victorian fiction" (p. 168). Bernard DeVoto goes even further:

> If Warner invented the cumbersome story of "The Gilded Age", Mark Twain consented to it. Wasn't such melodrama the condition of fiction? For twenty years he had been reading novels in which female infants of mysterious parentage were hurled before the reader by expedients quite as violent as a steamboat wreck, and in which their compelling beauty produced a seduction that had to be paid for with the villain's life, leaving the seduced under obligation to die of a broken heart. He consented. It was quite impossible for this newcomer to fiction, this newspaper humorist, to do anything else. He had no reasoned philosophy of literature; it is unlikely that he ever analyzed, beyond its mere grammar, an effect of his own or any one's else; he completely lacked the discipline of art. . . .[43]

Carl Van Doren writes: "Neither man shrank from melodrama or hesitated to set it side by side with the most scrupulous realism." And Andrews calls the plot "an imperfect amalgam of Mark's unsureness in structure and Warner's early deference to the sentimentalism of Mrs. Stowe."[44]

That the structure is weak and the plot, or rather group of plots, obvious and melodramatic is unquestionable. Clemens himself declared in retrospect that he and Warner had worked "in the superstition that we were writing one coherent yarn, when I suppose, as a matter of fact, we were writing two *in*coherent ones."[45] But that the use of stock patterns and devices was the result of ignorance, ineptitude, or carelessness is an entirely unwarranted conclusion. It is significant that this conclusion coincides with the evaluation of Mark Twain by certain twentieth-century critics as an unconscious genius, a "divine amateur,"[46] molded by the genteel tradition, by his mother and wife, by Howells, or by the frontier—anything but a conscious craftsman aware of what he was writing.

It is not necessary to look farther than the Appendix to the novel (written by Twain but signed "The Authors") to demonstrate the intentional burlesque in the plot:

> Perhaps some apology to the reader is necessary in view of our failure to find Laura's father. We supposed, from the ease with which lost persons [the manuscript originally had "lost parents"][47] are found in novels, that it would not be difficult. But it was; indeed, it was impossible; and therefore the portions of the narrative containing the record of the search have been stricken out. Not because they were not interesting—for they were; but inasmuch as the man was not found, after all, it did not seem wise to harass and excite the reader to no purpose. (II, 353)

There are several passages in the novel proper that provide corroborative internal evidence of burlesque intent. When, for example, Philip is piqued at Ruth's seeming lack of interest in him at Fallkill, he would like to be able to bring himself to quarrel with her ". . . and fling himself out of the house in tragedy style, going perhaps so far as to blindly wander off miles into the country and bathe his throbbing brow in the chilling rain of the stars, as people do in novels; but he had no opportunity" (I, 256). Later, Alice, who we are to believe has fallen secretly in love with Philip, is described thus:

> Whatever her thoughts may have been they were unknown to Philip, as they are to these historians; if she was seeming to be what she was not, and carrying a burden heavier than any one else carried, because she had to bear it alone, she was only doing what thousands of women do, with a self-renunciation and heroism of which men, impatient and complaining, have no conception. Have not these big babies with beards filled all literature with their outcries, their griefs, and their lamentations? It is always the gentle sex which is hard and cruel and fickle and implacable. (II, 210)

More effective even than these bits of editorializing is the pernicious formative effect upon Laura attributed to her reading of contemporary fiction, a falsifying of her concept of social values described in terms strongly reminiscent of the *Backlog* conversations.

> Much of her reading had been of modern works of fiction, written by her own sex, which had revealed to her something of her own powers and

given her, indeed, an exaggerated notion of the influence, the wealth, the position a woman may attain who has beauty and talent and ambition and a little culture, and is not too scrupulous in the use of them. She wanted to be rich, she wanted luxury, she wanted men at her feet, her slaves, and she had not—thanks to some of the novels she had read—the nicest discrimination between notoriety and reputation; . . . (I, 217-18)

The small private libraries of Hawkeye were "largely made up of romances and fictions which fed her imagination with the most exaggerated notions of life" (I, 206). Reinforcing such passages are frequent small jibes ("Such disappointments seldom occur in novels, but are always happening in real life") which have the effect of maintaining a tone of literary banter through much of the book.

In the original manuscript occurs a touch of Gothicism of the kind with which current sensation fiction was redolent. It has been deleted, probably because it neither had sufficient purpose in the story nor clearly conveyed its intended satirical effect. Toward the end of Chapter IX, during Si Hawkins' deathbed scene, "There was a sound at the door, as if something had fallen against it, & a listening look came into the startled faces; but only the wailing & moaning of the wind was heard, & presently the circumstance was forgotten." A little while later, toward midnight, "sounds were heard at the door as if some one were there," but at this moment Mr. Hawkins, rousing out of a doze, distracts the listeners' attention. Hawkins dies, and the mother and children give final vent to their pent-up grief.

When this ebullition had presently subsided into moanings & occasional plaintive ejaculations, sounds were again heard at the door—mutterings, accented with excited interjections.
Dan [Clay] got up & opened the door, & a blast of wind that brought a whirling mist of snow with it blew out his candle. He[48]

(Here the page, the final one of Chapter IX, comes to an end.) What Clemens had in mind will probably never be known. But the burlesque Gothicism is unmistakable.

The most dramatic and, from the standpoint of burlesque, the most effective handling of melodramatic material is the insertion of deliberate anticlimax after the jury has returned a verdict of not guilty in Laura's trial for murder.

. . . The verdict of the jury having left no doubt that the woman was of an unsound mind, with a kind of insanity dangerous to the safety of the community, she could not be permitted to go at large. "In accordance with the directions of the law in such cases," said the judge, "and in obedience to the dictates of a wise humanity, I hereby commit Laura Hawkins to the care of the Superintendent of the State Hospital for Insane Criminals, to be held in confinement until the State Commissioners on Insanity shall order her discharge. Mr. Sheriff, you will attend at once to the execution of this decree."

Laura was overwhelmed and terror-stricken. She had expected to walk forth in freedom in a few moments. The revulsion was terrible. Her mother appeared like one shaken with an ague fit. Laura insane! And about to be locked up with madmen! She had never contemplated this. Mr. Braham said he should move at once for a writ of *habeas corpus*.

But the judge could not do less than his duty, the law must have its way. As in the stupor of a sudden calamity, and not fully comprehending it, Mrs. Hawkins saw Laura led away by the officer.

With little space for thought she was rapidly driven to the railway station, and conveyed to the Hospital for Lunatic Criminals. It was only when she was within this vast and grim abode of madness that she realized the horror of her situation. It was only when she was received by the kind physician and read pity in his eyes, and saw his look of hopeless incredulity when she attempted to tell him that she was not insane; it was only when she passed through the ward to which she was consigned and saw the horrible creatures, the victims of a double calamity, whose dreadful faces she was hereafter to see daily, and was locked into the small, bare room that was to be her home, that all her fortitude forsook her. She sank upon the bed, as soon as she was left alone—she had been searched by the matron—and tried to think. But her brain was in a whirl. She recalled Braham's speech, she recalled the testimony regarding her lunacy. She wondered if she *were* not mad; she felt that she soon should be among these loathsome creatures. Better almost to have died, than to slowly go mad in this confinement.

—We beg the reader's pardon. This is not history which has just been written. It is really what would have occurred if this were a novel. If this were a work of fiction, we should not dare to dispose of Laura otherwise. True art and any attention to dramatic proprieties required it. The novelist who would turn loose upon society an insane murderess could not escape condemnation. Besides, the safety of society, the decencies of criminal procedure, what we call our modern civilization, all would demand that Laura should be disposed of in the manner we have described. Foreigners, who read this sad story, will be unable to understand any other termination of it.

But this is history and not fiction. There is no such law or custom as that to which his Honor is supposed to have referred; Judge [O']Shaunnessy would not probably pay any attention to it if there were. There is no Hospital for Insane Criminals; there is no State Commission of Lunacy. What actually occurred when the tumult in the court room had subsided the sagacious reader will now learn. (II, 289-92)

This deliberate anticlimax is consonant with the total anticlimactic effect of the plot, which leads the reader to anticipate the typical grand reunion of the sensation novel. The grand reunion, however, which would be expected at the least to reunite Laura and her father and Clay and some unknown relative-benefactor, is, as we see, mockingly dropped in favor of realism. Clay is brought back only intermittently for melodramatic effect.

The satirical intent is heavily underlined in Clemens' Chapter XXXVI (II:V), "The Book-store Clerk," in which the plot movement is temporarily suspended to allow for a sort of interlude on contemporary poor taste in literature. An excuse is provided by Laura's browsing at a bookstore near Mr. Buckstone's lodgings while she waits for this gentleman to put in an appearance. When Laura asks the dapper young clerk for Taine's *Notes on England,* he has no idea what she is referring to, though the bookstore has advertised it for sale, and politely suggests that she must mean George Francis Train. When she asks for *The Autocrat of the Breakfast Table,* he replies "with cold dignity" that cookbooks are "somewhat out of their line." Finally, having conned over the Hawthornes, the Longfellows, the Tennysons, and "other favorites of her idle hours,"[49] she picks up "a copy of 'Venetian Life'" and begins "running over a familiar passage here and there." (This was intended partly as a *quid pro quo* compliment to Howells for his mention of *The Innocents Abroad* in the latest instalment of *A Chance Acquaintance* in the *Atlantic*.)[50] At this point, the clerk intrudes himself to recommend to her such titles as *The Pirate's Doom, or the Last of the Buccaneers, The Hooligans of Hackensack, Gonderil the Vampire,* and *The Phunny Phellow's Bosom*

From The Gilded Age, *First Edition*

Laura and the Bookstore Clerk

Phriend; whereupon, Laura turns to him and delivers herself of three pages' worth of courteous but devastating sarcasm, much to the bewildered discomfort of the smugly ignorant young salesman.

". . . Now some people would think it odd that because you, with the budding tastes and the innocent enthusiasms natural to your time of life, enjoyed the Vampires and the volume of nursery jokes, you should imagine that an older person would delight in them, too—but I do not think it odd at all. I think it natural—perfectly natural—in you. And kind, too. You look like a person who not only finds a deep pleasure in any little thing in the way of literature that strikes you forcibly, but is willing and glad to share that pleasure with others—and that, I think, is noble and admirable—very noble and admirable. . . ." (II:60)

On the basis of internal evidence such as is afforded by the foregoing excerpts, one literary historian, Everett Carter, has, indeed, called *The Gilded Age* "an attack in fiction upon sentimentalism in literature as it operated in the social and economic and political life of America."[51]

There is, as well, external testimony to the authors' striving after satirical effect. In a letter from Clemens to Mrs. Fairbanks on April 16, 1873, when the collaborators were nearing the end of their project, he wrote that Livy and Susie Warner

. . . pleaded so long & vigorously for Warner's heroine, that yesterday Warner agreed to spare her life & let her marry—he meant to kill her. I killed my heroine as dead as a mackerel yesterday (but Livy don't know it yet). Warner may or may not kill her to-day (this is in the "boss" chapter.) We shall see. . . .

I'm not half done this letter, but I have an itching desire to get back to my chapter & shake up my heroine's remains. . . .

P.S.—(Night.) My climax chapter is the one accepted by Livy & Susie, & so my heroine, Laura, remains dead.

I have also written another chapter, in which I have brought Clay Hawkins home from California & the Chinchas, made Washington tear up the tax bill, & started him & Col. Sellers home, to appear no more in the book. Do you think that was best? Or would it have been better to let Sellers go over into Pennsylvania first, & give Philip a lift with his mining troubles? He could have passed through Philadelphia, then, & had a chance to see Ruth (poor Ruth!) & the Boltons. (*Fairbanks Letters,* pp. 171-72)

Such thinking aloud, so to speak, has been mistaken for unsureness and stumbling. Actually, when viewed in relation to the historical and biographical facts presented heretofore in this chapter, such a glimpse into the workings of Clemens' mind during composition of the novel indicates his and Warner's desire to fulfil their self-appointed task of outdoing the contemporary popular novel on its own ground. It should be added that not one reviewer at the time caught the burlesque intent. The (London) *Graphic* reviewer was puzzled by the dropping of Clay from an obviously intended "leading part in the tale."[52] *Hearth and Home,* which, it will be remembered, had "thought the whole would prove an inimitable burlesque of the modern novel," found it instead "as genuine a novel as any, . . . on the whole, rather a pathetic than a humorous production."[53] And the Hartford *Courant* said:

The authors apparently had no regard for the rule which requires every novel to end like the standard play, with the happiness of all the agreeable characters and the discomfiture of all the rascals. Apparently after satirizing the shams of the age, they considered their work accomplished and decided to let their characters with a few exceptions take care of themselves. . . .[54]

Though most of the obviousness, melodrama, and sentimentalism in *The Gilded Age* is deliberately burlesque, it is undeniable that the structure is weak and that there is a noticeable lack of cohesion. These defects can be, as they have been, attributed to the lack of experience of the collaborators in writing fiction. But only in part. They are attributable also to the speed with which the book was written—it was begun in January and finished in April—and to what Mrs. Fields called "always a more or less unsatisfactory scheme," collaboration itself.[55] The speed was necessitated by the extreme topicality of the book, several of the events portrayed actually taking place while it was being written.

The collaboration has been interpreted variously. Contemporary reviewers were disturbed in particular by the lack of fusion of the two writers' separate styles. Fred Perkins said:

Probably no admirer of Mr. Clemens nor of Mr. Warner will be satisfied with the quantity he will find of either writer's peculiar product in their joint book. The child has not the traits, in full force, of either parent; or, it may be said, one is reminded of the optical doctrine, that beams of light may so clash as to nullify each other, and leave a dark spot. The peculiar subtlety, and delicate, quiet, graceful humor, of Mr. Warner's best work, are of too cool a tone to mix well with the broader and more ridiculous and literal fun of Mr. Clemens. . . .[56]

The reviewer in *Appleton's Journal* found that the book had "the faults which will possibly cling to the results of most joint author-ship to the end of time."

It is good in episodes from which to make a novel—unsatisfactory as a combination of them. It is like a salad-dressing badly mixed, wherein one comes upon the mustard in lumps, the salt in masses, pools of vinegar, and collections of oil which might have softened the whole. . . . (XI, 59)

The condemnatory *Chicago Tribune* had this to say:

Every one . . . had a right to expect the book, when given to the world, though it should lack the unity and coherence of a work conceived and brought out by a single mind, should at least be redeemed with passages of the refined and delicate beauty which distinguishes the one writer, and with the quaint and fertile humor that has created for the other even a trans-Atlantic popularity. . . .[57]

Where the reviewers were not concerned with the individual au-thors as such they still commented on the lack of cohesion. "It is not so much a well-wrought story, with a unity running through it," said the *Independent*, "as a series of sketches strung together." The *Pall Mall Budget* remarked that "the fortunes of the numer-ous persons introduced are told in a somewhat rambling fashion."[58] The Hartford *Daily Times* decided that

. . . a certain characteristic of abruptness and unexpectedness in the method of developing the story may mean that two hands did fashion the work, all the way through, and find [*sic*], moreover, some difficulty in dovetailing all the chapters, characteristics and incidents, so as to make a nice job of it. . . .[59]

Howells wrote later that "such coherence as it had was weakened by the diverse qualities of their minds and their irreconcilable ideals in literature"; and Brander Matthews commented that the novel was written "not so much in collaboration as in conjunction."[60]

If it was true, as Howells said, that their qualities of mind were diverse and their literary ideals irreconcilable—and that it *was* true can be seen by a merely desultory glance at their individual writings of the same period—why was a collaboration seriously undertaken at all? One answer, the most obvious and superficial one, is that it became the excuse for an enjoyable close association of the two couples for several weeks. A far more decisive answer is the fact outlined above that despite divergence of tastes and mental processes the two authors were in agreement that they could readily outdo the popular novel of the day. On the one hand the collaboration has been called "an enthusiastic coöperative venture,"[61] and on the other the claim has been made that only the character Colonel Sellers "kept the two humourists gayly interested" and that "they made up the rest of the book in a perfunctory way at a low pitch of creative enthusiasm."[62] For the latter of these two extremes of interpretation there is not a shred of evidence. A far more prevalent view is that expressed by Brashear in comparing the collaboration with that of Joseph Conrad and Ford Madox Hueffer. Stating that Clemens "had no experience to help him chart the way for a full-length story," she continues that "Charles Dudley Warner was an experienced and successful literary man" and that "the westerner was canny enough to realize the advantage of working with him . . . ."[63]

Convenient as this theory is for the "divine amateur" concept of Twain, it is without foundation in fact. The only books Warner had written were *My Summer in a Garden*, a series of humorous nature essays that had originally appeared in the Hartford *Courant,* of which he was editor, published in 1870 at the urging of Henry Ward Beecher, *Saunterings*, a collection of travel letters published in 1872, and *Backlog Studies*, a series of social and literary essays published as a volume in the winter of 1872-73. The rest of his output prior to the writing of *The Gilded Age* had consisted of contributions to the *Knickerbocker* during his college days and to *Putnam's* later, a volume of selections from English and American authors entitled *The Book of Eloquence*, issued two years after his graduation from college, and travel letters to the *Courant* when he was abroad on vacation. He did not begin writing his novels until late in life when *The Gilded Age* was a memory.[64] So little was Clemens in awe of this literary man, whom he quickly got to speak of as "Charley"—he always spoke of Howells as "Howells"—that as early as December, 1870, he wrote to Twichell from Buffalo, "I didn't know Warner had a book out."[65] Clemens, therefore, cannot be said to have sought out the assistance of an experienced novelist or writer of fiction; and in the area of journalistic sketches the author of the best-selling *Innocents Abroad* and *Roughing It* had little need for reliance on the author of the far less brilliant volumes *My Summer in a Garden* and *Saunterings*. It is hardly an exaggeration to say it was an instance of the blind leading the blind.

Though it is untrue that Clemens could have derived any substantial benefit from Warner's experience (as he could have from Howells', let us say), there is reason to suppose he may have had a certain timidity at facing a novel for the first time alone. Isabel Lyon, Clemens' secretary during most of the last decade of his life, recorded in her notebook for September 27, 1907, that he had told her that evening not only that he had been the one to propose the collaboration but that he had done so out of apprehension that his recently acquired great reputation might not be sufficient to sustain him by himself.[66] It must be remembered that this was said in retrospect after thirty-four years and that the notes and correspondence of 1872-73 give no indication of such hesitancy, so that the probable honesty of a later admission must be weighed against the probable distortion of reminiscence. In 1933 Miss Lyon reported in her notes on a copy of the contract for *The Gilded Age* that Clemens had told her he slid easily into the arrangement to work with Warner but became irked by the association before he got through.[67] This statement of Clemens' divested of its probable exaggeration can be taken as undoubtedly true. It is only necessary to examine the division of labor in the text and the few extant fragments of manuscript to recognize how quickly Clemens outstripped Warner in imaginativeness, how pervasive his influence was—even on the portions of the novel written by Warner, to how great an extent the original and memorable elements of the story were his, and how frequently his interpolations and emenda-

tions saved the day. As Van Wyck Brooks has said, the irony of
Warner's fate "lay in his having worked with Clemens, . . . the
man of talent collaborated with the man of genius. The result was
that this excellent writer, this competent, ready, industrious craftsman, was only recalled in later years for the weakest work he ever
did. . . ."[68]

CHAPTER III

The Collaboration

CHARLES WARREN STODDARD has given the most succinct account of the collaboration, as it was described to him by Clemens in the winter of 1873-74 during the London sojourn:

He [Clemens] wrote a dozen chapters and read them to the domestic critics.

"Do you catch the idea?" said Mark to Warner. The latter thought he did, and took up the thread of the narrative where Mark dropped it, and spun on until he felt fagged. The story was passed from hand to hand like a shuttle, and came at last to a conclusion. Whenever it flagged under one roof it was carried over to another, where it took a fresh start. The changes were frequent, a chapter or two bringing the writer to a halt; or in consequence of the business of the book, falling naturally to one hand or the other—the love-making to Warner and the melodrama to Mark. . . .[1]

Once the authors had agreed to the undertaking, Clemens, who it will be recalled had a story in mind, immediately set to work and wrote the first eleven chapters, 399 manuscript pages, "before the early flush of enthusiasm waned."[2] These chapters, which were written right out of his early childhood experience, apparently came easily and with great speed, as much as fifty-five pages at one sitting.[3] At the end of Chapter XI, on MS page 399, Clemens scrawled the note, "Now comes in Warner's first Chapter," and circled it.[4] According to Paine, Warner then came over and Clemens read this beginning aloud to him. "Warner had some plans for the story, and took it up at this point, and continued it through the next twelve chapters . . . ."[5] Paine assigned the chapters thus:

Clemens wrote chapters I to XI; also chapters XXIV, XXV, XXVII, XXVIII, XXX, XXXII, XXXIII, XXXIV, XXXVI, XXXVII, XLII, XLIII, XLV, LI, LII, LIII, LVII, LIX, LX, LXI, LXII, and portions of chapters XXXV, XLIX, LVI. Warner wrote chapters XII to XXIII; also chapters XXVI, XXIX, XXXI, XXXVIII, XXXIX, XL, XLI, XLIV, XLVI, XLVII, XLVIII, L, LIV, LV, LVIII, LXIII, and portions of chapters XXXV, XLIX, and LVI. The work was therefore very evenly divided. (II, 477, n. 1)

This division of labor is based on Clemens' own breakdown written in at least two letters of the period, one to Mrs. Fairbanks, February 25, 1874, and one to Dr. John Brown, February 28.[6] To Brown he added, ". . . I wrote 32 of the 63 chapters *entirely* and part of 3 others beside." Tabulated by chapter numbers and titles the division appears as follows:

TWAIN	WARNER
I Squire Hawkins' Tennessee Lands	
II Squire Hawkins Adopts Clay	
III Uncle Daniel's First Sight of a Steamboat	
IV Squire Hawkins on a Mississippi Steamboat	
V Laura Van Brunt Adopted by the Hawkinses	
VI Ten Years Later. Laura a Young Beauty	
VII Col. Sellers' Schemes for Money-making	
VIII Col. Sellers Entertains Washington Hawkins	
IX Squire Hawkins Dies, Leaving Lands to His Children	
X Laura's Discovery. Mrs. Hawkins's Appeal	
XI A Dinner Party. Plain Fare, Brilliant Expectations	
	XII Harry and Philip Go West to Lay Out a Railroad

TWAIN   WARNER

XXXV (II:IV) How Majorities Are Secured

XXXVI (II:V) The Book-store
Clerk
XXXVII (II:VI) Laura Coquets
with Buckstone

XXXVIII (II:VII) Laura Sees Col.
Selby Again
XXXIX (II:VIII) Laura Again in
Love with Selby
XL (II:IX) How Washington
News Leaks Out
XLI (II:X) Harry Hopelessly in
Love

XLII (II:XI) Mr. Trollop Is Trap-
ped and Becomes an Ally
XLIII (II:XII) Newspapers Attack
the University Bill

XLIV (II:XIII) Philip Shows His
Friendship for Brierly

XLV (II:XIV) Why Mr. Buckstone Supported the University
Bill

XLVI (II:XV) Laura Kills Colonel
Selby
XLVII (II:XVI) Laura in the
Tombs
XLVIII (II:XVII) Mr. Bigler Help-
ed Out While Mr. Bolton Runs
in Debt

XLIX (II:XVIII) Philip Just Misses Striking Coal

L (II:XIX) A Bad Fix. Philip Sees
a Way Out of It

LI (II:XX) Congressional Prelimi-
naries. Sellers Justly Offended
LII (II:XXI) Moral Influences to
Help the University Bill
LIII (II:XXII) Dilworthy at
Saint's Rest, Prepares for Re-
election

LIV (II:XXIII) Laura's Trial. An
Intelligent Jury and Model
Judge

As can easily be seen, Mark Twain's characters are the Hawkinses, Laura, Clay, Colonel Sellers, Senator Dilworthy (once
Warner has introduced him), the Washington society group, and
the venal congressmen; his part of the story involves the fortunes
of the Hawkins family, the Tennessee Land, the Knobs University
Bill, Colonel Sellers' several speculative ventures, the lobbying at
Washington, and the vote-buying scandal and Senate investigation
of Senator Dilworthy. Warner's characters are Philip Sterling,
Harry Brierly, the Bolton family, Squire Montague and his daughter Alice, the promoter Bigler, Colonel Selby, the lawyer Braham,
the minor characters associated with the Salt Lick Pacific Extension,
and the court group; his part of the story concerns the adventures
and trials of Philip and Harry, Mr. Bolton's speculations, Ruth
Bolton's education, the Ilium coal field venture, the love affairs
of Laura and Colonel Selby and of Philip and Ruth, Harry's flirtation with Laura, and Laura's trial for murder. In other words,
Twain produced the principal socially critical, satirical parts of the
novel, while Warner, though contributing a lesser share of satire,
handled the more obviously melodramatic elements and provided
the love interest.

   In 1937, Ernest E. Leisy made a valuable examination of

Clemens' own annotated copy of *The Gilded Age,* in the margins of which the author had indicated what he had written, what Warner had written, and what was the result of mutual interpolation or rewriting.[8] Though the marked volume for the most part corresponds with Clemens' account in his correspondence, Leisy found that the task was not as neatly divided as Clemens and Paine had implied.

In reality a number of passages were written by one author and rewritten by the other, and in others they wrote alternate portions. For example, the first two paragraphs of the Preface were written by Warner, the next two by Clemens, the next paragraph was by Warner, and the last by Clemens. Clemens's portions explained the introduction of scraps from foreign literature to serve as chapter heads, and concluded with the remark, "There is scarcely a chapter that does not bear the marks of the two writers of the book."

Space does not allow nor careful judgment condone a detailed restatement of Leisy's findings in the present study. A few examples, however, will serve to indicate the nature of the modifications he discovered.

Although Paine attributes Chapter XVIII ["Laura Deceived by a Mock Marriage"] to Warner, Clemens notes it "was mapped out by C, written by W." Chapter XXIX, moreover, is not wholly Warner's. It relates Philip's experience with the surly conductor who threw him off the train for his kindness to a woman passenger. In this connection Clemens observes, "This incident is fact—recounted by C and written by W." Clemens supplied the ironic passage on bad citizenship beginning at bottom [*sic*] of p. 268 and extending to bottom p. 269 [I, 321-22], "He confessed . . . rest of the people."[9]

. . . .

Concerning Chapter LVI Clemens says, "This was first done in narrative style by W and afterward broken up into dialogue by C." Warner wrote the first part, up to p. 506 [II, 269], "The wrangle continued." On page 508 he wrote, "Narrative done by W—turned into dialogue by C." [The dialogue begins with the oratorical monologue delivered by Sellers to the jury while the counsel and bench are distracted by their wrangle over technicalities and continues with the cross-examination of the Colonel.] Warner resumed the narrative at the bottom of p. 509 [II, 273], "The defense then spent a day," and continued to the end of the chapter. Clemens's ebullience enlivened the trial scene of Laura Hawkins.[10]

Study of the extant portions of the manuscript reveals interesting refinements even within the modifications reported by Leisy.
In Chapter VI, for example, Leisy states that there occurs an interpolation by Warner. "It begins with the third paragraph, and includes the fourth and the sixth." This is the passage describing
Laura Hawkins as a schoolgirl (I, 67-69). In a letter to Livy,
April 26, [1873], Clemens implies that he himself wrote the final
version. This is how he describes the difficulties he and Warner had
with the passage:

> Warner failed on his description of Laura as a school-girl—as a *pic-
> ture* of her, I mean. He had simply copied Miss Woolson's pretty descrip-
> tion almost word for word—the plagiarism would have been detected in
> a moment. I told him so—he saw it & yet I'm hanged if he didn't hate to
> lose it because there was a "nip" & a pungency about that woman's phrases
> that he hated to lose—& so did I, only they weren't ours & we couldn't
> take them. So I set him to create a picture & he went at it. I finally took
> paper & pencil, had a thought, (as to phraseology) & scratched it down.
> I had already told him what the *details* of the picture should be, & so
> only choice language was needed to dress them in. Then we read our two
> efforts, & mine being rather the best, we used it. And so it *ought* to have
> been the best. If I had been trying to describe a picture that was in *his*
> mind, I would have botched it.[11]

The manuscript for this portion of Chapter VI bears out both
Clemens' annotation cited by Leisy and his statement in the letter
to Livy. Halfway down the Clemens page originally numbered
163 occurs the note "[insert 163 $\frac{1}{8}$, $\frac{1}{4}$, $\frac{1}{2}$, $\frac{3}{4}$]." Page 163 $\frac{1}{8}$ is
missing, but 163 $\frac{1}{4}$ and 163 $\frac{3}{4}$ are in Warner's hand, the last bear-
ing emendations by Clemens. Page 163 $\frac{1}{2}$, the one describing Laura
"as a *picture*," is in Clemens' hand and replaces a differently conceived, less evocative image by Warner, crossed out remnants of
which appear on the adjoining leaves of manuscript.[12] The fragments of the Warner version of the "picture" read as follows: "In
the street, where she was likely to be the center of an eager bunch
of talking, pushing and laughing companions, she was conspicuous
by some graceful cast of her scarf over her shoulders, by a saucy
dip of her hat, or by the superior earnest-[163 $\frac{1}{4}$]"; ". . . secrecy.
Secrets? She lived on momentous secrets, and taffy, molasses candy
and other sweetmeats, which she ate in the street, going to and from

school, with other chattering and skipping girls of her age, who wore their hair braided down their backs, braided and tied with colored ribbons" [163¾].[13] In the last paragraph of the interpolation (on 163¾), where Warner has applied a string of adjectives to Laura, "willful, generous, forgiving, imperious, affectionate, improvident, charming," Clemens with a characteristically impatient flourish strikes out the last adjective, throws in a dash, and adds: "—bewitching, in short" (I, 69).

The question of the collaboration, indeed, is more complex than Leisy's report would suggest. Clemens obviously did not have the manuscript at hand when he jotted down his marginalia, or if it was available he did not consult it. Though his crediting of portions of chapters to himself or to Warner is in general fairly accurate, his always fallible memory appears to have led him astray in several places. At any rate, two or three passages involving interpolations by one author in the other's text were, judged by the evidence of final manuscript at least, inaccurately assigned. Chapter XLIX, for example, concerning the prospecting of Mr. Bolton's coal mine by Philip and Harry, had been listed by Paine as the joint work of the collaborators; and according to Clemens' annotations of his copy of the novel "all the matter on pp. 443, 444, and 445, except the last paragraph on p. 445" (II, 194-96 plus two lines at the top of 197) he had written himself. Yet almost a third, including the last fourth, of this passage is in Warner's hand.[14] And the seven-line paragraph, later in the chapter, that describes the coal "find" as worthless, though also claimed by Clemens is entirely in Warner's hand.[15] Similarly, the paragraph in Chapter LVIII describing Laura's hypothetical commitment to the Hospital for Lunatic Criminals (II, 290-91), though marked by Clemens "W and C," is in Warner's hand.[16] In view of these discrepancies, it is reasonable to assume that Clemens' annotations of such passages were intended to indicate authorship not so much of the final written version as of the ideas incorporated. (It is significant, for example, that Clemens failed to credit Warner with the passage in Chapter XLV that sets forth the provisions of the Knobs Industrial University Bill [II, 149-52], a considerable proportion of which is the latter's hand.)[17]

Chapter XXXV (II, 46-55), "How Majorities Are Secured," is one of the three chapters that Clemens told Mrs. Fairbanks and Dr. Brown he wrote "portions of." It consists of two parts: first a conference between Laura and Senator Dilworthy in which Laura reports progress on her lobbying and receives advice from Dilworthy, and then an informal interrogation of Colonel Sellers by the Washington correspondents on Newspaper Row; and it covers such matters as pushing private interests for the "public good," bribery of congressmen, and abuse of the franking privilege. Clemens' marginalia state "written first by C, but rewritten by W, who incorporated half of C's MS in it and the rest was discarded." What is not apparent from this annotation, however, is that discarded material was not necessarily thrown away but, in this instance at least, found its way into other sections of the novel. There are extant three discarded holograph pages of Clemens' MS which from their numbering and content clearly were intended for this chapter.[18] One of these ends with a retained fragment almost exactly in the form published (II, 50):

".. . leave you, now, & go & convince that Chairman."
And humming a cheery air from some opera, she departed to .. ."[19]

Another reads as follows:

"Laura, my child, there is a tone about your remarks which is unpleasant. Do not be disrespectful."
"Far from it. I could not be, knowing these gentlemen as I do. A great many of them have bought their seats in Congress, with money, & the whole country recognizes that as right & legitimate; & so why should any one complain if they try to get back some of the money they have spent? I am sure I would not find fault with them."

The first two sentences of dialogue, by Senator Dilworthy, have been crossed out and replaced by the following sentence in Warner's hand:

"It strikes me, sir, that your remarks are a little disrespectful[.]"

The page, originally intended for the first part of Chapter XXXV (Laura and Dilworthy), was transferred to the second part (news-

men and Sellers) by Warner, then discarded entirely and its content assigned to Chapter LI, "Congressional Preliminaries . . . ,"
in which Colonel Sellers explains the inexplicable ways of Congress
to his Sancho Panza, Washington Hawkins. The subject matter,
the buying of seats in Congress for money, has been retained but
the concept of the dialogue has been changed and the passage entirely rewritten as it appears in the published version (II, 220).[20]
The third page, having to do with committee investigations (or
"trials") of bribery and vote-buying, has similarly been reassigned
to Chapter LI, expanded, and rewritten (II, 220-21). The reference in it to Senator Balloon's eloquent speeches about upholding
the ancient dignity of the Senate has been transferred to the Dilworthy investigation scene in Chapter LIX (II, 301).[21]

The combined results of Leisy's examination of Clemens' annotated copy of *The Gilded Age* and my examination of the manuscript do not show any substantial inaccuracy in Clemens' original
outline of the division of labor; but they do reveal two general
modifications of it: (1) that the mutual interpolations and rewritten passages, though minor in nature, were frequent and caused
a greater interweaving of the collaborators' work than would appear from the basic division, and (2) that to a greater degree than
would appear from the division Clemens' ideas and even phraseology were absorbed into many of the portions written by Warner.
The available evidence suggests the logical hypothesis, moreover,
that this cross-strain from Clemens is particularly strong in the
borderline chapters, such as XIII or XVIII, where Warner found
it necessary to handle characters originated by Clemens. Though no
manuscript evidence at present exists for Clemens' influence on
Warner's handling of Colonel Sellers in Chapter XIII, for example,
such an utterance as "I'm down here now with reference to a
little operation—a little side thing merely" is assuredly phrased in
the Mark Twain manner.[22]

A passage that illustrates the process of interpenetration occurs
in Chapter LVIII, "The Verdict. Laura Acquitted." It presents
Laura's interview with the lecture agent, J. Adolphe Griller (II,
293-95), and was credited to himself by Clemens. The extant
manuscript page that contains the end of this paragraph shows,

however, only a partial rewriting by Clemens of a version already written by Warner. Here is that portion; all deletions and additions (in italics) are by Clemens:

     twelve   [."]
. . . a liberal offer,—~~five~~ thousand dollars for thirty nights, ~~and expenses.~~"
 Laura thought. She hesitated. Why not? It would give her employ-
ment, money. She must do something.
 "I will think of it, and let you know ~~very~~ soon.~~"~~ *But still, there is
very little likelihood that I—however, we will not discuss it further now."*
 "Remember, that ~~now is the time, Miss Hawkins. Au revior.~~" *the
sooner we get to work the better, Miss Hawkins, public curiosity is so
fickle. Good day, madam."*
 The close of the trial . . . [Remainder of page in Warner's hand
only.][23]

It is not to be inferred, of course, that Warner was dependent upon Clemens' editing to restore such passages to a presentable tone and style. If the following excerpt, for example, from what must have been an earlier draft by Warner of his own Chapter XL is compared with the same passage in his published version, it can be seen that by careful reworking of his own material he could produce a text which while lacking the liveliness and pungency of Clemens' work caught its general spirit.

 Col. Sellers entered into this plan as far as the selling of the Hawkins Land to the govmt was concerned with great heartiness. He believed with Washington that the land was worth millions of money, but he was willing that the govmt should share in it, and he probably would not re-fuse a competence out of it[.][24]

This rather pallid bit of exposition he expanded and enlivened into the following narrative passage punctuated with dialogue:

 It must not be supposed that the Colonel in his general patriotic labors neglected his own affairs. The Columbus River navigation scheme absorbed only a part of his time, so he was enabled to throw quite a strong reserve force of energy into the Tennessee Land plan, a vast enterprise commensurate with his abilities, . . .
 "We must create a public opinion," said Senator Dilworthy. "My only

interest in it is a public one, and if the country wants the institution, Congress will have to yield."

. . . .

When Washington Hawkins read [a newspaper dispatch stating that Senator Dilworthy was inflexibly opposed to any arrangement that would not give the government absolute control of the land] . . . , he went to the Colonel in some anxiety. He was for a lease, he didn't want to surrender anything. What did he think the government would offer? Two millions?

"Maybe three, maybe four," said the Colonel, "it's worth more than the Bank of England." (II, 92-93)

If Mark Twain doctored the passage, there is no surviving evidence to prove it.

It appears, furthermore, that Clemens' ideas not only permeated much of Warner's portion of the novel but also served to strengthen Warner's uncertain plan of action. There is no direct evidence, to be sure, that it was Clemens who resolved Warner's dilemmas; but there *is* evidence that Warner was unsure of the outcome of the plot, and it can be assumed that Clemens was instrumental in shaping it. A page of manuscript in Warner's hand presents his projected outline for the second half of the novel, roughly from Chapter XXV to the end (MTP, DV 137). This outline, though very bare and lacking numerous episodes, corresponds fairly accurately with the finished novel up through Chapter XLIV. At this point the main characters are in Washington, the "Tennessee scheme" is under way, and Philip Sterling is developing the coal project. Then Warner proposes that the following summer the "Tennessee scheme" (Knobs University Bill) "will blow up (in the long July session of congress)" owing to the discovery of vote-buying by Dilworthy (called Bumroy throughout the outline),[25] or as an alternative "you can let the scheme cook *all* summer and blow up in the winter more untimely" when Dilworthy fails to be re-elected. Still unsatisfied, he offers the further alternative that the murder and trial take place in the summer and the exposure of Dilworthy follow in the winter. Whether or not Clemens devised the dramatic timing of the murder trial, the vote on the bill, and the Dilworthy exposure to follow one another in a sequence calculated to heighten and sustain suspense cannot be proved, but the fact that both Laura and Dilworthy were his characters and Laura's machinations as a lobbyist his work strongly suggests that the combination of denouements was also of his contrivance. Such firsthand evidence as the fragment of Warner's outline dispels the false doctrine, chief apostle of which is Bernard DeVoto, that the literary man Warner laid out the plot and Clemens, the crude outlander, merely acquiesced.

No better indication of the superior quality of Clemens' imagination can be cited than the manner in which Chapter LX, describing Laura's posttrial fate (the "boss" chapter, as Clemens called it) was handled by the two authors. As we have seen, Clemens and Warner, following their plan of both writing versions of key chapters and then appealing to their wives to choose the better, submitted their separate versions of this chapter for approval, and Clemens' was the one chosen.[26] An extant holograph page of Warner's rejected chapter contains the following account of Laura's lecturing fiasco and its aftermath:

The reporters took no notes, and very soon, they all arose and went out, talking and laughing. And one by one most of the men dropped out, having seen the woman enough.

Before Laura had half finished, she broke down in a nervous agitation and abruptly left the stage. This was the brilliant triumph she had fed her imagination on! The world had not even curiosity about her!

She hastened from the hall and to her hotel. There, locked in her room, she threw herself upon the bed, and gave way to a paroxism [sic] of rage and disappointment. This was the end. There was nothing now to hope.

Her whole life passed before her in those hours of anguish, the struggle, the passion, the pride, the sin of it, . . . (MTP, DV 137)

Compare this with Clemens' vivid presentation of the same sequence of events in the published chapter:

There were only a handful of coarse men and ten or twelve still coarser women, lolling upon the benches and scattered about singly and in couples.

Her pulses stood still, her limbs quaked, the gladness went out of her face. There was a moment of silence, and then a brutal laugh and an explosion of cat-calls and hisses saluted her from the audience. The

From The Gilded Age, *First Edition*
The Terrible Ordeal

clamor grew stronger and louder, and insulting speeches were shouted at
her. A half-intoxicated man rose up and threw something, which missed
her but bespattered a chair at her side, and this evoked an outburst of
laughter and boisterous admiration. She was bewildered, her strength was
forsaking her. She reeled away from the platform, reached the anteroom,
and dropped helpless upon a sofa. The lecture agent ran in, with a hurried
question upon his lips; but she put forth her hands, and with the tears
raining from her eyes, said:

"Oh, do not speak! Take me away—please take me away, out of this
dreadful place! Oh, this is like all my life—failure, disappointment, misery
—always misery, always failure. What have I done, to be so pursued!
Take me away, I beg of you, I implore you!"

Upon the pavement she was hustled by the mob, the surging masses
roared her name and accompanied it with every species of insulting
epithet; they thronged after the carriage, hooting, jeering, cursing, and
even assailing the vehicle with missiles. A stone crushed through a blind,

wounding Laura's forehead, and so stunning her that she hardly knew what further transpired during her flight.

It was long before her faculties were wholly restored, and then she found herself lying on the floor by a sofa in her own sitting-room, and alone. So she supposed she must have sat down upon the sofa and afterward fallen. She raised herself up, with difficulty, for the air was chilly and her limbs were stiff. She turned up the gas and sought the glass. She hardly knew herself, so worn and old she looked, and so marred with blood were her features. The night was far spent, and a dead stillness reigned. She sat down by her table, leaned her elbows upon it, and put her face in her hands.

Her thoughts wandered back over her old life again and her tears flowed unrestrained. Her pride was humbled, her spirit was broken. Her memory found but one resting-place; it lingered about her young girlhood with a caressing regret; it dwelt upon it as the one brief interval in her life that bore no curse. She saw herself again in the budding grace of her twelve years, decked in her dainty pride of ribbons, consorting with the bees and the butterflies, believing in fairies, holding confidential converse with the flowers, busying herself all day long with airy trifles that were as weighty to her as the affairs that tax the brains of diplomats and emperors. She was without sin, then, and unacquainted with grief; the world was full of sunshine and her heart was full of music. From that— to this! (II, 321-23)

In this connection, something should be said about Laura's immediately subsequent death "from heart disease," which occurs as she is sitting quietly at her table, upon which her elbows are propped, her face in her hands. The modern reader may well be struck by the sentimentalism of this death, particularly as it is preceded by Laura's prayer: "If I could only die! . . . My God, I am humbled, my pride is all gone, my stubborn heart repents— have pity!" (II, 323). It is surprising to find that Warner, generally considered far more the sentimentalist than Twain, in his (unused) version disposed of Laura with admirable realism by sending her into western retirement and obscurity (Leisy, p. 447). It is to be further noted that the apparent pathos of Laura's prayer is in sharp contrast with Clemens' attitude toward the scene: "I killed my heroine dead as a mackerel"; as has repeatedly been shown, Clemens was an enemy and lampooner of sentimentalism.

The most obvious explanation of this seeming lapse on his part is that Laura's death scene was part of the burlesque of contempo-

From The Gilded Age, *First Edition*

Retrospection

rary fiction. *Some* heroine had to die, and Laura was the most likely candidate. There was a definite tragic irony in her fate that afforded a nice contrast with the meaningless and merely bathetic death of the average sentimental heroine. The story of this beautiful, intelligent, resourceful woman, who when victimized by circumstances and by a society she never made retaliates with full vigor only to bring about her own destruction, has the makings of true tragedy, however imperfectly realized. That her destruction takes the form of ostracism and attack by the society that molded her rather than that of enforced death by court order heightens the tragic irony. Consequently, by the time Clemens disposes of her he has already made his point, and though the account of her death may be in the nature of a sop thrown to the yellowback audience Clemens must have felt that this was a minor concession. Besides, he knew that the novel had narrowly escaped a genuinely bathetic death of the minor heroine Ruth. Warner had intended to have Ruth die (apparently so that Alice's constancy could be rewarded by her marriage to Philip) and was prevented from perpetrating such a banality only by the good sense of his wife and Olivia Clemens.[27]

Another possible explanation, though one far more conjectural, is that Clemens intended to imply suicide, a denouement appropriate to the sensation novel. At least two reviewers inferred this. The *Literary World* said that the heroine apparently poisons herself, an inference for which there is not the slightest evidence.[28] The *Golden Age* spoke of Laura's "death by her own hand."[29] There is little indication that this was Clemens' intent, however. Though Laura turns up the gas, there is no suggestion that it is not lighted! The description of her haggard appearance and of her head injury from a stone hurled at her, an injury possibly producing trauma,[30] gives a sort of justification to heart failure or cerebral hemorrhage. (Laura is depicted as high-strung, hardly even neurotic, certainly not frail.) The only excuse for the interpretation of suicide is the final paragraph, with its possible implication of hushed-up truth: "The jury of inquest found that death had resulted from heart disease, and was instant and painless. That was all. Merely heart disease" (II, 323).

The fact that the corruptibility of the American jury plays so large a role in *The Gilded Age,* coupled with Clemens' long-standing anger at the abuse of the jury system, lends some credence to this interpretation. If Clemens meant to imply suicide, he did so very clumsily. "Merely heart disease" is probably intended only as a comment to point up the irony of Laura's actual destruction by society, whether this destruction was effected indirectly through the shock of social opprobrium or directly in a possibly implied literal stoning. As *The Gilded Age* was written in burlesque of the sensation novel, the achievement of the heroine's violent end in accordance with the formula of sensation fiction and at the same time in terms of meaningful satire constitutes a tour de force not contemplated by Warner. Retributive justice has ended the cycle of violation of the moral code, and the victimization of the individual by a corrupt society has been illustrated, at one and the same time. The simple morality of a Sylvanus Cobb has been given a new, socially critical dimension. There is only slight exaggeration in Pattee's claim that to compare Warner's portions of *The Gilded Age* with Mark Twain's "is like looking from a still-life picture on a parlor wall out upon an actual steamboat pulling showily up to a Mississippi wharf."[31]

Mark Twain's creativity was a flame that flared and burned at intense heat, sometimes destructively and wastefully, whereas Charles Dudley Warner's slower imagination smoldered with intermittent flickerings like the backlog in his fireplace. The wastefulness of manuscript sheets seems to have been in almost direct proportion to the heat generated. Clemens was a little envious of his partner's economical writing method. "Have written many chapters twice, & some of them three times—have thrown away 300 clean pages of MS. & still there's havoc to be made when I enter on final polishing. Warner has been more fortunate—he won't lose 50 pages."[32]

The extant manuscript pages bear out this difference. The small, unvarying, almost illegible lines of Warner's manuscript, containing very few corrections, gain much greater mileage page for page than Clemens' large, clear, penman hand, continually interrupted with deletions, rephrasings, interpolations, even whole paragraphs crossed out.[33] Both sought to improve their diction even as they wrote—Clemens to gain greater explicitness, Warner to achieve more accuracy or purer idiom.[34] Both embellished their texts with interpolated words or phrases as they went along: "Sellers threw a lot or two on the market, ∧ and they sold well"; the court was opened ∧ the case called, and the sheriff was directed."[35]

<small>"as a feeler,"</small> (interlineated above "∧ and they sold well")

<small>with the 'oi yis, oi yis' of the officer in his native language,</small> (interlineated above "∧ the case called")

Yet Clemens' alterations and emendations are the result of rapid thinking, immediate commitment to paper, and impulsive changes of mind, the original word often being abruptly abandoned only half written.[36] Warner's, on the other hand, which are far less frequent, show a slow thinking process and considerable uncertainty, a crossed-out phrase often being restored immediately.[37] Similarly, Clemens' interpolations are characteristically short and interlineated: "Mr. Buckstone rose, ∧ & said it was evident . . .";[38] whereas Warner's are afterthoughts, often taking the form of lengthy insertions added on the reverse of a leaf.[39]

<small>with an injured look,</small> (interlineated above "∧ & said it was evident")

Both authors frequently "weakened the English tongue," particularly in dialogue, by subservience to the middle-class gentility with which they were surrounded—Clemens deleting an irrepressible "infernal" and changing "come right out and say so" to "come out and prove it"; Warner changing "Perhaps it isn't" to "Possibly it might not be" and "Divil a bit" to "No, sir, not to my knowledge"; both formalizing verb-phrase contractions.[40] Clemens, moreover, had a running battle against old habit not shared by Warner. This was his conscious effort to enforce restraint upon his impulsively bantering, low-comedy manner, a manner born of long apprenticeship in journalistic burlesque and platform humor. Regardless of whatever "refining" influence he may have received from Livy and Howells—a favorite topic of the pundits—the *Gilded Age* manuscript abounds with instances of a self-censorship that was imposed well in advance of the oral reading sessions. When, for example, Colonel Sellers is eulogizing his Universal Expectorant, he just begins to warm up to his subject ("One of these days I'll have all the nations of the earth expecto—") when he is interrupted by his wife. In the manuscript the sentence is finished and then the latter part crossed out. It reads: "One of these days I'll have all the nations of the earth expectorating in brotherly unison like one grand cosmopolitan watering pot, & blessing the name of Eschol Sellers the world's benefactor between discharges—firing everlasting salutes of honor, as you may say."[41]

The last is admittedly an extreme example; the softening of the burlesque tone generally involves only the change of an ill-chosen word or two.[42] More prevalent are the deletions of exaggerated concepts or language. When Washington Hawkins falls in love with Louise Boswell, he at first (in a discarded fragment) longs for some catastrophe that will allow him to attract Louise's attention by his heroism. But it does not seem that Louise is "ever going to get into serious peril" when he is by. "For some time he depended on robbers; but none ever molested the house, & he had to give them up; then he put his trust in fire, but this failed him too; riots were out of the question—the place was too hopelessly peaceful. There was no chance but in wealth; . . ."[43] This passage was replaced with the simple, straightforward statement that appears in the published text: "Some instinct taught Washington that his present lack of money would be an obstruction, though possibly not a bar, to his hopes, and straightway his poverty became a torture to him which cast all his former sufferings under that head into the shade" (I, 106). Again, in describing the curiosity of Hawkeye inhabitants about Laura's origins Clemens writes: "They meant no harm—they only wanted to know. Villagers always want to know" (I, 121). A deleted continuation of the passage belabors the point with digressive self-indulgence:

they even want to know who lives next door to you; & when you confess that you don't know, they often seem surprised; & when they find out that you not only don't know but don't want to know and never even thought of the subject before, they think there is a screw loose about you somewhere.[44]

All of this excision is the kind of self-censorship he had used when he was editing his Holy Land letters for publication as *The Innocents Abroad*,[45] only this time the process was simultaneous with the writing itself.[46]

The difference in the writing methods of the two collaborators is closely related to the most criticized weakness of *The Gilded Age* as a novel, its overly episodic structure. As the *Independent* put it, the novel was "not so much a well-wrought story, with a unity running through it, as a series of sketches strung together." If Warner's portion is considered by itself, this criticism hardly applies to it. There is a fairly well-wrought story of the Bolton family, with the unity of Ruth's relationship with Philip Sterling running through it. The love affair, with its subplot of Alice Montague's secret love for Philip and overt friendship with Ruth, is utilized with some skill to show the maturing of the young man and woman—Philip in endurance and in strength to meet adversity, Ruth in endurance and also in ability to know herself—so that its happy outcome is in a sense a prize won rather than a gratuitous gift of the author. Harry Brierly's volatility and Philip's steadfastness are thrown into contrast with considerable craftsmanship. Unoriginal, yes; sentimental, yes; but sketchy, no. Therefore, if the criticism applies at all, it applies to Clemens' portion. The deliberately wasted episodes concerning Clay and concerning Laura's parentage I have already shown to be part of the paraphernalia of burlesque on the sensation novel. The fortunes of the Hawkinses, however, are not told with neat precision or flowing continuity. There is, nevertheless, a strong unity of theme that runs through their entire history and this is the all-pervading, corrupting speculative fever which motivates Colonel Sellers' several schemes and finds symbolic embodiment in the Tennessee Land. As I have shown earlier, the murder and trial sequence involving Laura Hawkins, though in part an obvious parody of sensation fiction, is incorporated into the central theme of corruption. Even Warner's characters Harry Brierly, Eli Bolton, and Squire Montague all fall prey to the pervasive mania of speculation.

What, then, is the source of the quite apparent sketchiness of the novel? One answer lies in Mark Twain's writing habits. His was an episodic method, the natural result of individual characteristics reinforced by environmental conditioning. Clemens had a quick, vivid imagination, making him highly susceptible to shocking or suggestively dramatic experiences, an acuity of vision that allowed him to perceive a total scene at a given moment (remember his accounts of riverboat piloting), and a nervous sensitivity that as a boy made him a sleep-walker and as a man a night owl who found it necessary to coax his "reluctant sleepiness" with lager beer or a hot scotch before retiring. His organism had undergone a conditioning favorable to the development of these somatic characteristics—the alertness acquired in river navigation, the exposure to excitement, instability, and violence accompanying the silver-mining life, and the rapid impressionability necessary to good travel reporting. By the time he set about writing *The Gilded Age,* therefore, the episodic method had become the mainstay of his craft, as exemplified in *Innocents Abroad* and *Roughing It.* The method is easily traceable throughout the entire corpus of Mark Twain's writings, but in later novels such as *Huckleberry Finn* and *The Prince and the Pauper* he had learned how to set off episodes in a continuum of story development. In *The Gilded Age,* his first attempt at novel writing, the continuum remains in the background and is not sufficiently integrated to be readily seen at first reading. Moreover, the diversity of elements in *The Gilded Age,* the transitional state of the society it reflects, and the attempted national scope of its coverage combine to accentuate its episodic quality. Writing in 1901, Clemens' friend and sympathetic critic Howells summed up the matter in what I believe is still the best statement of it:

Mr. Clemens uses in work on the larger scale the method of the elder essayists, . . . The end you arrive at is the end of the book, . . . You have noted the author's thoughts, but not his order of thinking; he has not attempted to trace the threads of association between the things that have followed one another; his reason, not his logic, has convinced you, or rather it has persuaded you, for you have not been brought under conviction. It is not certain that this method is of design with Mr. Clemens; that might spoil it; and possibly he will be as much surprised as any to know that it is his method. It is imaginable that he pursues it from no wish but to have pleasure of his work, and not to fatigue either himself or his reader; and his method may be the secret of his vast popularity, but it cannot be the whole secret of it. Any one may compose a scrap-book, and offer it to the public with nothing of Mark Twain's good fortune. Everything seems to depend upon the nature of the scraps, after all; . . . there is no doubt that people like things that have at least the appearance of not having been drilled into line. Life itself has that sort of appearance as it goes on; it is an essay with moments of drama in it rather than a drama; . . .[47]

The decisive answer, however, to the sometimes bewildering lack of cohesiveness in *The Gilded Age* lies in the mechanical division of labor in the collaboration itself. As can readily be seen from the tabulation of chapters, each author developed his own story independently, finding a common meeting-ground of plot only occasionally in chapters written more nearly in *collaboration* in its usual sense of working together. The first twenty-three chapters were divided into two roughly equal parts assigned exclusively to one author or the other, the first eleven to Clemens, the following twelve to Warner. Thereafter, the collaborators alternated by chapters or groups of two or three chapters. In only a few chapters was there a division of responsibility within the chapter itself, and in most instances this was again a segmenting into passages ranging from an occasional single paragraph to several pages. The even less frequent interpolations and rewriting of individual lines and phrases of one author by the other, though significant stylistically and in terms of overall tone, failed to fuse structurally the independently conceived chapters and groups of chapters. So Clemens' admission that the book was two tales in one cover is fairly accurate—what the *Queen* called "the 'patchwork' order of composition" and Brander Matthews writing "in conjunction."[48] By a running series of switchbacks the reader goes ahead with one set of characters, then shifts to the other set, catches up and goes on ahead, then returns to the first set and brings them up to and beyond the others in a fashion akin to the alternating advancement of checkers on a checkerboard.

If the mechanical division of labor had not already made the novel's incohesiveness a foregone conclusion, the final assembling of chapters must have guaranteed it. In his April 26 letter to Livy, marked "10:30 P.M.," Clemens wrote: ". . . to-day we began the work of critically reading the book, line by line & numbering the chapters & working them in together in their appropriate places. It is perfectly fascinating work."[49] On May 5 he wrote his brother, Orion, that the task was completed: "We finished revamping & refining the book tonight—ten days' labor. It is near midnight & we are just through."[50] Though the collaborators had of course kept in close communication throughout the composition of the novel, the fact that with very few exceptions their separately written chapters were assigned their "appropriate places" *as units* only compounded the initial defect in the collaboration. Since there was almost no attempt at effecting a continuity between the alternating segments of material, the novel can at best be said to have been solidified, not synthesized. The extant portions of the manuscript, to be sure, reveal through several series of canceled folios earlier attempts at partial collation, and their physical state shows a good deal of cutting and pasting. With the exception of the jointly written chapters, however, the shifts of material remain largely within each writer's own part of the story.[51] Surely the idea of voting for the better of the two candidates' versions of the same chapter presaged inevitable difficulties!

The significant fact about this awkward, hasty, ill-defined collaboration was not, however, the structural incohesiveness of its product. It was not the divergence of the collaborators' writing methods and styles. Nor was it their patently dissimilar, frequently antipathetic habits of thought and standards of esthetic values. The truly significant and overriding fact was the unity of purpose of Clemens and Warner, so compensating in its effect that it cut through the unresolved problems of design, structure, and refinement. Developing out of the general discontent with current fiction among the American intelligentsia, out of the specific intellectual environment of the Nook Farm colony, and out of the immediate impulse of Clemens and Warner that transformed belief into action, *The Gilded Age* gained in conviction more than it lost in artistry. As the authors stated in their preface to the British edition, "all-pervading speculativeness" and "shameful corruption" were their themes. The strength of the satire outweighed the weakness of the construction and made the novel an immediate best-seller and the controversial harbinger of a period of socially critical realism.

PART II

Roman à Clef and Exposé

CHAPTER IV

Senator Dilworthy

IT WILL BE remembered that when Mark Twain first announced his forthcoming novel written in partnership, he stated that Warner had "worked up the fiction" and he had "hurled in the facts."[1] Facts as such had a fascination for Clemens. From his earliest years he had had a great interest in history, and he much preferred factual and expository reading matter to fiction. He told Rudyard Kipling, "Personally I never care for fiction or story-books. What I like to read about are facts and statistics of any kind."[2] This predilection had undoubtedly been strengthened by his reportorial experience, which had run the gamut from legislative assemblies to fancy-dress balls. Though it is his ability at farcical portraiture that most delights his readers in *The Innocents Abroad* and *Roughing It,* there is much of factual observation in these books; and the interestedness with which he handles statistics is well exemplified in his reports on Hawaiian economy written in 1866 for the Sacramento *Union.*[3] Brander Matthews, a keen appraiser of Mark Twain's writing, wrote that Twain "needed to have the sustaining solidity of the concrete fact, which he could deal with at will."[4] As Clemens himself put it, in his historic interview with the young Kipling, "Get your facts first, and . . . then you can distort 'em as much as you please."[5]

It is not surprising, therefore, that when he set about writing his first novel Clemens, together with his collaborator, produced a *roman à clef* (or *Schlüsselroman*), a story based upon barely disguised current events. Though a large part of *The Gilded Age* also

reflects the youthful experiences and personal associations of both
Clemens and Warner, the elements of the novel that evoked an
immediate response from its readers and that catapulted it into
best-selling status were the direct hits at vulnerable contemporary
institutions and personages. It was these elements that drew the
wrath of the *Chicago Tribune* and other mouthpieces of the ruling
administration down upon the authors' heads. For it must be under-
stood that *The Gilded Age* was a *roman à clef* not in the more commonly applied general sense of "scandalous fiction involving real
persons." It was not written in the spirit of the early eighteenth-
century "key novels" such as Mrs. Manley's *Secret Memoirs and
Manners of Several Persons of Quality,* nor in that of George
Meredith's later novel *Diana of the Crossways,* which made such
obvious use of the Caroline Norton adultery case that Meredith
found it necessary to publish a disclaimer for fear of lawsuit.[6] It
was a "key novel" in the more particular sense of fiction that
"acquires a kind of meretricious interest by the support which it
lends to one side of a current controversy."[7] Yet this narrower
definition is inadequate when applied to *The Gilded Age,* for the
interest the novel aroused, directed as it was against the most
flagrant corruptions of American capitalist enterprise and the
subservient federal government, can by no means be considered
meretricious.

Though the topicality of the novel has become obscured with
the passage of time, readers in 1874 easily recognized events and
personages depicted. It is true that only a very few readers could
possibly have identified all of the many originals; yet hardly anyone in the United States who glanced at a newspaper could fail to
identify at least one or two figures who had been prominent in
recent headlines, and though the newspaper reader might not have
been able to name the actual occurrence upon which any specific
episode was based he would have immediately realized its general
authenticity. The authors, indeed, had underscored the novel's
topicality by giving it the subtitle *A Tale of To-Day.*[8] Seventeen
out of thirty-eight reviews, or nearly half, acknowledged that
actual persons and events were portrayed, and nine of these seventeen named names. As was to be expected, most of these reviews

appeared in American publications; however, two British newspapers were represented. As was also to be expected, all but four
of the reviews were published in metropolitan newspapers.

The two lengthiest and most prominent episodes of *The Gilded
Age*—the Senate investigation of Senator Dilworthy for vote-
buying and Laura Hawkins' trial for murder—were quite literally
drawn from two events of nationwide interest, the investigation of
Senator Samuel C. Pomeroy of Kansas and the murder trial of the
San Francisco adventuress Laura D. Fair. The Pomeroy scandal had
been in the headlines almost continuously from the end of January
until the first week of March, 1873; the Laura Fair trial had been
headlined intermittently from June, 1871, until January, 1873.
Five of the reviews openly identified Dilworthy as Pomeroy
(another one did so indirectly), and three reviews, one of them
British, saw Laura D. Fair in Laura Hawkins.[9] Both episodes in the
novel, it should be noted, were climactic to the political satire, and
the reviews that stopped short of naming names clearly indicated,
none the less, that the most easily identifiable characters were well-
known political figures. The Hartford *Courant*, for example, drily
expressed doubts that the book would be popular among Washington or Kansas politicians; the *New York Herald* said that the
novel transferred "incidents and institutions bodily into its pages"
and the London *Evening Standard* that "every line of the work
can find a parallel in the New York press alone."[10] In addition to
Pomeroy, the Boston *Saturday Evening Gazette* claimed to recognize such other senators as Cameron, Nye, and Harlan and such
national scandals as the Crédit Mobilier exposé.[11] Two of the railroad group of characters were recognized by *Hearth and Home,*
and Laura Hawkins' counsel, Braham, was mentioned in several
reviews as a thinly disguised attorney of prominence.

Some years after publication of the novel the process of identification was resumed, largely by historians and literary investigators, who not only corroborated the early reviews but found further originals for characters, things, and episodes, and the process
is not finished even yet. The evidence found to date, however, is
so nearly complete that it can be stated without qualification that
wherever *The Gilded Age* is not primarily autobiographical or

closely associated with its authors' personal experiences it is at least a *roman à clef*. In fact, the novel is such a detailed *roman à clef* as to justify the conclusion that Clemens and Warner were pillorying the contemporary scene for the sheer enjoyment of it, were it not for the fact that practically every identifiable person or thing was at the time the book was written sufficiently well-known to be recognized by *some* reader, thereby to some degree fulfilling a satirical role.[12]

Senator Dilworthy, as Albert Bigelow Paine says, was familiar enough.[13] In fact, not only was he the character most widely recognized by contemporary readers, but of the several characters identified he was the one who continued to be cited by historians and critics alike as based on an actual public figure.[14] Not until 1954, however, did any investigator examine in detail Twain's use of the Pomeroy case. At that time Albert R. Kitzhaber published an article showing by references to the *New York Tribune, Congressional Globe, Senate Reports* of the 42nd Congress, and several histories of Kansas that the entire episode of the Dilworthy exposure and investigation was drawn, down to the minutest detail, from published reports of the Pomeroy case.[15] The dramatic revelation of Dilworthy's vote-buying by State Senator Noble of the Happy-Land-of-Canaan on the floor of the state legislature at Saint's Rest, the consequent defeat of Dilworthy for re-election, the investigation of the charges of bribery by the Senate at Dilworthy's request and the resultant exoneration of the accused and indictment of the accuser, the particularized testimony of Noble and its rebuttal by Dilworthy—nearly all of these minutiae of incident contained in chapters LIII, LVII, and LIX find their counterparts in the Pomeroy case.[16] Making use of the same sources Kitzhaber points out further that in the principal aspects of the characterization—his professed devotion to the public weal, his hypocritical piety, his championship of religion and temperance, and his concern for the Negro and the Indian—Abner Dilworthy is a caricature of Samuel C. Pomeroy. "In fact, the more closely one studies Pomeroy's career the more clearly one sees that Twain's account in *The Gilded Age*, far from being ovedrawn, is a surprisingly exact copy."[17]

Senator Dilworthy, I have discovered, is indeed an even more exact copy of Senator Pomeroy than has generally been supposed. Take, for example, his often-expressed concern for the Indian and the Negro. The parallel drawn by Twain is much more specific than would appear at the present distance in time. As Kitzhaber has stated elsewhere, the Washington newspaper *Daily Love-Feast*, which takes Dilworthy's side when the rest of the press attacks the Knobs University Bill, is none other than the Washing-

From The Gilded Age, *First Edition*
Brother Balaam

ton *Chronicle*, at that time run by Pomeroy's friend Senator Harlan of Iowa (Twain's "Brother Balaam").[18] Harlan, who had been Secretary of the Interior under Andrew Johnson, was notorious for his role in swindling the American Indians. ("There's old Balaam, was in the Interior—used to be the Rev. Orson Balaam of Iowa—he's made the riffle on the Injun; . . .")[19] A "high priest of his church,"[20] Harlan maintained a lobby at Des Moines composed largely of Department of Interior men and "Methodist Preachers, without number or piety,"[21] and all that he did "emitted an odor of sanctity," even as the works of Brother Balaam. As early as 1865 Harlan had been accused of diverting large sums intended for feeding and clothing Indians in the Southwest, and in 1868 he was charged with the illegal sale of Cherokee Indian lands in Kansas in such a way as to enrich his friends, a charge that was repeated in 1872.[22] The scandalous Indian affairs of the federal government were handled for many years by Harlan and Pomeroy,[23] and Pomeroy's seat on several influential senate committees, including those on public lands and territories, must have been of inestimable value to him and his colleague.[24] The Cincinnati *Gazette*, speaking of the Osage Treaty as a "nice plum," remarked pointedly that "some Kansas men who showed a vast amount of righteous indignation over it, before their re-election, are, now that their places are assured, helping the swindle on."[25] No wonder that Senator Dilworthy attends so many "gatherings for the benefit of the Indians." The Indian frauds, like other abuses satirized in *The Gilded Age,* were almost constant and were farspread in their effects,[26] so it was no accident that Twain chose to emphasize this theme in his portrayal of Pomeroy.

Pomeroy's interest in the cause of the Negro was similarly no passive or disinterested one. The Chiriqui colonization plan, whereby Negroes were to be gently ousted from their homeland by being urged to emigrate to the Chiriqui Isthmus in Central America, a plan espoused with zeal by Senator Pomeroy, was actually a project for land stealing and plunder.[27] Pomeroy volunteered his services as "friend, agent and protector" of Negroes, received a twenty-five-thousand-dollar appropriation, set up an office in Washington, and procured a steamer. Fortunately the plan was abandoned.[28] It is evident that "Old Subsidy," as Pomeroy was nicknamed, "judged all public measures by the cash that was in them."[29] (In *The Gilded Age,* when Senator Balloon learns about the Knobs University Bill he remarks that it is doubtless a good thing. Laura reports to Dilworthy: "He said . . . if Senator Dilworthy was in it, it would pay to look into it" [II. 49].)

Even Dilworthy's physical appearance is unmistakable when coupled with his other characteristics.

Senator Dilworthy was large and portly, though not tall—a pleasant spoken man, a popular man with the people. (I, 225)[30]

"There! that's him, with the grand, noble forehead! . . . There, that's him, with the peeled head!" (II, 235)

According to the Washington correspondent of the *Chicago Tribune,* George Alfred Townsend ("Gath"), Pomeroy was "baldish, large, cheerful-faced" and looked "like the proprietor of a large hotel who was fond of having a clergyman for a guest."[31] The well-known woman journalist Emily Edson Briggs ("Olivia") spoke of his having "a broad brow and capacious enough for Jupiter."[32] The pious apostrophes of Dilworthy's utterances such as that concerning "soldiers of the cross in the rude campaigns of life, and ransomed souls in the happy fields of Paradise hereafter" are hardly exaggerations of Pomeroy's figures of public speech when he talked about "the mountains near where God dwells" or proclaimed, "While one plants and another sows, it is God who giveth the increase."[33] This cant, indeed, was so characteristic of Pomeroy that the Angola goats on his farm in Atchison, Kansas, were reputed to "utter a cry . . . said to sound wonderfully like the word 'Amen.' "[34]

It is evident that no one who was informed in Washington politics regarded seriously Pomeroy's "comedy of temperance and religion" except a close associate such as Harlan, who because of his own double-faced conduct could hardly afford not to keep a sober countenance.[35] Regardless of the extent to which he may have rationalized his own successes as tokens of divine approval, Pomeroy was well aware, as were many politicians of the day, particularly those from the frontier territories, of the estimable value of sanctimoniousness and the advocacy of temperance in impressing constituents favorably. The religious pose paid especially well, as is attested by the fact that some of the most consummate scoundrels in the post-Civil War congresses—Pomeroy, Harlan, Schuyler ("Smiler") Colfax, and a few others—were sarcastically called the "Christian Statesmen."[36] The religious hypocrite has been a well-known figure in literature from Chaucer's Pardoner to Lewis' Elmer Gantry. Twain's Dilworthy, however, unlike Molière's Tartufe or Dickens' Pecksniff, is a more dangerous member of society, for his swindles are perpetrated in the name of social welfare, not merely friendship or family loyalty: "I never push a private interest if it is not justified and ennobled by some larger public good" (II, 48).[37]

Clemens was familiar with the type of the "Christian Statesman." In his Nevada days, when his brother Orion had been secretary to "Jim" Nye, then governor of the Territory, he had had
ample opportunity to observe this "jolly, unctuous, oleaginous
old Body,"[38] who later became Senator from Nevada. Though he
became a "cronie" of Nye's, he clearly saw through his pretense,
knew him to be a liar, and frequently lampooned him in his news
dispatches much to the victim's enjoyment.[39] It is obvious that
Pomeroy was the principal sitter for Dilworthy's portrait; even
so, the image reflects bits of Nye's personality as well. Townsend described Nye as having a "fat, priest-like face" and a "stout-
ish, genteel body" and as making an "appeal to the Deity in every
apostrophe."[40] Like Dilworthy also, he was a tireless friend of the
Sunday school.[41]

Another hypocritical rogue whom Clemens knew well and
many of whose characteristics were undoubtedly blended into the
delineation of Dilworthy was Senator William M. Stewart. "Bill"
Stewart, whom Clemens had known in Virginia City and for
whom he served as an erratic secretary for a few weeks in Washington in the winter of 1868-69, had been elected to the Senate
at the same time as Nye.[42] Personally a millionaire and politically
a servant of corporate mining interests,[43] Stewart was in his own
way as great a hypocrite as Dilworthy and found it necessary to
protest his innocence in the face of attacks upon his probity.[44]
His legislative practices, which Clemens had witnessed both in
Nevada and in the national capitol, had provided Dilworthy's
creator with suitably intimate knowledge of senatorial rascality.[45]
And it is interesting to note that Stewart served as chairman of the
Committee on Indian Affairs.[46] It would be incorrect to state that
Dilworthy is a composite character, but at the same time that he
is a portrait of Pomeroy he is a well-rounded representation of
senatorial corruption in the post-Civil War congresses.[47]

A point left unelaborated by Kitzhaber is that of Twain's
sources for the details of the Pomeroy case and his use of these
sources.[48] It is well known, of course, that Clemens read both the
New York Herald and the *New-York Tribune* with some fre-
quency.[49] What has not been sufficiently realized is that he was a

From The Gilded Age, *First Edition*
Senator Dilworthy Addressing the Sunday School

fairly constant reader of the *New York Times* as well.[50] The Hartford *Courant*, besides, did exceptionally well at excerpting opinions of the press in various parts of the country.

In using the news reports and editorial comment, Twain not only transformed actual incidents into episodes but selected salient details or phrasings to elaborate upon for satiric effect. There are two prominent examples of the latter process in Chapter LIX (II, 298-313). In the summary of testimony by B. F. Simpson, counsel for State Senator York of Kansas (Noble in the novel), it was pointed out that Pomeroy had paid cash, without interest, without security, without receipt to a person he had met only once, to help him establish a national bank. "Is not this a remarkable business transaction? At the same time, does it not demonstrate the trusting and confiding nature of short friendships formed in the midst of a senatorial strife?"[51] This testimony is built up to well over a page of caustic sarcasm by Twain:

> The statement of Senator Dilworthy naturally carried conviction . . . . It was close, logical, unanswerable; it bore many internal evidences of its truth. For instance, it is customary in all countries for business men to loan large sums of money in bank bills instead of checks. It is customary for the lender to make no memorandum of the transaction. . . . It is customary to lend nearly anybody money to start a bank with, . . . It is customary to hand a large sum in bank bills to a man you have just been introduced to (if he asks you to do it). . . . [etc.] (II, 308-9)

The other example is Twain's use of the speech made by his old Nevada friend Senator "Jim" Nye. In this spread-eagle bit of oratory defending Pomeroy, Nye spoke of the necessity to "bear aloft the ancient dignity" of the Senate.[52] As the *New-York Tribune* editorialized: "Very few Senators of the period could bear it so far aloft or so much of it at one time."[53] In the novel, a senator is quoted as saying that it was high time the Senate should crush a cur like Noble and thus show "that it was able and resolved to uphold its ancient dignity."

> A bystander laughed at this finely-delivered peroration, and said:
> "Why, this is the Senator who franked his baggage home through the mails last week—registered, at that. However, perhaps he was merely engaged in 'upholding the ancient dignity of the Senate,' then."

"No, the modern dignity of it," said another bystander. "It don't re-
semble its ancient dignity, but it fits its modern style like a glove." (II,
301)[54]

More of Nye's speech is echoed in the fictional Senate debate upon
acceptance of the committee report:

One Senator—indeed, several Senators—objected that the committee had
failed of its duty; they had proved this man Noble guilty of nothing,
they had meted out no punishment to him; if the report were accepted,
he would go forth free and scathless, glorying in his crime, and it would
be a tacit admission that any blackguard could insult the Senate of the
United States and conspire against the sacred reputation of its members
with impunity; . . . (II, 310)

Nye's words had been:

Who would arraign an honorable Senator before the public, before the
world, upon the petition of a man who, on his own assertion, is steeped
in the very depths of fraud? . . . I ask the Senators to be careful how they
trifle with the reputation of a brother Senator, or how they allow outside
rascals to trifle with it.[55]

For Clemens vote-buying epitomized legislative immorality.
Commenting in later life on the charge that Senator Guggenheim
had bought the Colorado legislature to elect him to office, "which
is almost the customary way, now," he says that the Senator "is
not aware that he has been guilty of even an indelicacy, let alone
a gross crime."[56] In an early chapter of *The Gilded Age* the theme
is planted when Major Lackland is described as formerly "a man
of note in the State" who has been irretrievably disgraced by selling his vote just as he was to be "elevated to the Senate" (I, 113-
14). Pomeroy, notorious for his buying and selling of votes,[57]
afforded an excellent example of governmental practitioners of
this form of bribery. As the public exposure of Pomeroy's latest
and most flagrant knavery occurred at the very time Clemens and
Warner were beginning the novel,[58] the almost daily news dispatches supplied ready-made copy for the Dilworthy episodes.

CHAPTER V

Laura

ONLY LESS QUICKLY recognized than the Pomeroy case by readers of *The Gilded Age* in 1874 was the murder trial and acquittal of Laura D. Fair thinly disguised in the trial of Laura Hawkins. The Laura Fair scandal was less familiar internationally than the Pomeroy case only because Mrs. Fair was not a political figure; her prolonged series of court trials and appeals was emblazoned in American headlines from coast to coast. Though known before locally, she came into nationwide prominence because her trial epitomized an abuse of the court system in the United States that was currently the subject of heated controversy—the plea of temporary insanity. With the passing of time, however, both Mrs. Fair and the issue she had served to dramatize were relegated to obscurity and their role in *The Gilded Age* was forgotten.[1]

In 1936 Franklin Walker wrote a well-documented pioneering article showing the exactness with which Clemens and Warner had transferred the Laura Fair case into the pages of their novel.[2] Walker pointed out: "Laura Hawkins's motive for killing her paramour, her means of accomplishing the act, and her defense and the grounds for her acquittal are in essential points the same as those of the Western murderess. . . ." He further suggested that Warner wrote the trial chapters "because he was more familiar with New York court procedure" but that the idea itself of satirizing the Fair case was Clemens', conclusions borne out by my own research and examination of the manuscript;[3] and he showed that Clemens had based the episode in which the acquitted Laura at-

tempts to lecture on a similar venture by Mrs. Fair.[4] Finally, he
suggested that as Mrs. Fair had created excitement by an earlier
shooting—this one not fatal—in Virginia City, Nevada, at the
time Clemens was on the *Territorial Enterprise,* the latter undoubtedly knew her and may for that reason have had more than
passing interest in her later trial for murder.[5]

The Laura Fair case had begun in November, 1870, and had
extended through September, 1872, flaring up again only briefly
in January, 1873 (when Mrs. Fair attempted her lecturing), so
that rather than being concurrent copy for the novel it was recent
history. The scandal was sensational enough, however, to be fresh
in the minds of the novel's readers. For purposes of artistic unity
and compression, the authors took certain unimportant liberties
with the facts. For example, though Mrs. Fair's first trial had ended
in conviction, an appeal to the Supreme Court secured a reversal
of judgment on a technicality, and not until her second trial in
September, 1872, was she acquitted.[6] In *The Gilded Age,* the second, acquitting trial is the only one used. The venue is changed
from San Francisco to New York in order to keep the court proceedings in proximity to the episodes in Washington, give an
excuse for satirizing a well-known New York criminal lawyer in
the character of Braham, and allow the notoriously corrupt practices of the New York courts to be satirized. The scene of the
shooting is similarly changed from the deck of the Oakland–San
Francisco ferryboat to the public parlor of a New York hotel,
though the motive is exactly the same.[7] And the postacquittal lecture is actually attempted in the novel to heighten the dramatic
irony and provide an excuse for Laura Hawkins' death. (Mrs.
Fair did not dare venture to the public hall where her lecture had
been scheduled. Instead, she published a pamphlet on her experiences.)[8]

The pattern of attacking a social abuse by means of satirizing
a notorious example of it is followed in utilizing the Fair trial. Just
as the investigation of Pomeroy's electioneering highlighted the
practice of vote-buying among congressmen, a practice which in
turn epitomized Congressional corruption in general, so the Laura
Fair trial focused national attention on the corruption of the

United States judiciary system, the most flagrant examples of which were to be found in New York City courts. At the time that a retrial was ordered for Laura Fair, seven months after her original sentencing, the *New York Times* cited the case as a prime example of thwarting justice through delaying tactics on the one hand and incompetence on the other. In its editorial "Balking Justice," the *Times* lambasted the incompetence of the bench as the principal cause of procrastination:

. . . all through the trial the course of a Judge nowadays is weak, wavering, without dignity, without authority. The counsel for the prisoner is allowed to set up all sorts of frivolous pleas and pretenses, and to support them by long, tedious, quibbling arguments that weary and confuse the jury, and retard and often pervert the course of justice, when they ought to be swept aside with the prompt and decided exercise of a little common sense and authority. . . .[9]

When even the retrial of Laura Fair was postponed for three months until September, 1872, the *Times* pointed out that a "fearful mortality" had already occurred among those connected with the case.[10] In *The Gilded Age,* Colonel Sellers is jubilant when he receives a telegram stating that the Hawkins trial had been postponed. ". . . Bless my life, what lawyers they have in New York! Give them money to fight with, and the ghost of an excuse, and they would manage to postpone anything in this world, unless it might be the millennium or something like that. . . ." (II, 225-26)

Warner's depiction of the presiding judge at the Hawkins trial, Judge O'Shaunnessy, who had worked his way up from street arab to magistrate via the route of police court politics, not by study of the law (II, 245-46),[11] corresponds to the general informed view of the New York bench, particularly of the judges installed by the Tammany Ring. "Most of the justices in charge of criminal business in New York," stated the *North American Review,* "are coarse, profane, uneducated men, knowing nothing of law except what they have picked up in their experience on the bench. One of the best of them was a butcher until he became a police justice; another was formerly a bar-keeper."[12]

O'Shaunnessy's original, indeed, appears to have been Judge

John McCunn, a Ring protégé, who had immigrated from Ireland at sixteen, learned a smattering of law as a messenger boy in the offices of attorney Charles O'Conor, been admitted to the bar in his early twenties, and, having barely escaped court-martial during the Civil War, been elected Judge of the Superior Court in 1863 and again in 1870. At the height of his career, McCunn, who was described as "outwardly good-natured and even jovial" though notoriously corrupt, treacherous, and vain, had accumulated a fortune of a million and a half dollars through fraud and speculation and maintained a manorial estate in Ireland, on which his mother lived.[13] In the novel, Judge O'Shaunnessy has a "rather jovial face, sharp rather than intellectual," and "a self-sufficient air," is "descended from a long line of Irish Kings" (though the first to have come into his kingdom), and "believing that a dependent judge can never be impartial" has "prudently laid away money" and has acquired lands and houses worth several hundred thousand dollars (II, 245-46).

The novel's principal attack against court corruption, however, is directed toward abuse of the jury system, at the time a nationally recognized disgrace. Half a chapter is devoted to an appallingly amusing account of the empaneling of Laura Hawkins' jury. After "four weary days" the process is completed fairly satisfactorily—only two jurymen can read! "Low foreheads and heavy faces they all had; some had a look of animal cunning, while the most were only stupid. The entire panel formed that boasted heritage commonly described as the 'bulwark of our liberties' " (II, 252). This jury selection is drawn with telling accuracy from that of the Laura Fair trial, described by the *Times* as "the most ignorant jury of her countrymen that could be obtained."[14]

Informed opinion among the leading newspapers and magazines of the time was strongly aroused concerning the jury system, and among the chief voices of protest was that of Mark Twain. In *Roughing It* he had written that "the jury system puts a ban upon intelligence and honesty, and a premium upon ignorance, stupidity, and perjury"; a year later, he was still insisting that "its efficiency is only marred by the difficulty of finding twelve men every day who don't know anything and can't read."[15] While *The Gilded Age*

was in the making, he took time to write a blistering letter of sarcasm concerning the Foster murder trial, which again had been long-drawn-out despite overwhelming evidence. In it he described the ideal criminal juror as "an intellectual vacuum, attached to a melting heart, and perfectly macaronian bowels of compassion."[16] A British observer of American mores of the time described the

From The Gilded Age, *First Edition*

Judge O'Shaunnessy

unemployed vagabonds hanging about the courts for the chance to be put upon a jury for a dollar and a half a day, many standing "open-handed for a bribe far outweighing that pay."[17] The reference is strikingly similar to a deleted passage in one of Warner's manuscript pages for the empaneling episode:

It is one of the mysteries, even to those most familiar with the ignorance and crime of the city of New York, where the sheriff finds the men he summons for jury duty. He must have some process of detection unknown to the census taker, or he could not bring in such an array of incapables, men whose intellectual and moral perceptions are not equal to those of the codfish and the ferret. Bad as the lot offered in this case was, however, it was too good to suit Counsellor Braham, who had great difficulty in finding among them twelve men ignorant enough for his purpose.[18]

In *The Gilded Age* four other juries are mentioned outside that of the Hawkins trial: the inconclusive jury of inquest on the steamboat explosion (I, 54), the jury of asylum inmates and graduates of Sing Sing who vindicate the unscrupulous Weed and O'Riley (II, 25), the quibbling jury of inquest on Selby's death (II, 170), and the inferentially indifferent jury of inquest on Laura's death (II, 323). As all of these except the Selby jury are certainly Clemens' creations, the question suggests itself as to how influential Clemens may have been in what the internal evidence shows to be totally Warner's chapter, at least in its final draft.[19] As Daniel McKeithan has pointed out, by 1870 Clemens had probably acquired knowledge of trial procedure sufficient to describe a trial effectively.[20] Howells mentioned his friend's reading "a volume of great trials."[21] Between 1864 and 1872 Clemens had put at least eight trials into his writings, half of them murder trials.[22] Therefore, although Warner's practice as a lawyer[23] had undoubtedly given him a firsthand knowledge of legal technicalities that strengthened his depiction of courtroom scenes, Clemens was by no means unversed in court procedures. Most significant of all, the Clemens scrapbook for 1872-73 is devoted largely to reports of crimes and includes clippings on the Foster murder trial, a *New-York Tribune* editorial on the "Impunity of Murder" containing specific references to Laura Fair,[24] and a *New York Times* article concerning the alleged encouragement of homicide by acquittals based on technicalities.[25]

It is unquestionable that Clemens established the theme of the Laura Hawkins acquittal—beneficent insanity. To be sure, because the acquittal of Laura D. Fair had been based on the defense plea of "emotional insanity,"[26] the authors of its fictional counterpart could hardly have been true to their original without using the same grounds. The fact is, however, that Clemens was eager for an excuse to satirize what he called the "beneficent insanity plea" in full dress and for this reason must have chosen the notorious Fair trial as best suited to his purpose. He had for several years been fulminating against the plea as a legal device for evading justice. As a target for public attack it was, indeed, second only to the jury system. Mark Twain joined with enlightened journalists of the time in what today might appear at first glance a highly reactionary stand against a forward step in the psychology of crime and the consequently more intelligent and humane treatment of the mentally ill criminal. Actually, the field of psychology in its modern, scientific sense had scarcely begun to develop, and the outcry was quite justifiably against a new legal technicality or "gimmick" whereby a clever defense counsel could induce an ignorant jury and an incompetent bench to acquit and set free a pathological killer. Like many advanced concepts the insanity plea, before it could find scientific foundation and be safeguarded by socially beneficent laws, was turned into a mockery of itself. It was this contradictory form that aroused public wrath and that, incidentally, because it obscured the positively good underlying concept, seriously delayed the latter's proper development.[27]

In this spirit Twain had, two years before, written and sent to Elisha Bliss a proposed dedication for *Roughing It* which he thought would be "worth the price of the volume" but which was never used. It dedicated the book "To the Late Cain . . . out of a mere human commiseration for him that it was his misfortune to live in a dark age that knew not the beneficent Insanity Plea."[28] Far from being the "humoristic impulse of the moment," as Albert Bigelow Paine suggests, it was only the latest in a succession of Mark Twain diatribes against the plea, the first of which appeared in the *Alta California* in July, 1867.[29] In "A New Crime: Legislation Needed" (1870) he summed up the Baldwin, Lynch Hackett, and Bridget Durgin [*sic*] cases with the conclusion that "what we want now, is not laws against crime, but a law against *insanity*."[30] He decided in "The 'Tournament' in A.D. 1870" that if the bloodthirsty heroes of medieval romance should come to life again "nothing but a New York jury and the insanity plea could save them from hanging."[31] The most devastating of Twain's attacks on the insanity plea prior to *The Gilded Age* was his Buffalo *Express* article, "Our Precious Lunatic" (1870), which is a mock verdict of the jury in the famous McFarland murder trial, listing fifteen ludicrously phrased reasons for considering the defendant insane, each successively more far-fetched.[32] Of especial interest in this parody is the manner in which the author anticipates the handling of Laura Hawkins' acquittal, first reporting McFarland's insane rage, capture, and committal to an asylum, then adding in a postscript ("LATER") that instead of sending him to the asylum " (which I naturally supposed they would do, and so I prematurely *said* they had) the court has actually SET HIM AT LIBERTY."[33]

Public reaction to Laura Fair's acquittal tended to be polarized. There were those on the one hand who felt that a personal score had been paid off by the shooting, that a family man "who would meddle with a woman as he [Crittenden] did with Mrs. Fair, should do it at his own risk."[34] Walter M. Fisher, a contemporary historiographer who considered the California spirit "very Gallic" in this respect, wrote that "Mark Twain and Mr. Dudley Warner are only stating a simple fact when they assert in 'The Gilded Age,' that 'the woman who lays her hand on a man, without any exception whatever, is always acquitted by the jury;' . . ."[35] On the other hand were those whose male guilt at their social domination over women led them to self-righteous condemnation of Mrs. Fair, "a woman," as the *New York Times* declared editorially, "who has outraged nearly all the fundamental principles on which society rests."[36] The dilemma was effectively expressed by the San Francisco *Bulletin* in an editorial entitled "A Mockery of Justice":

While the enforcement of a capital sentence upon a woman would shock most persons as much as the crime with which she was charged, and while many many think that, so far as mere punishment goes, the wretched woman has already suffered more than death, the fact of a total quittance will seem to all right thinkers an occurrence calculated to lessen the restraints upon crime, . . . The lax code that would condone murder on such grounds would soon make murder common and law a farce. . . .[37]

The division is reflected in the novel. There are, for example, the newspaper commentaries that speak of Colonel Selby as having " 'reaped the harvest he sowed' " and say that it is " 'the old story' " (II, 178-79) and the Colonel's dying deposition that he had wronged Laura and deserved his fate (II, 256). Yet, as the authors state, "upon the first publication of the facts of the tragedy, there was an almost universal feeling of rage against the murderess" (II, 179).

This polarity of viewpoints was significantly altered when Mrs. Fair proposed to take to the public lecture platform. Many who had originally condoned or been indifferent to the murder of Crittenden were now outraged. Had Mrs. Fair gone into retirement and disappeared from public view, as was provided for Laura Hawkins in Warner's rejected draft of the "boss" chapter,[38] popular opinion would have remained relatively static. But Mrs. Fair attempted to make of her history a *cause célèbre*—a purpose implicit in her topic, "Wolves in the Fold."[39] She had throughout her trials received the ardent support of a group of extremists in the women's rights movement. These "strong-minded" women, advocates of direct action against their male oppressors, had demonstrated at her first-trial conviction.[40] Thereafter she had become a martyr to "the women of San Francisco of the school of Mrs. EMILY PITT STEVENS, known to fame as the 'Heroine of the Revolver,' and as the editress of a woman's journal."[41] Needless to say, the anarchistic position of these women was a serious handicap to nineteenth-century feminism.

Though kept in the background, this theme is also reflected in *The Gilded Age*. One of the Journals reporting the crime adds: " 'Laura, straying into her Thessaly with the youth Brierly, slays her other lover and becomes the champion of the wrongs of her sex' " (II, 178). When the lecture agent interviews Laura, he suggests that she make "woman" the subject of her address, "the marriage relation, woman's fate, anything of that sort. Call it The Revelations of a Woman's Life" (II, 294-95). Residing at Nook Farm, a colony strongly under the influence of women's rights advocacy, particularly that of Isabella Beecher Hooker, Clemens and Warner could hardly ignore the issue as it related to the trial of Mrs. Fair. Yet the theme remains undeveloped in the novel. Laura Hawkins' motivation for lecturing is not that implied in her agent's suggestions: she turns to "that final resort of the disappointed of her sex, the lecture platform" because the "one thing left that could give a passing zest to a wasted life . . . was fame, admiration, the applause of the multitude" (II, 318). In view of Clemens' later championship of women's rights, this shallow, negative, and unconsciously cynical handling of Laura's motivation, so at variance with her maturity and experience, can be explained partly by Clemens' lifelong tendency to idealize and romanticize women—a subject beyond the scope of the present study. It can to a large degree be explained also by the fact that in 1873 his convictions concerning the woman question had not as yet crystallized.[42]

Though Laura Hawkins never emerges as a fully visualized personality in the way Dilworthy does but to the end remains a lay figure representing certain elements of the satire, she is endowed by her creators, in her trial scenes, with a physical appearance and behavior pattern modeled on Mrs. Fair. When Laura enters the courtroom, she is

very pale, but this pallor heightened the luster of her large eyes and gave a touching sadness to her expressive face. . . . There was in her manner or face neither shame nor boldness, . . . her eyes were downcast. A murmur of admiration ran through the room. The newspaper reporters made their pencils fly. (II, 246-47)

The San Francisco *Chronicle* described Mrs. Fair on her first day of trial.

Mrs. Fair has doubtless been a handsome woman, though anxiety and long sickness have left their indelible marks upon her face. . . . Her expression is that of great sadness, weariness and passive suffering—such a face as would be likely to materially aid the efforts of counsel in such a case as the present.[43]

Laura Hawkins' initial shock at her own act and her arraignment are described thus:

The statement from Laura was not full, in fact it was fragmentary, and . . . was, as the reporter significantly remarked, "incoherent." . . . When the reporter asked:
"What made you shoot him, Miss Hawkins?" Laura's only reply was, very simply,
"Did I shoot him? Do they say I shot him?" . . . (II, 172)

Mrs. Fair's behavior was similarly incoherent but far more violent. She "raved wildly," "was in a condition of apparent delirium," and

From Official Report of Trial

Laura D. Fair

"talked in a rambling way about what she had done"; she was put under opiates and was constantly attended by a nurse.[44]

It is perfectly evident that the exigencies of the novel's propaganda against the insanity plea necessitated a softening of the actual behavior of the defendant. Laura Hawkins could not be allowed to be convincingly hysterical. Though she is momentarily cast in the role of Mrs. Fair, she has her own history in the novel and is decidedly a sympathetic character, following in her emotional, passionate nature and in the circumstances of her death the tradition of sensation fiction. Mrs. Fair was quite another person, whose antecedent life could not have been portrayed in the novel without altering its entire tone and conception, and it is obvious that neither author for a moment contemplated doing so.

Mrs. Fair was a highly neurotic and unstable person, and the true story of her life, which today might be told with understanding from the viewpoint of psychological realism, in the moral climate of the 1870's would have met with outrage and indignation. Married at sixteen, she had had four husbands, one of whom had committed suicide and two of whom had been divorced from her, and had carried on her sexual activity so openly that she became "a household word in the land."[45] Whereas in the novel Laura Hawkins receives the devoted ministrations of her adopted mother, Laura Fair actually sued her mother for misappropriating money intended for the daughter she had had by Crittenden.[46] So thoroughly debased and desperate had Mrs. Fair become that before her second trial she had plotted to poison the judge who had sentenced her at her first one.[47]

That the trial and acquittal of Laura Hawkins was intended by Mark Twain primarily as an exposé of the American jury system and the abusive insanity plea and only secondarily as a parody of the Fair case—that it therefore fulfilled the purpose of the *roman à clef* in the more profound, sophisticated sense, is made abundantly clear by the play he based on the novel. This play, *Colonel Sellers* (considered at length in the Epilogue, below), was presented in a long initial run and revived many times by the comedian John T. Raymond, whose performance in the leading role of Sellers established his own reputation. The fact that Warner relinquished all rights to the play and that Clemens wrote the acting script himself, avowedly based on his own material from the novel,[48] also gives conclusive proof that though the trial chapters of *The Gilded Age* are ostensibly Warner's the concept is Clemens'.

The final scene of the play as originally written by Clemens ends as follows:

Judge.

What say you—Guilty, or Not Guilty? (*Pause.*)

Foreman.

Guilty, of murder in the first degree.
    (Sensation in the court. Mrs Hawkins faints away.)

Judge.

(Rising.) Gentlemen of the Jury, this painful, but righteous verdict—
    (Laura begins to sink back—Clay shoulders his way to her.)

Clay.

Laura, Laura, speak!

Laura.

There. There. it is just. let me rest.
    (Sinks back in Clay's arms and dies.)

Clay.

God send it may be in peace - - - for it is eternal.

Tableau.

and

Slow   *Curtain.*[49]

In the prompter's copy, all the dialogue and action after the word
"*Foreman*" have been crossed out with the single exception of the
line "*Sensation in the court. Mrs. Hawkins faints away,*" and on the
blank page following, opposite the verdict line, are penciled the
words "Not Guilty." On the opening night, September 16, 1874,
Clemens made a curtain speech just before the trial scene. It began
as follows:

I thank you for the compliment of this call, and I will take advantage
of it to say that I have written this piece in such a way that the jury can
bring in a verdict of guilty or not guilty, just as they happen to feel
about it. I have done this for this reason. If a play carries its best lesson
by teaching what ought to be done in such a case, but is *not* done in real
life, then the righteous verdict of guilty should appear; but if the best
lesson may be conveyed by holding up the mirror and showing what *is*
done every day in such a case but ought *not* to be done, then the satirical
verdict of not guilty should appear. I don't know which is best, strict
truth and satire, or a nice moral lesson void of both. So I leave my jury
free to decide.[50]

The curtain speech *appears* to be a clever showman's trick—appropriate to this veteran of the public platform—intended to enhance the satire of the play. In reality, Clemens himself apparently did not decide until almost the last moment what the more effective ending would be. Whether one accounts for this by Clemens' unsureness as a playwright, by the fact that the play, unlike the novel, ended with the verdict, making no allowance for the anticlimax of Laura's lecturing attempt, by the author's sensitivity to criticism of the novel, or by a possible dispute with Raymond over the denouement, the real significance of the combined evidence is Clemens' concern about the play's satire. One might have guessed what his choice would be.

The play brings the issues of the ignorant jury and the insanity plea into sharp focus in a way that the novel, with its greater complexity and its multiplicity of interests, could not do. For one thing, since the murder of Selby, which in the novel is only related, is brought to life on the stage, it allows the introduction of the insanity theme immediately and in a melodramatic fashion that Clemens no doubt thought highly theatrical.

Col Selby.

Peace, child, you are—

Laura.

Mad, and you have made me so. *(backing away, with hand on her bosom.)*

Col Selby.

(Starting back.) Laura, Laura!

Laura.

Do you know what it is to drive a woman like me to madness? It is— *(Drawing pistol from her bosom and leveling it.)* Death!! *(Kneels over body, caresses face—looks up with vacant expression.)* I have killed the only man I ever loved.

   (Enter Col Sellers, Lafayette & others.)

All.

Laura, Laura, What is this?

Laura.

It is death![51]

Then in the trial scene, the final summations by the prosecution and the defense, instead of being indirectly described in Warner's own words (II, 274-75), are uttered directly, and they present sharply and succinctly the opposing points of view. The District Attorney, in resting the case for the prosecution, uses heavy sarcasm:

Gentlemen of the jury *(sneeringly)* of course we cant find her guilty.— Nobody expects that. Everybody knows, in these wise latter days that *murder* laws are made for men, not women. If a woman kills a man in cold blood, whom she fancies has wronged her, she is'nt [*sic*] a murderess —O, certainly not! She is a heroine—*that's* the new name for it. She must be petted, and coddled, and made much of. Juries shed tears over her— the whole tender-hearted public cry over her sufferings—the weeping pulpit intercedes—romantic young girls beg for an autograph from her red hand, and treasure it as a sacred thing. Gentlemen, this woman has done murder—black, hideous *murder*. Do you comprehend? Let me beg that you will not belie the character of the American jury. Set her free, gentlemen, set her free! and let us all bow down to the sublime heroine and glorify her! . . .[52]

The defense counsel, Duffer (the Braham of the novel), then makes this rejoinder:

Gentlemen, our benignant laws casting about the helpless the sheltering arms of their protection, have decreed that children, and poor creatures stricken in mind by the heavy hand of God, shall not be held responsible for the deeds they do. . . .

   Gentlemen of the Jury, I charge you to remember that the law forbids you to punish this poor ruined mind for this distressful deed which it's [*sic*] subject hand has wrought. I have done. I leave this sad wreck in the pitying hands of God—and you to utter the voice of His forgiving mercy.[53]

   Though I have been unable to find an exact original for Laura Hawkins as a woman lobbyist, there are many clues as to her identity; and, as *The Gilded Age* is so thoroughly a *roman à clef*, there is no reason to suppose that an original or, for that matter, two or three originals did not exist. The records mention several notorious figures in detail, such as the voluptuous "Comanche" and the handsome and notorious Mrs. Lucy Cobb.[54] A very suggestive fact is that handbills were distributed in Topeka, Kansas, accusing Pomeroy of having a mistress—a certain Alice Caton of Baltimore—[55] a circumstance which may well have been known to Clemens.

There are two eligible candidates for Laura's original in Washington. One is Mrs. General Straitor, a "handsome castaway in one of the Southern towns," who infatuated General Straitor (even as Laura infatuated Colonel Selby) and who later, as his widow, was brought to Washington "to influence the Interior Department in the matter of Indian contracts." Perry Fuller and "one of the Western Senators" paid her bills.[56] The other, known as the "Queen" of the lobby in 1868-69, was kept by Jay Gould, a circumstance seemingly made to order to fit the satire on the railroad lobby described in the next chapter. Her eligibility is enhanced by the fact that before Senator Benjamin Hill made an exhaustive railroad speech on the floor of the Senate, the "Queen" had his ear.[57] Indeed, ghost-writing of Congressional speeches by women, particularly women lobbyists, so effectively illustrated in Laura's writing Congressman Trollop's speech on soldiers' pensions and then blackmailing him (II, 118-21), was a very common practice.[58]

In any case, Clemens was obviously fascinated by the figure of the woman lobbyist, who, in Allan Nevins' much-quoted words, "was seen everywhere, making the streets and hotels disreputably gay."[59] In the winter of 1868-69 Clemens discovered a type of politicized woman who did not demand appropriations to supply Congress "with paregoric, Jayne's carminative, sugar plums, &c," as he had heard in his youth.[60] Rather, he found the female rascal who would work and bribe "with all her might,"[61] not, however, as a voter or elected representative but as a behind-the-scenes manipulator. At the time of writing *The Gilded Age,* Clemens jocosely advocated a woman's party, not so much as a positive good as a palliative to the fact that "both the great parties" had failed and the highest offices of the land continued "to be occupied by perjurers and robbers."[62] The women who invited Mark Twain's satire were a key part of this hierarchy of perjurers and robbers.

In her role as woman lobbyist Laura Hawkins is drawn with

Ladies' Reception Room, Capitol, Washington

the greatest accuracy. In Chapter XXXIV Twain describes her thus:

Laura was on excellent terms with a great many members of Congress, and there was an undercurrent of suspicion in some quarters that she was one of that detested class known as "lobbyists"; but what belle could escape slander in such a city? . . . She was very gay, now, and very celebrated, . . . She was growing used to celebrity, and could already sit calm and seemingly unconscious, under the fire of fifty lorgnettes in a theater, or even overhear the low voiced "That's she!" as she passed along the street without betraying an[n]oyance.

. . . Laura was considered to be very wealthy and likely to be vastly more so in a little while. Consequently, she was much courted and as much envied. Her wealth attracted many suitors. . . . Some of the noblest men of the time succumbed to her fascinations. . . . (II, 39-41)

Compare this passage with the following description of the typical woman lobbyist by Clemens' brilliant contemporary, the journalist Mary Clemmer Ames:

The calmness of assured position, the serene satisfaction of conscious beauty, envelop her and float from her like an atmosphere. . . . Look, and the unveiled gaze which meets yours will tell you, as plainly as a gaze can tell, that adulation is the life of its life, and seduction the secret of its spell. . . . She glides through the corridors, haunts the galleries and the ante-rooms of the Capitol—everywhere conspicuous in her beauty. All who behold her inquire, Who is that beautiful woman? Nobody seems quite sure. Doubt and mystery envelop her like a cloud. "She is a rich and beautiful widow," "She is unmarried," "She is visiting the city with her husband." Every gazer has a different answer. There are a few, deep in the secrets of diplomacy, of legislative venality, of governmental prostitution, who can tell you she is one of the most subtle and most dangerous of lobbyists. She is but one of a class always beautiful and always successful. . . .[63]

Laura's earlier background is typical of such women, many of whom "had drifted from home localities where they had found themselves the subjects of scandalous comments."[64] The themes of adoption, ambiguous antecedents, and bigamous marriage may be part of the paraphernalia of sensation fiction; in Laura's story they become effective motivation for her later role as well.

Some women lobbyists were highly paid prostitutes; the munitions manufacturer Colt, for example, maintained a whorehouse on C Street.[65] A contemporary observer wrote that he "never knew a woman to exert an 'influence' here, who did not become common, descend to lobbying, lose her credit, and increase the skepticism of men."[66] That Clemens at first had this kind of lobbyist in mind as a model for Laura is shown by a discarded page of manuscript, which states that "the hidden fires were making wasteful destruction within."

In the fulness of time there came a day when she threw off the mask, & gave everybody the opportunity to say, "There, I told you so!" She went boldly into the places in & about the Capitol where lobbyists congregate, & labored for all sorts of disreputable bills; Mr. Dilworthy was getting uncomfortable; she took a house in the suburbs & set herself up with showy carriage & servants; she received & entertained no end of Parvenus there; she drove through the public streets with various rather questionable characters. She was down, but she had the satisfaction of knowing that she had brought more than one man of high position & blemishless character down with her—for when she had once taken an adorer captive, nothing could free him from his slavery. These ruined creatures followed her down into the dirt helplessly.—They were cast out from society; they despised themselves; they tore themselves away from her & said their bondage was broken; this [*sic*] did this again & again; but they always came back penitent & worshiping. . . .[67]

Wisely for purposes both of the novel and historical accuracy, Twain decided to cast Laura as the more influential sophisticated type of lobbyist, one of the "Grand Duchesses of the tribe," who skilfully lured their prey with a decoy of sex—who, so to speak, knew how to use sex as a weapon without allowing themselves to be disarmed.

Flirt they certainly did, but it was just a flitting smile, the flicker of an eyelid, the faint suggestion of a blush. Was the lady "prudishly quick to interpret anything as an insult?" All the more proof that she was of the aristocracy of her kind. And yet the cynical correspondent, studying her methods, noted that "she will flare up at a mere glance of curiosity from a stranger, and pardon a kiss red-hot on the lips from a man who has a vote."
    . . . That there was no little blackmailing we may be sure. But, on the whole, the system was by no means crude or vulgar. . . .[68]

So the portrait of Laura was altered:

She frowned upon no lover when he made his first advances, but by and by, when he was hopelessly enthralled, he learned from her own lips that she had formed a resolution never to marry. Then he would go away

From Ellis, Sights and Secrets
Lobby Members

hating and cursing the whole sex, and she would calmly add his scalp to
her string, . . . (II, 41)

To maintain, as Van Wyck Brooks does, that Twain "was both
afraid and unable to present her character truly, and, in consequence, too impatient, too indifferent, too little interested, even to

attempt it,"[69] shows a lack of knowledge of the historical period. It assumes, in the words of DeVoto, that "young women, women of marriageable age, women who could be objects of desire, would not live for him."[70] This interpretation, because of its one-dimensional, neo-Freudian approach, confuses restrained delineation of a type with the psychological inhibition of the writer and succeeds only in distorting these critics' judgment of Twain's intentions. It conveniently overlooks such revealing thoughts of Laura's as: " 'Free! I wonder what Dilworthy *does* think of me, anyway?' " (II, 51) or "this is a desperate game I am playing in these days—a wearing, sordid, heartless game. If I lose, I lose everything—even myself" (II, 69).[71] In spite of the fact that she falls far short of being a fully realized individual character, Laura Hawkins is not the mere stick or the untrue portrayal so often alleged. She is a carefully drawn type of the historically significant woman lobbyist and in her life story and motivations is not far from reality.

CHAPTER VI

Other Persons,
Events, and Things

IN BOTH *The Gilded Age* and its dramatization, *Colonel Sellers*, the parody of Mrs. Fair's trial is neatly punctuated with unmistakable allusions to the Tweed Ring, allusions that strengthen the satire of the New York court system, which at that time was in abject captivity to the Ring. It has been shown how obviously Judge O'Shaunnessy is portrayed as one of the chief minions of Tammany. Similarly, the defense counsel for Laura Hawkins is none other than the counselor who defended Tweed in his sensational trial for graft, John Graham, one of the ablest legal talents in New York. As the *Hearth and Home* review of *The Gilded Age* noted, "People in New York will not be at a loss to know who sat for the portrait of Mr. John Braham the noted criminal lawyer."[1]

In Clemens' 1872-73 scrapbook is a newspaper clipping concerning the Tweed trial, which states, in a manner reminiscent of the comment on the Fair trial: "By strict adherence to the absurd law which excludes from the jurybox men who read the daily papers and have intelligence enough to form an opinion on what they read, a jury of ignorant men has been obtained, . . ."[2] The newspaper article goes on to describe how the prosecution considered discontinuing suit when information was presented that jurymen were in Tweed's pay. Known for his shrewd selection of jurymen likely to be responsive to the pleas of the defense, John Graham was adept as well in legal maneuvering and in the calculated use of grandiloquent emotionalism—a type of conduct successfully employed by his fictional counterpart. At the Tweed trial,

Graham "invoked the Universal Prayer and other pleas for the quality of mercy, and finally broke into sobs at the picture of misery he had himself painted."[3] In *The Gilded Age*, Braham's similarly emotional summation visibly affects the jury and puts "half the court room . . . in tears" (II, 275).[4] Then, in the final scene of the Hawkins trial, when the verdict of "Not Guilty" is announced, occurs "one of those beautiful incidents which no fiction-writer would dare to imagine."

> The women could not restrain their long pent-up emotions. They threw themselves upon Mr. Braham in a transport of gratitude; they kissed him again and again, . . . in the words of a newspaper of the day they "lavished him with kisses." It was something sweet to do; and it would be sweet for a woman to remember in after years, that she had kissed Braham! . . .
> This beautiful scene is still known in New York as "the kissing of Braham." (II, 288-89)

Though to the modern reader such an episode must seem another instance of Mark Twain's sometimes overdrawn burlesque, the scene is a faithful reproduction of the conclusion of the McFarland trial, which had so aroused Clemens in 1870—a trial in which the successful acquittal of the defendant had been effected by John Graham and the setting of which, it might be added, was the Ring's famous county courthouse.[5] According to the *New-York Tribune*, "the court-room was a perfect tumult . . . and the ladies commenced an indiscriminate kissing," leaving "approving and enthusiastic traces of their saliva upon his [Graham's] countenance."[6]

The Tammany Ring, the third national scandal treated in *The Gilded Age*, came to focus in the graft practiced in connection with construction of the county courthouse. Had Judge O'Shaunnessy "not helped to build and furnish this very courthouse? Did he not know that the very 'spittoon' which his judge-ship used cost the city the sum of one thousand dollars?" (II, 246) This subject is given its principal attention in a passage in Chapter XXXIII concerning the unscrupulous New York politician Patrick O'Riley, whose original was apparently one Thomas Murphy, "an experienced Republican ward heeler of New York City, a

notorious shoddy contractor during the war, and sometime business associate of William Tweed."[7]

Mr. O'Riley furnished shingle nails to the new court-house at three
thousand dollars a keg, and eighteen gross of 60-cent thermometers at
fifteen hundred dollars a dozen; the controller and the board of audit
passed the bills, and a mayor, who was simply ignorant but not criminal,
signed them. (II, 24)

The real courthouse, which was supposed to cost a quarter of a
million dollars, in fact cost eight million and the City of New York
was charged, among other items, $470 apiece for chairs, $400,000
apiece for safes, and $7,500 for thermometers.[8] The "controller,"
"board of audit," and "mayor" unquestionably refer to the Ring's
quadrumvirate in control of the city government—Mayor A.
"Elegant Oakey" Hall, Controller Richard B. "Slippery Dick"
Connolly, Treasurer Peter B. "Brains" Sweeney, and William Marcy
"Boss" Tweed himself, President of the Board of Supervisors.[9]

Though not a precise thumbnail biography of Murphy, the life
of O'Riley is representative of the Ring politician's. An Irish
immigrant, O'Riley begins as a hod carrier, then starts a low rum
shop, and, having made a practice of giving straw bail at the police
courts for his customers, gets a petty office in the city government
and opens a stylish gambling saloon higher up town. Becoming an
alderman, he closes the saloon and turns to contracting for the
city. With his "bosom friend" Wm. M. Weed (Tweed) he is
elected to his "proper theater of action," the legislature in Albany.[10]
As the North American Review stated, the "absolute exclusion of
all honest men from any practical control of affairs" in New York
and the supremacy of "pickpockets, prize-fighters, emigrant run-
ners, pimps, and the lowest class of liquor-dealers, are facts which
admit of no question."[11]

The story of the ascendancy of Tammany Hall and its subsequent downfall once a seemingly apathetic citizenry had been
aroused is so well known as to need no recounting here. Suffice it
to say that Clemens had watched developments with keen interest
while the New York Times under its fearless English editor, Louis
J. Jennings, almost singlehandedly conducted its 1871 campaign
against the Ring and against the scandalous whitewashing by

Charles Dana's New York *Sun*. He must also have relished the series of brilliant cartoons of his friend Thomas Nast in *Harper's Weekly*, which courageously lampooned members of the Ring by name.[12] After the September mass meeting of outraged New Yorkers in the Cooper Institute, Mark Twain could no longer contain himself. In the September 27 issue of the *New-York Tribune*, one month before Tweed's arrest and while the controversy was at white heat, he published an ingeniously contrived burlesque on the Ring entitled "The Revised Catechism." Based on the Westminster Shorter Catechism, it depicted each of the principal "saints" of Tammany in terse and telling epithets—"St. Hall's Garbled Reports, St. Fisk's Ingenious Robberies," etc. Consisting of questions and answers, it began by posing what four years later was to be the central theme of *The Gilded Age*:

> What is the chief end of man?
> A. To get rich.
> In what way?
> A. Dishonestly if we can; honestly if we must.
> Who is God, the one only and true?
> A. Money is God. Gold and greenbacks and stock—father, son, and the ghost of the same—three persons in one: these are the true and only God, mighty and supreme; and William Tweed is his prophet.[13]

As in his use of the figures of Senator Pomeroy and Laura Fair, Mark Twain singled out Tweed and his Ring for attack because they dramatically epitomized a widespread abuse. He had strong feelings about officials who ascended to their positions "by a jump from gin-mills or the needy families and friends" of other officials.[14] "Rings" were the order of the day, and practically all the great cities of the nation found their corporate government controlled to a greater or lesser degree by a group of law-evading manipulators. They were, indeed, only the localized manifestations of a practice that pervaded the entire governmental structure of the nation. The contemporary British observer, G. Manigault, clearly placed Tweed in overall perspective:

> . . . let no man imagine that Boss Tweed is an anomalous character, or has run an anomalous career. He is simply a well-marked type of a

numerous, and in many cases still prosperous, class of officials, to be found in every considerable municipal corporation, in every State government, in every department of the United States government, in the House of Representatives and the Senate, in the Cabinet and the diplomatic corps. . . .[15]

One passage in Manigault's little book, *The United States Unmasked*—a book which, according to the author, American publishing houses had consistently refused to publish[16]—states that since the end of the Civil War,

frauds and plundering in high places have multiplied and grown to gigantic stature. Millions, untold millions, have been the prize; for no one knows to what extent the government and the country have been robbed. What a startling narrative of rascality in high places, involving senators and representatives in Congress and the Vice-President, is furnished by the history of the 'Credit Mobilier,' and the sixty millions of government bonds lent to aid the Pacific railroad; . . . (p. 125)

Though it has long been recognized that *The Gilded Age* satirized railroad speculation and its concomitant Congressional bribery in general, it has been assumed by several commentators that Mark Twain made no pointed allusion in the book to the famous Crédit Mobilier scheme, the exposure of which revealed bribe-taking by several prominent congressmen and ruined the careers of congressmen Oakes Ames and James Brooks. One critic, indeed, has stated that because Clemens later supported the presidential ticket of Garfield, who "came before the people carrying in his clothes the stench of the Credit Mobilier," he seems to have "swallowed the Credit Mobilier" and not given it the "antiseptic treatment" it deserved.[17] The facts are quite to the contrary.

In a passage about a page and a half in length (II, 116-18) Twain presents a conversation between Laura Hawkins and Congressman Trollop concerning a certain National Internal Improvement Directors' Relief Measure. She says, "My dear sir, by and by there is going to be an investigation into that National Internal Improvement Directors' Relief Measure of a few years ago, and you know very well that you will be a crippled man, as likely as not, when it is completed." To this Trollop replies, "It cannot be shown that a man is a knave merely for owning that stock." Laura then proceeds to detail the manner in which the transaction was handled:

Several of you gentlemen bought of that stock (without paying a penny down) received dividends from it (think of the happy idea of receiving dividends, and very large ones, too, from stock one hasn't paid for!), and all the while your names never appeared in the transaction; if ever you took the stock at all, you took it in other people's names. Now, you see, you had to know one of two things; namely, you either knew that the idea of all this preposterous generosity was to bribe you into future legislative friendship, or you *didn't* know it. That is to say, you had to be either a knave or a—well, a fool—there was no middle ground. . . . (II, 116-17)

At this point Trollop points out that "some of the best and purest men in Congress took that stock in that way."

The procedure outlined by Laura Hawkins in this passage is precisely that used by Oakes Ames in bribing fellow congressmen to vote huge appropriations for construction of the Union Pacific railroad. The controlling stockholders in the Union Pacific organized a construction company, the Crédit Mobilier,[18] and awarded themselves the contract by means of this front organization at such terms as to acquire complete ownership of all assets—land, railroad, bonds, and stocks.[19] The stock issued by this structure was thus based upon credit built upon credit, and generous blocks of it were distributed among congressmen where, in the famous words of Oakes Ames, "they will do most good."[20] Permitted to "subscribe" at par, the recipients did not put up a cent of money, Ames obligingly carrying the stock for them. Among those so favored were the Vice-President, Colfax; his successor, Wilson; and a future President, Garfield.[21]

To point up his allusion to the Crédit Mobilier scandal itself, as distinguished from other similar machinations, Mark Twain dubbed his organization the National Internal Improvement Directors' Relief Measure. In the parlance of the time any large project for opening up the interior, or frontier, areas of the United States to commercial exploitation was known as an "internal improvement." The key phrase that reveals the Crédit Mobilier as the particular internal improvement meant is "Directors' Relief Measure." It was brought out in the subsequent Poland committee investigation, which was taking place even as *The Gilded Age* was being written, that the idea of the Crédit Mobilier "was to *relieve the directors* and shareholders of the Union Pacific Railroad Company from any individual responsibility in building the road, . . . the design was to cover up anything that might have been done to *relieve* individuals from responsibility; . . . [italics mine, B. F.][22]

As a result of the investigation by the committee chaired by Congressman Luke P. Poland, the House passed a resolution to "absolutely condemn" the two most convenient scapegoats, Oakes Ames and James Brooks.[23] This face-saving act on the part of Congress is alluded to by Twain in Chapter XX during Colonel Sellers' innocently damning elucidation to Washington Hawkins of the ritualistic and meaningless process of self-purification regularly indulged in by Congress.

"Congress has inflicted frightful punishments on its members—now you know that. When they tried Mr. Fairoaks [Oakes Ames], and a cloud of witnesses proved him to be—well, you know what they proved him to be —and his own testimony and his own confessions gave him the same character, what did Congress do then?—come!"

"Well, what *did* Congress do?"

"You know what Congress did, Washington. Congress intimated plainly enough, that they considered him almost a stain upon their body; and without waiting ten days, hardly, to think the thing over, they rose up and hurled at him a resolution declaring that they disapproved of his conduct! Now *you* know that, Washington."

"It *was* a terrific thing—there is no denying that. If he had been proven guilty of theft, arson, licentiousness, infanticide, and defiling graves, I believe they would have suspended him for two days." (II, 223-24)

An earlier draft of this passage, in which Senator James W. Patterson appears as "the College professor from New Hampshire,"[24] is thoroughly explicit:

". . . Now let's see. First, there's the Credit Mo*b*iler business."

"Why *you* know that if they try every Senator & Representative that the Hon. Mr. Hamfat[25] bought with that stock, they never can get through, because there were so many."

"Yes, I know; but they won't try *all* of them. All they need is some examples—just a sort of sop you know to throw to the press & the people & keep them quiet. Just a few examples—& they have got to be prominent simple-hearted people who have been honest before & didn't know enough about sharp practice to cover up their tracks this time. Now there's the Vice President; he'll catch it, guilty or not guilty; & there's one of the Senators from Massachusetts, they'll make it sultry for him; & there's Cro [Croker?] a New York man or so—the idea of a New York public man not knowing how to conspire to rob a government without getting caught at it! Ain't that the oddest thing? Well, you know, they'll try those fellows; & the College professor from New Hampshire—bless you, *he* has been simple enough to write letters that tell the whole thing on him—but what could you expect of one of those trustful, unpractical cultivated people? . . ."[26]

Revealing as this earlier version is as to Clemens' detailed knowledge of the facts,[27] one can be glad that his sense of artistry led him to condense and to satirize more indirectly. His allusions as published certainly were not lost on his contemporary readers.[28]

The Senate investigation of Senator Pomeroy's vote-buying, which epitomized for Mark Twain an almost endless chain of similar Congressional malpractices, shared the headlines at the time *The Gilded Age* was written with the Tammany Ring exposure and the Crédit Mobilier hearings. As "Philip Quilibet" wrote in his "Drift-Wood" columns in the *Galaxy*, it was "a bad show for one winter."[29] The three scandals revealed appalling corruption at all levels of government, and of the three the Crédit Mobilier affair was the most grandiose in conception and national in scope, signaling as it did the building of a corporate empire at government expense. The story of the financing of the Union Pacific is a classic nineteenth-century example of the federal government's acting as a servant of private capitalist enterprise.

A single symptom such as the Crédit Mobilier was not, however, to be mistaken for the main disease infecting the body politic and economic. Mark Twain recognized that an "all-pervading speculativeness" with its concomitant "shameful corruption," as he phrased it, was the subject of the novel and that its principal manifestation in midcentury lay in the attempt to possess and exploit the vast frontier West—particularly by means of the railroad.[30] Because this phenomenon was so all-pervading and the competition it engendered so great, Twain, in satirizing it, did not confine himself to writing a consistent parody of one specific speculation, but instead created an original fiction that drew upon various real railroad projects and that limited the *roman à clef* aspect to occasional allusions. This fiction—the most original story element in *The Gilded Age*—is contained in two large episode sequences, one concerning the Columbus River Slackwater Navigation Company and the Salt Lick Extension of the Pacific Railroad, and the other concerning the Knobs Industrial University Bill. Both of these sequences were intimately associated with the personal lives of the authors; nevertheless, they both follow the unmistakable pattern of Gilded Age railroad empire building. If this pattern is divided into its basic elements of land exploitation on the frontier, financial speculation on Wall Street, and Congressional lobbying in Washington, it can readily be seen that the Salt Lick Extension with its riverhead terminus at Stone's Landing represents the first, the Columbus River Slackwater Navigation Company the second, and the Knobs University Bill the third.

Though the Salt Lick Extension of the Pacific Railroad, the laying out of which involves Philip Sterling, Harry Brierly, and Colonel Sellers, represents in part the Hannibal and St. Joseph Railroad, it is also strongly suggestive of a branch of this road known as the Atchison (later Central) Branch of the Union Pacific Railroad. The construction company for the branch, which used the Kansas charter of the Atchison and Pike's Peak Railroad, finished the hundred miles for which it could receive government bonds in 1868; and just as the Salt Lick Extension was to have ended at Stone's Landing on Goose Run, the Central Branch ended in the valley of the Little Blue River in northern Kansas.[31] The president of this branch, which like the Salt Lick had its headquarters in New York, was none other than Samuel C. Pomeroy.[32] Labeled "Pomeroy's little private Atchison Pacific," it was described as "one of the nicest and fattest speculations ever concocted."[33] The Fortieth Congress, the machinations of which Clemens had observed as first hand, was notorious for the quantity of railroad bills introduced, and in this frenzied activity Senator

Pomeroy distanced "all competitors in the number and extent of his jobs."[34] He was strongly abetted by his friend James Harlan, himself an active speculator, always for the ostensible national good and for the actual private benefit of friends.[35] In the Salt Lick sequence Mark Twain is in part filling out his satire of Pomeroy, and in so doing is again hitting at a major abuse through a representative practitioner. Just as the Salt Lick Pacific Extension is laid out to go "miles out of its way" to build up the projected city of Napoleon, Pomeroy was accused of diverting the northern Kansas road from its intended course, due west from St. Joseph, many miles south "to accommodate the town of Atchison."[36] The name "Salt Lick" (partly a parody of Salt Lake), of course, carries the same ambitious connotation as Atchison and Pike's Peak,[37] and without doubt alludes to the route of the Union Pacific, which was to extend to the Great Salt Lake at Ogden, Utah, passing through the valley of the Platte River.[38]

To the extent that Colonel Sellers' project to convert Goose Run into the commercially navigable water artery Columbus River, with its crucial rail-water junction at the city of Napoleon, is a memory of prewar visions of tying the new commercial carrier, the railway, to the old-established and theretofore omnipotent one, the steamboat line, to that extent it reflects historical background rather than contemporary events. But to the extent that it provides the excuse for the anticipated boom town of Napoleon that will mushroom out of the sleepy hamlet of Stone's Landing, it depicts the uncontrolled land speculation that was the ever present camp-follower of the Pacific railroads of the sixties and seventies as they pushed their way across the continent.

In Harry Brierly's interview with the president of the Columbus River Slackwater Navigation Company, presented in Chapter XXVIII, and in part of the Knobs University Bill sequence not only is there general satire of railroad lobbying, but there are also details highly suggestive of the actions of the financier Jay Cooke in promoting the Northern Pacific. The planting of favorable stories in influential newspapers, particularly in a religious newspaper of enormous circulation ("Your religious paper is by far the best vehicle for a thing of this kind") is, for example, re-

markably similar to Jay Cooke's payment of $15,000 to Henry
Ward Beecher for the support of the *Christian Union,* in which
appeared a series of articles eulogistic of the northwest territory
being opened up by the Northern Pacific.[39] Among secular newspapers bribed for their support was the Washington *Chronicle,*
Brother Balaam's *Washington Daily Love-Feast* in *The Gilded
Age.*[40] The newspaper debate touched off by introduction of the
Knobs University Bill in Congress (II, 130-36) is very much like
the public debate surrounding the Northern Pacific bill. Just as
the *Public Ledger* denounced the "huge robberies of the public
domain,"[41] the newspapers in the novel speak of "highway rob-
bery" and an "iniquitous scheme."

Again, the tug-of-war in the House of Representatives over
winning votes for or against the Knobs University Bill, followed
blow by blow by daily reports in the newspapers (II, 134-36),
finds its counterpart in the struggle around the Northern Pacific
bill. As the debate approaches a climax, Senator Dilworthy sends
a note up from the floor to the chairman of the Committee on
Benevolent Appropriations. It says (II, 148):

"Everybody expects a grand assault in force; no doubt you believe, as
I certainly do, that it is the thing to do; we are strong, and everything is
hot for the contest. Trollop's espousal of our cause has immensely helped
us and we grow in power constantly. Ten of the opposition were called
away from town about noon . . . . Six others are sick, but expect to be
about again *to-morrow or next day* . . . . Go for a suspension of the rules!
You will find we can swing a two-thirds vote—I am perfectly satisfied
of it. The Lord's truth will prevail.

"Dilworthy."

On May 6, 1870, after a stormy scene in the House the preceding
day, Henry Cooke wrote to his brother Jay:

Blaine is doing us great service; so is Schenck . . . . Blaine dropped in
specially to say . . . that we must not be in the least disturbed; that when
the House again meets our relative strength will be considerably stronger
than it was yesterday; that we have got the bill in such shape that all the
business of the House is suspended until it passes . . . .[42]

Though Clemens could not possibly have known this correspon-

dence—it was not published until 1907—the similarity of his
own passage in tone and even in wording clearly indicates how
thoroughly familiar he was with the actions of the Northern Pacific
and other railroad lobbies.[43]

I have not been able to find any satisfactory original for the
Knobs Industrial University Bill. Still, it is not difficult to find
valid reasons for Clemens' invention of such a bill as a vehicle for
his satire on lobbying. Disregarding for the moment his desire to
use his family's "Tennessee Land" in the plot of the novel,[44]
Clemens had good reason to make a land grant bill for Negro
education a high point of his satire. The "Reconstruction" Congresses were notorious for granting appropriations to aid all kinds
of projects ostensibly designed to "uplift" the freed slave and
simultaneously manipulated for the benefit of private investors and
landowners. In these projects the Christian Statesmen were prominently active.[45]

Among the several responsibilities assigned the famous Freedmen's Bureau was the supervision of educational enterprises, practically all of which were of a technical rather than liberal arts
nature. In the page of Clemens' manuscript containing the passage
in which the bill is first given notice in Congress, it is at first called
"a bill 'To Found and Incorporate the Knobs University' " (it
has been previously referred to as the "Knobs University bill");
then the word *Industrial* is added as an afterthought and thereafter is consistently incorporated in the name.[46] It is evident that
Clemens revised the name to reflect more accurately such enterprises as Hampton Normal and Agricultural Institute, founded in
1870 by General Samuel C. Armstrong, an officer of the Freedmen's Bureau; for General Armstrong's first purpose was to ele-
vate manual work.[47] Then, too, Senator Stewart, for whom Clemens acted briefly as secretary, was a member of the Committee on
Judiciary, chaired by Lyman Trumbull, the chief proponent of
the Freedmen's Bureau bill. Stewart himself claimed to disapprove
of the bill, for, as he hypocritically stated, "There was unlimited
power given the commission to purchase land for educational
purposes."[48] Most significant of all, Senator Pomeroy had procured
passage of a bill donating three acres in Nashville, Tennessee, for

Fisk University.[49] Again Mark Twain wrote with full knowledge of historical events.

It should be noted in this connection that Charles Dudley Warner in a later novel, *A Little Journey*, makes a brief, caustic allusion to freedmen's education. His character Henderson goes to a Negro college to dedicate a building he has donated and travels there in a special train, the cost of which ". . . 'would have built and furnished an industrial school and workshop for a hundred Negroes; but this train was, I dare say, a much more inspiring example of what they might attain by the higher education.' "[50] Also in this connection it may be significant that in early March, 1873, as *The Gilded Age* was being written, an Agricultural College bill, having passed the House, reached the Speaker's table, where, its sponsor reversing his own request for a conference committee, it was dropped.[51]

One or two other Congressional measures of dubious legitimacy, though not given as extensive treatment, are alluded to satirically in *The Gilded Age*. One of these is the 1872 subsidy voted for extending the service of the already heavily subsidized Pacific Mail Steamship Company. Originally founded on the federal government postal contract of 1866 to connect San Francisco with New Zealand and Australia via the Sandwich Islands, the Pacific Mail had had one subsidy denied by Congress, even though recommended unanimously by the influential Senate Committee on Post Offices, on which Pomeroy was second ranking member.[52] Therefore, in order to secure a subsidy of half a million dollars to finance more frequent service with Asia, the company placed $900,000 in the hands of an agent to pay lobbyists, influence congressmen, and bribe editors. Termed "a reckless robbery of a corporation under the temporary control of speculators," the scheme was later referred to a Congressional committee, who recommended a judicial investigation. Meanwhile, on June 1, 1872, the desired subsidy bill was enacted by Congress.[53]

In *The Gilded Age* Laura Hawkins, as part of her blackmailing of Mr. Trollop, reveals that the lobbyist who induced him to vote for the "Steamship Subsidy bill," a bill that "was a fraud on the government," was her agent and that she herself, accompanied by a second witness, had secretly overheard the entire conversation. " '. . . Mr. Trollop, you would not sell your vote on that subsidy bill—which was perfectly right—but you accepted of some of the stock, with the understanding that it was to stand in your brother-in-law's name' " (II, 115).[54]

Another, much more scandalous measure satirized was the famous "Salary Grab Act," or "Back Pay Steal," as it was alternatively called, by which Congress on its last day of session before Grant's second term, March 3, 1873, passed a bill doubling the President's salary, raising those of Cabinet members and Supreme Court justices, and increasing those of members of Congress by 50 per cent, retroactive for two years.[55] A wave of indignation swept the nation and the Salary Grab "became a theme of denunciation in every hamlet in the land."[56] As could be expected, Clemens was among the most wrathful. His Mr. Trollop, one of the "back-pay gang of thieves,"[57] is "pledged to support the Indigent Congressmen's Retroactive Appropriation." In the words of Laura Hawkins, "The man that will vote for that bill will break the eighth commandment in any *other* way" (II, 118). When the measure does come up, Senator Dilworthy, who has occupied his purchased seat to the last hour of the session, casts his vote for the last time,

in support of an ingenious measure contrived by the General from Massachusetts [Ben Butler][58] whereby the President's salary was proposed to be doubled and every Congressman paid several thousand dollars extra for work previously done, under an accepted contract, and already paid for once and receipted for. (II, 312)

So great was the public outcry against the Salary Grab that it had to be repealed in the next session.[59] The full extent of Clemens' indignation at the whole spectacle can best be seen in a proposed footnote to the foregoing passage, fully written out but eventually discarded:

47½

When the above was written, a full month had elapsed since the renowned Congressional embezzlement, & up to that time only 18 of the membership had declined to take their shares of the spoil. *After* that, under the lash of the newspapers, several culprits came meekly & reluctantly back & delivered up their several proportions of the property so shamefully wrested from the Treasury. As long as histories of America shall continue to be written, they will probably always contain a mention of the curious fact that in the year 1873 the Republic of the United States was represented by a Congress *sixteen-seventeenths* of whose membership actually could not be trusted with a pocket-book while the owner's back was turned. Fine-spun explanations & arguments are one thing & figures are another. Facts are stubborn things.[60]

A third bill mentioned by Laura in her conference with Mr. Trollop is his "great Pension bill," the speech for which Laura, as its ghost-writer, uses as a part of her blackmail (II, 111-12, 118-21). There were, however, so many soldiers' pension bills at the time—a sure way for a favorite son to curry favor with his constituents in the postwar period was to sponsor a pension bill—that finding an original for Mr. Trollop's unspecified one defies accomplishment.

Besides the legislative measures, which he gave more or less full treatment, Mark Twain made pointed allusions to a number of lesser actions and customs associated with Grant's administration. One of these was Grant's attempt to get Congressional support for his pet scheme of annexing Santo Domingo, once in 1870 and again in 1871. Termed a "shady adventure in imperial expansion," the proposed treaty failed of ratification by the Senate. Grant meanwhile sent his military aid to negotiate a secret treaty with the "puppet" dictator Baèz, the affair made headlines in the press, and several political heads fell.[61] In *The Gilded Age*, Colonel Sellers, the reconstructed rebel, who represents among other things the unconsciously arrogant expansionist attitude of the period, which later developed into full-blown "Yankee imperialism," says: " 'I go for putting the old flag on all the vacant lots. I said to the President, says I, "Grant, why don't you take Santo Domingo, annex the whole thing, and settle the bill afterwards." That's my way' " (II, 91).

A popular cause that typified the postwar years was the Greenback movement, an attempt to maintain an inflated currency of only partially redeemable paper money. As the greenbacks by law had to be accepted in all the transactions of the mass of the people, whereas gold could be demanded by holders of government bonds, the Greenbackers argued against deflation, which would compel investors in frontier speculations to pay in a cheaper currency than they had borrowed and would deprive the smaller capitalist of the new West and the reconstructed South of a supply of currency needed for development. The issue became, therefore, a sectional one between the financial centers of the East and the money-borrowing West and South.[62]

Colonel Sellers is a typical Greenbacker, in favor of the policy that has been defined as giving "the man without capital an equal opportunity in business with his rich competitor."[63] Just as he is an expansionist in foreign policy, so domestically he is a laissez faire private enterpriser, for whom government exists not as a control but as an instrument of capitalism. In the fall of 1872 five million dollars in retired greenbacks were put into circulation "to move the crops,"[64] and with this action in mind Mark Twain has the Colonel state:

". . . What we want is more money. I've told Boutwell so. Talk about basing the currency on gold; you might as well base it on pork. Gold is only one product. Base it on everything! You've got to do something for the West. How am I to move my crops? We must have improvements. . . ." (II, 141)

George S. Boutwell, the Secretary of the Treasury, who had released the greenbacks and who came under fire for his policies, was both timid and obstinate and served as the whipping-boy in the Greenback struggle.[65] In the novel Colonel Sellers voices this opinion: "You've got to conciliate the South, consolidate the two [war] debts, pay 'em off in greenbacks, and go ahead. That's my notion. Boutwell's got the right notion about the value of paper, but he lacks courage" (II, 91).[66]

A custom prevalent in the days before the press release became the popular mode of spreading Washington opinion, one that was so virulent in the Grant administration as to arouse much public comment, was the news "leak." The Washington correspondents were adepts at getting leaks. Senator Logan's wife, in her reminiscences, has outlined the procedure. She writes that when a congressman has made a statement in his own favor and detrimental to his opponent the correspondent

has only to see the opponent to obtain another "leak." Thus little by little the whole story comes out, and possibly not one of the Congressmen or officials thinks that he contributed in any way to it. Each thinks that his opponent is responsible for the disclosure, but the correspondent has only put the "leaks" together.[67]

Clemens himself had been a member of Newspaper Row in Washington and was entirely familiar with the habits of the press.[68] In *The Gilded Age* he attributes the Washington leaks to the loquacious and convivial Colonel Sellers, "a great favorite in Newspaper Row," who was forever "dropping bits of private, official information, which were immediately caught up and telegraphed all over the country."

People used to wonder in the winters of 187- and 187-, where the "Specials" got that remarkable information with which they every morning surprised the country, revealing the most secret intentions of the President and his cabinet, the private thoughts of political leaders, the hidden meaning of every movement. This information was furnished by Colonel Sellers. (II, 91-92)

In May, 1871, the *New-York Tribune* published the full text of the Treaty of Washington, generally referred to as the "Alabama Claims treaty" or "Alabama Treaty,"[69] before it appeared anywhere else. This scoop caused consternation and envy in newspaper circles, as well it might.[70] The *Gilded Age* passage continues:

When he [the Colonel] was asked, afterwards, about the stolen copy of the Alabama Treaty which got into the "New York Tribune," he only looked mysterious, and said that neither he nor Senator Dilworthy knew anything about it. But those whom he was in the habit of meeting occasionally felt almost certain that he did know. (II, 92)

Another custom that was prevalent and the subject of public comment was the abuse of the franking privilege. Mrs. Logan tells of congressmen sending free through the mails not only papers, documents, books, and maps, but typewriters, clothing, bedding, and other household effects as well.[71] Indeed, packages "occupying an entire mail-bag" were franked home "by Congressmen with tough consciences," and it was said that certain members franked their dirty linen home to be washed in order to economize.[72] In the novel, Laura Hawkins tells Dilworthy that Senator Balloon seemed to be packing on the day she saw him.

From The Gilded Age, *First Edition*
All Congressmen Do That

". . . His rooms were full of dry goods boxes, into which his servant was crowding all manner of old clothes and stuff. I suppose he will paint 'Pub. Docs' on them and frank them home. That's good economy, isn't it?"

"Yes, yes, but, child, all Congressmen do that. It may not be strictly honest, indeed, it is not unless he had some public documents mixed in with the clothes." (II, 50)[73]

Besides the principal characters of the novel already discussed, a sufficient number of minor ones are identifiable to justify the assertion that in almost all of its dramatis personae *The Gilded Age* is a key novel. What few characters are not images of public figures are based nonetheless upon real persons known to Clemens and Warner. The minor *public* characters are largely divided between two groups, those associated with the Washington scenes and those associated with the railroad episodes. With two or three exceptions both groups are made up of personages not nationally recognizable in the manner of Dilworthy or Laura Hawkins, yet identifiable by readers close to the areas and events satirized. The general effect of these characters is, consequently, that of giving authenticity and convincingness to the novel rather than stretching the game of identification to the breaking point. The average contemporary reader must have sensed, without knowing why, that these were real persons.

Next to Dilworthy himself, the most easily identified Washington characters are Brother Balaam, Senator Balloon, General Sutler, and the "dapper young Senator from Iowa." Brother Balaam, as we have seen, is James Harlan. The name of the character in itself makes a witty satirical comment on the original, for the biblical Balaam, who loved the wages of unrighteousness, was ready to prophesy as desired, for a price.[74] Senator Balloon, who upholds the ancient dignity of the Senate (II, 301) and franks his baggage home (II, 50 f., 301), is Clemens' old Nevada acquaintance James Nye.[75] Formerly governor of "one of the Territories" and "ex-officio Indian agent," this "whole-hearted," "waggish," "handsome old gentleman," who "knows the Scriptures" better than anyone else in the Senate (II, 49-50), has milked the Indians for all they are worth and for his devotion is spoken of for an ambassadorship (II, 53-54). General Sutler of Massachusetts, who defies England on the Alabama claims (II, 74) and engineers the Salary Grab (II, 312), is Senator and ex-general "Ben" Butler. It is no accident that when Colonel Selby passes the equestrian statue of General Jackson in Lafayette Square he says to himself, "Old Hickory ought to get down and give his seat to General Sutler—but they'd have to tie him on" (II, 81), for Butler was described as "the very incarnation of force and will" and as "seeming always poised for a leap."[76] The unnamed "dapper young Senator from Iowa," who stands where he can exhibit his feet to Laura Hawkins, sitting in the gallery, whereas his usual custom

is "to prop them on his desk and enjoy them himself with a
selfish disregard of other people's longings" (II, 7), is undoubtedly
William B. Allison, congressman from Dubuque. Allison, who was
accused of accepting a large railroad bribe, was dubbed by the
New-York Tribune the handsomest man in Congress.[77]

Other congressmen, who figure less prominently in the novel,
have names tantalizingly close to those of members of the 39th,
40th, and 41st Congresses. Mr. Buckstone, Chairman of the House
Committee on Benevolent Appropriations, could be Ralph P. Buckland of Ohio or Charles W. Buckley of Alabama. Mr. Hopperson,
the congressman who has serious doubts about casting his vote for
any measure sponsored by Dilworthy, could be Benjamin H.
Epperson of Texas. And two others, barely mentioned in passing,
Jex and Huffy, sound like Thomas A. Jenckes of Rhode Island
and John Taffe of Nebraska, and a third, Spatters, may be another,
oblique reference to James W. Patterson of New Hampshire.[78]
These last, and a few others for whom there are virtually no distinguishing characteristics presented, defy identification at this
distance in time; their names, however, are suggestive of a well-
rounded *roman à clef*. Mr. Trollop, on the other hand, appears to
be nothing more than a convenient foil for Laura and a catchall
for parodies on congressional bills.[79]

In the Washington chapters there also occurs an allusion to one
of the most controversial feminists of the time, Victoria Woodhull. When, after Colonel Selby's reappearance in Washington and
hypocritical profession of love to her, Laura rationalizes to herself
the sudden resurgence of her former passion, she recalls women
lecturers who have advocated free love and common-law marriage.

Not even the religious atmosphere of Senator Dilworthy's house had
been sufficient to instill into Laura that deep Christian principle which
had been somehow omitted in her training. Indeed, in that very house
had she not heard women, prominent before the country and besieging
Congress, utter sentiments that fully justified the course she was marking
out for herself? (II, 85)

Among the most eloquent advocates of free love was the aggressive, beautiful Victoria Woodhull, whom, as she had scandalized

and divided the Nook Farm community, Clemens most certainly knew by reputation. The most famous episode of her career was when she "besieged Congress" with a memorial on woman suffrage, her presentation of which electrified that male assemblage.[80]

The railroad men associated with the Salt Lick Pacific Extension are Warner's contribution to the *roman à clef*. Warner had been on a railway surveying team for a while as a young man and had known the originals of these characters personally; still, the real persons were sufficiently well known, particularly in the Middle West, to allow their recognition in fictional guise by a certain proportion of the novel's readers. Two of them, Jeff Thompson and Duff Brown, were singled out for mention by the *Hearth and Home* review:

. . . we have Jeff Thompson, without any mask at all, as the engineer who of all others was the man to make a preliminary survey for a railroad, it being the principal business of the preliminary surveyor to make the road seem certain to pass through every town, and intersect every big plantation within thirty miles of its probable route. We have Mr. Duff Brown too, whom every Western man will recognize simply by substituting for Brown another color. . . .[81]

Fortunately, a letter from Jeff Thompson to his old friend "Charlie" Warner has survived and goes far toward identifying persons and places.[82] M. Jeff Thompson, an ex-Confederate brigadier general—who had begun life as a dilettante and ladies' man, "polkaed at Newport" and "ridden at tournaments in the Old Dominion"—had later turned into a hard-drinking frontiersman and railroad surveyor and had been associated with Warner in the opening of the Hannibal and St. Joseph Railroad,[83] a line also closely linked with the Clemens family. At the time of his letter to Warner, he was chief state engineer of Louisiana and had retained his reputation as an accommodating surveyor. "A very queer chicken," said *Harper's Weekly*, "possessing the necessary faculty of closing an eye to a cheap piece of canal or levee, and submerging his politics beneath the water-level of interest."[84]

Thompson, who had known Clemens back in his steamboating days, writes that he "was exceedingly anxious to get a copy [of

The Gilded Age], not knowing that it was a joint work, and wondering what Sam Clemens had told on me, unless it had been the opening of the H & St Jo—or some of my steamboat adventures about the beginning of the war." The moment he saw Warner's name, however, he "suspected something about the One Hundred and Two or Third fork of Platte, would appear." These names seem not to refer—as might be supposed from the route of the Union Pacific—to the third fork of the Platte River in Nebraska, where it divides into its north and south branches only some 160 miles east of the 102nd parallel of longitude, but instead to the much smaller Platte River that flows southward east of St. Joseph, Missouri, and has two tributaries named the "Third Fork" and the "Hundred and Two," both of whose confluences with it came within a mile or two of the Hannibal and St. Joseph route.

Jeff Thompson identifies in his letter the original for Duff Brown, who is not primarily Duff Green, as the *Hearth and Home* reviewer evidently thought.[85] He is principally the portly John Duff of Boston, an early director of the Union Pacific with an exceptionally keen interest in the road, who took advantage of every opportunity to make trips over the completed part of the line and who, at the time *The Gilded Age* was written, was becoming vice-president of the company.[86] Duff Brown, who with Rodney Schaick controls the construction of the whole line of the Salt Lick Pacific Extension (I, 149), is a member of the surveying expedition and is described as a "great railroad contractor," "a bluff, jovial Bost'n man, thick-set" (I, 143). He is also "subsequently a well-known member of Congress" like Duff Green, whose similarity of name and connection with the Crédit Mobilier[87] no doubt suggested the double parody. Brown's associate, Rodney Schaick (not mentioned by Thompson), the "sleek New York broker," "dainty in his dress, smooth of speech," and noted for his "assurance and adroitness" (I, 143), is in all probability Sidney Dillon of New York, soon to be made chairman of the board of Union Pacific, who was "a self-made man of brisk but courtly address, . . . of the English type." Primarily a railroad contractor, "who had constructed probably as many railroads as any other living man," Dillon, acting as director of subsidiary con-

tractors, was personally involved in the construction of the Union
Pacific, "frequently traveling backward and forward along the
line and aiding the builders out of his abundant experience."[88]
Grayson, the surveyor whom Jeff Thompson tells to get out his
sighting iron to see if he "can find old Sellers's town" (I, 193) is
also a real person in the original crew.[89]

Another Warner character, one who figures largely in the story
of the Boltons, is at least in part a real person. Mr. Bigler of "the
great firm of Pennybacker, Bigler & Small, railroad contractors,"
who in planning the financing of the Tunkhannock, Rattlesnake,
and Youngwomanstown Railroad[90] proposes to "arrange things"
in the Pennsylvania legislature, is described as "one of the most
important men in the State; nobody has more influence at Harris-
burg" (I, 167-70). Here is an obvious allusion to Governor, and
sometime Senator, William Bigler of Pennsylvania,[91] who had been
involved earlier in the contest between the Pennsylvania Railroad
and the Baltimore and Ohio to secure the state charter authorizing
incorporation.[92] Here also is an allusion to the notorious laxity of
the Pennsylvania legislature in its framing of the Crédit Mobilier
charter.[93] Senator Simon, whose re-election leaves Bigler "cleaned
out" because the Senator fails to recompense his financial backers
with the usual lucrative legislative measures (II, 183-84), is Simon
Cameron, senator from Pennsylvania in 1856-61 and 1867-77.[94]
Earlier in the novel occurs an anticipatory pun on his name. Bigler
tells Mr. Bolton that "the price is raised so high on United States
Senator[s] now, that it affects the whole market; you can't get
any public improvement through on reasonable terms. Simony is
what I call it, Simony" (I, 170).

Certain places and publications actually have more meaning
in *The Gilded Age* than would appear on the surface. The Washington bookstore at which Laura Hawkins loiters watching for
Mr. Buckstone (II, 51, 56) is near his place of lodging and is
described in a deleted sentence in the manuscript as "the showy
new bookstore."[95] This is not, of course, James Guild's disorderly,
overflowing bookshop on Pennsylvania Avenue at the turn of
First Street, where Clemens loved to browse, but appears to be
William Duane's bookstore farther along the Avenue at the corner

of Sixth Street, adjoining Woodward's Tavern and Mrs. Wilson's
boarding house (possibly Buckstone's lodgings).[96] As it was opposite the *National Intelligencer* office, it is likely that Clemens
had occasionally patronized it while a Washington correspondent.

In writing about Philip Sterling's residence in New York,
Warner makes a number of allusions that, though lost upon a
modern reader, had a familiar ring to readers in the 1870's. Telling
of Philip's theater-going, he says, "Philip was too young to remember the old Chambers street box, where the serious Burton led his
hilarious and pagan crew" (I, 133). The Chambers Street Theatre
(1848-1856), originally Palmo's New York Opera House, had a
very small auditorium that would seat barely eight hundred. It
was the stamping ground of the famous comedian William E. Burton, creator of "Toodles."[97] When Philip receives an offer to take
charge of a country newspaper, he seeks advice from Mr. Gringo,
"who years ago managed the *Atlas*." He explains to Gringo his
qualms about accepting the post because the owners want him to
change it into an opposition paper, a proposal that goes against his
principles. Gringo tells him that if he is going into newspaper work
he "can't afford a conscience like that" (I, 137-38). The *Atlas*
(1828-1881) was one of the oldest New York Sunday papers, a
serious journal long associated with the name of Anson Herrick,
at one time a congressman,[98] who was probably the original for
Mr. Gringo.

While Philip is waiting for the appropriation to materialize, he
devotes himself to studying and writing. During this time he sub-
mits some papers to the journal *The Plow, the Loom, and the Anvil*,
and they are reprinted in the British *Practical Magazine* (I, 260).
These titles, which sound very much like satirical fictions, were
actual periodicals. *The Plough* [*sic*], *the Loom, and the Anvil*,
described as "one of the ablest agricultural journals of the times,"[99]
in reality covered not only agriculture and husbandry but also the
coal trade, markets, domestic economy, the iron trade, textiles,
agricultural chemistry, and foreign trade, among other things.[100]
Hence, Philip's subjects, "strength of materials" and "bridge-
building," are not as farfetched as they seem. They are even more
appropriate to the British publication, the lengthy subtitle of

which begins, "an illustrated cyclopedia of industrial information, inventions and improvements, collected from foreign and British sources, for the use of those concerned in raw materials, machinery, manufactures, building and decoration," and then gives a list of professions covered, including "Civil and Mechanical Engineers." Comparable in seriousness to *Machine Design* or *Architectural Forum* in the present time, it was a brand new publication begun the very year *The Gilded Age* came out.[101]

Though there are a few other scattered allusions, so fleeting as not to justify extended research,[102] the evidence presented in this and the preceding two chapters proves that *The Gilded Age* was a thoroughgoing exposé of its times and that, though its minor characters and incidents fell short of the full *roman à clef* role assigned to its major ones, they still had a fresh topicality that served as a running commentary on the period.

PART III

The Larger Satire

CHAPTER VII

The Clemens Background

IT WILL BE REMEMBERED that, when the writing of a partnership novel was first proposed, it was decided that as Clemens had the beginning of a story in mind he should be the one to begin; and that he immediately proceeded to write eleven consecutive chapters with great speed before he relinquished the manuscript to Warner. These first eleven chapters are drawn almost entirely from Clemens' childhood experiences and riverboat piloting days. Indeed, so highly personal are they in their nostalgic glimpses and their allusions to family legends that, taken by themselves, they might constitute the opening of an autobiographical romance. It is no wonder that the words flowed easily and with a lyricism that Clemens was not to achieve again until *Huckleberry Finn*. For the story he had to tell had occupied his thoughts, often irritatingly, sometimes tantalizingly, always hauntingly, for many years past, and this story centered around the subject announced in the title of the very first chapter—"Squire Hawkins' Tennessee Lands."

The story of the Tennessee Land was the story of Samuel Clemens' father, John Marshall Clemens, and the latter's aspirations for his children's future security. It is true that during the course of the novel Mark Twain skilfully molds the Tennessee Land into a symbol of "all-pervading speculativeness," the focal point of a centripetal circle of corruption. This fact, however, should not obscure the intensely personal origins of the tale—a tragi-comic tale of great expectations that affected the lives of the Clemens family and those of two or three individuals in particular. Here is the way that Mark Twain has described it in his *Autobiography:*

> The monster tract of land which our family own in Tennessee was purchased by my father a little over forty years ago. He bought the enormous area of seventy-five thousand acres at one purchase. The entire lot must have cost him somewhere in the neighborhood of four hundred dollars. . . . When my father paid down that great sum, and turned and stood in the courthouse door of Jamestown, and looked abroad over his vast possessions, he said, "Whatever befalls me, my heirs are secure; I shall not live to see these acres turn to silver and gold, but my children will." Thus with the very kindest intentions in the world toward us, he laid the heavy curse of prospective wealth upon our shoulders. . . .
>
> . . . .
>
> When he died in 1847 he had owned it about twenty years. The taxes were almost nothing (five dollars a year for the whole), and he had always paid them regularly and kept his title perfect. . . .
>
> . . . .
>
> Forty years afterward we had managed it all away except 10,000 acres, and gotten nothing to remember the sales by. About 1887—possibly it was earlier—the 10,000 went. . . .
>
> . . . It kept us hoping and hoping during forty years, and forsook us at last. It put our energies to sleep and made visionaries of us—dreamers and indolent. We were always going to be rich next year—no occasion to work. It is good to begin life poor; it is good to begin life rich—these are wholesome; but to begin it poor and *prospectively* rich! The man who has not experienced it cannot imagine the curse of it.[1]

Mark Twain returns to the subject several times during his *Autobiography.* The first passage concerning the Tennessee Land was written about three years before *The Gilded Age.*[2] This was the first time the subject had been formally committed to paper; the informal record is large. As early as 1857, when Clemens was about twenty-two, he offered a few thousand acres to Horace Bixby in lieu of cash to pay for his instruction in riverboat pilot-ing, an offer firmly declined.[3] A year later, he was writing to Orion and his wife, "I seldom venture to think about our landed wealth, for 'hope deferred maketh the heart sick.' "[4] When he visited the clairvoyant Madame Caprell in New Orleans in 1861, she told him, "The land he [Orion] has now will be very valuable after a while," to which Clemens laconically replied, "Say 250 years hence."[5] In 1866 Orion was made a considerable offer for the land by some winegrowers but refused it because he had, temporarily, become a prohibitionist; and Sam wrote in a fury to his sister-in-law, Mollie, "It is Orion's duty to attend to that land, . . . if he lets it be sold for taxes, all his religion will not wipe out the sin."[6] It is not surprising, therefore, that by 1870 he was writing Orion, "I beseech you never to ask my advice, opinion or consent about that hated property,"[7] and that he felt moved to draft the fragment later incorporated in the *Autobiography*.

Though the land petered out as an investment for John Clemens' family, it indirectly contributed a substantial income to Sam, as the latter recognized.

It furnished me a field for Sellers and a book. Out of my half of the book I got $20,000, perhaps something more; out of the play I got $75,000—just about a dollar an acre. It is curious; I was not alive when my father made the investment, therefore he was not intending any partiality; yet I was the only member of the family that ever profited by it. . . .[8]

From the opening chapter of *The Gilded Age*, in which Squire Hawkins announces his purchase of the land, to Clemens' own next-to-last chapter (LXI), where Washington Hawkins tears up the real estate tax bill with the words, "The spell is broken, the life-long curse is ended!" (II, 332),[9] the Tennessee Land runs like a leitmotif through the novel, serving as the physical symbol of the idea of speculativeness. So much is it a symbol that the phrase is always capitalized; and an indication of what a personally meaningful symbol it was for Clemens is the fact that in the *Autobiography* he consistently referred to it by the same simple phrase— apparently a catchword among the Clemens clan.

Less obvious than the role of the Tennessee Land as a talisman in *The Gilded Age* is the detailed extent to which the episodes concerning it are drawn from life. Though there are occasional inconsistencies, the fictional account on the whole corresponds point by point with the actual events as they appear in surviving records. The principal source is the *Autobiography*, and because it was written by the same author—one, moreover, who was not always successful at distinguishing between recollection and fantasy—it is not entirely reliable. The correspondence of the time and the remembrance of others, however, support the main facts as given by Clemens.

The land that John Clemens bought was in Fentress County midway between the two main arteries of commerce for the region, the Cumberland and Tennessee rivers.[10] It apparently contained coal, copper, and iron, and bore "thousands of acres of the finest yellow-pine timber," which could be "rafted down Obeds River to the Cumberland, down the Cumberland to the Ohio, down the Ohio to the Mississippi, and down the Mississippi to any community" that wanted it. It produced a promising variety of wild grape.[11] Located only a few hundred miles from Knoxville, it was in the probable path of some future railroad leading south from Cincinnati.[12] Considering that the seventy-five thousand acres[13] probably did not cost him more than five hundred dollars, the purchase, far from being a harebrained venture, was a good long-term speculative investment.[14] Though the land might never have been worth the millions envisioned by John Clemens, the prospects for realizing tens of thousands of dollars were entirely reasonable, particularly as the maintenance amounted to only five dollars a year in taxes. It is important to stress this point, for in many respects John Clemens was a gambler with the welfare of his family. In the land transaction, however, he played the shrewdest hand in his life. It was not the investment itself that brought anxiety and frustration to his children but the lack of judgment that kept him and his visionary son Orion from selling out at a good profit, in the hope of raising the ante still further, until the speculative boom evaporated and the land dropped in value to less than its purchase price. It is this self-deception born of greed that Mark Twain successfully illustrates in hurling the facts of his family's great expectations into the novel.

In *The Gilded Age* Si Hawkins, speaking of his children, echoes the words of John Clemens when he says to his wife, *"We'll* never see the day, Nancy— . . . but *they'll* ride in coaches, Nancy! They'll live like the princes of the earth" (I, 22). Squire Hawkins' discussion of his purchase, in fact, is a hyperbolic expansion of the remarks Clemens attributes to his father in the *Autobiography:*

" 'Even you and I will see the day that steamboats will come up that little Turkey River to within twenty miles of this land of ours—and in high water they'll come right *to* it! . . .' " (I, 20) In his 1870 passage in the *Autobiography* Clemens states that his father might have listed the probable intersecting of a railroad as one of the "eligibilities" of the land but failed to do so presumably because "he never had seen a railway, and it is barely possible that he had not even heard of such a thing." "Curious as it may seem, as late as eight years ago there were people living close to Jamestown who never had heard of a railroad and could not be brought to believe in steamboats. . . ."[15] Fortunately, when he adapted his material to fiction three years later, Clemens dropped this fairly obvious comic exaggeration of his father's supposed innocence and relegated the naïveté to the backward local squatters. Squire Hawkins clearly foresees the coming of the railroads and the value of coal; it is "these cattle" of Obedstown who scoff at even the idea of steamboats and who use coal to build dams with.[16]

John Clemens lived thenceforth with a sense of reassurance that regardless of what happened to him his children's future was secure; and on his deathbed he admonished his family, " 'Cling to the land and wait; let nothing beguile it away from you.' "[17] This utterance is built up in *The Gilded Age* to a complete deathbed scene, culminating in a sudden, final burst of energy in which the dying Hawkins rouses himself and says,

> "I am leaving you in cruel poverty. I have been—so foolish—so short-sighted. But courage! A better day is—is coming. Never lose sight of the Tennessee Land! Be wary. There is wealth stored up for you there—wealth that is boundless! The children shall hold up their heads with the best in the land, yet. . . ."

and then dies with the unfinished words, "But you are—safe. Safe. The Ten—" (I, 110-11).

During his lifetime, though, John Clemens was frequently tempted to sell the land at a reasonable profit when the opportunity offered itself.

Negotiations looking to the sale of the land were usually in progress.

When the pressure became very hard and finances were at their lowest ebb, it was offered at any price—at five cents an acre, sometimes. When conditions improved, however little, the price suddenly advanced even to its maximum of one thousand dollars an acre. Now and then a genuine offer came along, but, though eagerly welcomed at the moment, it was always refused after a little consideration.

"We will struggle along somehow, Jane," he would say. "We will not throw away the children's fortune."[18]

In 1846, sixteen or seventeen years after the purchase, John Clemens was asking a minimum of only twenty cents an acre,[19] and by 1850, three years after his death, the market value had decreased to ten cents an acre;[20] still the family clung to it. In the novel, two successive offers, one of $1,500 and one of $3,000, are mentioned as having tempted Hawkins in times of financial stress. A third offer, of $10,000, is described in a fully developed episode, in which Hawkins, resisting his initial impulse to accept at once, argues himself into making the unrealistic counteroffer of the "iron property" alone for $30,000. When the agent departs with this counterproposal, an amused look on his face, the Squire kicks himself for not having held out for fifty thousand—a quarter of a million, even. When his wife reminds him, however, that they "haven't a cent in the world" yet have "sent ten thousand dollars a-begging," he rushes out to find the stranger—who has vanished forever—ready to settle for almost any price.[21] Comic exaggeration though it is, the episode captures the spirit of the torturing vacillation that haunted John Clemens and his heirs.

Forty years after John Clemens' death, the family had "managed it all away except 10,000 acres, and gotten nothing to remember the sales by."

"About 1887 . . . the 10,000 went. My brother found a chance to trade it for a house and lot in the town of Corry, in the oil regions of Pennsylvania. About 1894 he sold this property for $250. That ended the Tennessee land."[22] In the novel, the end of the Tennessee Land is signalized in a much more dramatic fashion. When, after all schemes for turning the real estate into money have completely collapsed, Washington Hawkins receives a bill for the current year's taxes amounting to "more than twice the market value of the land," he for a moment vacillates in typical Clemens fashion ("I wish I had someone to decide for me"), then tears up the bill, saying, "It shall go for taxes . . . and never tempt me or mine any more" (II, 332)—the outcome Sam Clemens had in real life always feared.[23]

It is obvious that the character Squire Hawkins was based largely on John Marshall Clemens.[24] Like Hawkins, John Clemens had "a heart full of hope and dreams" as a young man, "an unerring faculty for making business mistakes," and a basic optimism which "led him from one unfortunate locality or enterprise to another."[25] Like Hawkins he tinkered in all seriousness with a perpetual-motion machine, that trap of ingenious but undisciplined minds.[26] The career of Squire Hawkins is in all of its principal events, motivations, and effects only the slightest exaggeration of that of John Clemens.

The Gilded Age opens in Obedstown, East Tennessee, where "Squire" Hawkins, who has got his title from being postmaster, keeps store in a part of his house in the intervals between the monthly deliveries of mail (I, 13-14). A deleted passage in the original manuscript for this section adds: "He had removed from Virginia 'well off,' but had broken himself up, here, by going people's security, allowing credit for goods, & so on."[27] John Marshall Clemens, who came from Virginia stock (his father had lived in Mason County, Virginia),[28] moved with his wife, Jane Lampton Clemens, and their first child, Orion, from their first home in Gainsborough, Tennessee, to "the remote and secluded village of Jamestown," on the Obed River, in the heart of Fentress County, the Obedstown of *The Gilded Age*.[29] "Judge" Clemens, who had studied law in Columbia, Kentucky, was one of the commissioners who established the county seat at Jamestown, built the courthouse, and was elected circuit clerk of the court, thereby acquiring his title ("in those regions the chief citizens always must have titles of some sort").[30] Four or five years later the Clemenses moved to a hamlet known as the Three Forks of Wolf and shortly thereafter to Pall Mall, also on the Wolf River, where the father kept the combined crossroads store and post office described in the novel.[31]

When John Clemens came to Jamestown he built a substantial house with plastered walls and real glass windows, the talk of the neighborhood. In *The Gilded Age* one of the tobacco-spitting, rail-sitting gossips speaks of a certain Si Higgins who has

. . . ben over to Kaintuck n' married a high-toned gal thar, outen the fust families [Jane Lampton, whom John Clemens married, was a Kentucky girl descended from an aristocratic English family], an' he's come back to the Forks [Three Forks of Wolf?] with jist a hell's-mint o' whoop-jamboree notions, folks say. He's tuck an' fixed up the ole house like they does in Kaintuck, he say, an' tha's ben folks come cler from Turpentine for to see it. He's tuck an' gawmed it all over on the inside with plarster-in'."

"What's plarsterin'?"

"*I* dono. Hit's what *he* calls it. Ole Mam Higgins, she tole me. She say she warn't gwyne to hang out in no sich a dern hole like a hog. Says it's mud, or some sich kind o' nastness that sticks on n' kivers up everything. Plarsterin', Si calls it." (I, 17)[32]

The financial crash of 1834 wrecked John Clemens' modest and short-lived prosperity.

From being honored and envied as the most opulent citizen of Fentress County—for outside of his great landed possessions he was considered to be worth not less than three thousand five hundred dollars—he suddenly woke up and found himself reduced to less than one-fourth of that amount. He was a proud man, a silent, austere man, and not a person likely to abide among the scenes of his vanished grandeur and be the target for public commiseration. . . .[33]

When, therefore, a letter arrived from John Quarles, the husband of Jane Clemens' sister, who had settled in the "almost invisible village" of Florida, Missouri, urging John Clemens to come to this new and promising frontier country, he "gathered together his household and journeyed many tedious days through wilderness solitudes, toward what was then the 'Far West.' "[34] The "happy-hearted, generous, and optimistic" Quarles wrote with enthusiasm, exaggerating the size of Florida from its actual twenty-one houses to fifty-four. Responding with matching enthusiasm, an enthusiasm born of release from frustration, John Clemens sold his store and farm and, with the few hundred dollars realized, departed hastily with his family in a two-horse barouche and on horseback.[35]

In *The Gilded Age* Si Hawkins, who feels he is rotting away in the midst of shiftlessness and poverty, receives a letter from his ebullient friend Colonel Sellers, which says in part: " 'Come right along to Missouri! . . . sell out for whatever you can get, and come along, . . . It's the grandest country—the loveliest land . . . no pen can do it justice. . . . there's enough for all, and to spare. . . . Come!—rush!—hurry!—don't wait for anything!' " Si says to Nancy, "I am going to Missouri. I won't stay in this dead country and decay with it." And "with an activity and a suddenness that bewildered Obedstown and almost took its breath away, the Hawkinses hurried through with their arrangements in four short months and flitted out into the great mysterious blank that lay beyond the Knobs of Tennessee." (I, 19, 26)[36]

The first episode along the way is the finding and adoption of the boy Clay, who has just been orphaned by his mother's death from fever. There is no autobiographical counterpart of this episode. It is designed, as has been indicated, to introduce one of the clichés of sensation fiction that are burlesqued in *The Gilded Age*— that of the heroically devoted foster child.[37] It should be mentioned parenthetically, however, that in the opinion of the French critic Lemonnier the weakening of Clay's parental ties absolves Mark Twain psychologically from a feeling of disrespect in depicting his own father in fiction, a hesitancy completely avoided in *Tom Sawyer*.[38] The theory finds some support in the fact that Warner's old friend Jeff Thompson, who had also known Sam Clemens, assumed that Clay was Clemens himself.[39]

The next episode is "Uncle Daniel's First Sight of a Steamboat," Chapter III. Uncle Dan'l was a middle-aged slave of the Quarleses, whom Sam Clemens had got to know and love during the many idyllic months he spent on the Quarles farm in his early years. The original of Jim in *Huckleberry Finn*, Uncle Dan'l was "a faithful and affectionate good friend, ally, and adviser . . . , whose sympathies were wide and warm."[40] Mark Twain's brief sketch of him in *The Gilded Age* is significant as a "literary rehearsal" for Jim, but not in its humorous depiction of superstitious fear (when the fiery steamboat rushes out of the night, coughing and glaring, Uncle Dan'l solemnly says, "It's de Almighty! Git down on you' knees!"); it is significant in its portrayal of human courage and self-sacrifice ("Oh, Lord, spah de little chil'en, . . . jes' let 'em off jes' dis once, and take it out'n de ole niggah").[41]

The last episode in the Hawkins migration to Missouri is the steamboat race and its resultant wreck, which provide the excuse for introducing the second orphan, Laura, into the story. Laura's introduction as an orphaned survivor of the steamboat explosion, though entirely suited to the burlesque of sensation fiction, takes advantage, for the purpose of the story, of an episode that Mark Twain wanted to write anyway for its own sake. Indeed, Clemens had a twofold motivation for describing the disaster in all its breathtaking and gruesome detail:[42] to write out of his system the explosion of the steamboat *Pennsylvania,* as a result of which his younger brother, Henry, perished, and to criticize the ineffectuality of American courts in the face of such calamities.[43]

Clemens was similarly motivated in giving his heroine the name Laura and in describing her girlhood appearance and personality the way he did in the early chapters of *The Gilded Age.* The young Laura is very evidently based on Laura M. Wright, a charming fourteen-year-old Missourian with whom Clemens had fallen in youthful love in 1858 when as a cub pilot of twenty-two he was steering on the *Pennsylvania.* The point is of some interest because Albert Bigelow Paine assumed that Clemens' childhood sweetheart, Laura (Annie Laurie) Hawkins, the original of Becky Thatcher in *Tom Sawyer,* was also the young Laura Hawkins of *The Gilded Age*—that, indeed, there was for Clemens only one "real Laura." In portraying Laura at the age of twelve, according to Paine, Clemens "had a picture of the real Laura in his mind," though, as Paine notes, "the story itself bears no resemblance to her life."[44] Dixon Wecter has pointed out that Clemens borrowed only her name for "the ill-starred *femme fatale* of *The Gilded Age.*"[45]

Samuel C. Webster, Clemens' grandnephew, first suggested that the true original of the fictional Laura Hawkins was probably Laura Wright (whom Webster calls by her married name, Laura Dake), "the only girl he had any trouble forgetting." As Webster notes, Clemens had never had more than a childhood crush on the actual Laura Hawkins; but he had had an avid flirtation with Laura Wright, which had been abruptly ended by the interception of his letters by her mother—a circumstance calculated to rankle in Clemens' mind—and he was quite possibly writing this poignant memory out of his system (as he had that of his brother's disaster) after three years of happily married life.[46]

The story of Clemens' brief, romantic encounter with Laura Wright, "that fresh flower of the woods and the prairies,"[47] is charmingly and nostalgically related in the *Autobiography*. In New Orleans, the young pilot made frequent visits to the *John J. Roe*, a steamboat owned by Indiana farm people "overflowing with good-fellowship," who had "brought the simple . . . farm spirit" to the boat "and had domesticated it there." On one of these occasions, out of the midst of the congenial company aboard, "floating upon my enchanted vision," Clemens writes,

came that slip of a girl of whom I have spoken—that instantly elected sweetheart out of the remoteness of interior Missouri—a frank and simple and winsome child who had never been away from home in her life before, and had brought with her to these distant regions the freshness and the fragrance of her own prairies.

"I was not four inches from that girl's elbow during our waking hours for the next three days," he continues. "Then there came a sudden interruption." Someone shouted that the *Pennsylvania* was backing out; Clemens ran and leaped and just managed to scramble aboard his boat as it passed astern the *John J. Roe*.[48]

He never saw Laura Wright again, but he never forgot her. When in 1861 he called on the New Orleans clairvoyant Madame Caprell, she told him, ". . . you can get the girl you have in your eye, if you are a better man than her mother— . . . *she* caused the trouble and produced the coolness which has existed between yourself and the young lady for so many months past— . . . ." In relating this interview to Orion shortly afterward, Clemens added,

And the woman had the impudence to say that although I was eternally falling in love, still, when I went to bed at night, I somehow always happened to think of Miss Laura before I thought of my last new flame—

and it always would be the same (which will be devilish comfortable, won't it, when both she and I (like one of Dickens' characters,) are Another's?) But drat the woman, she *did* tell the truth, and I won't deny it. . . .[49]

In March, 1880, he heard indirectly from Laura Wright, now Laura Dake, through the agency of a twelve-year-old admirer in Dallas, Texas, David Watt Bowser. Mrs. Dake, it appears, was "Master Wattie's" teacher and principal; and when the boy mentioned that she had known Clemens when he was "a little boy and she was a little girl," the latter replied warmly,

> No indeed, I have not forgotten your principal at all. She was a very little girl, with a very large spirit, a long memory, a wise head, a great appetite for books, a good mental digestion, with grave ways, & inclined to introspection—an unusual girl. . . .[50]

Five years later, Clemens made the following entry in his *Notebook*:

> May 26, 1885. This date, 1858, parted from L. (Laura Dake). Who said "We shall meet again 30 years from now."[51]

And in July, 1906, he was replying to an appeal for financial help from Mrs. Dake, now sixty-two, and her disabled son of thirty-seven, a letter which, he noted, "shook me to the foundations" and revived the nostalgia.[52]

The descriptions of the two Lauras tally well. Laura Wright was "not remarkably pretty, but very intelligent . . . slender—dark-brown hair and eyes," a "peachy young face," and "entirely too proud."[53] Laura Hawkins in *The Gilded Age* "had a proud bearing and a somewhat mature look; she had fine, clean-cut features, her complexion was pure white and contrasted vividly with her black hair and eyes; she was not what one calls pretty—she was beautiful" (I, 78). One can see that Clemens had more personal reasons for rewriting Warner's "picture" of Laura than that of rectifying the latter's unconscious imitation of Constance Fenimore Woolson.[54]

Finally, it seems more than coincidental that Laura Wright was involved in a steamboat wreck shortly after Clemens had last seen her. The *John J. Roe* had hit a snag in the night, and when the passengers vacated the sinking vessel it was discovered that the young girl was missing. When finally sought out, she was found trying to repair a hoopskirt; and when she was urged to abandon the skirt and come as she was, she replied with characteristic calmness and pride that she would come ashore when she had completely dressed, and proceeded to do exactly that.[55]

When, in *The Gilded Age*, the Hawkinses eventually arrive at St. Louis, they transfer to a smaller steamboat, sail 130 miles up the Mississippi, and disembark "at a little tumble-down village on the Missouri shore."[56] For two days more they travel by team into the "almost roadless and uninhabited" interior until they come to a small roadside hamlet, their future home.

> By the muddy roadside stood a new log cabin, one-story high—the store; clustered in the neighborhood were ten or twelve more cabins, some new, some old.
> In the sad light of the departing day the place looked homeless enough. . . . (I, 59-60)

This desolate hamlet, little more than a clearing, to which the Hawkinses have been lured by the optimistic Colonel Sellers, seems from its locale to be somewhere in Marion or Monroe County, Missouri, not far from Florida, the village to which the Clemenses were drawn by the urging of the no less optimistic John Quarles. Its appearance is strikingly close to that of the "almost invisible" Florida of less than three hundred inhabitants described in Mark Twain's *Autobiography* in a passage written only four years after *The Gilded Age*.[57]

> It had two streets, each a couple of hundred yards long; the rest of the avenues mere lanes, with rail fences and cornfields on either side. Both the streets and the lanes were paved with the same material—tough black mud in wet times, deep dust in dry.
> Most of the houses were of logs—all of them, indeed, except three or four; these latter were frame ones. There were none of brick, and none of stone. There was a log church, with a puncheon floor and slab benches.
> . . .

Stone's Landing

From The Gilded Age, *First Edition*

Such was the village in which Sam Clemens was born and which he left when he was four years old. His memory of it, therefore, is of its period of decline, when he returned for summer vacations on the Quarles farm as a lad of ten or twelve.[58] Florida figures more prominently in the novel, however, as Hawkeye, the village thirty miles distant to which the Hawkinses follow Colonel Sellers a few years later—"a pretty large town for interior Missouri" (I, 83).

The historical Florida, which had been laid out early in 1831 on a ridge between the north and south forks of the Salt River,[59] boasted, within a few weeks, of two good grist mills, a saw mill, and "enough water power to put in operation an immense quantity of machinery." By 1837 it had, in addition, four or five whiskey and brandy distilleries, a pottery, and "an extensive hemp manufactory." Safely within the official frontier line of the United States, about thirty miles from Hannibal, Palmyra, and New London, with "no probability of any Village being established between," Florida was considered an ideal location for a large commercial metropolis.[60]

The future growth of Florida depended, however, upon the Salt River's being made a navigable outlet to the Mississippi and the outside world. At the time of the township's official founding, settlers from forty miles around were already bringing corn to be ground in its mills and produce to be shipped to St. Louis, and one of the mill owners was running boatloads of flour to Louisiana, Missouri, where the Salt flows into the Mississippi. Though Salt River was navigable for keels, batteaux, and flatboats several months of the year, it often became a thin rivulet in the summer. Plans were immediately made for opening the river from Florida to the junction of the forks half a mile away and for establishing the town as the county seat of Monroe County.[61]

In January, 1837, the Missouri legislature passed an "act to incorporate the Salt River Navigation Company," capital stock was issued, and a list of sixteen commissioners was drawn from three counties, at the head of which was John M. Clemens. It was hoped to raise funds sufficient to construct a series of dams and locks that would make Salt River navigable by steamboat the entire eighty-five miles from its junction with the Mississippi to the docks of

Florida. Congress was petitioned for an appropriation. Florida, in a frenzy of excitement, established a shipyard and began boat building. John Clemens, in addition to heading the navigation company, threw himself into the fight to secure the county seat.[62]

It is this actual attempt at creating an internal improvement, in which John Clemens was so actively involved and to which his son must have heard references as a boy, that Mark Twain used as the basis of his Columbus River Slackwater Navigation Company. The Goose Run of the novel, which Colonel Sellers intends to rename Columbus River, "sweeps round the town—forty-nine miles to the Missouri" (I, 229) and if enlarged and deepened will carry steamboat traffic. Like its prototype, it depends for its improvement upon a Congressional appropriation. As in the case of its prototype also, the appropriation never materializes, and Stone's Landing, the visionary site of the metropolis of Napoleon, sinks back into bucolic oblivion: ". . . the wary tadpole returned from exile, the bullfrog resumed his ancient song, the tranquil turtle sunned his back upon bank and log and drowsed his grateful life away as in the old sweet days of yore" (I, 315). The still unreclaimed Salt River has, as Wecter states, "long past changed to muddy slate and . . . built alluvial flats and sand bars to its own frustration."[63]

The Salt River itself appears to figure as Goose Run. Whereas Stone's Landing is probably a purely fictional representative of incipient frontier boom towns, the topography of Goose Run is visualized fairly clearly in Mark Twain's mind: "They turned their first attention to straightening the river just above the Landing, where it made a deep bend, and where the maps and plans showed that the process of straightening would not only shorten distance but increase the 'fall' " (I, 276). This description tallies with the actual contour of the Salt River. It is evident, besides, that Clemens remembered the geography of the area well, for as late as 1861, during his unenthusiastic and aborted enlistment in the Confederate forces, he skirmished through the neighborhood and encamped briefly on Salt River "in a hollow near the village of Florida."[64]

In *The Gilded Age* the project for reclamation of Goose Run is undertaken at the same time as advance surveying of the Salt

Lick Pacific Extension is going on.[65] It is hoped that the railroad company may be induced to construct its line passing through Napoleon (Stone's Landing) so that a rail-water junction will be effected. Such a scheme is entirely typical of the frontier development in midcentury, for transportation by any and all means was the key to the profitable exploitation of interior land resources. Though the plan is typical, it even more significantly epitomizes the transition from waterway to rail transportation that occurred in the United States during the middle years of the nineteenth century and completely bridges a historical period of some fifteen or twenty years from the pre-Civil War to the post-Civil War frontier. That it does so is important to the theme of all-pervading speculativeness, for many a frontier boom town became a ghost town as a result of the changeover in the means of transportation and of the shifting of routes of competing railway branches. In the novel, Stone's Landing succumbs to defeat not only from loss of the lifeblood of a Congressional appropriation but even more from being bypassed by the railroad in favor of neighboring Hawkeye.

. . . before Colonel Sellers knew what he was about, Hawkeye, in a panic, had rushed to the front and subscribed such a sum that Napoleon's attractions suddenly sank into insignificance, and the railroad concluded to follow a comparatively straight course instead of going miles out of its way to build up a metropolis in the muddy desert of Stone's Landing.

. . . Hawkeye rose from her fright triumphant and rejoicing, and down went Stone's Landing! One by one, its meager parcel of inhabitants packed up and moved away, as the summer waned and fall approached. Town lots were no longer salable, traffic ceased, a deadly lethargy fell upon the place once more, . . . (I, 314-15)

Even as the Columbus River Slackwater Navigation Company was based on John Clemens' Salt River Navigation Company, the Salt Lick Pacific Extension found a counterpart, at least spiritually, in the Florida and Paris Railroad Company, headed once again by John Clemens.[66] The Florida and Paris never was built, and Florida lost the bid for county seat to Paris. Once again John Clemens had guessed wrong. There is no direct evidence that Sam Clemens recollected his father's involvement in this railroad project, but as he did recall the Salt River Navigation business,[67] it is reasonable to assume that he had at some time heard of the railroad venture also.

Colonel Sellers' description of the proposed route of the Salt Lick Extension bears a remarkable resemblance, also, to the configuration of the Salt River channel from beyond New London in adjoining Ralls County to Florida. According to the Colonel's map,[68] the railroad is to go all over the river (Goose Run) "and all through it—wades right along on stilts." "Seventeen bridges in three miles and a half—forty-nine bridges from Hark-from-the-Tomb to Stone's Landing altogether—forty-nine bridges, and culverts enough to culvert creation itself! . . . perfect trestle-work of bridges for seventy-two miles" (I, 299). The fact that Salt River twists and turns back on itself in an exaggerated snake dance, so that a straight line must cross it many times, provides convincing corroboration that throughout this part of the novel Clemens was writing about the river so familiar to his boyhood summers.

Though the Salt Lick Extension is a fictional composite of several small branches of the Union Pacific system, not least of which was Samuel C. Pomeroy's "Atchison Pacific,"[69] a likely inspiration was the Hannibal and St. Joseph Railroad, the Kansas rights of which Pomeroy's company secured in 1864.[70] This road was another venture sponsored by John Marshall Clemens. In the fall of 1839, John Clemens, having finally despaired of his earlier hopes for Florida's future, moved his family to the up-and-coming Mississippi River town of Hannibal, which had good prospects of becoming the commercial pivot of northeast Missouri.[71] In 1846 he met in his office with a group of local businessmen to organize a company to build a railroad from Hannibal on the Mississippi to St. Joseph on the Missouri River. The next year, the Missouri legislature chartered the Hannibal & St. Jo.[72] Sam Clemens was then eleven.

In May, 1853, when Sam was seventeen, working on his brother Orion's *Hannibal Journal*, he wrote "Our Assistant's Column" in three issues. In the column for May 23 appeared the doggerel poem "The Burial of Sir Abner Gilstrap," a parody of "The Burial of Sir John Moore," Sam's "first literary venture." The satirical verses were directed at one Abner Gilstrap, editor of the Bloomington *Republican,* who had become heatedly and polemically involved in Bloomington's struggle to secure the Hannibal and St. Jo through its boundaries, a struggle which was lost. As county seat of Macon County, Bloomington was of sufficient importance to make a strong bid, and much political maneuvering had gone on.

. . . Abner Gilstrap, who was something of a fire-eater, had charged certain Hannibal business men, responsible, as he thought, for the success of Hannibal and the slight to Bloomington, with having bribed the railway authorities, by holding out to them a vision of immense profits to be realized from the sale of new town lots. Abner Gilstrap was a candidate for the legislature, and his political opponents made the most of his quarrels. . . .[73]

Though Clemens disclaimed any knowledge of his father's part in railroad promotion,[74] his remembrance of this first plunge into journalism was sufficiently vivid,[75] and it is possible that as a boy he had unconsciously absorbed some knowledge of the Hannibal & St. Jo from family talk. In any event, six years before the writing of *The Gilded Age* Mark Twain wrote some recollections of Hannibal for the *Alta California,* in which he commented on the Hannibal & St. Jo and its effect on his home town.

They got into a perfect frenzy and talked of a railroad—an actual railroad—a railroad 200 miles long—a railroad from Hannibal to St. Joseph! And behold, in the fullness of time—in ten or fifteen years—they built it.

A sure enough prosperity burst upon the community, now. Property went up. It was noted as a significant fact that instead of selling town-lots by the acre people began to sell them by the front foot. Hannibal grew fast—doubled its population in two years, started a daily paper or two, and came to be called a city— . . .

. . . .

Well, Hannibal's prosperity seemed to be of a permanent nature, but St. Louis built the North Missouri Railroad and hurt her, and Quincy tapped the Hannibal and St. Joe [*sic*] in one or two places, which hurt her still worse, and then the war came, and the closing years of it almost finished her.

. . . A railroad is like a lie—you have to keep building to it to make it stand. A railroad is a ravenous destroyer of towns, unless those towns are put at the end of it and a sea beyond, so that you can't go further and find another terminus. . . .[76]

The outstanding example of Clemens' use of real persons of his acquaintance as characters in fiction is his transference of his mother's cousin James Lampton onto the pages of *The Gilded Age* as Colonel Sellers. Equally as memorable as Aunt Polly, based on Jane Lampton Clemens herself,[77] Colonel Sellers not only is based on her cousin James but is a vividly accurate, detailed portrait of him. In the *Autobiography* Mark Twain states quite frankly that James Lampton "figures in the *Gilded Age* as Colonel Sellers." "I merely put him on paper as he was; he was not a person who could be exaggerated."[78] So apparently effortless, indeed, was Clemens' bodily lifting of his relative from reality to fiction that he told Howells "any scrub of a newspaper reporter could have done the same thing."[79] Yet no scrub of a reporter, unless he were a genius, could have made out of his copy one of the great characters of American fiction, one sometimes called the American Micawber.[80]

Despite the fact that Clemens always insisted that Colonel Sellers was not his "creation" but merely a carbon copy of James Lampton,[81] critics and biographers have persisted in their attempts to find other originals for this character. Much of the speculation has had to do with possible literary influences; yet there is one pretender to the Sellers throne who has found several advocates, including the careful Twain scholar Minnie Brashear. This alleged original is Colonel William Muldrow, projector of Marion City in Marion County, Missouri. Muldrow was "a promoter of the first magnitude," who was entrusted with large sums of money "to invest in wild lands all over the county by speculators who were convinced that the wonderful pictures that had been painted . . . spelled unbounded profits."[82] The Marion City project included, in addition to urban development, plans for a railroad running east to Philadelphia and west to the Pacific Coast and for an academy, Marion College. The entire enterprise, however, collapsed in the economic depression of 1837-40, the destructive effects of which induced John Marshall Clemens to abandon Florida in favor of Hannibal.[83]

Marion City was the principal inspiration for Dickens' "Eden," in the American chapters of *Martin Chuzzlewit*, that devastating satire of frontier land exploitation and fraud. There is a slim possibility, of course, that Clemens may have had the British writer's earlier novel in mind when he was writing the Stone's Landing passages of *The Gilded Age,* though there is no direct evidence that he had read *Martin Chuzzlewit* by 1873.[84] A more likely hypothesis is that Clemens drew independently upon Marion City as a source. That he knew of Muldrow's project and had personally viewed Marion City as early as 1846 is clear from his two-paragraph mention of the town in Chapter LVII of *Life on the Mississippi,* a passage which hints that the downfall of Muldrow's town was connected with the rise to prosperity of the neighboring town of Quincy, much in the *Gilded Age* pattern.[85] A more significant reference is found in his letter to the *Alta California* dated April 19, 1867: "Marion City used to be an important shipping point. The railroads killed it."[86]

In view of the overwhelming evidence that the town of Florida and John Marshall Clemens' own Salt River Navigation Company and Florida and Paris Railroad were the prime sources of Mark Twain's chapters, it is vain to look elsewhere for his inspiration except for the very limited purpose of finding reinforcing impressions. To claim, moreover, that William Muldrow was the original for Colonel Sellers, as has been done in one Twain biography, is entirely unwarranted.[87] Even Minnie Brashear, ardent Missourian though she is, admits that no real case can be made for this identification.[88] That Colonel Sellers is so true to type that he has given rise to many local claims of proprietorship is only a tribute to Clemens' genius for capturing and embodying the spirit of the historical period. That he is closely modeled on Clemens' cousin James Lampton, as will be seen, proves merely that this family relation was himself an ideal prototype of his times.

Toward the end of 1872, Clemens wrote his sister, Pamela, "I wish you would get all the gossip you can out of Mollie about Cousin James Lampton & Family, *without her knowing it is I that want it.*" ("Mollie," as she was called, was Mary Eleanor [Stotts] Clemens, Orion's wife.)

I want every little trifling detail, about how they look & dress, & what they say, & how the house is furnished—& the various ages & characters of the tribe. Mollie does up gossip mighty well. I have preserved the other letter she wrote you about that gang. I wish to write the whole thing up— but not publish it for a great many years. That is, if the story I write from it could be recognized by him or the family.[89]

This request, which occurs as a postscript, has significance in two ways. First, it not only corroborates Paine's statement that Clemens had a story about James Lampton in mind at the time he undertook the collaboration,[90] but it reveals the degree of accuracy Clemens wished to achieve in his fictional portrait. Second, it underlines his desire to run no risk of hurting or embarrassing Cousin Jim,[91] a consideration that, along with his known sensitivity to the feelings of others and reticence in alluding openly to persons of his own acquaintance, testifies to the genuine regard in which he held his eccentric relative. This point is important in evaluating the underlying pathos of the comic Colonel and in understanding the ingredients Clemens blended into his characterization.

James Lampton, Jane Lampton Clemens' favorite cousin, "the courtliest, gentlest, most prodigal optimist of all that guileless race," had married first at eighteen and lost his wife within a year and their only child shortly afterward. He then married Ella Hunter, "who seems to have been a strong-minded woman," and by her had four daughters and a son. The eldest daughter, Jennie, the beauty of the family, became psychotic and imagined that she was Judas Iscariot. James Lampton himself had wanted to be a doctor but had had to give up medical studies because he could not stand the sight of blood. In spite of the frustration and half-tragedy of this life—or perhaps because of it—he "floated, all his days, in a tinted mist of magnificent dreams," a "happy light in his eye, . . . abounding hope in his heart," possessing a persuasive tongue and a "miracle-breeding imagination."[92]

James Lampton's two most noticeable characteristics were his expansive speculativeness—his favorite expression was "there's millions in it"—and his fondness for alluding to his descent from nobility: "The bare mention of the Tennessee land sent him off into figures that ended with the purchase of estates in England adjoining those of the Durham Lamptons, whom he always referred to as 'our kindred,' casually mentioning the whereabouts and health of the 'present earl.' "[93] The first of these characteristics Mark Twain emphasized in the Sellers of *The Gilded Age,* the second in the almost grotesquely exaggerated revival of Sellers in *The American Claimant.* Lampton's speculativeness, so hyperbolically expressive of frontier psychology, especially that of the young men who were seeking a fortune in the hills of Nevada and California, had already impressed Clemens in his own Nevada days. In 1861 he wrote Pamela from Carson City,

> you *must* persuade Uncle [*sic*] Jim to come out here . . . . I have written to him twice to come. I wrote him today. . . .
> This is just the country for Cousin Jim to live in. I don't believe it would take him six months to make $100,000 here, if he had 3,000 dollars to commence with. . . .[94]

Possibly the best testimony as to the accuracy of the portrait is to be found in the famous visit of James Lampton to Clemens' hotel room when the latter was in St. Louis on his reading tour with George W. Cable in 1884. Though it had been many years since Clemens had seen his Cousin Jim, the moment Lampton entered, his immortalizer said to himself, "I did not overdraw him by a shade, I set him down as he was; . . . Cable will recognize him."[95] According to the Mark Twain account, when Lampton departed, Cable, who had been in the next room with the door ajar, put his head in and said, "That was Colonel Sellers." Cable's own version of the incident, hastily jotted down in pencil on the hotel stationery, reveals that he had actually come in and been introduced to Lampton.[96] The discrepancy is unimportant, however, for the two accounts jibe perfectly in their depiction of Sellers' original. In the Twain account, Lampton tells of a "small venture" he has begun in New Mexico through his son.

> . . . "only a little thing—a mere trifle—partly to amuse my leisure, partly to keep my capital from lying idle, but mainly to develop the boy—develop the boy. Fortune's wheel is ever revolving; he may have to work for his living some day—as strange things have happened in this world. But it's only a little thing—a mere trifle, as I said."

In Cable's notes Lampton is quoted as saying,

Well, Mr. Cable I want you to come down with Cousin Sa-a-am &
see my daughters. They're school-ma'ams, you know, self-sustaining institutions—women air, you know, ah, ha, ha, ha! And if you'll come down
to our very plain little place—you're a southern man & used to rusticity
—I'll take you down to the edge of my pond surrounded by willows &—
gold fish in it that long, Cousin Sam. And I've got—you know—I've got
a brewery! Pipes leading to the house. Just turn on the fasset. . . .

The context is different but the accent and underlying personality are unmistakable. Twain, as is to be expected, emphasizes
the speculative. Cable records Lampton's reactions at their introduction to one another. Yet in both versions there is the same
Lamptonian blend of false modesty and irrepressible boastfulness.
In the Twain version some of Lampton's remarks are virtually in-
distinguishable from those of Colonel Sellers: "I suppose there's a
couple of millions in it, possibly three, but not more, I think."
Just as the Colonel finds he is without his pocketbook when he is
about to pay for the drinks to which he has treated Philip Sterling
and Harry Brierly,[97] so Lampton finds he has forgotten his when
he starts to buy tickets to the Twain-Cable performance; and even
as Philip comes to the rescue in the novel and pays for his own
treat, Clemens gives his cousin complimentary seats for the evening's entertainment.[98] As author both of the Colonel Sellers episodes and of the descriptions of James Lampton in the *Autobiography,* Clemens is vulnerable, to be sure, to the charge of confusing
fact and fiction in the retrospect of fourteen years—the *Autobiography* passage concerning the 1884 Cable episode was written
in 1897-98—hence of recollecting Lampton through Sellers-colored
glasses. As pointed out earlier,[99] the threshold between the actual
and the vividly imagined was easily overstepped by Clemens. Still,
the testimony of other relatives and of Clemens' own pre-*Gilded
Age* references to his Cousin Jim leaves no doubt about the essential accuracy of the Sellers portrait regardless of the heightened
coloration of artistic license.

The last point is well illustrated by the turnip-dinner episode.
In this episode, the poverty-stricken Sellers entertains Washington Hawkins at a dinner consisting entirely of raw turnips and
water, which the host to cover his embarrassment offers as the

rarest, most exotic, and most health-bestowing delicacy.[100] In the phenomenally successful dramatization of *The Gilded Age,* the five-act play *Colonel Sellers,* in which the comedian John T. Raymond made his fame in the leading role,[101] the turnip-dinner scene was a high point, which invariably brought down the house. As Mark Twain tells it,

John T. Raymond's audiences used to come near to dying with laughter over the turnip-eating scene; but, extravagant as the scene was, it was faithful to the facts, in all its absurd details. The thing happened in Lampton's own house, and I was present. In fact, I was myself the guest who ate the turnips. . . .[102]

On the only extant page of manuscript for this episode in *The Gilded Age,* Clemens had originally written "dried apples" then struck it out and substituted "turnips."[103] It can probably never be determined whether the change represented the author's correction of an initially faulty remembrance or whether raw turnips seemed an inherently more ludicrous food for his purpose.[104] The important element in the scene is the spirit of Colonel Sellers—the desire to gloss over his dire poverty and turn misfortune into a positive virtue, a characteristic both of the Colonel and of his original, James Lampton.

Clemens' criticism of Raymond's acting of the turnip-eating scene leads him directly into a statement of his own conception of Colonel Sellers:

In the hands of a great actor that piteous scene would have dimmed any manly spectator's eyes with tears, and racked his ribs apart with laughter at the same time. But Raymond was great in humorous portrayal only. . . . The real Colonel Sellers, as I knew him in James Lampton, was a pathetic and beautiful spirit, a manly man, a straight and honorable man, a man with a big, foolish, unselfish heart in his bosom, a man born to be loved; and he was loved by all his friends, and by his family worshiped. It is the right word. To them he was but little less than a god. . . .[105]

Some moving anecdotes about this man, who was "as brave as a lion and as upright and stern as a covenanter," are recounted by

Clemens' bosom friend and distant relative, Henry Watterson,[106] anecdotes which serve to bear out Clemens' own feeling for Cousin Jim.[107]

The original Sellers . . . [was] a second and perfect Don Quixote in appearance and not unlike the knight of La Mancha in character. It would have been safe for nobody to laugh at him—nay, by the slightest intimation, look, or gesture, to treat him with inconsideration, or any proposal of his—however preposterous—with levity. . . .

As Clemens once told a fellow correspondent, "He had some funny traits about him, but these never counted with me. It was the pathos in his life that got me."[108]

It is vain to search through *The Gilded Age* for explicit statements of Colonel Sellers' pathos or for its deliberate underlining in individual episodes. The closest Mark Twain ever comes to such overtness is a comment upon the Colonel's dividing his remaining bank account among the unpaid railroad construction workers at Stone's Landing; he describes it as "an act which had nothing surprising about it because he was generally ready to divide whatever he had with anybody that wanted it, and it was owing to this very trait that his family spent their days in poverty and at times were pinched with famine" (I, 280). Nor is it undeniable that Sellers is first and foremost a comic character. It is as a comic character that readers of the novel have unquestioningly accepted him. It is as a comic character that John T. Raymond enacted him on the stage and that Raymond's audiences greeted him with roars of laughter. Yet the pathos is there—in Sellers' irresponsibly childlike generosity, in his not very convincing attempts to cover up his chronic poverty, in his obstinate resilience under misfortune, in his unbounded, almost desperate optimism and his ability to live gloriously in a future that never appears.

It is a tribute to Twain's artistic understatement that the pathos of Colonel Sellers remains implicit in the circumstances of his existence and maintains only a soft diapason against which his scherzo is played. That the pathos often escapes the reader is not because it is absent but because the rollicking comic burlesque, which Twain still had not learned to control, throws it far into the background. It escaped Raymond, much to Clemens' chagrin. Henry Watterson once showed Raymond a sincere, hospitable, and pitiably bombastic invitation from James Lampton to his daughter's wedding. "He read it through with care and re-read it. 'Do you know,' said he, 'it makes me want to cry. That is not the man I am trying to impersonate at all.' "[109]

Though the original of Colonel Sellers was indubitably James Lampton, the visionary, optimistic impracticality of his nature was apparently a transmitted trait of the Clemenses as well. "Prone by temperament to the visionary and unsophisticated," as Wecter states, the Clemens clan "found itself disadvantaged in the Western country, whether vis-à-vis the more affluent Southern stock or the aggressive Yankee, and thus was foredoomed to the disappointment of its great expectations." In Virginia, Samuel Clemens' ancestors "had contrived to miss the Tidewater and the Shenandoah Valley, to light upon the Blue Ridge uplands of Bedford County, and beyond the Alleghenies to choose the less fertile tracts of western Virginia and Kentucky."[110] The fictional embodiment of John Marshall Clemens, to be sure, is Squire Hawkins, yet the Sellers optimism has the persistent quality of John Clemens' re-iterated cry "Cling to the land!" and the Colonel's fascination with potentially fortune-making inventions is closely akin to John Clemens' absorption in his perpetual-motion machine.[111]

Again, though Orion Clemens, Sam's brother, was avowedly Washington Hawkins in the novel,[112] his propensity for visionary inventiveness was a Sellers-like inheritance from his father. He was, at the very time *The Gilded Age* was being written, pursuing the age-old Icarian dream of a flying machine that would cross the Atlantic or, failing this, at least a paddle wheel that would enable a steamboat to cross it in twenty-four hours.[113] In the novel Washington Hawkins' own inventiveness is dropped once the Colonel makes his appearance—it would not do to allow Washington to develop except as a foil for Sellers—yet his devotion to Sellers shows the vicarious fulfilment he finds in the older man's stronger imagination and confident experimentation. It is to be noted, however, that Washington's youthful inventions (which include a method of making window-glass opaque and another for coloring hen's eggs through the hen's diet)[114] are as impracticable as Orion's were and almost as fantastic as those of the later Mulberry Sellers in *The American Claimant*.

Finally, in a very profound sense, Colonel Sellers is Samuel Clemens himself. As Albert Bigelow Paine has said, Colonel Sellers "is a character that only Mark Twain could create, for . . . it embodies—and in no very exaggerated degree—characteristics that were his own."[115] His close friend Howells wrote that "Clemens satisfied the Colonel Sellers nature in himself (from which he drew the picture of that wild and lovable figure), . . ."[116] And since Howells' time, critic after critic has recognized this autobiographical element.[117] Even Clemens himself admitted it.[118]

For one thing, like Colonel Sellers Clemens was an inventor of sorts and delighted in concocting contrivances that would save time, effort, and exasperation. Sellers' inventions, it is true, are typically ludicrous, like his Universal Expectorant, yet they are always strongly motivated by the expectation of large profits resulting from their indispensability—the Infallible Imperial Oriental Optic Liniment and Salvation for Sore Eyes will sell millions of bottles among the ophthalmia-ridden populations of Asia (I, 97-100). Clemens' inventions were of the "better mousetrap" variety, simple devices for making life easier: a vest that enabled the wearer to dispense with suspenders, a shirt that required no buttons or studs, a notebook that always opened at the page last written, a scrapbook that required no paste.[119] All of these, it is to be noted, were remedies for his intense personal annoyances.[120] Yet all of them were, if successful, potential money-makers, and Mark Twain's Scrap Book was a considerable financial success.[121]

Like Colonel Sellers also, Clemens was a keen speculator, with equally grandiose expectations and with equally mistaken judgment. As Henry Watterson said, "his mind" like that of Sellers "soared when it sailed financial currents."[122] Henry Seidel Canby, who considers Clemens both the father and the child of Colonel Sellers, has put his finger on the principal difference between them: "Sellers lived in a dream of rivers, cities, railroads, and millions in each. Mark, like a half-analyzed patient of a psychiatrist, had reduced his dreams of money to possible realization in present reality."[123] As Samuel Webster says, "When it came to figuring profits Uncle Sam could make his cousin James Lampton look like a pessimist."[124]

Indeed, Clemens from his youth on was frequently guilty of talking in millions.[125] As a boy he carried a purse which Paine later conjectured had been a symbol of Sellers optimism.[126] When in 1856 he started out on the journey that converted him into a river pilot, his intended destination was the headwaters of the Amazon, where he hoped to make a fortune collecting coca.[127] When he arrived in Nevada in 1861 he already had the "get-rich-quick" fever, and there he had his "organ of hope preposterously developed."[128] On May 11, 1862, he wrote Orion from Esmeralda that he owned an eighth of the "Monitor Ledge, Clemens Company" and asserted, "I *know* it to contain our fortune."[129]

These two traits, inventiveness and speculativeness, intermingled in Clemens' nature to an even greater degree than they do in Colonel Sellers'. Where the Colonel limits his interest in inventions primarily to his own and directs his speculativeness into the traditional channels of land promotion and frontier development, Clemens was continually risking his money on other people's inventions. If he himself lacked the genius to invent revolutionizing devices or processes, he felt that he at least could recognize the immense potential in another person's ideas and by acting as angel promote that person's fortune and his own. As has been seen, he began his speculative investments long before the writing of *The Gilded Age* and he continued them, through failure after failure, nearly to the end of his life. His daughter Clara wrote: "Sometimes I think Father's propensity for investing in all sorts of business propositions was not dictated entirely by the desire to make more money, but largely because it was difficult to refuse aid to any man so enthusiastic as the inventor of a new device. . . ."[130]

To relate the details and circumstances of Clemens' numerous investments is far beyond the scope and purposes of this volume. Suffice it to say that among the principal ones were a considerable expenditure on a steam generator that would not generate, thirty-two thousand dollars on a steam pulley that would not pull, twenty-five thousand on a marine telegraph that never carried a message, and fifty thousand on a chalk-plate engraving process that was vanquished by its successful rival, photoengraving. Ironically enough, when Alexander Graham Bell offered him what would have been almost priceless shares in the telephone, he declined because he had barely recovered from a risky insurance company scheme. "I was the burnt child and I resisted all these temptations, resisted them easily, went off with my check intact, and next day lent five thousand of it on an unendorsed note to my friend who was going to go bankrupt three days later."[131] Surely his father's and brother's miscalculations about the Tennessee Land were no more obstinately perverse!

Most disastrous of all was the venture with the Paige typesetting machine. Having been a typesetter in his youth, Clemens was eager to see mechanized the tedious hand process of loading a composing stick. But with a fateful contrariness he poured a small fortune into a delicate machine, which its perfectionist inventor could never keep working for long, and by the time the Mergenthaler linotype had proved its supremacy Clemens' funds were so low that it only needed the bankruptcy of his own publishing firm to send him on a round-the-world lecture tour to pay off his accumulated debts.[132] During the prolonged period of experimentation with the machine Clemens kept sending cables to Livy, who was in London—"Look out for good news," "Nearing success," etc. "They make me laugh," Livy wrote her sister, "for they are so like my beloved 'Colonel.' "[133]

Though the character Colonel Sellers is thus intimately associated with Clemens' family and with his own personality, the name was contributed by Charles Dudley Warner.[134] There are a number of inaccuracies in the *Autobiography* and in the Paine *Biography* about Warner's proposal of the name. According to Arthur Hobson Quinn, when Warner was studying law at the University of Pennsylvania in 1856-58 his landlord had a business associate by the name of Escol Sellers, a Philadelphia engineer and a member of a well-established Philadelphia family.[135] The use of the name in the novel may have been suggested by the daughter of an old partner of Sellers' while she was visiting the Warners in Hartford;[136] or it may have occurred to Warner as the result of comment about Sellers by a mutual friend, Dr. J. H. Barton of Lock Haven, Pennsylvania—apparently Warner's old law partner[137]—with whom he was on the most intimate terms.[138] At any rate, Warner, according to Clemens, thought the name "just the right and fitting" one for the Colonel "since it was odd and quaint and all that."[139]

Far from being "a farmer in a cheap and humble way," as Clemens in retrospect apparently believed, George Escol (not Eschol) Sellers was "a man of culture and refinement," who besides being an able mechanical engineer was an inventor, like others of his family, an archeologist and collector of American Indian artifacts, and an art patron and painter (he was the grandson of Charles Willson Peale and nephew of Rembrandt Peale). He came from a wealthy Quaker family, who for generations had possessed a tract of land in Upper Darby, Delaware County, Pennsylvania, under the patent of William Penn, and who were prominent in the machine tool and locomotive industry, his father, Coleman Sellers, being a manufacturer of carding machinery in Upper Darby at a place he named Cardington. George Escol in 1854 had become proprietor of the Saline Coal & Manufacturing Company in the salt spring region of Gallatin County, Illinois, on the lower Ohio, in which Philadelphia capital was invested. This Sellers, like his namesake, was "a man of much and varied information, and like most enthusiasts, a fluent talker." In 1859 he had built an expensive paper mill in adjoining Hardin County, Illinois, overlooking the Ohio, and had established a town about it, which he named Sellers' Landing. The mill, based on an invention of his own for manufacturing brown wrapping paper out of Mississippi river-bottom cane and vegetable fiber, failed; and Sellers' Landing, the name of which may have suggested that of Stone's Landing, decayed even as the latter and sank into oblivion.[140] Apparently, the influence of George Escol Sellers found expression in more than name.

Irritated by newspaper references to him as Colonel Sellers' original, George Escol Sellers wrote to Warner demanding redress. Warner, within a matter of days, reported to Sellers, "We have stopped the press and struck out from the stereotype plates the name of 'Eschol' whenever it appeared," and, finding that Sellers was in Philadelphia, arranged an appointment for him with Bliss in Hartford, to forestall a possible libel suit. The first printing of the novel was suppressed as far as practicable and in all further printings the name *Beriah* Sellers was substituted.[141] In the dramatization of the novel, *Colonel Sellers, Beriah* had to be dropped "to satisfy another member of the race," and *Mulberry* was substituted; Mulberry Sellers remains the name of the Colonel in his revival in *The American Claimant*.[142] As George Escol Sellers had himself acquired the nickname "Mulberry" from the mulberry trees he planted to cultivate silkworms,[143] and as he had been born in or near *Mulberry Court*, Philadelphia,[144] the final form of the name also seems more than coincidental, if not indeed retaliatory![145]

It is regrettable, perhaps, that the name Eschol had to be dropped, for it had clever and subtle satirical overtones. Harold Sellers Colton relates that George Escol Sellers received his middle name because of a dream his father had had on the night George Escol was born. "He saw four men carrying a large bunch of grapes. This dream recalled the brook of Eschol [*sic*] from which Moses' henchmen carried back to Moses a bunch of grapes (Num. XIII:23) 'and they came unto the brook of Eschol [*sic*] and cut down from thence a cluster of grapes.' "[146] The brook (or "valley" [Deut. 1:24] or "wady"[147]) of Es*h*col (not Es*ch*ol) was so named from the incident involving Moses' henchmen (Num. 13:24), *Eshcol* meaning "Cluster of grapes."[148] And the cluster of grapes was brought back to Moses from this wady in Canaan, along with such other "fruit of the land" as pomegranates and figs, as evidence of a land "flowing with milk and honey" (Num. 13:27, Ex. 3:8)—the Missouri of Colonel Sellers, "the loveliest land," that no pen could do justice. No wonder Warner thought the name just the right and fitting one!

As a replacement, however, the name *Beriah* is not lacking in irony. It means "unfortunate,"[149] and an Arabic root of the word has as one of its senses "be munificent."[150] The biblical Beriah was a son of Asher (Num. 26:44), whose territory has been described as "especially fertile and fitted to promote prosperity."[151]

In the second half of *The Gilded Age* Colonel Sellers is set against the background of postbellum Washington, where "a clamorous, competing crowd of flashy men, and sometimes worldly women . . . besieged the Capitol in force, buttonholing the politicians everywhere, plying them with liquor, cigars, and money. . . ."[152] So clearly did Mark Twain visualize his frontier promoter and aspirant to fortune, so typical of the pathetic home-grown emulator of the successful flashy men did he make him, that as late as 1922 the Washington historiographer Shackleton wrote: ". . . you may still see the immortal character, shabby, hopeful, broad-brimmed, string-tied, black-clad, wandering about the lobbies of the minor hotels and the corridors of Congress."[153] This character, drawn from life out of Clemens' early background, becomes here a part of the satire on the national capital, a city also drawn to the life out of Clemens' experience and his intimate knowledge of it.

By the time he set about writing *The Gilded Age* Clemens had visited Washington on at least three separate occasions and had lived there for a period of several weeks during the winter of 1867-68. His close observation of the city is evident throughout the later chapters of the novel. It is interesting to note also that the Washington he describes is physically that of the later sixties, the city as it was when he knew it best and the city which, because of its raw condition just after the war, lent itself best to satire. By 1873 improvements had been made, but in 1868 Washington was about as the war days had found it. Many of Clemens' impressions went back even farther, to his flying visit from Philadelphia in January or February, 1854, when as a lad of nineteen he was setting type for the *Inquirer* and *Public Ledger*.[154] His observations on that occasion he recorded in the pages of Orion's Muscatine *Journal* as part of his correspondence to that paper during his journeyman printer days.[155]

The first thing that impressed Clemens about Washington, as, indeed, it did many people, was its muddy thoroughfares. "When I came out on the street this morning," he wrote in the *Journal* letter, ". . . there being no sidewalk, I sank ankle deep in mud and snow at every step." The very month *The Gilded Age* was

published, Zina Peirce was writing in the *Atlantic*, "Five years ago
the National Capital was a magnificent mud-hole."[156] And in the
novel occurs the following Twainian summation: "If the thaw is
still going on when you come down and go about town, you will
wonder at the short-sightedness of the city fathers, when you come
to inspect the streets, in that they do not dilute the mud a little
more and use them for canals" (I, 266).

When, in *The Gilded Age*, Mark Twain carries Colonel Sellers
and Washington Hawkins to Washington, he uses the occasion to
introduce a sort of entr'acte chapter on "The City of Washington," in which he ridicules the city's principal shortcomings as he
had encountered them—the hacks, the hotels, the weather, the
slums, the violent contrasts afforded by magnificent public build-
ings set in the midst of unkept marshes.[157] In the *Journal* letter he
wrote:

> The public buildings of Washington are all fine specimens of architecture,
> and would add greatly to the embellishment of such a city as New York
> —but here they are sadly out of place looking like so many palaces in
> a Hottentot village. . . . But the [other] buildings, almost invariably, are
> very poor—two and three story brick houses, and strewed about in clus-
> ters; . . . They look as though they might have been emptied out of a
> sack by some Brobdignagian gentleman, and when falling, been scattered
> abroad by the winds. . . .

In the novel, the Treasury building, similarly, is described as "an
edifice that would command respect in any capital" and the "city
at large" as "a wide stretch of cheap little brick houses, with here
and there a noble architectural pile lifting itself out of the midst."

One of the most telling passages in the Washington chapter is
the description of the notoriously unfinished Washington Monument towering out of the mud ("—sacred soil is the customary
term"), which "has the aspect of a factory chimney with the top
broken off."

> The skeleton of a decaying scaffolding lingers about its summit, and tra-
> dition says that the spirit of Washington often comes down and sits [the
> MS originally had "roosts"][158] on those rafters to enjoy this tribute of
> respect which the nation has reared as the symbol of its unappeasable
> gratitude. The Monument is to be finished, some day, . . .[159]

This "memorial Chimney" stands "in a quiet pastoral locality," where with a glass "you can see the cow-sheds about its base, and the contented sheep nibbling pebbles in the desert solitudes that surround it, and the tired pigs dozing in the holy calm of its protecting shadow."[160] This ridicule is apparently prompted by twenty

From The Gilded Age, *First Edition*
Reared by a Grateful Country

years of waiting for the Monument's endlessly delayed completion; for in his 1854 version Clemens had been content with a brief statistical description ending in the comment, "If Congress would appropriate $200,000 to the Monument fund, this sum, with the contributions of the people, would build it in four years." In the manuscript for the passage in the novel, however, appears a final, sarcastic apostrophe, later deleted:

If all our forty millions of free men could gather upon Capitol Hill with their glasses and gaze upon the emblem of their gratitude & its meet surroundings, they would be overcome—they would mingle their grateful tears together & say with one voice, "Oh, princes and peoples of the Earth, behold how we loved our benefactor!"[161]

Similarly, Clemens' ridicule of "the marvelous Historical Paintings," bas-reliefs, and frescoes inside the Capitol, a veritable "delirium tremens of art," as it appears in *The Gilded Age,* is a product
of the later Washington impressions, postdating those of the icono-
clastic *Innocents Abroad.* Wagenknecht, writing seven years before
publication of the *Journal* letter, in which "noble" pictures are
said to "embellish" the Capitol, was therefore mistaken in his quite
natural surmise that Clemens' distaste may have derived from the
earlier visit.[162] As one literary historiographer has observed, the
interior of the Capitol is not taken as seriously in *The Gilded Age*
as in Atherton's *Senator North* or Grant's *Unleavened Bread.*[163]

Léon Lemmonier has said that one senses with Mark Twain's
description of Washington "a mind made up for disparagement, a
naïve and sincere execration of everything men might build."[164]
"Shabby furniture & shabby food—*that* is Wash^n," Clemens wrote
his family in 1868, after changing his residence five times, "—I
mean to keep moving."[165] Indeed, it is quite probable that Clemens'
reactions to the national capital were inextricably interwoven with
his reactions to its inhabitants—or at the least, heavily influenced
by them. The city was raw enough, the Washingtonians even rawer.
"This is a place to get a poor opinion of everybody in," he wrote.[166]
He had seen much rawness in the West, it is true; but that was
the expected rawness of a frontier environment. What he witnessed
in Washington in the winter of 1867-68 was the rawness of pre-
tension, the vulgar display and crude politicking of the "great
barbecue." The Brahminical *Atlantic Monthly,* commenting on the
heterogeneousness of Washington society and deploring its lack of
a unified set of values and tastes, denied that *The Gilded Age* gave
a "true delineation" of this society but at the same time was forced
to admit that "there is something in it which furnishes a basis for
such burlesques."[167] Half a century later, historians showed that
during the Gilded Age the "cash nexus" was the basis of social
relations in the capital and that Twain's burlesques were far more
reliable than the *Atlantic's* apologies.[168]

The cross-currents of Washington society, particularly the bad
taste and false manners of the *nouveaux riches*, Mark Twain illustrates with devastating effect in his sketching of the women. The

men—politicians, lobbyists, promoters—he satirizes in connection
with the Congressional maneuverings.[169] But where the social life
of the capital is concerned he turns to the women, who, as non-
political attachés of their husbands, occupy themselves with the
expected entertaining and conduct of amenities. Whether engaged
in upholding the ancient dignity of the older families or in adapt-
ing frontier manners to resplendently sophisticated surroundings,
the women of *The Gilded Age* provide the perfect medium for
comment.

Using the intelligent woman lobbyist Laura as a foil, Clemens
devotes two entire chapters to burlesquing the social climbers he
had observed at first hand in the winter of 1867-68.[170] The task
was not new to him. Ten years before, he had burlesqued the
fashions at the San Francisco Pioneer Ball.[171] And in 1867 he had
written the *Alta California* that "the old, genuine, travelled,
cultivated, pedigreed aristocracy" of New York found themselves
"supplanted by upstart princes of Shoddy, vulgar and with unknown grandfathers."[172] Never had he struck a richer vein, however, than he did in the Washington salons of the "new people."
Mary Clemmer Ames wrote of the "new woman," "Her bearing
and her honors do not blend. The sun of prosperity may strike
down to a rarer vein, and draw it outward, to tone down this
boastful commonplace; but we must bear the glare, the smell of
varnish, and the crackle of veneering, during the process." And she
added that there is all the difference "in the quality of the put-on,
puckering manner, and the simple dignity of real ladyhood" that
there is between a persimmon and a pomegranate.[173]

Washington society divided itself basically into two contrasting
groups, which have been labeled variously as the "real inhabitants"
and the "barbarians," the "exclusives" and the "mob," or, as Mark
Twain called them, the "Antiques" and the "Parvenus."[174] "The
aristocracy of the Antiques ignored the aristocracy of the Parvenus;
the Parvenus laughed at the Antiques (and secretly envied them)"
(II, 15). The old families, the Antiques—some called them "cave-
dwellers,"[175] "more respectable than loyal,"[176] are represented in
The Gilded Age by the fictitious Mrs. Major-General Fulke-
Fulkerson and daughter, who come to call "in a rather antiquated

vehicle with a faded coat of arms on the panels" and converse with "easy grace and dignity" about the acceptable watering places (II, 17-20). Laura, undoubtedly reflecting Clemens' own reactions, knows them to be people "respected for their stainless characters and esteemed for their social virtues" and thinks it a pity that they have to be "icebergs" when out of their own waters.[177]

The Parvenus are depicted in another group of Laura's callers, the Hon. Mrs. Oliver Higgins, the Hon. Mrs. Patrique Oreillé, Miss Bridget Oreillé, Mrs. Peter Gashly, Miss Gashly, and Miss Emmeline Gashly (II, 20-34). Though these women are revealed as the Parvenus they are by their conversation, they are in part defined as the spouses of certain new members of the Reconstruction Congress. The Hon. Mrs. Oliver Higgins is the wife of "a delegate from a distant Territory," who has kept the principal saloon of his village, been chief of the fire department, and killed several "parties," all of which qualifies him as his constituency's fittest representative. Always regarded as the most elegant gentleman in his Territory, he wears immaculate shirt fronts, a watch chain weighing a pound, and a diamond cluster pin, and parts his hair behind. He may be based on Tom Peaseley, owner of the colorful Sazerac saloon in Virginia City or on the Nevada Indian agent and sometime representative Harry Worthington.[178] The Hon. Mrs. Patrique Oreillé (pronounced Ore*lay*)" and her daughter, Miss Bridget "(pronounced Breezhay)," are the wife and daughter of Patrick O'Riley, who has been shown to be based on the New York ward heeler Thomas Murphy.[179] Mrs. Oreillé's gushing about Parry (Paris) and her pedigreed lap dog named François reminds one of the anecdote in *Innocents* about a certain Gordon who recognized his name only when pronounced Gor-r-*dong* and who called his old friend Herbert Er-bare.[180] Such Gallicized Irish, to use DeVoto's phrase,[181] were not untypical of the Washington scene; the Irish-American politican was much in evidence.[182] The origins of the Gashlys are left at the single comment that petroleum had suddenly transformed them "from modest hard-working country village folk into 'loud' aristocrats."

The conversation of this group of Parvenu callers, a conversation in which Laura has little to say, begins with a competitive

series of allusions to Paris, by means of which the women vie with
one another at appearing cosmopolitan and traveled. It soon de-
generates into a nauseating discussion of health measures (as an

Hon. P. Oreillé and Lady

From The Gilded Age, First Edition

Pat O'Riley and the Ould Woman

excuse for mentioning the fashionable spas) and ends with a ludicrously serious exchange of experiences with sick lap dogs, a sort
of mock epic of canine illnesses. The general tone of the utterances
fluctuates amusingly between affectation and vulgarity, the latter
as unconscious as the former is deliberate. "Laura's scorn" is
"boundless." At the end of the passage occurs the following footnote by "The Authors":

As impossible and exasperating as this conversation may sound to a person who is not an idiot, it is scarcely in any respect an exaggeration of one which one of us actually listened to in an American drawing-room; otherwise we could not venture to put such a chapter into a book which professes to deal with social possibilities. (II, 34)

Mark Twain distinguishes a third social group, the aristocracy of the Middle Ground, composed of the families of public men of both the legislative and executive branches of government, unostentatious, cultured, well educated, beyond reproach. As an honest reporter, he is compelled to recognize their existence—he calls them "really the most powerful, by far." As a satirist, he must realize that his admiring comment upon them strengthens his contrasting burlesque of the others. They are, so to speak, his own people. Little has been written about them as a class, though biography is replete with representative individuals. Perhaps they have been as nearly defined as anywhere outside Mark Twain by the Beards: "It was within this group that the early Puritan characteristics of thrift, sobriety, and self-denial appeared to survive and unfold in the most natural fashion."[183]

Merely defined in the chapter on the "aristocracies," the Middle Ground is illustrated four chapters later in the person of Mrs. Representative Schoonmaker.[184] "A sweet woman, of simple and sincere manners," she entertains with little ostentation in a house to which people like to come because the atmosphere reminds them "of the peace and purity of home." Mrs. Schoonmaker is "as natural and unaffected in Washington society as . . . in her own New York house," and her husband, though "not exactly a leader in the House," is "greatly respected for his fine talents and his honesty." The delineation may be a compliment to Mrs. John G. Schumaker, whose husband was a representative from New York.[185]

As a prelude to narrating Laura's reception of fashionable calls, Mark Twain devotes over two pages to a detailed outline of the " 'society' custom" of calling.

When a lady of any prominence comes to one of our cities and takes up her residence, all the ladies of her grade favor her in turn with an initial call, giving their cards to the servant at the door by way of introduction. . . . If the lady receiving the call desires a further acquaintance, she must return the visit within two weeks; to neglect it beyond that time means "let the matter drop." But if she does return the visit within two weeks, it then becomes the other party's privilege to continue the acquaintance or drop it. . . . (II, 15)

He enumerates the various ways of turning down one corner of the calling card to signify "called in person" or "congratulations" or "condolence." "It is very necessary to get the corners right, else one may unintentionally condole with a friend on a wedding or congratulate her upon a funeral."

That observance of the custom of calling was a source of some little anxiety is attested by various contemporary writings. According to the *Atlantic,* "The rule in Washington is that all strangers pay visits first,—a rule which, like most social rules, is observed with strictness by foreigners, and with considerable laxity by natives" (XL, 658). Twain's fellow journalist Donn Piatt puts it more laconically: "It is the etiquette in Washington, soon as you arrive, to empty your trunk, and hire a hack to drive around and call on people. It is not necessary to know them, or to be known. If you have a paper collar and a pair of kids, the official people are glad to see you. . . ."[186] The niceties of the convention, generally considered *de rigueur,* went back, as a matter of fact, to a set of rules established by Washington, Adams, and Hamilton, which rules were set forth in an 1870 newspaper article, "Official Etiquette. Rules Therefor as Drawn by President Washington—The Existing Code."[187] In connection with the portrayal in *The Gilded Age* it is interesting to note the *Atlantic's* comment that the custom "tends to make society altogether too easy of entrance, and to foist upon it gradually many characters whom, if left to itself, it would not recognize."

As has already been indicated, Clemens gleaned the greatest proportion of the Washington impressions that he incorporated into *The Gilded Age* during his few weeks' stay in the city in the winter of 1867-68. While still on the Quaker City tour of Europe and the Holy Land, he had written to his Nevada friend, Senator Bill Stewart, from Naples, accepting an offer previously made by the latter to become his private secretary when the excursion was over.[188] To quote Paine, "Stewart no doubt thought it would be considerably to his advantage to have the brilliant writer and lecturer attached to his political establishment."[189] Clemens, of course, desired a not too arduous berth, which would allow him the leisure to get his *Alta* letters in shape for publication as a volume. Therefore, after disembarking on November 19, he spent only a day and a half in New York—a stopover that included dinner with "the whole editorial corps" of the *Herald*—and was off to Washington on the twenty-first.[190]

The secretaryship did not last long. As Paine says, "It is impossible to conceive of Mark Twain as anybody's secretary."[191] Twain himself burlesqued the episode in two sketches written shortly afterward, "My Late Senatorial Secretaryship" and "The Facts Concerning the Recent Resignation," which when divested of their obvious exaggerations reveal the author's natural incompatibility with the post.[192] But Clemens had other irons in the fire. Declining "18 invitations to lecture, at $100 each, in various parts of the Union," he spent the hours not required by his secretarial duties in supplying special correspondence to several newspapers and magazines, writing satirical sketches on national affairs and curiosa, trying to get Orion placed in the Patent Office (where, presumably, Orion's inventiveness could thrive!), and working on his book.[193] Though the clerkship for Orion never materialized, Clemens himself was offered several sinecures, including the San Francisco postmastership, a consulship, and the post of United States Minister to China.[194]

Socially, he "found himself all at once in the midst of receptions, dinners, and speech-making; all very exciting, for a time at least."[195] The correspondent "Olivia" (Emily Edson Briggs) gave the following picture of him at the time:

. . . quite a lion, as he deserves to be. Mark is a bachelor, faultless in taste, whose snowy vest is suggestive of endless quarrels with Washington washerwomen; but the heroism of Mark is settled for all time, for such purity and smoothness were never seen before. His lavender gloves might have been stolen from some Turkish harem, so delicate were they in size; but more likely—anything else were more likely than that. . . .[196]

It is no wonder that he could quote reception-room conversations almost verbatim.

As a correspondent Mark Twain wrote for several of the principal journals of the day: the *New-York Tribune* and *Herald*, the *Chicago Tribune* and *Republican*, the San Francisco *Alta California*, the Virginia City *Territorial Enterprise*.[197] In addition, he formed with William Swinton what he claimed to be the first American "syndicate," to supply regular Washington letters to a list of newspapers.[198] William Swinton was the brother of John Swinton, then chief of the *New York Times* editorial staff and later the publisher of *John Swinton's Paper*, the leading labor paper of its time.[199] As a war correspondent for the *Times*, William Swinton was so critical of the Union army's conduct of the war that he was saved from reprisals only by the intervention of Secretary Seward.[200] Later in life, when he was professor of English language and literature at the University of California, he was a leader of the Henry Georgite revolt within the university that came into head-on collision with the administration.[201] What Mark Twain recollected of him in his *Autobiography* was that he was "one of the dearest and loveliest human beings I have ever known . . . refined by nature . . . highly educated . . . pure in heart and speech" and that he "kept a jug" of scotch, "sometimes full, but seldom as full as himself."[202] Yet the critical intellect of this Scottish Presbyterian rebel must have stimulated Clemens' own critical faculty, as indeed that of his earlier Scot friend, Macfarlane, had.

In his journalistic capacity Clemens became one of that group described by Senator Harlan as "people hanging around Washington writing for newspapers, styling themselves correspondents, and occupying seats in that [press] gallery by the courtesy of the Senate."[203] In other words, he became a member of "Newspaper Row." Newspaper Row was both a coterie and a locality, the latter endowing the former with its designation. Along the 500 block of Fourteenth Street were to be found the Washington offices of most of the country's principal newspapers, with George W. Childs' Philadelphia *Public Ledger* at one end and the *New York Times*, under Justin E. Colburn, at the other. Here, in this "veritable rabbit warren of journalism," Clemens may have hobnobbed with such notable colleagues as E. V. Smalley of the *New-York Tribune* and Cincinnati *Commercial*, Finley Anderson of the *New*

York Herald, Ben: Perley Poore of the Boston *Journal,* and George W. Adams of the New York *World.*[204] It was here, too, that

> in the leisurely evenings, the leading statesmen of the day would drop in upon their particular cronies among the correspondents to talk politics, discuss the latest gossip in congressional circles, and to see to it in person that news of interest to their constituents and to themselves was properly placed in the hands of the writers.[205]

In *The Gilded Age* Mark Twain gives his impressions of Newspaper Row as Colonel Sellers comes in contact with it. The Colonel, who has access to the government departments, the offices of senators and representatives, the lobby, even the President himself, is "consequently a great favorite in Newspaper Row," where he is often found "lounging in the offices there, dropping bits of private, official information," which are immediately telegraphed across the nation, "embellished to that degree" that he hardly recognizes them.[206] As Twain says, "They were always talking in the Row, everlastingly gossiping, bantering, and sarcastically praising things, and going on in a style which was a curious commingling of earnest and persiflage" (II, 52).

His firsthand knowledge of the Row and of journalistic behavior at the capital is reflected, indeed, throughout these later chapters, as, for example, in the account of the news coverage of the debate over the University Bill.[207] The chief characteristic of Washington correspondents that emerges from these pages is a zeal to expose the very corruption being satirized in the novel. Obviously, Clemens had great respect for his fellow journalists. The only exception to the novel's friendly treatment of newspapermen is the caricature of James Harlan's corrupt Washington *Chronicle* in Brother Balaam's *Daily Love-Feast.* Regardless of Clemens' known partiality and loyalty to friends and associates whom he might violently oppose if they were strangers, his regard for the Row correspondents was shared by others. In the view of the *Atlantic,* fifty-five of the sixty correspondents customarily resident in Washington during the winter season were "honorable and industrious"; the other "corrupt five," the exceptions only, were "vulgar, unscrupulous, and rich."[208]

From his vantage point, then, in Newspaper Row and in the press galleries of Congress, Clemens confirmed to his lasting satisfaction his earlier impressions of legislators and their behavior. He wrote in retrospect in 1891 that he "was reporter in a legislature two sessions and the same in Congress one session, and thus learned to know personally three sample bodies of the smallest minds and the selfishest souls and the cowardliest hearts that God makes."[209] Though it is undoubtedly true that the winter of 1867-68 contributed most to his store of anathema against congressmen (". . . there is no distinctly native American criminal class except Congress")[210] and made the unforgettable impact recorded in *The Gilded Age*,[211] his skepticism regarding the integrity and probity of the people's elected representatives began as early as his Washington visit of 1854 and was intensified by his visits of 1867 and 1870.

On his 1870 trip, he wrote Livy that he had "spent half the day in the House Gallery" and added: "Drove up to the Senate & staid till now (10:30 P M) . . . Oh, I have gathered material enough for a whole book! This is a perfect gold mine."[212] Yet he had begun panning this congressional gold in 1854 when he wrote:

I passed into the Senate Chamber to see the men who give the people the benefit of their wisdom and learning for a little glory and eight dollars a day. The Senate is now composed of a different material from what it once was. Its glory hath departed. Its halls no longer echo the words of a Clay, or Webster, or Calhoun. They have played their parts and retired from the stage; and though they are still occupied by others, the void is felt. . . .

Or again:

In the House nearly every man seemed to have something weighing on his mind on which the salvation of the Republic depended, and which he appeared very anxious to ease himself of; and so there were generally half a dozen of them on the floor, and "Mr. Chairman! Mr. Chairman!" was echoed from every part of the house. Mr. Benton sits silent and gloomy in the midst of the din, like a lion imprisoned in a cage of monkeys, who, feeling his superiority, disdains to notice their chattering.[213]

What is lacking here, of course, is the descriptive power of the mature observer and writer that vivify *The Gilded Age*:

From Ellis, Sights and Secrets
Congressional "Buncombe"

Below, a few Senators lounged upon the sofas set apart for visitors, and talked with idle Congressmen. A dreary member was speaking; the presiding officer was nodding; here and there little knots of members stood in the aisles, whispering together; all about the House others sat in all the various attitudes that express weariness; some, tilted back, had one or more legs disposed upon their desks; some sharpened pencils indolently; some scribbled aimlessly; some yawned and stretched; a great many lay upon their breasts upon the desks, sound asleep and gently snoring. The flooding gaslight from the fancifully wrought roof poured down upon the tranquil scene. Hardly a sound disturbed the stillness, save the monotonous eloquence of the gentleman who occupied the floor. . . . (II, 153-54)

Long before Clemens encountered national legislators, he had developed a contempt for the corruptness of the state and territorial variety. Starting with "Blabbing Government Secrets" in Orion's Hannibal *Journal* in 1852,[214] the record of his experience with legislatures, whether in Missouri, Louisiana, Nevada, California, or Hawaii, was a disheartening one.[215] The gist of his appraisals was that American and American-influenced legislators as a group were composed almost exclusively of thieves, liars, and idiots. The Washoe Territorial Legislature, the sessions of which he had covered as Carson City correspondent of the *Enterprise*, had been particularly rich in material to be lampooned; and his career as Speaker of the "Third House," with its ludicrous proceedings, is too well known to require comment here.[216]

So too at the national capitol, where they carry the whiskey into committee rooms "in demijohns and carry it out in demagogues."[217] Congressmen were also largely made up of thieves, liars, and idiots. In his admonition to the burglars who broke into his house he said, "They'll send you from here down to Bridgeport jail, and the next thing you know you'll be in the United States Senate."[218] One congressman who "proved himself a good Democrat at the White House, and a good Radical at the Capitol," became so expert in duplicity "that he couldn't tell, himself, when he was lying and when he wasn't."[219] And all Congresses had a kindly feeling for idiots and a compassion for them, "on account of personal experience and heredity."[220] Their vanity also elicited his scorn, and he described in his notebook the "pigmy Congressmen" who opened their mail conspicuously in the breakfast room of the Arlington.[221]

Clemens was not alone in his opinion of congressmen. Henry Adams quotes a cabinet member as saying, "A Congressman is a hog! You must take a stick and hit him on the snout!"[222] Yet no other writer of the period brought to such a state of perfection the art of congressman-baiting. In *The Gilded Age* Washington Hawkins, in a burst of admiration, says to Colonel Sellers, ". . . if the people only knew you as I do, . . . you would be in Congress."

The gladness died out of the Colonel's face, and he laid his hand upon Washington's shoulder and said gravely:
"I have always been a friend of your family, Washington, and I think I have always tried to do right as between man and man, according to my lights. Now I don't think there has ever been anything in my conduct that should make you feel justified in saying a thing like that." (II, 227)

One is reminded of Clemens' telling Kipling that he had a notion to write the sequel to *Tom Sawyer* in two ways. " '. . . In one I would make him rise to great honour and go to Congress, and in the other I should hang him. Then the friends and enemies of the book could take their choice.' "[223]

Something needs to be said here about the elements of *The Gilded Age* that stem directly out of Charles Dudley Warner's personal experience. Although he was content to allow Clemens to hurl in the facts of the events of the day, when it came to drawing upon autobiographical material Warner did not hesitate to do so any more than his partner did. Because he lacked the equivalent of a Cousin Jim or an eccentric older brother and also lacked the talent for strong characterization, his figures remain pallid by comparison, even when they are based on real persons. Similarly, the events of his life did not stimulate him in the way that Clemens' experiences did him; so not only was a leitmotiv such as the Tennessee Land impossible for Warner, but even the trivia of everyday living failed to elicit the lively, imaginative responses that they did in the excitable Clemens. More of Warner's background appears in *The Gilded Age* than might be suspected, however, and much of it dovetails interestingly and productively into the Clemens material.

Born in 1829 on a farm near Plainfield in western Massachusetts, the descendant of "sturdy Puritan yeoman" stock, Charles Warner was acquainted with the world of books from an early age. His father, who was a "man of cultivation," died when Charles was five, and the boy went to Charlemont, on the banks of the

Deerfield River, where he lived with a guardian-relative until he was twelve. His father had owned the largest library in town except the minister's, and when, at twelve, he moved with his mother to Cazenovia, New York, among her relatives, he once again had access to the books for which he had been starving. There in Cazenovia he attended the Oneida Conference Seminary, a preparatory school under the auspices of the Methodist Episcopal church. In 1848 he entered Hamilton College, and he was graduated in 1851. Like his future friend and collaborator he for a time set type in a printing office and assisted in a bookstore.

Never robust, Warner took a course of treatment in a sanatorium at Clifton Springs and then, as an open-air life was recommended, went on a railroad surveying expedition to Missouri in 1853-54, during the course of which his health was restored. After studying law for a season in Binghamton, New York, he went to Philadelphia in 1855 at the behest of an acquaintance, Philip M. Price of that city, and formed a partnership with another young man, a former employee of Price named Barton, in the legal conveyancing of real estate. In 1856 he was married to Susan Lee of New York City. The young couple lived with the Prices while Charles studied law at the University of Pennsylvania, receiving the LL.B. degree in 1858. The Warners then moved to Chicago, where Charles went into a law partnership with another friend. In 1860, when Charles's former classmate Senator J. R. Hawley invited him to become associate editor of the *Evening Press*, the Warners finally settled in Hartford, Connecticut. A year later Hawley entered the army, leaving Warner in charge of the *Press*. This paper was consolidated with the *Courant* in 1867. Charles Dudley Warner's adult career was at last launched.[224]

From this brief outline of Warner's early life a number of general deductions can be made. First of all, Warner's knowledge of railroad surveying was of inestimable value in writing the passages of *The Gilded Age* concerning the laying out of the Salt Lick Extension. (These passages, largely chapters XII, XVI, and XXIII,[225] were Warner's.) Second, his firsthand knowledge of Philadelphia gave authenticity to the setting of the Bolton family episodes. Third, his knowledge of law and court practice probably supplied the technicalities of the courtroom scenes and the depiction of attorneys and bench in Laura Hawkins' trial, filling out the bare essentials of the Laura Fair trial undoubtedly suggested by Clemens. (It must be remembered that the bulk of the trial chapters were written, at least in their final form, by Warner.)[226] Other inferences, though lacking direct evidence, seem clear. For example, the Seminary at Fallkill (a name suggestive of Catskill) may well represent the Oneida Conference Seminary at Cazenovia.[227] Again, the Quaker atmosphere and speech of the Bolton household, even Ruth Bolton's attendance at a Quaker school in Westfield, are nicely explained by a statement in Mrs. Field's biography of Warner that is not to be found in other biographies. According to her, young Warner lived for a time with a Quaker aunt, at the latter's invitation, in the town of De Ruyter in order to go to the De Ruyter school, "of very high repute."[228]

Suggestive as the foregoing parallels are, there are also very specific bits of evidence that Warner drew heavily upon his own history. It is patent that Philip Sterling is Warner himself. It was quite apparent to his old friend Jeff Thompson: "I know you to be Philip."[229] Philip, like Warner, is "a New England boy." His mother, like Mrs. Warner, is "a widow, living on a small income in a remote Massachusetts village" (II, 187). Philip is a Yale graduate—Warner went to Hamilton—and like his creator he has "a very good use of the English language and considerable knowledge of its literature." After he leaves college he takes the advice of friends and reads law, meanwhile scribbling on the side. "In an unfortunate hour," he has two or three papers accepted by first-class magazines (Warner had contributed to the *Knickerbocker* and *Putnam's*)[230] and decides to try for a literary career by way of journalism. Philip therefore reads "diligently in the Astor Library" (I, 137). Warner, prior to his preparation for the bar, "devoted several months to special studies at the Astor Library."[231]

When Philip Sterling sets off for Missouri with his friend Harry Brierly, he continues to re-enact many of his creator's experiences. As has already been pointed out, the Salt Lick Extension, for which the surveying expedition is laying out the route, is based on the Hannibal & St. Jo. Even if Clemens is taken at his word that at the time *The Gilded Age* was in preparation he knew nothing of his father's association with railroad building, not to mention the Hannibal & St. Jo,[232] Warner could have supplied and unquestionably did supply the necessary details concerning that road. For that was the line on which Warner had been surveying engineer in 1854.[233] Philip's friend, the vain, impulsive, unstable Harry Brierly, is apparently based on a friend of Warner's who was also in the surveying party.[234]

It will be remembered that after the work of "improving" Goose Run and renovating Stone's Landing has been in progress for several weeks, during which time no funds have been forthcoming from the New York headquarters of the Columbus River Slackwater Navigation Company, the crews finally mutiny and are quieted only by Colonel Sellers' distributing town lots and dividing his bank balance among them (I, 277-80). The episode has a striking parallel in Warner's experiences on the surveying expedition and may well have been inspired by it. On November 14, 1853, the subcontractors Duff & Learned wrote to the President and Directors of the Hannibal & St. Joseph Rail Road Company as follows:

> We have been repeatedly informed by Col. Stewart, that on our arrival here we would be paid the monies to which we are entitled under our Contract with the Company, as he had obtained the necessary funds at the East from Subscribers to the Capital Stock of the Company.
>
> The Company having failed on several former occasions to provide us with funds according to the terms of our Contract, & having otherwise failed to perform its obligations to us, and also having failed to pay us now according to promise, we are compelled in protection of our rights & interests to notify the Company, through you, that our Contract has been violated on the part of the Company, and that we shall claim our legal & just, present and prospective damages. . . .[235]

This letter and another, to a Messrs. Harding Mills & Co. giving notice of violation of contract for grading and masonry, were served upon the respective parties the next morning by "Chas. D. Warner."[236] Less than a week later, on November 19, Warner gave Duff & Learned a promissory note for fifty thousand dollars, in return for which he was issued one hundred certificates of Hannibal & St. Jo stock. A little short of two months later, on January 10, he returned the stock and redeemed his note for the consideration of one dollar![237] In *The Gilded Age*, Philip declines to give his IOU for a prospective share (I, 199) and the worthless engraved stock is eventually thrown into a bonfire (I, 279). The similarities of fact and fiction surely are more than coincidental.

The character Eli Bolton, Ruth's father and Philip Sterling's future father-in-law, plays a considerable role in Warner's half of the plot as the dupe for various promoters such as Mr. Bigler. Arthur Hobson Quinn stated that Mr. Bolton was based on Philip M. Price, the prominent Philadelphian with whom Warner and his bride lived in 1856-58.[238] Even as Bolton is entangled in his Ilium coal lands in Pennsylvania, lands which finally yield their precious deposits only through Philip's diligent prospecting, Philip M. Price, at the time Warner was living with him, had an investment in George Escol Sellers' Saline Coal Mines in Illinois, a project which unlike its fictional counterpart seems eventually to have failed. Price, for many years Surveyor of Spring Garden in Philadelphia, had an interest in building, railroads, and other improvements that "amounted almost to a passion," and he sometimes pursued them "to his own injury, and at the imminent risk of health and life."[239] He was active in launching the Pennsylvania Railroad and lent his support to the Erie and to tributary roads, even as Eli Bolton is involved in railroad projects by Mr. Bigler, the fictional embodiment of Senator William Bigler.[240]

Philip had an older brother Eli K. Price, who was a specialist in the law of real estate and conveyancing.[241] As it was in legal conveyancing that Warner and his partner Barton had been engaged in 1855 at the behest of Philip Price, it seems obvious that Warner took Mr. Bolton's first name from that of Eli K. Price and that it is more than coincidental that the names Barton and Bolton are so nearly alike. It also seems apparent that Warner, who appropriated Sellers' middle name for the fictional Colonel, also took the first name of his hero from that of Philip M. Price; and it is not too far-fetched to surmise that, in the subtle alchemy of satirical adaptation, *Price* was coined into *Sterling*. The further facts that Philip Price had begun his career as a practicing physician and that his sister Hannah married an H. Barton, M.D., could well account for Ruth Bolton's interest in medicine.[242]

More, perhaps, than in any other part of the novel, Warner and Clemens must have pooled their experiences in the coal-mining episodes. Unfortunately, there is almost no internal evidence. The Ilium chapters are ascribed to Warner with the exception of the last one, Chapter LXII, which is ascribed to Clemens, and Chapter XLIX, ascribed to both. Yet of the ten extant manuscript pages, three of which are ascribed to Clemens, nine are in Warner's hand.[243] Consequently, it is logical to conclude that Clemens not only wrote the bulk of the coal-prospecting material but contributed numerous suggestions and technical details to Warner's pages. Though Clemens' mining experience was of a different type—gold and silver, not coal—there would have been similarities that could be put to use, particularly in the psychology of the prospector. It is interesting to note, for example, that although Clemens' Chapter LXII is written entirely around Philip Sterling, it is concerned with the young man's successful strike and his reactions to it, a type of circumstance with which Clemens was familiar from his Nevada mining days. And whenever he needed information specifically concerning coal prospecting, he had a source ready at hand. He had married into a coal merchant's family; therefore, when in doubt, he consulted the Langdon miners.[244]

Clemens also, in all probability, contributed substantially to the conception of Mr. Bolton. Jervis Langdon, Clemens' father-in-law, was a mine owner and wholesaler of anthracite coal, whose dealings extended as far as Chicago and who "had important branches of his business in a number of cities." Not unlike Eli Bolton, his agents "were usually considerably in debt to him, and he was correspondingly in debt" to the other mine owners in the combine.[245] Interesting to note in relation to Eli Bolton's Illium tract in Pennsylvania is the fact that Jervis Langdon also had "interests in the budding coal-oil fields of Pennsylvania."[246] Furthermore, Clemens, writing to his fiancée in February, 1869, complained that on a visit to Jervis Langdon he could not get much of his company except his coal company. He added:

I hardly like to tell on him—but Livy you ought to have seen what sort

of characters he was associating with. He had his room full of them all
the time. He had two abandoned coal-heavers there from Scranton, & two
or three suspicious looking pirates from other districts, & that dissolute
Mr. Frisbie from Elmira, & a notorious character by the name of Slee,
from Buffalo. . . .[247]

Compare this with the situation in the Bolton household:

> The Bolton house was a sort of hotel for this kind of people. They
> were always coming. Ruth had always known them from childhood, and
> she used to say that her father attracted them as naturally as a sugar
> hogshead does flies. . . .
>
> . . . .
> "I wish," said Ruth to her father, . . . "that you wouldn't bring home
> any more such horrid men. . . ." (I, 167, 170)[248]

Again, even as Mr. Bolton suffers a devastating loss by going
security for Bigler on a contract to pave the city of Mobile (II,
185-86, 202-3), Jervis Langdon "had suffered some severe losses
through a relative, . . . who had paved Memphis, Tennessee, with
the wooden pavement so popular in that day." And in this instance
conclusive evidence of Clemens' influence is provided by the fact
that in Warner's manuscript the "contract for Dobson's Patent
Pavement for the city of Mobile" (II, 185) originally read "contract for Dobson's Wood and Tar Pavement for the city of
Memphis."[249]

The great extent to which Clemens guided the destinies of
The Gilded Age, and put his oar in many times when Warner was
presumably rowing his own boat, has been discussed in an earlier
chapter. It can now be seen as well that even where Warner was
writing out of his personal experience, this experience became interwoven with that of his dominant collaborator.

There remains to be mentioned here but one more allusion by
Clemens to his own experience. It concerns his lecturing.

As has been remarked before, Laura, upon being acquitted
from the charge of murder, is approached by a lecture agent and
induced by him to undertake the platform appearance that proves

to be her swan song. The agent, J. Adolphe Griller, is depicted in graphically repugnant terms:

> He was a small man, slovenly in dress, his tone confidential, his manner wholly void of animation, all his features below the forehead protruding —particularly the apple of his throat—hair without a kink in it, a hand with no grip, a meek, hang-dog countenance. He was a falsehood done in flesh and blood; for while every visible sign about him proclaimed him a poor, witless, useless weakling, the truth was that he had the brains to plan great enterprises and the pluck to carry them through. That was his reputation, and it was a deserved one. (II, 293-94)

On the margin of Clemens' own annotated copy of the novel is his note: "This is the late Mr. Brelsford."[250] Clemens had reason to detest Brelsford (or Brelesford—see below), an agent of the American Lecture Bureau, and vented his animosity in the thumbnail sketch of Griller. It seems that Brelsford had, at the very time *The Gilded Age* was being written, tried to make a deal with Clemens' regular Philadelphia agent, T. B. Pugh, to split gross receipts if he could manage to book Clemens for a lecture in the city. Pugh declined the "preposterous proposition" and wrote Clemens:

> . . . I am very certain that you would not think of coming to Phila this season, after declining to come to me. I have intimated to Brelesford [*sic*] that Phila is one of your "Pet places" as you once informed me, and that I did not think that you would consent to come as "a show"—
>
> . . . .
> I wish you would write to him and settle him on this subject.[251]

One can only imagine Sam Clemens' wrath upon reading this![252]

With the exception of certain bits of reportage and prose opinion, Mark Twain's writings up until the *Prince and the Pauper* were largely drawn from personal or family experience. On this fact rests the charm of *Innocents* and *Roughing It*. On it rests the magic of *Tom Sawyer*. And despite such later departures from the personal as *Connecticut Yankee*, *Joan of Arc*, and *Pudd'nhead Wilson*, he returned to his past over and over, notably in *Life on the Mississippi* and *Huck Finn*. What has not been sufficiently realized, because left unexplored, is the fact that *The Gilded Age,* a satire on contemporary public events and a collaboration at that, was highly autobiographical in the sense of being personally and subjectively associative. It was this reliance on personal background in turning for the first time to extended fiction that set for Clemens a precedent leading directly into the richly autobiographical and sensitive novels *Tom Sawyer* and *Huck Finn.*

CHAPTER VIII

The Historical *Gestalt*

"WITH ALL its ingenuities and cleverness, the book can hardly be called a literary success." So wrote Mrs. Fields about *The Gilded Age* thirty years after its publication.[1] It is an opinion that has been echoed one way or another by the majority of literary critics and conceded, often tacitly, by the literary historians. This is not to say that the book was not a marketable commodity. As has already been pointed out, it was an immediate best seller; and, though overshadowed in ultimate sales by such perennial favorites as *Huck Finn, Tom Sawyer,* and *Innocents Abroad*, it retained its popularity until almost the turn of the century.[2] In fact, in view of the highly topical nature of its allusions and the contemporaneousness of its satire, its popularity waned with a slowness that is seldom achieved by the highly competitive best sellers of today. Its tenacity is to be explained in part, probably, by the exceptionally great reputation of its principal author. It is to be accounted for also, and much more significantly, by the authenticity with which the novel caught the feeling of the times and by the appeal of its immortal protagonist, Colonel Sellers.

Sales alone, however, cannot constitute the essential measure of literary achievement; witness the yellow-backs of Clemens' time and the drugstore pocketbooks of ours. The fact remains that the reviewers of 1874—those who bothered with the book at all—evaluated it principally as a satire, a social document, hardly at all as a work of art, a novel. With a few notable exceptions, the critics glossed over its literary deficiencies with such deprecatory phrases as "the 'patchwork' order of composition."[3] The precedent established by contemporary critics has been generally followed ever since. Typical of later evaluations is Stephen Leacock's laconic verdict: "*The Gilded Age* is a mixed product, to place where one will."[4] Granville Hicks puts it more specifically when he says that "a good novel requires understanding quite as much as observation, the kind of understanding that leads to mastery and to structural unity. For this, burlesque, melodrama, and even shrewd portraiture are poor substitutes. . . ."[5] Typical also is a certain ambivalence that holds the condemnation in check. Hicks in the same breath calls *The Gilded Age* "one of the most ambitious novels written in the decades after the war" (p. 70). And Arthur Hobson Quinn, while calling it "more interesting as a social study than as a novel," hails it as "the prose epic of the age" preparatory to the post-Civil War period.[6] Most typical of all is a total avoidance of any opinion based upon literary criteria, a deferring to the noncommittal biographical or historical outline of the book's creation and its satirical content.

Yet despite the temptation to follow the safe path of recording facts and ignoring values, critics have been unable on the whole to resist the gnawing of their consciences regarding *The Gilded Age*. After all, the role of the critic is to measure values, to evaluate, and he cannot escape this necessity of his craft. Consequently, the critics who have devoted special attention to Mark Twain often arrive at a state of confused apology when they come to this particular novel. Bernard DeVoto, for example. For many years the literary executor of the Mark Twain estate, hence thoroughly conversant with the original Twain manuscripts and notes, DeVoto recognizes that with this novel "something memorable has happened in American literature." After reciting all the formal weaknesses of the book—its "amorphousness," its "absurd plot," its "set pieces of femininity"—with no attempt to account for them other than the ordinary clichés about Warner's influence and Clemens' inexperience, DeVoto admits that "the book is nevertheless literature." "Defaced and disfigured, it is still much more than a ruin above which an occasional column rises."[7]

This critical ambivalence is illustrated even better in the verdict

of Henry Seidel Canby, who takes it to the verge of equivoca-
tion.[8] To him *The Gilded Age* is a "curious phenomenon in the
nature and history of fiction." "As a book it is terrible," he writes,
"and Twain at his worst is quite as bad as Warner." Then he adds
the astonishing statement that "as a contribution to American
literature it is a certain proof of Twain's genius, for only genius
could make anyone now read it all." Only genius. What is the
criterion here? A clue is found in the following statement: "A
book does not have to be good as a whole in order to be famous,
if in parts or even in single characters it is excellent." This is close
to Fred Lewis Pattee's definition of *The Gilded Age* as "a book of
glorious fragments."[9] Canby compares Colonel Sellers with Falstaff,
"who also flourished in a good deal of melodrama much liked by
his creator." True; yet does Shakespearian criticism relegate the
two plays of *Henry IV* to obscurity, retaining only Falstaff? To
draw a parallel with Twain's famous older contemporary, does one
extract Pickwick, Pecksniff, and Micawber out of context and
ignore the rest of *The Pickwick Papers, Our Mutual Friend,* and
David Copperfield? How, then, is such critical extraction of *The
Gilded Age* to be explained?

It is to be explained by a number of contributing factors: lack
of sufficient investigation into the objective historical facts upon
which the novel was based; ignoration of the immediate literary
milieu into which it was launched; insufficient application of
known biographical facts about its authors to the circumstances of
its creation and the analysis of its contents; a proclivity for apply-
ing subjective, dogmatic, or formalistic criteria of literary criticism; and, closely allied to the last, want of a literary historical
method other than a superficially descriptive one.

What is the extent, for instance, to which *The Gilded Age* has
heretofore been placed in historical context? On the whole, literary
critics and biographers of Clemens have been content with the
general statement that the novel satirizes the post-Civil War period,
the times of the Johnson and Grant administrations. A few, such
as DeVoto, have intimated that real persons and events lay behind
the fictional characters and episodes. The first reviewers revealed
that Senator Dilworthy was Samuel C. Pomeroy and that Laura

Hawkins was Laura D. Fair, two identifications that prompted the richly rewarding investigations of Kitzhaber and Walker and that should have enticed researchers into a thorough testing of the *roman à clef* hypothesis. The historians—Oberholtzer, Josephson, the Beards, Nevins—have been uncovering the historical details of the time; yet no one except Walter Fuller Taylor has come close to seeing the potential of contemporary allusion in *The Gilded Age,* and because his subject was American economic novels in general he was strictly limited in the amount of attention he could give to any one.[10]

Outside a few discussions of the first eleven chapters as an outstanding depiction of frontier village life,[11] consideration of the historical background has largely been left to the historians, who have adopted the novel's title as a generic name for the period[12] and have frequently cited the novel itself as a valued contemporary source. One historian, Philip S. Foner, has written a critical biography of Mark Twain which not surprisingly devotes a much greater proportion of its length to *The Gilded Age* than does any other biography or critical work on Twain.[13] Also not surprisingly, he comes to the conclusion that "*The Gilded Age* is one of the few important novels produced in America in the last quarter of the nineteenth century" (p. 86).

Foner has done Twain scholarship a valuable service in pointing up Clemens' role as a serious social critic of his times. The humorist is a satirist, and, as has been shown earlier, his most extravagant burlesque often results from the deepest sense of outrage. It is known how he fretted at not being taken seriously, how he seemed unable to live down his initial reputation as the "Wild Humorist of the Pacific Slope," a reputation perpetuated by such literary historians as Charles F. Richardson and George Edward Woodberry.[14] In 1906, looking back over his career, he wrote:

> I have always preached. That is the reason that I have lasted thirty years. If the humor came of its own accord and uninvited I have allowed *ɪt* a place in my sermon, but I was not writing the sermon for the sake of the humor. I should have written the sermon just the same, whether any humor applied for admission or not. . . .[15]

Yet the Twain scholars, at least those in the United States, having failed to realize the thoroughness of political and social satire in *The Gilded Age*, have contented themselves with extracting Colonel Sellers and the village scenes of Obedstown and Hawkeye out of the novel as its only contributions to American literature and have dismissed the remainder as grossly exaggerated burlesque and imitative melodrama.

Had the American Twain scholars continued to explore the historical facts upon which the *Gilded Age* satire was based, as Kitzhaber and Walker had begun to do, they would have made the inescapable discovery that the novel was a detailed *roman à clef* embodying sharp criticism of the principal public abuses of its time. If this had been done, it would have been difficult for a Ludwig Lewisohn to say that even when Twain's satire is bitter in intent, "it lacks edge and point by the crinkled looseness and laxity of its vesture" or that he "cannot help being merely funny and merely 'folksy.' "[16] Mark Twain was well aware of the very trap into which Lewisohn claims he fell. Writing in the *Galaxy* three years before *The Gilded Age*, he made an admirable statement of the danger:

One can deliver a satire with telling force through the insidious medium of a travesty, if he is careful not to overwhelm the satire with the extraneous interest of the travesty, and so bury it from the reader's sight and leave him a joked and defrauded victim, when the honest intent was to add to either his knowledge or his wisdom. . . .[17]

The European scholars and critics have always taken Mark Twain's travesties seriously and, though not failing to appreciate his fun and humor, have not allowed the burlesque to obscure for them the underlying social criticism. The German scholar Friedrich Schönemann, for instance, calls Mark Twain's earlier humor "unrestrained and pugnacious, fraught with indignation and bitterness, full of protest and satire."[18] Rudolf Doehn speaks of *The Gilded Age* as "a satirical criticism of speculative mania, political intrigue, and corruption."[19] And Charles Alphonso Smith maintains that the superiority of Twain's humor lies in the fact that it is "socio-political."[20]

A French critic, Thérèse Bentzon, was among the first to present a detailed analysis of the book. Her review, published in 1875 and entitled "The Gilded Age in America," outlines the plot with a running commentary on its social significance. "Unhappily, we are much too disposed in France to take as a continuation of that golden age [of Franklin] the more or less *gilded* age that Messrs. Mark Twain and Dudley Warner present to us in its true light at last with its scars and blemishes; . . ."[21] Noting that "the Americans have reproached Messrs. Mark Twain and Warner for showing only one aspect of the facts," she adds that "while declaring that the depiction was gross and exaggerated, no one has denied that it was at bottom true."[22] Having expressed great concern throughout her article that the United States should find itself in such an appalling condition, she ends by saying, "let us hope that Mark Twain's personages, great oil barons, hired agents of intrigue, representatives who sell their votes and judges who sell their decisions, will also very shortly pass into the realm of myths and memories."[23] Another French critic, Maurice Muret, states, "It is difficult to see here anything other than a satire in cold blood—so much the more incisive—of democracy when it turns into demagogy."[24]

Even in the United States, Mark Twain was, at the outset of his career, taken as a potentially serious writer by more thoughtful critics. Edwin P. Whipple, for example, wrote in *Harper's* in 1876: "The serious portions of his writings indicate that he could win a reputation in literature even if he had not been blessed with a humorous fancy inexhaustible in resource."[25] Yet with the passage of time American critics refused to concede that Twain had in any significant way realized his potential as a serious writer. Not until his late, unfinished manuscripts were examined in the 1930's and parts of them published did there develop an appreciation of his serious concern with contemporary social values. Yet even then this discovery was quickly vitiated by a psychological interpretation that rationalized his social anger as an almost exclusively subjective phenomenon resulting from the frustration and bitterness of his later personal life.[26]

The story of Clemens' bankruptcy, the death of his favorite daughter from meningitis, the prolonged invalidism and final death of his adored wife, and the death of a second daughter, who had become his constant companion, on Christmas morning is indeed a painful one, filled with pathos and heartbreak. There is no doubt that Clemens was immeasurably crushed by these blows. But to imply that these circumstances completely determined his later outlook on life is not only to ignore the historical events at the turn of the century that engaged his lively interest but to distort his attitude toward them. Personal frustration cannot account for his fierce outcries against imperialism, colonialism, and other forms of oppression, particularly since these outcries were prompted by his own observation and reading. Though personal grief and despair might explain a *What Is Man?* or a *Mysterious Stranger,* how could it possibly account for such specific indictments as "A Salutation Speech from the Nineteenth Century to the Twentieth," "The Stupendous International Procession," "To the Person Sitting in Darkness," "In Defense of General Funston," or "The Czar's Soliloquy"?[27] Whether it is "Christendom, returning, bedraggled, besmirched, and dishonored from pirate raids in Kiao-Chou, Manchuria, South Africa & the Philippines, with her soul full of meanness, her pocket full of boodle and her mouth full of pious hypocrisies"[28] or the "Blessings-of-Civilization Trust" taking inventory of its "Glass Beads and Theology, and Maxim Guns and Hymn Books, and Trade-Gin and Torches of Progress and Enlightenment . . . good to fire villages with,"[29] the vitriol is that of a social prophet, not a self-pitying pessimist.

The chief differences between the quality of these utterances and that of *The Gilded Age* are a deepening of the sense of outrage (for now matters of life and death, war and peace are involved), an abandonment of bantering burlesque and ridicule in favor of grotesque caricature, and a dropping of the disguise of *roman à clef* in favor of direct naming of names. The neglect or, frequently, ignoring of these later sociopolitical writings by almost all the literary critics and scholars except those in the Soviet Union[30] has a direct connection with the neglect of *The Gilded Age.* It is a two-way connection. On the one hand, the fact that scholars have failed to investigate to any great extent the historical and topical material of the novel has blinded them to the socially critical tendency in Mark Twain, which culminates so strikingly in the later essays. On the other, the unquestioning acceptance of Twain as merely a humorist and glorified local colorist, which has prevented serious consideration of the later essays, has strengthened the neglect of *The Gilded Age* as being an unimportant, unsuccessful attempt at novel-writing.

Examination of the historical data reveals more about *The Gilded Age* than that it was a topical satire, a *roman à clef* of the postbellum years. In a broad manner it captured as well the essential quality of the business enterprise of its day, the spirit of headlong exploitation of the continental frontier for the profit of the northern capitalists. It was particularly successful in depicting the role of the middle-class promoters, lobbyists, and contractors who carried out the grandiose empire-building projects of the big bourgeoisie, the financial barons such as Jay Gould, and who emulated this finance capital in their own pitiful strivings to get rich quick. Much more than the specificity of topical allusion, it is the general overview of the period that has made the novel so valuable a social document to historians. This sweeping panorama of the early Gilded Age, from the mud flats of Stone's Landing to the halls of Congress, from a genteel seminary to a politics-ridden criminal court, is endowed with three characteristics that give it greatness—authenticity, satirical content, and social criticism.

The authenticity of *The Gilded Age* has always been, perhaps, its most noticeable feature. It was immediately noted by the more thoughtful reviewers such as Fred Perkins:

> Many of the scenes in the book are described with great force, and with the same obvious truthful-portrait character which belongs to its persons. Such are the steamboat race on the Mississippi, the lobbying transactions in Washington,—particularly the very well managed action by which the Knobs Industrial University Bill is carried in the House,— and the dramatic catastrophe of the bill in the Senate, where it fails within about two minutes of passing.[31]

Such recognition must have delighted Clemens in particular, for he continually strove for authenticity. "There is nothing," he had written Mrs. Fairbanks, "that makes me prouder than to be regarded by intelligent people as 'authentic.' A name I have coveted so long—& secured at last! *I* don't care anything about being humorous, or poetical, or eloquent, or anything of that kind—the end & aim of my ambition is to be authentic—is to be considered authentic."[32] DeVoto has made much of Twain's contribution to American literature in the frontier settings of *The Gilded Age:* ". . . it is possible, by 1872, to find several novels which undertook the honest portrayal of an American scene. Nevertheless, when the second paragraph introduces Obedstown, East Tennessee, we are on a higher level of realism than American literature had ever before attained. . . ."[33] Yet above anything else, the characterization of Colonel Sellers embodies the spirit of the times with sublimity, for Sellers' presence runs through the book, now in the foreground, now at one side, but always there, restless, impulsive, opportunistic, enthusiastic, ubiquitous. As protagonist for the theme of all-pervading speculativeness he is ably supported by minor characters—Si Hawkins, Eli Bolton, Harry Brierly and, to a lesser extent, Philip Sterling—even J. Adolphe Griller; but it is Sellers who epitomizes the "Gilded Age" personality.

More than sixty years ago William Dean Howells wrote that as a type Colonel Sellers

embodies the sort of Americanism which survived through the Civil War, and characterized in its boundlessly credulous, fearlessly adventurous, unconsciously burlesque excess the period of political and economic expansion which followed the war. Colonel Sellers was, in some rough sort, the America of that day, which already seems so remote, and is best imaginable through him. . . .[34]

It is a judgment the echo of which has rebounded from every crag of criticism—in Henderson, Parrington, Grattan, Josephson, Van Doren.[35] In Parrington's words:

A Colonel Sellers was to be found at every fireside talking the same blowsy doctrine. Infectious in their optimism, naïve in their faith that something would be turned up for them by the government if they made known their wants, they were hoping for dollars to be put in their pockets by a generous administration at Washington. . . .[36]

The Colonel, moreover, was recognized instantly by his contemporary audience. Apparently more vividly than in the novel itself, Colonel Sellers as a stage character made a deep impression on his fellow countrymen; for his personification by John T. Raymond, however inadequate Clemens may have thought it, brought his living presence before American spectators. Inspired by Raymond's performance as well as by the novel, the *New-York Tribune* devoted a long editorial to "The Tribe of Sellers." It read in part as follows:

Mulberry Sellers has taken his place in the galaxy of representative Americans. He is a caricature, an absurdity—this genial speculator who borrows ten cents while he divulges his scheme involving as many millions —but he is nevertheless a living and distinctive type of real American and peculiarly American character. He is no dramatic myth. American society is full of these interesting wrecks stranded on the shoals of misfortune, yet always basking in the sun. Every one knows Mulberry Sellers at once, and recognizes in him his next door neighbor, his chum at college, his wife's uncle—the one that ruined the family. He is to be seen every day in the street, every night at the club or the theater, every morning in the neighborhood of some cheap restaurant. Every man in New-York, every man in Washington, every man in Pike County, knows him. . . .

Of the tribe of Sellers there are many families, but the two great divisions are, perhaps, the honest and the dishonest. The honest Mulberry keeps himself, as well as every one around him, in perpetual poverty. He is always on the point of making a fortune too huge for the use of one man, Colonel though he be, and he announces his intention of sharing it with you; as a preliminary step he induces you to indorse his note or to lend him the little store you had laid up against a rainy day, and shoots it into the hopper of his enterprise. . . . The honest Mulberry went into oil, and was ruined; went into stocks, and was ruined again; went into real estate, and came out poorer than before; went into railroad bonds, and emerged a bankrupt, though no one could see what there was left to go smash. And every time he comes up smiling, with the light of a new "corner" or "strike" sparkling in his eye. He is a genuine Micawber flowered on American soil, but a greater than Micawber, for he is invincible. He is too American for despair; he steps up promptly to each new round with Fate—and gets thrown every time.

The dishonest Mulberry is a less pleasing fellow. He makes a precarious and disreputable living by the expenditure of ingenuity and industry which honestly exerted would make him a millionaire—if his name was anything but Sellers. His schemes are . . . all aimed at the appropriation of somebody else's money or thoughts or labor. . . . He plots a railroad swindle, and the reporters pry it out with their pencils; he worms himself into the confidence of defrauded bondholders, and is speedily discharged; . . .

At Washington, Mulberry Sellers is ubiquitous and influential. He has held a score of seats in every Congress within the memory of man, while in the lobby he is always in a majority. Mulberry, the lobbyist, lives a gilded, hollow sort of life, dining sumptuously during the session and starving during the recess. His bill fails of passage for want of three minutes' time on the morning of the Fourth of March, and is knocked on the head by the blow of the speaker's mallet which declares the Congress ended; or his project is referred to a Committee whose Chairman, he finds to his disgust, is virtuous. He inaugurates Pacific Railroads and lays the foundations for vast fortunes on which others build. . . .

Many a man is a Mulberry Sellers who would be astounded if you dubbed him so. . . . foolish fellows who think that real success is a thing to be stolen or bought or snatched out of the hand of Fate—these are representative Americans and representative of much that is raw and worthless in our civilization. . . .[37]

As one biography stated, "The public 'took' to Colonel Sellers, . . . it seemed as though he were part and parcel of reality."[38] Brander Matthews wrote,

. . . there was scarcely one of us who had not put money in schemes hardly more fantastic than the visionary Kentuckian's Oriental eyewater. Indeed, this general recognition of the truth of the character was pushed so far as to point out not one, but many originals, from whom the portrait had been drawn. . . .[39]

So authentic, indeed, did the Colonel seem, that the authors were besieged by claimants to having been the original of the character.[40] Raymond once told Brander Matthews that "in town after town he would be accosted by some man, who would say to him, 'I saw you to-night—and I recognized myself. Didn't Mark ever tell you? Well, he took Sellers from *me!* Why, all my friends knew me the first time they saw you!' "[41] The name Sellers, even as Micawber, became and for a long time remained a byword in the language.[42]

Other characters of *The Gilded Age* have been recognized as true to type, even when their "key" identity was unknown.

Among the American working classes, all save the most wretched had aspirations; . . . Brawny boys were constantly climbing upward to riches and circumstance; Patrick O'Riley of the saloon gang, who became Patrique Oreillé in Mark Twain's caricature of the passing show, was no mere creature of the imagination. . . .[43]

Warner's character Philip Sterling, idealized and stereotyped though he may be, has been noted as "a more or less lifelike sketch of the type of young New England men who were going West to seek their fortunes."[44] That this is how Warner himself envisioned Philip is made abundantly clear in the novel.

There are many young men like him in American society, of his age, opportunities, education, and abilities, who have really been educated for nothing and have let themselves drift, in the hope that they will find somehow, and by some sudden turn of good luck, the golden road to fortune. He was not idle or lazy; he had energy and a disposition to carve his own way. But he was born into a time when all young men of his age caught the fever of speculation, and expected to get on in the world by the omission of some of the regular processes which have been appointed from of old. And examples were not wanting to encourage him. He saw people, all around him, poor yesterday, rich to-day, who had come into sudden opulence by some means which they could not have classified among any of the regular occupations of life. . . . (II, 208-9)

That these and other characters of the novel—Si Hawkins, Washington Hawkins, Senator Dilworthy, Eli Bolton—should have been authentic to contemporary readers is not surprising, for, as has been shown earlier, Clemens and Warner knew them as real people. If their verisimilitude has faded somewhat for the modern reader, it is because the style of living in the United States has altered over the generations. A daguerreotype, stilted as it may now appear, is nonetheless an actual photograph.

Important as the authenticity of *The Gilded Age* may be as a measure of its worth in terms of literary realism, its value can best be seen in the support it gives to the novel's satire. As a novel of manners *The Gilded Age* is realistic, as a satire it is comic; as both it is comic realism in the great tradition of Fielding and Dickens. Were the fictive characters and episodes purely imaginary, the work might be considered merely farce. Since they are founded on solid reality, the work becomes satire of a high order.

The Gilded Age has had many detractors not alone of its literary merits but also of its satiric content. Detractors, once again, because of their ignorance of its great allusiveness; detractors because of their use of inadequate historical criteria. Some, like Russell Blankenship, feel that the book was only a harbinger of what might have been. According to him, the real tragedy of Clemens' life "was his failure to fulfill the promise of *The Gilded Age*" and "become the great American satirist."[45] Some, like Henry Seidel Canby, think that Clemens did not want to and could not do up the society he lived in and "proved his point in *The Gilded Age*."[46] Some, like Edgar Lee Masters, deploring the fact that Clemens was not Swift or Voltaire or Juvenal or Defoe or Thackeray or Tolstoy or Balzac, maintain that in this novel he has only staged "fools and grotesques."

He was old enough and of sufficiently wide experience and observation to have given America a novel which would have been a lasting history of one of its deepest periods of degradation. He didn't have the genius to do so. He was a humorist, soon ready to turn a cynic, a clown with a broken heart.[47]

Kenneth Andrews believes that the book is "more an attack on personal immorality in high places than a rounded satire of a new economic order" and that Clemens' "analysis of political corruption as the result of individual immorality indicates his subscription" to the Nook Farm point of view that excesses in the abuse of the basically sound American economic system were controllable.[48] In other words, what satire there is is largely a matter of personal ethics, hence is genial and innocuous. A similar point of view is expressed in Paul Schmidt's study of "Mark Twain's Satire on Republicanism."[49]

More effective in its detraction than the works of any of the foregoing critics, because clothed with a pseudoscientific plausibility, is Van Wyck Brooks's study *The Ordeal of Mark Twain*, which jolted literary circles when it was published in 1920.[50] What in Andrews' view is Clemens' conformity to Nook Farm values was to Brooks abject surrender. Attempting to make a Freudian psychoanalytic interpretation of Clemens and his writings, Brooks decided that Clemens found a mother-image in Olivia Langdon and thereupon surrendered to conformity. The capitulation was made permanent through the forcing of bourgeois values upon him by his wife, relatives, and friends. The Gilded Age, in conspiracy against the artist, and the Genteel Tradition of Howells finished the job. Hence his final sense of failure, his frustration, his despair, pessimism, pathological rage. This extraordinary piece of special pleading selected only the biographical facts and passages from the writings that fitted its hypothesis.[51]

Though Brooks's study of Twain is distorted out of all relation with reality, its matrix provides the hint of a historical approach, one which, unfortunately, leads him only to a vague, romantic cul-de-sac. Brooks characterizes the Gilded Age as that in which "the whole psychic energy of the American people was absorbed in the exploitation and the organization of the material resources of the continent," and he speaks of the "worship of success" of the "industrial pioneers," who tended to "romanticize their situation," believing as they did in the "myth of 'manifest destiny'" (pp. 77 and 83 ff.). Working consistently from this premise Brooks comes to the conclusion that the total effect of the novel *The Gilded Age* is idyllic, "the mirage of the American Myth lies over it like a rosy veil."

Mark Twain might permit himself a certain number of acid glances at the actual face of reality; but he had to redeem himself, he wished to redeem himself for doing so—for the story was written to meet the challenge of certain ladies in Hartford—by making the main thread the happy domestic tale of a well-brought-up young man who finds in this very stubbly field the amplest and the softest straw for the snug family nest he builds in the end. . . . (p. 277)

Other, more lenient detractors of the satire of *The Gilded Age* take the liberal point of view that, though the social criticism is well handled as far as it goes, it does not go far enough to be really significant. According to Edgar Branch, for example, the book is "not deeply penetrating satire." Twain's "observations of men and manners, acute and comprehensive as they are, do not get to the root of social and political corruption."[52] Parrington says that "with the innocence of his generation" Mark Twain "damned the agent and overlooked the principal."

The real sources of political corruption—the rapacious railway lobbyists that camped in brigades about the capitol building—are passed over, and attention is fastened on small steals—the Knobs University bill and the Columbus River Navigation scheme—that do not touch the real rascals of the day. . . .[53]

Had Parrington discovered to what a great extent such schemes as the University Bill and the Columbus River Navigation project were based on actual plunderings of the "real leaders of the great barbecue," he could never have made such a blunder.

The scholar who has come closest to placing *The Gilded Age* in its proper perspective as a satire is Walter Fuller Taylor. With Brooks's thesis in mind, he asks the question, "Did Mark Twain ever, in fact, really surrender to the plutocracy of the Gilded Age? Did he ever, in reality, abdicate the critical function of the satirist?" His answer is a definite no; and he cites as supporting evidence such works as "The Curious Republic of Gondour," *The Mysterious Stranger,* and *Connecticut Yankee.*[54] He concedes that the "genteel environment in New England was hardly congenial to free-spoken satire," but he points out that Twain was rich in the personal equipment of the satirist, "so rich, indeed, that satire overflows at some point or other into every one of his full-length works."[55] One of the latter was *The Gilded Age,* and Taylor presents an admirable outline of its satirical content.

Noting that as the story moves from the frontier to the commercial and political centers the satire grows sharper, Taylor enumerates the specific phenomena satirized—the phenomena dealt with earlier in the present volume—and summarizes that the "overwhelming majority" of the prevalent forms of business and political piracy are exposed. "Even the minor passages in the book," he continues, "are often salty with satirical thrust and epigram." He then speaks of "the code of middle-class prudence, thrift, and honesty" that constitutes the viewpoint from which the satire is directed.[56]

Apparently with Parrington's statement in mind that Twain "damned the agent and overlooked the principal," Taylor argues that the agents are represented in characters like Brown, Shaick, Bigler, and O'Riley and that other characters such as Laura Hawkins, Washington Hawkins, Sellers, and Sterling are either victims or dupes.[57] (Yet a director of the Union Pacific and [if Shaick may be taken as Sidney Dillon] the chairman of its board[58] come very close to being "principals," barring only the ruling oligarchy of the "first families" of the bourgeoisie.) Taylor further maintains that "the 'principal' force" in the novel is an intangible one, "the Spirit of Speculation."[59] He appears to believe that Mark Twain attributed the ills of the socio-economic system to the ideology born of that system rather than to the system itself. While there is much truth in this contention—for the ideology produced by a social system in turn reacts upon the system as a measurable force—it also comes close, if left by itself, to Andrews' contention that the novel's satire can be reduced to a matter of personal ethics. In other words, the fact that Taylor leaves the Spirit of Speculation as the ultimate "principal" implies an abandonment of social reality in favor of moral metaphysics.

In an attempt to evaluate *The Gilded Age* within the framework of a given set of criteria, a number of scholars and literary historians have presented rationales expressed in terms peculiar to their several viewpoints. Hazard, for example, considers Colonel Sellers as the type of the industrial pioneer.[60] Taylor, on the other hand, speaks of *The Gilded Age* as a preindustrial or "pre-machine" novel.[61] Parrington considers it a study of post-Civil War Whiggery.[62] Kenneth Lynn says it is written from the standpoint of "egghead Republicanism."[63] Kenneth Andrews calls it "a reactionary book" and implicitly antidemocratic,[64] a sentiment that finds an echo in Lynn.[65]

The liberals among the critics appear to be disappointed that Mark Twain had not read Ricardo or Marx and did not have the socially analytical insight into his material of fiction that is attributed to more recent, "proletarian" authors. Parrington states: "He asked no questions about unearned increment; to question that would have been treason to the frontier philosophy. . . . The eco-

nomics of history was a closed book to Americans of the seventies. . . ."[66] Similarly Taylor: "Of any formal economic philosophy,
he had none at all."[67] And the historian Harold Underwood Faulkner: "Warner and Twain . . . wrote a satire of American life without approaching the fundamentals that made such a picture possible."[68] More to the point, the researcher Thomas Bond Burnham
writes of Twain: "His mind was not a disciplined one, nor was it
of the type which reduce large phenomena to fit a formal pattern,
and it is doubtful whether it ever occurred to him to blame the
gilded age on a system, or even to figure out exactly what that
system was in all its implications. . . ."[69]

Of the evaluations by scholars of the American Left one of the
most provocative is that by Victor Francis Calverton. Writing in
1932, he declares that *"The Gilded Age* was one of the earliest and
best embodiments of the petty bourgeois philosophy of the frontiersman in his struggle against the corrupting influence of the
class in power. . . ."[70] According to his thesis, the American frontier offered, during the middle years of the nineteenth century, a
condition of exceptional social fluidity, in which the petty bourgeoisie were able to maintain dominance until after the Civil War.
The frontiersman, out of power, and escaping from the suppres-
sion of the big bourgeoisie in the East, pioneered new land in an
unfettered manner, established equalitarian communities, erased
class distinctions, and developed a strong, optimistic individualism.
The frontier also presumably provided an escape for the worker,
who developed a petty bourgeois rather than proletarian orientation, thereby retarding the growth of his own class consciousness
and leaving a legacy of illusion. In other words, the frontier environment, as Mark Twain illustrates in *The Gilded Age,* incul-
cated the rags-to-riches myth of the "American dream."[71]

This ingenious analysis, which has a certain amount of validity,
particularly in its emphasis on the "petty bourgeois" orientation of
The Gilded Age, is in other respects misleading and inadequate.
What, for example, is to be made of the fact that the Hawkinses
are slave-owners? How explain the presence in an "equalitarian
community" of the unregenerate, rail-sitting squatters of Obedstown, the flotsam and jetsam of the frontier, corresponding to the

lumpenproletariat of an industrialized region? Can the physical latitude offered by the American frontier solely account for the Micawber-like delusions of grandeur that are characteristic of the middle classes in other countries, or does it merely impart a national flavor?

Such questions are raised by Foner in his more recent study. As he points out, "the novel is by no means a complete mirror of the social and political history of the gilded age." He continues: "That the mass of Americans were not involved in the speculative fever of 'making money,' but rather were concerned in making ends meet, was not touched on by the authors. . . ." He speaks of "the book's tendency to make the moral corruption of the period universal."

Clearly, the authors believed that the debased values of the bankers, brokers, speculators, and corrupt politicians—get rich as fast as you can, even if you do it illegally and at every one else's expense—had become the moral values of all Americans. Yet this was a period when labor leaders, Negro leaders and agrarian leaders were upholding with passion entirely different values which emphasized the welfare and fraternity of all men.[72]

In delimiting the novel's satire in this way Foner is not, however, disparaging its merits ("The broad canvas of the novel covers many features of the gilded age which most deserved satire") (p. 72); he is merely showing that the novel, in spite of its "broad canvas," is not to be taken as an exhaustively representative Human Comedy. In fact, it is the very same "petty bourgeois" outlook underlined by Calverton that conditioned Clemens and Warner to endow their story unconsciously with a seemingly universal, or at least comprehensively national, significance.

Alone among Twain researchers published in the United States, Foner, a historian, maintains that Twain penetrated to the fountainhead of Gilded Age corruption. In this he comes into head-on collision with Parrington. How anyone can argue that *The Gilded Age* "purposely avoids sketching 'the real leaders of the great barbecue,' is," he writes, "beyond comprehension."

If the "real leaders" were not the bankers, brokers, and presidents of Wall Street corporations, who were they? . . . Twain was not, after all, writing a tract. He was performing the novelist's classic task—that of placing before us a group of characters and bringing them to life, causing the reader to say as he read, "Yes. This is right. This is the way the corporations buy legislators." . . .[73]

Of significance in this connection is the fact that around the turn of the century Clemens was jotting down notes (perhaps intended for a projected work on the "Fall of the Great Republic")[74] in which he outlined the growing depredations of the robber barons since the Civil War, giving specific names. The notes begin with the California gold rush, then continue:

Gould followed the California sudden-riches disease with a *worse* one, s. r. by swindling & buying courts. Cal. & Gould were the beginners of the moral rot, they were the worst things that ever befel [*sic*] Amer; they created the hunger for wealth when the Gr. Civ. had just completed its youth & its ennobling WAR—strong, pure, clean, ambitious, impressionable—ready to make choice of a life-course & move with a rush; *they* & *circumstances* determined the choice. . . .[75]

Though lacking a consciously articulated social philosophy, Clemens was greatly concerned with authenticity and with observed facts, two guiding lights that led him far along the road to understanding.

In depicting the manipulation of the national legislature by large corporate interests for their own benefit and in revealing the role of the middle-class promoters and speculators in carrying out the "manifest destiny" of these interests—victimizing themselves in the process—Mark Twain was dramatizing in probably the most effective way he could the headlong plundering of the national domain that was to lead to monopoly control of the economy. The notorious open corruption and graft associated with this process was its Achilles' heel, exposed to satirical attack. In *The Gilded Age*, the controlling interests, the "real leaders," the hidden rulers, are there in the background—Duff Brown, Rodney Shaick, the New York headquarters of the Columbus River Slackwater Navigation Company—and their direct connection with the destinies of Stone's Landing, Hawkeye, and Sellers' land promotion is never lost sight of. That no similar connection with the economic centers is shown in the case of the Tennessee Land graft and its logrolling Knobs University Bill is relatively unimportant, for such independent action as Dilworthy's sponsorship of this bill is entirely typical of the behavior of the capitalists' henchmen in Congress. As Josephson says,

> . . . while the capitalists held a controlling interest in the concern, they were not always able to exercise genuine control over their partners, the professional politicians. Nor had the capitalists in their own minds arrived as yet at any consistent smooth-working scheme of relations with the political Government and the men who held it in charge. . . .
>
> . . . .
>
> In short, the new capitalism gave an immense impetus to official and political venality—*blindly,* by its own disorderliness and fiercely competitive character rather than out of regard for its own deeper interests. . . .[76]

Just as the Columbus River project and Salt Lick Extension are representative of the operations of the big capitalists, so the Tennessee Land scheme is representative of the attempt of the middle classes to rise to economic preferment. Both are equally symptomatic of the rampantly insurgent capitalism of the period.[77]

Notwithstanding Van Wyck Brooks's failure to pursue the socio-historical approach to Mark Twain that lay buried under the debris of his hybrid "Freudianism," he was the first to recognize a very important fact about the man Clemens. This was that Clemens was divided in his attitude toward the Gilded Age and in regard to his own relation to it. According to Brooks, Clemens was a child of the very same era he criticized and his surrender to its ideology prevented his fulfilment of himself as an American Rabelais, a frustration that ended in his despair.[78] In the Gilded Age, Brooks asserts, "business enterprise was virtually the only recognized sphere of action," and into that sphere the actively creative artist could not fit without prostituting his talent.[79] Though much exaggerated and though serving as the premise for quite unwarranted conclusions, Brooks's concept has basic validity.

This ambivalence, this spiritual dichotomy, this divided self of Clemens' has been commented upon by several critics and historians. Like Brooks, Lewisohn decides that Clemens succumbed to his environment and lived "the turbulent get-rich-quick life of the Gilded Age—the life of large earning, losing, spending, . . . a life uncritical, essentially unguided, . . ."[80] Similarly, Van Doren speaks of his plans for being "a sort of captain of letters" and of sharing in the furor of speculation "from which he had no literary ideals to deter him."[81] Josephson interprets the "capitulation" as a positive abandon:

> Not only did Mark Twain fail to contend with his age; he reveled in it, he frankly enjoyed his ill-fated business schemes, the whirl of great affairs, printing companies, newspapers, machines. He enjoyed "hobnobbing with generals, senators, and other humbugs." He was involved with the Rockefellers, the Rogerses, the nabobs of the time, whose intimacy he was proud to have won; and he frankly liked the power, the great public gestures which his success permitted, just as he liked the banquets he gave in his mansions and the charities he so lavishly distributed. . . .[82]

Such evaluations are, in fact, superficial in that they accept the surface realities as final and fail to search into the underlying complexity of Clemens' personality.

Several writers, to the contrary, recognizing that appearances can be deceiving, attempt to analyze more deeply, to discover something more about Clemens' apparently conflicting motivations than appears at the surface. Hazard, for example, attributes the "fatal cleavage which Mr. Brooks has traced in his nature" to the clash between his admiration of the gentility, ease, and power that are the "rewards of success" and his fierce contempt for the hypocrisy, greed, and cruelty "underlying the social conspiracy which assures the success of the successful."[83] Taylor says that the facts do not suggest his surrender "to the ways of capitalistic industrialism" but instead an unconscious adaptation, "a process that Mark Twain was able to understand well enough in others, if not in himself."[84] And Calverton, consistent with his interpretation elsewhere, maintains that "at no time did he 'sell out' his philosophy to the upper bourgeoisie of the East" but remained forthrightly petty bourgeois.[85]

It is clearly of critical importance, then, to analyze Clemens' ambivalent attitude toward the Gilded Age, for on it depends a correct evaluation of his purpose, method, and accomplishment in writing the novel dedicated to it. On this evaluation in turn de-

pends a valid judgment of the place of this novel in his development as a writer—the final goal toward which this volume is
directed.

The evidence touched upon by critic after critic, in the manner
outlined above, points irresistibly to a profound contradiction in
Clemens' personality, which existed as early as the writing of *The
Gilded Age*. As is well known, Clemens at that time had married
the daughter of a wealthy mine owner and coal merchant, had
moved to one of the choicest communities of cultured bourgeois
residence, and was living a life of apparently unmitigated affluence
and enjoyment. Yet only two years after publication of his and
Warner's best-selling novel, Mrs. Fields was recording in her diary:
"He is so unhappy and discontented with our government that he
says he is not conscious of the least emotion of patriotism in himself. He is overwhelmed with shame and confusion and wishes he
were not an American. . . ."[86]

Without going to the lengths Van Wyck Brooks did in claim-
ing Clemens as totally captive to a society in conspiracy against
the artist, one must acknowledge that that society, with its ag-
gressively bourgeois values, imposed a discernible drain upon his
energies. Given a man imbued from childhood with a typically
middle-class desire to "get ahead," to identify with the "finer"
life of the cultured sector of the upper strata, when that man
through unconsciously sought-after circumstances found himself
surrounded, almost miraculously, by the paraphernalia of wealth
and a leisurely way of life, it was difficult for him to resist the
seemingly endless opportunities afforded the enterprising. Add to
this his derivation from a strongly visionary family going through
life with perennially unfulfilled great expectations, and his resis-
tance to the all-pervading speculativeness became impossible.

At the same time, Clemens' clear-sighted objectivity, which
had for long made him the enemy of humbug, fraud, and hypocritically disguised injustice, kept asserting itself, as his almost
daily explosions at the newspaper headlines demonstrate. So while
living in a personal comfort that was inevitably accompanied by
the illusions associated with its base in society, Clemens was continually faced with reality, which his honesty could not ignore. The

conflict was personal, subjective, within him. The contradiction that produced it was objective and external, a natural concomitant of a society that sustained its purported values by constantly destroying them in one way or another. It is no surprise, therefore, that Clemens failed to achieve an integration. In so failing he was entirely representative of his class and time.[87]

Here can be seen the significance of the fact not only that John Marshall Clemens and Orion and John Quarles and James Lampton went into *The Gilded Age* but that *he himself* went into it, that he himself was much of Colonel Sellers. Samuel Clemens brought to this satire of all-pervading speculativeness, this study of middle-class Gilded Age society, an understanding that he was perfectly equipped to bring. The central conflict of *The Gilded Age* is one between the middle classes, both frontier and urban, with their aspirations to get rich quick, and the ruling class of corporation directors and financiers, who actually control the national economy. The novel's point of view is that of the Hawkinses, the Boltons, Colonel Sellers, and Philip Sterling, and these characters are drawn in full-length portraits. Significantly, the opposing force, that of the ruling class, remains largely impersonal, its representatives, such as the president of the Columbus River Slackwater Navigation Company, Duff Brown, and Rodney Shaick, being confined to fleetingly shown minor characters. The underlying conflict of these opposing forces sets up a tension that runs throughout the novel and expresses itself in several overt forms such as the attempted Congressional appropriation and the Knobs University Bill. *Clemens knew this tension.* Consciously or not, he lived with it day after day, so he was able with relative ease to transfer it to the pages of *The Gilded Age.*[88]

Not only did Clemens by his origins and by the circumstances of his environment have a personal understanding of and empathy with Gilded Age psychology, but he also happened to have had firsthand experience in the spheres of activity that provided the raw material of the novel's satire. He had been born and brought up in frontier Missouri. As a Mississippi pilot he had witnessed steamboat races and river disasters. He had been a Washington correspondent and had seen the Dilworthys in action, had indeed hobnobbed with some of them. He had been a miner. He had traveled the breadth of the land and had lived on both coasts. What he had not directly experienced he made up for in observation or in his constant, avid reading of the news and current affairs. The same can be said, to a lesser degree, of Warner. The latter had been in law practice and was familiar with court procedure. He had done surveying on the Pacific railroad system. And so on. The co-authors' personal knowledge of their material has been commented upon many times[89] and has been thoroughly elaborated in the present volume.

The obvious conclusion to be drawn from this fact of writing from experience would be that in their first attempt at extended fiction Clemens and Warner fell back on their own lives as source material,[90] were it not for two other equally important facts. One is that *The Gilded Age* was intended as a pointedly satirical *roman à clef* and as such drew upon the most salient news stories of the day to strengthen its satire. The other is that just as the topical allusions were selected deliberately to illustrate the principal public abuses of the time, even so were the main ingredients of the novel chosen from the most central economic and social phenomena of the time—government-subsidized exploitation of the continental frontier by means of the railroad, and speculative land promotion through Congressional graft.

It is no accident that the novel was so central in its theme. Though, as has been said, Clemens was devoid of any conscious social philosophy, or even rationale,[91] his own observation, reading, and experience directed him to a diagnosis which, if incomplete, was correct as far as it went. It will be remembered that the book was published during the great financial crisis of 1873-74, at the advent of a severe economic depression of several years' duration,[92] and that this crisis had been heralded by a Wall Street panic in April just as the manuscript for the novel had been completed.[93] The depression, which was classic in its formation and international in scope, began in earnest with the Vienna stock exchange panic early in May.[94] The cause of the crash was the same both in the economically advanced countries of Europe and in the United States—uncontrolled overspeculation, accompanied by swindling and corruption, which had produced the international boom of 1869-73.[95] At the heart of this boom, which was reaching its climax as *The Gilded Age* was being written, were, as far as the United States was concerned, the twin economic menaces of railroad expansion and land promotion.[96] New York at this time was swamped with railroad securities, and after the Vienna crash they were unmarketable in Europe. The New York crisis began with the downfall of firms heavily invested in the Pacific railway systems, and following the failure of Jay Cooke & Co. in September the crisis rapidly spread to all sectors of the economy.[97]

The reason that railroads took the lead in speculation and in the ensuing headlong crash was that in the United States their development was excessive, unprecedented, and certainly unparalleled in Europe. The railroads were, of course, the key to the opening up of the frontier West to economic exploitation, and for once they preceded settlement.[98] In 1869, 4,953 miles of road were built; in 1870, 5,690; in 1871, 7,670; in 1872, 6,167; in 1873, 4,190—a total of over 28,000 miles in five years, at an expenditure of $1,700,000,000.[99] In the wake of the railroads came the land sharks and settlers. Unless the newly available areas were quickly populated, there would be no freight or passengers to transport. So the East was propagandized for settlers, special reductions were offered, and in co-operation with European steamship lines the railroad companies recruited immigrants, using all kinds of lurid appeals including fake testimonials.[100] The seemingly miraculous boom produced a heightened form of Sellers-like frontier psychology. "The spread of luxury even in the villages of the far West was something astounding."[101]

In the course of this frenzied expansion the national domain was being given away right and left to the corporations, and Congress was appropriating vast sums from the public treasury for private gain. It was indeed the "great barbecue," or, as Josephson calls it, a "saturnalia of plunder."[102] The land-grant railroads often held the choicest parcels of land for their own speculation; four railroads alone received by 1870 an amount of public land equivalent to the states of Ohio, Illinois, Indiana, Wisconsin, and Michigan combined.[103] The scrupulous Senator Grimes expressed the

alarm of many when in the Senate he said, "Nearly all the grants
of lands to railroads and wagon roads find their way into the hands
of rich capitalists, . . ." "The 'New York World' was denouncing
the lobby of the Northern Pacific as a gang of 'plunderers,' and
describing it in the 'galleries, looking down on the scene like beasts
of prey.' "[104] And behind the scenes Wall Street financiers pulled
the strings. Hugh McCulloch told Gideon Welles about his own
role in the machinations. A rare and highly revealing bit of contemporary testimony, the following passage was entered by Welles
in his diary of March 14, 1867: "Certain Wall Street operators
know daily what is done in the Finance and Ways and Means Committee. He [McCulloch] gets information of the transactions of
that committee by way of Wall Street before the committee reports
to or advises with him, . . ."[105]

Samuel Clemens knew of these developments, had personally
witnessed the processes of the Gilded Age both out in the frontier
country and in the halls of Congress. Warner had seen his share,
too, though with less clarity. The critical question, then, arises:
Did Clemens and Warner write what they did because it appeared
to them as central to a proper diagnosis of the Gilded Age or because it reflected their own knowledge and experience of that era?
This question, however, poses a false, if enticing, opposition. There
is actually no choice to be made between mutually exclusive alter-
natives, no real polarity. That the authors wrote of those aspects
of their time they knew best there is no question. That they wrote
of matters they saw as central to their time is likewise clear, not
only from the evidence of the *roman à clef* ingredients of the
novel but also from the authors' own attitude toward the work.
In the preface to the American edition the authors stated, with a
straight-faced sarcasm worthy of Swift:

> It will be seen that it deals with an entirely ideal state of society; and
> the chief embarrassment of the writers in this realm of the imagination
> has been the want of illustrative examples. In a state where there is no
> fever of speculation, no inflamed desire for sudden wealth, where the poor
> are all simple-minded and contented, and the rich are all honest and
> generous, where society is in a condition of primitive purity, and politics
> is the occupation of only the capable and the patriotic, there are neces-

sarily no materials for such a history as we have constructed out of an ideal commonwealth.[106]

And in the revealing preface to the British edition, already referred to, Mark Twain wrote:

> . . . I have a great strong faith in a noble future for my country. A vast majority of the people are straightforward and honest; and this late state of things is stirring them to action. If it would only keep on stirring them until it became the habit of their lives to attend to the politics of the country personally, and put only their very best men into positions of trust and authority! That day will come.[107]

This fact, this coincidence of the authors' experience with the most significant phenomena of the early Gilded Age, can be explained very simply in terms of social need and inevitable fulfilment of that need. The rapid development of society in the United States after the Civil War, a development signalized, as has been seen, by widespread economic exploitation accompanied by official and semiofficial corruption, called for effective satire. In order to be effective the satire demanded a writer (or, as it turned out, writers) who could perceive and, it might be hoped, attest by personal experience the prevailing temper of the time and its social roots. Clemens and Warner had the ideal qualifications; hence they succeeded where others might have failed—where others, indeed, *had* failed.

If their famous decision to collaborate on a novel had never been made, such a novel would still have been written. It might have been written later; it might have taken a quite different form. Almost certainly it would have been inferior. The American people would never have had the glowing satisfaction of seeing as perfect an embodiment of the frontier promoter they knew so well as they did in the famous Colonel. Alternatively, Clemens, who "had a story in mind," might have produced the work single-handed; but again the chances are that without the sustaining stimulus of the competition with Warner and the almost nightly readings, discussions, and votes on the day's creation Clemens' end-product would have lacked some of the zest and sparkle that give delight to its reading. The point is that the era would have given rise to some such literary record out of the sheer inertia of its development.

What is the implication of all this as regards Mark Twain's genius? Does it reduce his talent to an accident in a deterministic literary history? Was he merely a puppet on the stage of social evolvement? Not at all. To maintain so would be absurd. The accomplishment of *The Gilded Age* (except for Warner's contribution) is peculiarly Twain's. How much the more so *Tom Sawyer, Huck Finn, Connecticut Yankee, Pudd'nhead Wilson.* What *is* to be inferred is the good fortune of American culture that through a complex of circumstances it befell the individual Samuel Clemens to fulfil the role of satirist of the early Gilded Age.

The good fortune of American culture is made vividly clear when *The Gilded Age* is compared with its contemporaries in the sphere of fiction. Chapter II of this volume has indicated the prevalent sentimentalism and sensationalism of the novels of the sixties and seventies. Pointing out the astonishing contrast between the work of such writers as Augusta Evans Wilson and E. P. Roe on the one hand and the Twain-Warner novel on the other, the student of socially critical American fiction Walter Taylor calls *The Gilded Age* "unique among American novels of its time."[108] It alone, as Foner states, "dared to deal with real problems of the era, to expose widespread corruption and the forces responsible for it, and to alert the people to a spreading decay in society."[109] Its only possible competitor, according to DeVoto, is Henry Adams' *Democracy* (1879), and he dismisses the latter as "just squeamish, a mere phobia of crowds."[110]

Though the general theme of politico-economic corruption had appeared in American fiction before *The Gilded Age*, it had never received more than passing attention. As early as 1792, Hugh Henry Brackenridge, in *Modern Chivalry*, proclaimed that it is a mistake to elect legislators incapable of understanding the nation's economic interests. Washington Irving in *Knickerbocker Holiday* (1809) also demanded economically competent solons. James Kirke Paulding, in *Konigsmarke* (1823), satirized public officials for using their public office for private gain, his character Wolfgang Langfanger, for instance, planning wharves for nonexistent shipping. The novels of James Fenimore Cooper made frequent allusion to incapability in government.[111] And Artemus Ward, in sketches such as "William Barker, the Young Patriot" (1862), exposed Civil War profiteering."[112]

Among its immediate contemporaries in works of American fiction were three in particular that attempted to satirize some of the abuses treated in *The Gilded Age*. These were the short story "An Inspired Lobbyist," by John W. De Forest, which appeared in the December, 1872, *Atlantic*, John Ferguson Hume's novel *Five Hundred Majority*, published by Putnam in 1872, and Edward Eggleston's *The Mystery of Metropolisville* (1873), which was serialized in the Eggleston brothers' magazine, *Hearth and Home*, December, 1872–April, 1873. All three departed from the usual run of popular fiction in having a socially critical viewpoint and had certain parallels with parts of *The Gilded Age*. None, however, attempted a satire national in scope, keeping for the most part to local or regional problems.

In De Forest's "An Inspired Lobbyist,"[113] Ananias Pullwool, "the most successful and famous lobbyist in Washington," who has the Devil in him, has been investigated for logrolling and filching and jailed. When he is let out, he goes into the hinterland for a season and plunges into the contest between the two towns of Slowburg and Fastburg to be made state capital. Working on both sides of the fence, he manipulates the lobby for Fastburg, then begins a similar one for Slowburg, with the result that when the legislature finally turns down Fastburg's bill both towns have spent over a hundred thousand dollars uselessly while Pullwool's capital ring, drawing from both sides, has lined its pockets.

To the lobbyists and members Pullwool was munificent; it seemed as if those gentlemen could not be paid enough for their "influence;" as if they alone had that kind of time which is money. Only, while dealing liberally with them, the inspired one did not forget himself. A thousand for Mr. Sly; yes, Mr. Sly was to receipt for a thousand; but he must let half of it stick to the Pullwool fingers. The same arrangement was made with Mr. Green and Mr. Sharp and Mr. Bummer and Mr. Pickpurse and Mr. Buncombe. It was a game of snacks, half to you and half to me; and sometimes it was more than snacks,—a thousand for you two and a thousand for me too.[114]

Interestingly suggestive of Mark Twain's later *Man That Cor-rupted Hadleyburg*, this semiallegorical story effectively preaches against the evils of lobbying. Ananias Pullwool, however, remains only a lay figure illustrating De Forest's theme, as do the other Dickensian-named characters, and in no way takes on the reality and vividness of a Senator Dilworthy. (It would be tempting, playing the game of literary influences, to speculate whether the name Ananias Pullwool suggested the name Brother Balaam in *The Gilded Age*, were it not that Clemens' own fondness for the satiri-cal use of biblical allusion quite adequately explains the latter.) [115]

The second contemporary work, *Five Hundred Majority: A Tale for the Times*, written by J. F. Hume under his pseudonym of Willys Niles,[116] is a novel that relentlessly exposes Tammany politics.[117] Compounded of many of the ingredients of the sensa-tion novel formula—murder, intended bigamy, self-sacrifice, dis-possession—with black villains (the Tammany Hall characters) and a pure hero and heroine (the idealistic young politician Clinton Maintland and his country-bred sweetheart Margaret Kortland), the novel yet contains new elements: exposure of rigged elections and electoral graft, city machine politics, legal frame-up by politi-cal enemies, and the moral degeneracy of political corruptness. Though cluttered up with the love motivations dear to the sensa-tion novel audience, it is a well-made story and has two notable characterizations, the Tammany sachem Barton Seacrist (who may be based on "Elegant Oakey" Hall)[118] and his completely corrupted daughter-secretary, Kate.

The novel is the prototype of a succession of novels of the next two decades having as their topic "the enormous strength of city political rings in the seventies and their power to wreck human lives."[119] As such it is definitely limited in its scope both as a social novel and as a progenitor; still, except for its almost total lack of humor, its general approach has similarities with that of *The Gilded Age*. Compare, for example, the following passage with the preface to the American edition of the Twain-Warner novel:

There can be no more beautiful system than we possess. Here justice and virtue are always triumphant, for the people rule. The will of the majority is the supreme law. Men are chosen to stations of honor and trust with sole reference to merit. The honest and capable are promoted—the undeserving cast down. Distinction and power are the rewards of the faithful, while punishment is swift to overtake the violator of public or private right. Integrity is the rule of official life and practice—knavery the exception—for the perfection of human wisdom has at last been attained. . . .[120]

The third work, Eggleston's *Mystery of Metropolisville*, instalments of which were appearing at the time *The Gilded Age* was being written,[121] was in part a study of the creation, rise, and eventual collapse of a typical frontier boom town, "the inevitable sequel and retribution of speculative madness."[122] This subject forms the background against which is enacted a rather grim melodrama of small-town personalities involving such sure-fire components as the victimizing and suicide of a young girl, attempted murder, jailing on false charges, and self-sacrificing devotion that redeems all. The "speculative madness" that holds the land shark Plausaby in its grip, causing him to sacrifice to his selfish gain the well-being of those around him and his own integrity as well, remains nonetheless a sort of local color setting. One has the feeling that Plausaby creates his own environment, rather than the other way around, and that he would be a villain anywhere, under any other circumstances. Eggleston, in other words, did not succeed in identifying Plausaby with the way of life that produced him as Mark Twain did in Colonel Sellers.

The setting and plot framework of Eggleston's novel, however, do outline the course of development of the Hawkeyes, the Stone's Landings, the Marion Cities and Edens of the period; and Eggleston admits that if he "were writing a History instead of a Mystery of Metropolisville" he would feel obliged to expand his sketchy treatment of the sociological element.[123] In spite of the fact that the melodrama plays itself out almost independently of its setting, Eggleston obviously had a sense of history and conceived of Metropolisville as a type of its period. He describes, for instance, the land speculators' advertisements in *The Wheat County Weakly Windmill*:

. . . as for the towns, it appears from these advertisements that there was one on almost every square mile, and that every one of them was on the line of an inevitable railroad, had a first-class hotel, a water-power, an academy, and an indefinite number of etcæteras of the most delightful and remunerative kind. Each one of these villages was in the heart of the greatest grain-growing section of the State. Each was the "natural outlet" to a large agricultural region. Each commanded the finest view. Each point was the healthiest in the county, and each village was "unrivaled." . . .[124]

In a short epilogue, "Words Afterwards," Eggleston writes, in a manner reminiscent of Twain, "Metropolisville is only a memory now. The collapse of the land-bubble and the opening of the railroads destroyed it."[125] And with a touch of topicality he adds the following stroke to his portrait of Plausaby: "He turned up afterwards as president of a Nevada silver-mine company, . . . and I have a vague impression that he had something to do with the building of the Union Pacific Railroad. . . ."[126]

The Mystery of Metropolisville came as close as any contemporary work of fiction to succeeding in the realm where *The Gilded Age* holds pre-eminence. It did not do so for two obvious reasons: it confined itself to a regional (Minnesota) study of speculative madness, never venturing toward the national centers of power, and it restricted its social theme to setting instead of integrating it into the human story. That *Metropolisville* and the other tales of the day fell so far short of fulfilling the social need for critcial satire points up the brilliance of Mark Twain's achievement in *The Gilded Age,* an augury that the United States had in its midst a rising genius of the first rank.

In addition to the foregoing, there are a few other contemporary fictional works of a socially critical nature which, though published slightly later than *The Gilded Age,* were so closely subsequent that they can be considered independent efforts uninfluenced by the Twain-Warner novel. All of them appeared as published volumes in 1875.

The first is a five-act farce entitled *Life in the Lobby,* by Donn Piatt, printed (apparently privately) in Washington, D.C., by Judd & Detweiler, Printers. Its author, Donn Piatt, who has been described as "the most sensitive, provoking, genial satirist in America,"[127] was a poet, playwright, and journalist who at this time was writing, under his pen-name Edmond About,[128] for his own journal, *The Capitol,* which he had started with George Alfred Townsend in 1871.[129] Clemens had know Piatt on the *Galaxy,* where Piatt had temporarily been his successor in the humorous department,[130] and probably even earlier on Newspaper Row, when Piatt had been Washington correspondent for the Cincinnati *Commercial.*[131] Obviously Piatt was as intimately acquainted with the Washington lobby as Clemens was, and his little farce contains many parallels with the *Gilded Age* version of the same milieu. If the play was ever performed, I have no evidence of the fact; it may have been written for the entertainment of Piatt's friends and privately printed by him for personal circulation.

The broadly burlesque plot of *Life in the Lobby* centers around the efforts of Colonel Ralph Stackpole, "Chief of the Lobby," to engineer an Indian appropriation fraud purportedly in behalf of an actually nonexistent tribe, the Omahogs. Champion of the move in the Senate is the "Christian Statesman" Senator Phineas Pilaster, "an Aaron Burr, covered all over with John Wesley,"[132] who is known as "Old Piety."[133] His Congressional maneuvering is strongly reminiscent of Senator Dilworthy's:

PILASTER. We must not, however, relax our efforts. Divine Providence favors the prudent. The Speaker must be seen so as to secure the floor at the right moment, and the Hon. Cockeye must move the previous question so as to cut off debate; and above all our forces must be well in hand. . . .[134]

Colonel Stackpole's brother is an unscrupulous Indian agent and a railroad promoter. Senator Pilaster is hypocritically threatening an investigation of his old friend Colonel Stackpole; but Stackpole's wife, disguised as a woman lobbyist, secures damaging evidence against Pilaster and suppresses equally damaging evidence against her husband, thus resolving the situation. The philandering Stackpole, who has been flirting with his own disguised wife, is taken home by her on his promise that he will henceforth behave himself! Minor episodes involve Dr. Gusset, a female woman's rights advocate, who is depicted as a ridiculous figure spouting a constant stream of feminist slogans, and Pat Doolan, an Irish-

American "baggage smasher," who runs for office, urging his constituents to get his principles from a bottle at his expense and "imbibe those principles until ye are full." There are also strongly chauvinistic treatments of the Indian delegation (members of the lobby in disguise) and of the Negro waiter Scipio, who becomes a professor at Howard Institute over night.

The most notable feature of the play is its biting satire on the Indian lobby, containing a barely disguised attack on Harlan, "our most Christian Secretary of the Interior." Describing the Indian ring, Colonel Stockpole says:

> It is nearer perfection, perhaps, than any work of the devil ever consummated. . . . It makes treaties only to break them, and the money appropriated, every dollar of which is stained with blood, it divides among its followers. If the Indians submit, profit doth accrue; if they rebel and blindly make war, war calls for heavier contracts and heavier appropriations, and corresponding profits. . . .[135]

Other themes touched on that have parallels in *The Gilded Age* are the Crédit Mobilier, vote-buying for re-election, and Negro colonization schemes.[136] There are even mentioned one or two Sellers-like schemes, which alone among the materials of the play slightly suggest Twain influence: the "Inter-Ocean Muskrat and Tadpole National Excavation Company" and the "grand National Interocean Gigantic Peashooter Company, that is to pierce the Rocky mountains with huge tubes, along which balls filled with freight and mails are to be propelled by compressed air—cold air from the lakes, hot air from the Pacific coast."[137]

The other 1875 works are two novels, De Forest's *Honest John Vane*[138] and Josiah Gilbert Holland's *Sevenoaks*,[139] both of which, unlike *Life in the Lobby*, have been commented on by other researchers. The first of these, the ironic title of which refers to its congressman hero, was based on the Crédit Mobilier.

> The directors and managers of the Great Subfluvial [Tunnel] had contrived what might be called a Sub-Tunnel for their own peculiar emolument, . . . It was a corporation inside of the original corporation. Its ostensible object was the construction of the Subfluvial, but its real object was the division of the capital into profits. . . .

O, it was a beautiful business idea,—this Floating Credit, or Syndicate, or whatever its inventors christened it. . . .[140]

Sevenoaks relates the story of a financial magnate who becomes rich by selling stock in a fake oil company, rejuvenating an old railroad as a speculation, and stealing inventions.[141] All three works, *Life in the Lobby, Honest John Vane,* and *Sevenoaks,* deal with serious social problems of the period but, like their earlier contemporaries, fail to present a satire of national scope, limiting themselves instead to single prospects of the total scene.[142] Needless to say, in their levels of writing and of human insight they fall far short of *The Gilded Age.*

With the appearance of *The Gilded Age,* therefore, fiction in the United States underwent a qualitative change. As is true of most such turning-points, the effect was not immediately noticeable; but as the decade of the seventies progressed and passed into the eighties the emergence of what Parrington has called the "realism of social protest"[143] became apparent. To be sure, a basis had been laid earlier, in the sixties, but only in a half-formed or incidental shape.[144] On the strength of *The Gilded Age,* indeed, Twain has been named "the first of the 'muckrakers.' "[145] The novel was, in the words of Calverton, "the precursor of those many attacks upon the exercise of power, which were to be made by the novelists and politicians of later generations" (p. 327).

If *The Gilded Age* seems today rather mild in its social criticism compared to the works of Frank Norris, Upton Sinclair, or Theodore Dreiser, it is partly because the progenitor is compared with its progeny; whereas the only just comparison of any innovation is with its siblings and contemporaries. It is also, to a great extent, because the form of the novel is comedy, to which we have grown unaccustomed as a vehicle for social criticism. The satires of Sinclair Lewis seem genial and permissive because they *follow* the muckrakers; his restoration of comic realism has the anticlimactic effect of most restorations. *The Gilded Age,* however, burst upon its audience with an energetic outspokenness and frankness that is attested to by the reviews and public reaction.

Another fact that must be kept in mind in correctly evaluating *The Gilded Age* is that until the turn of the century the majority of American novelists "held a position," as Taylor points out, "that may properly be defined as 'Left-Center.' "

Such novelists, although aware of the obvious evils of capitalistic industrialism, although capable of the sharpest examination of the corrupt practices of Big Business, although deeply concerned over certain disintegrating effects of industrialism in the lives of both the rich and the poor, nevertheless stopped short of advocating any fundamental change in the economic system. Moderate politico-economic reforms, or the alleviations offered by settlement work and slum-clearance, appeared to them sufficient.[146]

Typical examples are Robert Grant's *An Average Man* (1884), concerning machine politics; Thomas Stewart Dennison's *An Iron Crown* (1885), about manipulation of government by business; George Cary Eggleston and Dolores Marbourg's *Juggernaut* (1891), on the railroads' corrupting invasion of legislative bodies; Edgar Fawcett's *A New York Family* (1891), on Boss Tweed; and Hamlin Garland's *A Member of the Third House* (1892), on the Washington railroad lobby.[147] These novels are, certainly, a far cry from such giants as Norris' *Octopus*, Sinclair's *Jungle*, and Dreiser's *Titan*.[148]

In discussing any line of literary descent, critics have a predilection for tracing literary influences both real and imagined. Mark Twain has come in for his share of this somewhat unflattering treatment. In respect of *The Gilded Age* especially, Twain is supposed to have been strongly influenced by his older contemporary Dickens. The comparison of Colonel Sellers with Micawber began the moment the novel was published. *The Queen,* for example, in its review says, "There is a strong family likeness between this individual and our old friend Mr. Micawber," but hastens to add: "we must do the present authors justice to acquit them of plagiarism, for this character, which is a very prominent one throughout the novel, is drawn with originality and humour."[149] Stuart Sherman finds "a certain flavor of Dickens" in the book.[150] And Wagenknecht sees a Dickensian influence in Sellers' clock and says that "Senator Dilworthy's speech in chap. 53 (or chap. 22 of vol. II) might have been modeled directly on the remarks of the Reverend Mr. Chadband, in *Bleak House,* chapter 19" (p. 270, n. 9).

Schönemann, however, is highly skeptical of such influence, except in a general similarity between the two authors' portrayals of the petty bourgeois milieu, and points out that the most notable characters of *The Gilded Age* are drawn from life.[151] The sympathy between Micawber and Sellers he traces, rather, to their common descent from Don Quixote![152] There is no question of Clemens' familiarity with Dickens' novels from an early age[153] or of his love of the novelist; but efforts to find direct influence are rather silly in the case of such a deeply indigenous author and smack of a desire to do him discredit. If one is searching for parallels, the *American Notes* furnish more strikingly similar comparisons, such as this description of Congress:

I saw in them the wheels that move the meanest perversion of virtuous Political Machinery that the worst tools ever wrought. Despicable trickery at elections; under-handed tamperings with public officers; cowardly attacks upon opponents, with scurrilous newspapers for shields, and hired pens for daggers; shameful trucklings to mercenary knaves, whose claim to be considered, is, that every day and week they sow new crops of ruin with their venal types, which are the dragon's teeth of yore, in everything but sharpness; aidings and abettings of every bad inclination in the popular mind, and artful suppressions of all its good influences: such things as these, and in a word, Dishonest Faction in its most depraved and most unblushing form, stared out from every corner of the crowded hall.[154]

Still, in such passages, as in the American chapters of *Martin Chuzzlewit*, Dickens is only describing from personal observation the same conditions that Clemens described, also from personal observation.

In this game of literary influences, Beau Tibbs has been added to Micawber as a model for Colonel Sellers.[155] Domestically, Sellers' descent has been traced to the southwestern humorists—to Augustus Baldwin Longstreet,[156] to Johnson J. Hooper's Simon Suggs,[157] to Joseph G. Baldwin's Ovid Bolus.[158] Baldwin's visionary speculator, Ovid Bolus, does indeed uncannily anticipate the Colonel:

Bolus's lying came from his greatness of soul and his comprehensiveness of mind. The truth was too small for him. . . .

. . . .

His world was not the hard, work-day world the groundlings live in: . . .
he lived amidst the ideal and romantic. . . .

. . . .

He never higgled or chaffered about small things. He was as free with his
own money—if he ever had any of his own—as with yours. . . . —he
would fumble in his pocket, mutter something about nothing less than a
$100 bill, and direct the score [for drinks], with a lordly familiarity, to
be charged to his account.

. . . He was present at every important debate in the Senate at Washington, . . .[159]

Yet again, the originals of the Boluses and Sellerses were plentiful.
As DeVoto has wisely remarked, "Striking parallels and similarities appear in literature not because writers are influenced by one
another but because there are striking parallels and similarities in
human experience. . . ."[160]

What has been overlooked in this general concern with influences on Clemens is his interest in political fiction. In March,
1869, he wrote Livy that he was rereading *Gulliver's Travels*, which
had charmed him as a boy.

. . . now I can see what a scathing satire it is upon the English government, whereas, before I only gloated over its prodigies & its marvels.
Poor Swift—under the placid surface of this simply-worded book flows
the full tide of his venom—the turbid sea of his matchless hate. . . .[161]

Only a year before writing *The Gilded Age*, he wrote her that he
was reading *The Member from Paris*, "a very bright, sharp, able
French political novel."[162] It would seem that this interest contributed to stimulating his urge to write *The Gilded Age*, just as
his later reading of medieval history helped stir thoughts that took
form in *A Connecticut Yankee*.

The Gilded Age, then, standing as it does at the entrance of the
road along which American social realism was to travel, almost solitary, as a guidepost in the midst of uncultivated fields, is a significant landmark in United States literary history. Furthermore,
since in the constant interplay of idea and act, of society and the
individual, of culture and historical reality, the value of a single
phenomenon is measurable in more than one dimension, *The Gilded
Age* is seen to be important in the development of the art of Mark

Twain as well. Just as this novel, far from being a mere accident of fortunate circumstance, has been shown to have had inexorable causes that converged in its formation, so too it in turn had an almost predictable effect not only upon American fiction in general but in particular upon its own principal author.

Writing from the vantage point of a different cultural background and a fresh critical method, the Soviet scholar Maurice Mendelson states that *The Gilded Age* "represents the most important stage in the development of Twain as a satirist."[163] This is indeed true, in spite of the shortcomings of the novel as a work of art. That it *is* true becomes abundantly clear when one views the work in perspective—that is, in its place along the line of Mark Twain's development and in comparison with his earlier and later writings. Up through *Roughing It* Twain's burlesque had remained burlesque. True, he had eliminated most of the early crudity and horseplay still found lingering as late as the Quaker City excursion letters to the *Alta California;*[164] Scotty Briggs's funeral has an artistry unimagined in "The Burial of Sir Abner Gilstrap." Yet the alterations in style between 1853 and 1872, the developing sureness in caricature, the refining and eliminating of dross are all within the same general sphere of the funny.

In *The Gilded Age,* however, a qualitative change has occurred. The burlesque, to be sure, is still present but is strictly limited to such passages as Sellers' descriptions of his most outlandish projects or the dialogue of the Washington Parvenus. But the book seldom descends below the level of genuine farce, the broadly comic humor of situation viewed from a ludicrous perspective, which was anticipated in such episodes as that of the Doctor and "Christopher Colombo" in *Innocents Abroad.*[165] Instead, the prevailing tone is one of high comedy, partly resulting from the introduction of pathos. The comic is felt from within as well as seen from without, and the precious element of human sympathy, without which true comedy cannot exist, is there in good measure.

Even this noticeable change in the form of humor employed, though a sudden ascent to a new, higher level, occurs within the province of the humorist rather than that of the satirist. The truly important change is one of attitude. The comic no longer stays on the surface, playing lightly over the eccentricities and foibles of persons seen at a distance, but is used as an instrument to dissect the relationships of human beings with whom both author and reader have an inalienable kinship. Further than that, the humor becomes a weapon in defense of the basically innocent against the malevolent, of the pitiably injudicious but constructive idealist against the destructive power of vested interest, of the middle-class frontiersman and townsman against a centrally controlled national political machine. Twain had always lashed out at sham and humbug; but when sham and humbug become the tools of corruption and all-pervading speculativeness, his anger sharpens ridicule into the cutting edge of satire. The writer of entertaining burlesque becomes a social critic, and his mode of expression undergoes a corresponding transformation.

It is unimportant that *The Gilded Age* reveals no overt "plot" of Wall Street against the common people—to the disappointment of some liberal critics. That the speculativeness and corruption are depicted as evils indulged in, for the most part, voluntarily by the individuals involved is only a reflection of life itself. Twain is concerned not with agitational propaganda but with realism; and in human society the substructure of social activity is seldom obvious to the active participants. Herein, in fact, lies the insidious force of ideology: the individual commonly adopts the tenets of his society willingly and under the illusion that he is doing so entirely of his own "free will." It is a matter of conditioned reflex on a mass scale. So it is that Senator Dilworthy acts in his own self-interest in a piously hypocritical and politically remunerative manner that is logical to him and that has led him to inculcate a sublime talent for self-preservation. Colonel Sellers, Washington Hawkins, Eli Bolton, Si Hawkins—the "good" characters—are victims because their human decency recoils at complete acceptance of the indecent values imposed by rampant capitalism in its hunt for profits. The victimization of Laura can be traced almost directly to the clash of social values that characteristically produces neurotic personalities—in her case compounded by the predicament of an insecure yet beautiful woman in a milieu rife with male supremacism.

In other words, Mark Twain in *The Gilded Age* turned for the first time to a serious—one might truthfully say sober—examination of his society, a path from which there was no permanent return. From it he proceeded to his monumental probing of the American conscience in the mind of Huck Finn, tackling what is even yet the nation's number one social problem, the Negro question. He went on, to the eloquent fable of working-class oppression in *The Prince and the Pauper,* to a further analysis of capitalist society in *A Connecticut Yankee,* with its astonishing prediction of war and fascism, and to a second approach to the Negro question in the heroic figure of Roxana in *Pudd'nhead Wilson.* On the one hand, he had self-indulgent lapses into nostalgia (*Tom Sawyer*) and into burlesque (*American Claimant*). On the other, he made digressions into polemic, during which he momentarily forsook art for pamphleteering against imperialism and colonialism. Nevertheless, with the writing of *The Gilded Age* the stage had been set for the immortal work of America's first and, in the minds of millions, foremost social novelist.

The Play *Colonel Sellers*

ON SEPTEMBER 16, 1874, nine months after publication of *The Gilded Age*, a dramatization of the novel opened at Park Theatre in New York.[1] It at first bore the title of the novel, but, probably because of the stellar performance of John T. Raymond in the leading role, the name was quickly changed to *Colonel Sellers*.[2] An immediate hit, it ran steadily for 119 nights, not closing until January 9, 1875.[3] One of the most successful plays of its decade,[4] it was revived numerous times—in August, 1875, for a six-week run and almost annually from 1876 to 1888; and in its first year it toured the country, playing in cities as widely separated as Boston, New Orleans, and Chicago.[5] *Colonel Sellers* is deserving of consideration not only because it enjoyed, in Clemens' own words, "a success seldom achieved in this country,"[6] but also because it casts light upon certain ambiguities in the novel and especially because countless thousands of spectators who had never read the novel knew the Colonel and his fellow characters from their stage rendition. Yet this production, which as drama most assuredly merits little attention, has been almost completely ignored by Twain critics and biographers, receiving, outside Paine, barely more than a sentence here and there.[7]

The facts of the play's origination are these: On April 22, 1874, the California Theatre in San Francisco announced that on that and the following evening Mr. John T. Raymond, "the Popular Comedian" then in the third week of his engagement, would present "Mr. G. B. Densmore's dramatization of Mark Twain's latest satire, in four acts and a prologue, entitled The Gilded Age!'"[8] Densmore was drama critic of the San Francisco *Golden Era*.[9] He had apparently in all innocence adapted *The Gilded Age* to the stage, little knowing that Clemens and Warner had foresightedly taken out dramatic copyright on the novel a year before, the book later proving to be a best-seller,[10] and that he had thereby legally committed an act of piracy. David Belasco, who was playing in San Francisco at the time, gives some interesting sidelights on the circumstances.

While that play was building Densmore talked it all over with me. As it was originally written it was in five long acts and had in it a curious medley of melodrama. . . . When the script was eventually read to him [Raymond], all the comment he made, with a few of those choice expletives which he knew so well how to choose, was that he hated all courtroom scenes, except those in "The Merchant of Venice" and in Boucicault's "The Heart of Midlothian." . . . It was in this frame of mind that he was finally persuaded to try "The Gilded Age." Of course, the play needed a lot of re-writing, and I don't believe anyone really thought it would be successful. It was put on as a try-out because the man was in such sore need of a vehicle, and, like so many other plays which are produced as makeshifts, it soared its way into instant popularity. . . .[11]

On April 30 Warner wrote Clemens, who was in Elmira:

I see by the San Francisco papers that The Gilded Age has been dramatized and was to be put on the stage, at once, of the California Theater. I think one Dinsmore [*sic*], Editor of a Sunday paper, dramatized it. The story is mainly that of Laura—leaving out the political parts that would create a row.

The transplanters don't seem to have considered it necessary to consult the authors. Probably don't know that we have a little copyright stowed away. Let us see if the thing comes to any thing, and if it is worth while to interfere.[12]

Meantime, Clemens' old Virginia City friend Joe Goodman, former editor of the *Territorial Enterprise,* wrote him concerning the performance.[13] Characteristically Clemens was unwilling to wait and see if the thing came to anything but immediately telegraphed, enjoining further performances.[14] On May 5 he wrote Warner,[15]

"I know Mr. D. mighty well and he shan't run any play on MY brains.—He is the chap who finished Bret Harte's story for him without Bret's asking it."[16] He told Warner that "a San Francisco friend" [Goodman?] had sent him a *Chronicle* in which it was stated that only his own portions of the novel were used. He therefore proposed to Warner that they each relinquish "dramatic ownership" of characters created by the other. Then, he continued, "I will buy this play of Densmore, re-write it if it is worth it—or burn it, and write one myself . . . ." He also asked Warner to forward to him a copy of their printed dramatic copyright page.[17]

Warner immediately agreed to this arrangement,[18] and Clemens entered into correspondence with Densmore and Raymond, meanwhile, according to Paine, starting on a version of his own.[19] Some confusion has existed as to how much use Clemens made of Densmore's version in his own.[20] The source of the confusion, which is more apparent than real, seems to have been an article in the New York *Sun* of November 2, 1874, implying that Clemens had made extensive but unacknowledged use of Densmore's material.[21] (It may be that the *Sun* wanted to "get" Clemens for his earlier attack on the Tweed Ring in "The Revised Catechism" and his continuance of the pillorying in *The Gilded Age*.)[22] Both Clemens and Raymond replied to the insinuation, Raymond in a letter to the editor of the *Sun*, which was published the following day, Clemens in a letter to the editor of the Hartford *Post*, which was apparently never sent. Raymond wrote that "not one line" of Densmore's dramatization was used in the Clemens play "except that which was taken bodily from the novel . . .";[23] Clemens, that he did "not think that there are now twenty sentences of Mr. Densmore's in the play."[24] Though Howells, writing after Clemens' death, said, "Clemens never pretended, to me at any rate, that he had the least hand in it," he was sufficiently vague about the whole incident to attribute Densmore's play to an "unknown dramatist," "some one in Utah."[25]

In his unpublished letter to the Hartford *Post* Clemens wrote, ". . . I used so much of his plot that I wrote and told him that I should pay him about as much more as I had already paid him in case the play proved a success. I shall keep my word. . . . Most of the *plot or skeleton* was furnished by Densmore. . . ."[26] He paid Densmore $200 for his script and another $200 after the play became a success.[27] Densmore thanked him in a letter of August 4 "for the very handsome manner" in which he had acted.[28] On the same day, Clemens was writing Densmore, apparently spoofing him about his inspiring certain newspaper stories that had implied plagiarism on Clemens' part. Distressed at the apparent accusation, Densmore replied on August 26 that he did not "in any way prompt or suggest a single notice" but on the contrary had let it be known that he was "thoroughly satisfied with the arrangements."

As you say the feature of the play is yours. I don't recollect that I originated anything for Col. Sellers to say unless it might be some commonplace to make connection between scenes. The character is distinctly yours and the arrangement of incidents became yours by purchase, . . .[29]

This letter of August 26 is of further interest in that it reveals Densmore's dissatisfaction with what he considered Raymond's somewhat haphazard way of sending Clemens sections of the script representing various states of cutting and revision. Such a circumstance might in part account for Clemens' assertion that he *"entirely re-wrote his* [Densmore's] *play three separate & distinct times,"*[30] especially as he had presumably begun work on his own before any of Densmore's script had arrived.[31]

When the play was finished, Clemens wrote Howells, "I don't think much of it, as a drama, but I suppose it will do to hang Col. Sellers on, & maybe even damn him. *He* will play tolerably well, in the hands of a good actor. . . ."[32] According to Henry Watterson, Clemens designed the part of Sellers for Edwin Booth.

I do not know what Edwin Booth thought of Sellers, or indeed, whether he so much as read the part which had been intended for him. That Booth and Sellers were in Mark Twain's mind conjointly tells its own and quite a different story.[33]

It is certain that he offered it to Lawrence Barrett, who in declining recommended Raymond for the role.[34] This reluctance to engage Raymond at once is significant considering Clemens' subsequent dissatisfaction with the comedian's interpretation of the Colonel, particularly as Raymond had already proved himself a success in the role[35] and had apparently approached Clemens independently to secure it.[36]

However, Raymond was engaged and rehearsals were begun. In mid-September Clemens, with his wife, made a ten-day visit to New York to buy carpets and furniture and see how the play was shaping up. He wrote Orion later:

> I staid on the stage 2 to 4 hours several days in succession showing them how I thought the speeches ought to be uttered. The consequence was, the play went right through without a hitch on the very first night. They are better actors than I am, but of course I wanted the play played *my* way unless my way was radically wrong.[37]

He was apprehensive about his début as playwright, as indeed he was about any new form of public exposure. Earlier in the month he had written his Edinburgh friend Dr. John Brown that he

> would about as soon spend a night in the Spanish Inquisition as sit there and be tortured with all the adverse criticisms I can contrive to imagine the audience is indulging in. But whether the play be successful or not, I hope I shall never feel obliged to see it performed a second time. . . .[38]

The Park was a new theater, which had first opened its doors only the preceding April; yet so successful was the first night of *The Gilded Age* that September 16 was thought of thenceforth as the theater's real opening.[39] Supporting Raymond was a well-seasoned cast including Gertrude Kellogg, Milnes Levick, Sol Smith the younger, Welsh Edwards, John Matthews, and others, who had been walking the boards of Wood's Museum, Booth's, Wallack's, Niblo's Gardens, and the Lyceum for a number of years.[40] Gertrude Kellogg, who had cut her acting teeth in Wilkie Collins' *Man and Wife* at Daly's Fifth Avenue three years before and had played Desdemona the preceding season,[41] made a triumph as Laura second only to Raymond's Sellers. According to the *Tribune* she "played the heroine with infinite skill and grace" and "deserved all the applause she got."[42] As a whole, the play, which it was conceded was "by no means a model drama,"[43] was praised as going "a great way to solve the problem of the possibility of the American drama, resting not on the piles driven into the mud and slime of French sensationalism, but founded on American society

From the Park Theatre Playbill, November, 1874
Program for *Colonel Sellers*

and manners. . . ."[44] Clemens, who avowedly "detested the theatre" yet had a strong desire to succeed as a playwright,[45] was pleasantly surprised by this encouragement. The weekend after the reviews appeared, he wrote Howells: "I believe it will go. The newspapers have been complimentary. It is simply a *setting* for the one character, Col. Sellers—as a *play* I guess it will not bear a critical assault in force."[46] Examination of the acting script of the play bears out Clemens' own estimate; it is, dramatically, very little more than a patched-up vehicle for the Colonel.[47] Yet the same qualities of authenticity and satirical insight that infused the novel and made it a best seller were transferred to the play. As a consequence, while critics unanimously deplored the failure of the play as drama, they readily conceded its significance as social satire and its consequently great popular success. The later evaluations are represented most articulately by Howells' long review in the June, 1875, *Atlantic*.[48] Though he had passed up *The Gilded Age* as a book for review,[49] he wrote with warmth and enthusiasm about "The Play from 'The Gilded Age,'" devoting the entire "Drama" section of the issue to it.

It is scarcely more than a sketch, a framework almost as naked as that which the Italians used to clothe on with their *commedia d'arte* [*sic*]; and it is as unlike good literature as many other excellent acting-plays. Yet any one who should judge it from the literary standpoint, and not with an artistic sense greater and more than literary, would misjudge it. The play is true, in its broad way, to American conditions, and is a fair and just satire upon our generally recognized social and political corruptions. . . .[50]

Raymond made his fame in the role of Colonel Sellers. Howells, for example, classed him with Sothern in *Lord Dundreary* and Joseph Jefferson in *Rip Van Winkle*.[51] Critics and audiences alike were captivated by his rendition of the part. William Winter, drama critic of the *New-York Tribune*,[52] wrote that in acting Sellers "Raymond did something that was new," that, "possessing the humor which is akin to pathos, he could cause the laugh that is close to the tear."[53] Brander Matthews, who it will be remembered had discussed the Sellers role with Raymond, considered that the dramatization "had the good luck to be bought by the one actor who, by temperament and training, was capable of doing it justice."[54]

Born John O'Brien, in Buffalo, New York, a year later than Clemens, Raymond appeared first under his own name at the National Theatre in Boston in 1853 or 1854. As this time was the heyday of the Know-Nothing party, however, he quickly decided to adopt a stage name not obviously Irish.[55] In the season of 1861 he was in Laura Keene's company as Asa Trenchard in *Our American Cousin*. He went to Paris with Sothern and toured the provinces and England. Before *Colonel Sellers* he had become best known as Dick Swiveller in the Dickens-inspired travesty *Little Nell and the Marchioness*, a part for which he was highly praised by the *New York Herald* reviewer.[56]

In spite of Raymond's phenomenal success, Clemens was always, as Watterson says, "disgusted by the Raymond portrayal."[57] Mrs. Fields noted in her diary: "Raymond, who is doing the 'Gilded Age,' is so hopelessly given 'to saving at the spigot and losing at the bung-hole' that he [Clemens] is evidently not over-satisfied nor does he count the acting everything it might be."[58] At the hundredth performance, Clemens made a curtain speech in which he barely concealed his irritation under a guise of banter:

Neither can I criticize and abuse the actors, for I don't want to. I could abuse the play, but I have better judgment (Laughter and applause), and I cannot praise these actors of mine right here in their hearing and before their faces, for that would make anybody with flesh and blood unhappy, and indeed, to praise them would be like praising the members of my own family, and glorifying the lady who does our washing (Laughter).[59]

In his *Autobiography*, written for posthumous publication, Clemens sums up his real opinion of Raymond, an opinion which, by the time the passage was written, had been further prejudiced by a complete break with the actor.[60]

The real Colonel Sellers was never on the stage. Only half of him was there. Raymond could not play the other half of him; it was above his level. That half was made up of qualities of which Raymond was wholly destitute. For Raymond was not a manly man, he was not an honorable man nor an honest man, he was empty and selfish and vulgar and ignorant and silly, and there was a vacancy in him where his heart should have been. . . .[61]

Alone among the critics, Howells seems to have sensed some of the lack of genuine pathos in Raymond's performance that disturbed Clemens—some of the tendency to play the role for the plentiful laughs in it, plus a few gratuitously added. Though he writes that the "warm, caressing, affectionate nature of the man charms you in Mr. Raymond's performance," he ends his review with the seemingly contradictory caution that "Mr. Raymond might trust the sympathy of his audience in showing all the tenderness of the man's heart. We are loath to believe that he is not himself equal to showing it."[62] And again, in the middle of the review, Howells says, in praising the performance:

Only one point we must except, and we suspect it is not the author's lapse; that is where the Colonel borrows ten dollars of Clay Hawkins, and, being asked not to mention the return of it, stops on his way out and with a glance of low cunning at the audience says, "Well, I won't!" This is thoroughly false and bad, and the stupid laugh it raises ought to make Mr. Raymond ashamed. . . .[63]

This bit of dialogue, which appears in both extant amanuensis manuscripts of the play,[64] seems to have been a bone of contention between Clemens and Raymond, for in congratulating Howells on the review Clemens adds, "Raymond put that 'Well I won't' in & I can't get him to take it out."[65] Another bit of dialogue that may have originated with Raymond occurs in Act V, Scene 1:

> *Hawkins*
> . . . Let's all go to work and stop chasing first one and then another Ignis Fatuus.
>   *Sellers.*
> (*Aside. reflectively.*) Agnes *who?*
>   ·   ·   ·   ·   ·   ·   ·   ·   ·   ·   ·   ·   ·   ·   ·
>   (EXIT [*sic*] ALL BUT SELLERS.)
>   *Sellers.*
> (*Musing.*) We chasing Agnes Fatuous—That's a careless way for a man to talk. I never even heard the woman's *name* before. (EXIT)[66]

This excruciatingly bad pun is equaled only by a drunk scene in Act IV, which, though admittedly comic, has no possible excuse in the story except as an opportunity for more of Raymond's high jinks. Colonel Sellers' eye-water formula proves to be intoxicating.

> *Col Sellers.*
> (*Hic!*) I've got the lacking ingredient! The eye-water's a success now.

I tried it on one eye, and I couldn't see for an hour. Shows how strong it
is. I'll lose that eye may be. But this eye-water'll cure *anything* now—
anything that a man's got. Take it internally, Externally, and eternally.
I'll raise the price— . . . .

. . . .
    Sellers.
(*Holding Lafayette's hand and beaming.*) Ah, Lafayette, my boy, I've
foun' (*Hic*)—I've foun' (*Hic!*) (Pauses—summons all his faculties—
gets on a good ready—) —I've foun' (*Hic!*)—(*breaks into benevolent
smile*)—How's Laura?[67]

In order to appreciate the complete inappropriateness of this scene
to the spirit of Sellers one has only to turn to an anecdote told by
Henry Watterson about Sellers' original, Clemens' Cousin Jim
Lampton:

> When a very young man living in a woodland cabin down in the
> "Penny'rile" region of Kentucky, with a wife and two, or three, babies,
> he was so carried away by an unexpected windfall that he lingered over
> long in the village, dispensing a royal hospitality; in point of fact, he
> "got on a spree." Two or three days passed before he regained possession
> of himself. When at last he reached his home, he found his wife ill in
> bed and the children nearly starved for want of food. He said never a
> word, but walked out of the cabin, tied himself to a tree, and was literally
> horse-whipping himself to death when the cries of the frightened family
> called the neighbors and he was cut loose and brought to reason. He never
> touched an intoxicating drop from that day to the day of his death.[68]

If Clemens himself wrote any of the foregoing material from the
play, he must be held responsible for encouraging much of the
superficiality in Raymond's interpretation for which he blamed the
actor. It may be that such passages are due to another of Clemens'
sporadic lapses into his earlier, crude burlesque.

Discontented though he was with John T. Raymond, Clemens
was jubilant at the financial success Raymond was bringing to the
play. Clemens sent along an agent, who kept a record of the
author's share of the box office and reported back to him every day
by postcard. Howells writes:

The postals used to come about dinner-time, and Clemens would read
them aloud to us in wild triumph. One hundred and fifty dollars—two

hundred dollars—three hundred dollars were the gay figures which they
bore, and which he flaunted in the air before he sat down at table, or rose
from it to brandish, and then, flinging his napkin into his chair, walked
up and down to exult in.[69]

The play brought Clemens a profit of some $70,000.[70]

The critical importance of the play today is in the light it casts
on the author's probable intentions in certain ambiguous passages
in the novel and the consequent strengthening of interpretations
that might otherwise remain purely inferential. Some use of *Colonel
Sellers* has already been made in the present volume for this purpose.[71] Two additional points should be mentioned, however. The
first concerns a somewhat greater outspokenness in the play about
railroad exploitation and the accompanying governmental graft.

> *Clay.*
> But Col. the whole appropriation is only $200,000.
>
> *Sellers.*
> True—but it breeds the railroad—the railroad breeds population—up goes
> your town-lots into the thousands. And there you are! See?
> . . . .
> *Sellers.*
> No man can know what a straight line is until the Engineers have been
> over it. I have talked with Jeff Thompson, the Division Engineer. Jeff
> understands the wants of Napoleon. Jeff says railroads ought to be run
> for the benefit of the company, and the general country round—not for
> the benefit of towns already built. Now how is the company to make
> money out of a railroad? Is it by going to old towns where the land is
> all owned by Tom, Dick, and Harry? *No* Sir! It's by going to new places
> where the land is owned by the company.
> . . . .
> *Clay.*
> And the government finds the million, while the Rail-road company owns
> the town?
> *Sellers.*
> Exactly, my dear boy, exactly. That's what Governments are for. It is
> only within the last few years that the science of government has been
> thoroughly understood. . . .[72]

The second point has to do with Clemens' and Warner's burlesque of contemporary sensation fiction. One of the stock themes

of the yellow-back novel was the titillating suggestion of incest. The possibilities for this theme in Laura's story, which remain unrealized in *The Gilded Age*, are made use of in *Colonel Sellers*. In the scene of Laura's trial (Act V, Scene 2) the defense counsel draws out of Sellers the fact that Laura's "mania" had for many years taken the form of anxiety to find her real father.

> *Sellers.*
> . . . There were some old letters that described him as being a man with one eye, and a lame leg. The sight of a stranger bearing those peculiar trade-marks, so to speak, always set her wild. She never could look at a one-eyed man without emotion! She never could contemplate a game leg without whirlwinds of joy. Let her flush a stranger with one eye, *and* a game leg, and she'd hound that cripple to the ends of the earth, but she'd bring him to cover, and make him show up. . . ."[73]

When Colonel Selby, Laura's false husband, makes his entrance (in Act III), he has a slight limp and uses a cane.

Besides the contracting and combining of episodes into the same scene that is a normal feature of all dramatizations, a consideration far too detailed for this epilogue, the principal changes between novel and play are the following. First of all, the adopted Clay Hawkins comes into his own. The entire first scene of Act I is a stilted love scene between Clay (age 23) and Laura (age 16), and Clay's love for the heroine, replacing that of the deleted Warner character Harry Brierly, leads to the verge of a duel with Colonel Selby in Act III, which is prevented only by the intervention of Sellers. Clay also replaces Washington Hawkins as a foil for Sellers in the Hawkeye scenes, enduring the raw turnip dinner and listening to Sellers' schemes with more of skepticism than awed gullibility. A new character, John Peterson, servant in the Dilworthy household, is introduced to give testimony as a surreptitious witness of Laura's shooting of Selby (presumably to add to the irony of the verdict), and a Prosecuting Attorney emerges as a voluble individual character. Senator Dilworthy, though referred to, never appears. And, as mentioned elsewhere in this volume,[74] the murder takes place on stage.

A few minor changes might also be mentioned. Washington Hawkins becomes Lafayette, the name of one of the Sellers children in the novel.[75] Squire Hawkins remains alive throughout the play and is the one who lets the Tennessee Land go for taxes in the last act. The humanity of Uncle Daniel is completely obscured by his conversion into a jimcrow character in the minstrel show tradition, who must needs have been played for laughs. He is endowed with a stammer, which is made the excuse for a low comedy bit by Colonel Sellers in his drunk scene about a man who cured himself of stammering by learning to whistle.[76]

Clemens' fascination with his character Colonel Sellers persisted intermittently for more than two decades, reaching one brief high point in a second, very bad play, *The American Claimant*, and culminating in a novel of mixed virtues bearing the same title.[77] The play, which during its several years of sporadic creation was called variously *The Steam Generator*, *Orme's Motor*, and *Colonel Sellers as a Scientist*, began as a collaboration with that other impossible playwright Howells in the form of a nebulous farce on Clemens' brother, the visionary Orion. Not much came of the effort, except to provide the two friends with hilarious recreation, until Clemens revived Sellers as the central character in place of Orion and introduced the theme of a paranoic American claimant to an English earldom.[78] Howells, with good sense, withdrew from the joint venture, but Clemens, with characteristic impulsiveness, went ahead on his own. Mulberry Sellers, as a visionary inventor, became exaggerated to such an extreme caricature that Raymond refused to play the role of what he considered a mere "lunatic."[79] The play was produced, however, for a few misbegotten performances in 1887, with A. P. Burbank, an ambitious elocutionist, in the lead.

In the novel *The American Claimant*, published in 1892, Clemens reworked the material of the play thoroughly,[80] placing emphasis on the claimant theme. In spite of the crudity of construction and the unfortunate deterioration of Sellers into a ridiculous travesty of himself, the novel draws a rather good contrast between the deluded aspirations of a frustrated American promoter to an aristocratic inheritance and the attempt of a born nobleman, heir to an earldom, to find a democratic way of life for himself among the American working class. The moderate success of this novel led Augustin Daly, ironically enough, to consider negotiating with Clemens for dramatization rights.[81] But Clemens had at last written Colonel Sellers out of his system and was no longer interested.

The entire account of Mark Twain's relationship with his character Colonel Sellers, from his earliest impressions of James Lampton up through the later reincarnations, which combined more family legends, another relative, by the name of Leathers, and the famous Tichborne case, is a story in itself and one well worth telling. But that is for another time.

Appendices

British Copyright

AT THE TIME that the first British edition of *The Gilded Age* was published, the statute by which British copyright was regulated was the Act of 1842 (5 and 6 Victoria, c. 45). This statute was not clear as to whether it gave protection "to every author who first published in the United Kingdom, wheresoever he might then be resident." In 1865 or 1868[1] occurred the famous test case of *Routledge* v. *Low*, L.R. 3, H.L. 100, concerning violation of the British copyright of the American author Maria Cummins, who had assigned the copyright of her novel *Haunted Hearts* to the London publisher Samson Low and Company and had then gone to Montreal to reside during its publication. Samson Low and Company duly registered both novel and assignment at Stationers' Hall and proceeded to publish the work in two volumes "at the monstrous price of sixteen shillings." Shortly afterward, George Routledge and Sons, "always thinking of the poor and needy," issued a one-volume edition at two shillings, whereupon Low filed a bill in Chancery. The unanimous decision of the court was that "an alien friend (like Miss Maria Cummins) who published in the United Kingdom whilst residing in a British colony is entitled to the benefit of English copyright."[2]

Apparently on the basis of this precedent, Clemens, Warner, and Harriet Beecher Stowe all followed the practice of "beating a path for Quebec" to be in residence there on the publication date of the volume they wished to register in the United Kingdom.[3] In anticipation of the issuance of *The Gilded Age*, indeed, Clemens and Warner drew up a formal document attesting to permanent residence in Canada.[4] And their contract with Routledge stipulated that for three days before and four days following the agreed-upon date of publication the authors were to reside "in some part of the Dominion of Canada or some other parts of the British Empire" and that immediately afterward they were to "make a solemn Declaration before some competent authority" that they had so resided during the seven days.[5] The affidavit of Canadian residence remained unsigned, however, and, as has been seen, Clemens took up extended residence in London instead.

Clemens' anxiety about British copyright of *The Gilded Age* was grounded on the fact that the book was to be published simultaneously in England and the United States, a circumstance that conceivably could obscure the priority of the copyright. The *Routledge* v. *Low* decision had "clearly affirmed the view" that *first* publication of a book must occur in the United Kingdom in order to assure British copyright.[6] This anxiety accounts for Clemens' frantic eleventh-hour precautions to insure exact timing of the two editions on opposite shores of the Atlantic Ocean.[7]

The "Fake" Title Page

THE DETECTIVE WORK of Denis Woodfield[1] has proved that copies of *The Gilded Age* containing a tipped-in "fake" title page were bound in Hartford under circumstances that suggest double-dealing on the part of Elisha Bliss and consequently indicate that Clemens' later cry of swindle may have had foundation in fact. The most significant characteristics of the "fake" title pages are the following: (1) Whereas the title pages of copies to be sold bear the local imprint of the distributing agent in combination with that of the American Publishing Company,[2] the fakes carry the imprint of the Company alone. (2) They are all dated 1873. (3) They were run from the setting of type from which the sample title page in the prospectus-dummies of the book was run; and this type had been set in a separate shop, for it had faces entirely different from those of the book's title page.

This internal evidence, which on first thought appears damaging, is at curious variance with other circumstances of the book's publication. For instance, so many copies of *Innocents Abroad* and *Roughing It* had been bootlegged that with *The Gilded Age* the American Publishing Company changed policy. "Instead of running the names of all their agents on the title page . . . The books were . . . made up for each wholesale agent with only his own name and that of the American Publishing Co. on them. This made it an easy matter to trace a guilty agent."[3] Furthermore, this first policy change may account for a second one. The title pages of *Innocents Abroad* and *Roughing It* had carried the statement,

"Issued by subscription only, and not for sale in the book-stores. Residents of any state desiring a copy should address the publishers, and an agent will call upon them." In *The Gilded Age* this was reduced to the simple phrase, "Sold by Subscription Only."

On the other hand, the elimination of the appeal to the potential buyer to address the publishers and the deletion of the phrase "not for sale in the book-stores" can be interpreted as subtly inviting bootlegging[4] in order to increase total sales or at least as leaving the door farther ajar for secret connivance on the part of Bliss. Reasoning along such lines, Jacob Blanck in a more recent treatment of the subject offers the conjecture that "the publishers may have violated their own injunction regarding sales to bookshops and by means of the variant title-page hoped to escape detection and at the same time throw suspicion on an agent."[5] The very small percentage of additional profit, however, that might have been squeezed out of a few hundred smuggled copies would hardly have seemed worth Bliss's effort in an edition running to tens of thousands and by no means would account for the large-scale swindling claimed by Clemens.

A simple yet logical explanation might be that the "fake" title pages were tipped into copies intended for reviewers and that when the publication date was changed to 1874, copies of the second (1874) issue were sent to reviewers instead and those containing the 1873 title page used to fill orders received directly at Hartford. It may have been less expensive to tip these extra leaves into a few score of an already printed first signature bearing the double imprint of the company and one of its agents than to make a special short run of the signature.

APPENDIX C

Date of the British Edition

AT THE TIME that *The Gilded Age* was published, British copyright could be secured only if a book was issued *first* in the United Kingdom.[1] As the novel was to be published simultaneously in the United States and England, it was important, therefore, that the American edition should not come out even one day before the British. The fact that proofsheets pulled in Hartford were being shipped to London for resetting constituted some measure of control. So anxious was Clemens, nevertheless, that simultaneous publication be assured that he wrote Elisha Bliss from London on July 16 asking him always to send duplicate sheets and casts of the pictures by successive steamers so that if one set were lost the British edition would not be held up. He adds: "Be sure to write on to Routledge and state as nearly as you can the exact day at which you can publish. Routledge will publish on that day or the day before. If you change the date of publication telegraph Routledge." On the same day he wrote Warner asking him to see that the plan for duplicates was carried out, adding: ". . . don't let a sheet be carelessly kept back for a week or two, scaring a body to death with the idea that it is lost; but have the sheets sent in their regular order faithfully. Don't wait for a quantity, but send it right along, signature by signature." Farther on he says, "if Routledge makes a mistake in the publishing day of Bliss it may cost us our copyright."[2]

An announcement by Routledge in the London *Times*, Tuesday, December 23, 1873,[3] states: "This day is Published, in 3 vols.,

cloth price £1 5s. 6d., The Gilded Age: a Novel. By Mark Twain
and Charles Warner." The announcement was repeated verbatim
the following day.[4] A previous announcement in the same newspaper on Thursday, December 18,[5] had said, "Will be ready at all
the libraries on the 20th inst.," a prediction that coincides with the
announcement in the December 20 issue of the *Athenaeum* (published every Saturday) that the novel was *"Now ready."*[6] The
Times announcement of Thursday, December 18, was repeated
verbatim on Friday, December 19, Saturday, December 20, and,
significantly, Monday, December 22. The following Saturday,
December 27, the *Athenaeum* included the novel in its "List of
New Books,"[7] and the *Publishers' Circular* listed it under "New
Works" published December 18-31 in the issue of December 31.[8]
(The more selective monthly *Bookseller* ignored it.) Obviously,
therefore, a literally simultaneous publication in the United States
and England was effected, and the issuance in the two countries
occurred according to plan, apparently within forty-eight hours.[9]

The foregoing facts correct the following misinformation in
Merle Johnson's *Bibliography*: "The English edition was listed in
the *Publishers' Circular* for June 16, 1874, several months after
American publication. It is described as three volumes, 1873-1874,
which possibly means that the three volumes were simultaneously
issued."[10] The implied publication date of June 16, 1874, though
having no relation with reality, has been accepted as final by later
investigators such as Robert M. Rodney.[11] The three-volume edition
was the first British edition, in crown octavo, published in December, 1873, as described above. The edition listed in the *Publishers'
Circular* for June 16, 1874, was a second, less expensive one in
duodecimo at twelve shillings and appeared under the heading
"New Works Published from June 1 to 15."[12] It is described in
Blanck as "Cloth, leather shelfback. Also, pictorial boards."[13]

APPENDIX D

The *Gilded Age* Manuscript

THE EXTANT PORTIONS of holograph manuscript of *The Gilded Age* of which I have knowledge are principally in ten separate institutional depositories: the Willard S. Morse Collection, Yale University Library, New Haven, Connecticut; the Henry E. Huntington Library, San Marino, California; the C. Waller Barrett Collection, Alderman Library, University of Virginia, Charlottesville; the Lilly Collection of Americana, Indiana University Library, Bloomington; the University of Pittsburgh Library; the Mark Twain Papers, University of California Library, Berkeley; the Mark Twain Library and Memorial, Hartford, Connecticut; the Henry W. and Albert A. Berg Collection, New York Public Library; the University of Wisconsin Library, Madison; and the Columbia branch library of the Missouri Historical Society. Of the ten the Morse Collection contains the greatest number of leaves, representing some 212 pages of final MS.[1] Next in size is the group in the Huntington Library, which comprises the complete chapters XXIII, XXXIII (II:II), XL (II:IX), XLVIII (II:XVII), LV (II:XXIV), and LVII (II:XXVI); chapters XXXVII (II:VI) and LX (II:XXIX), complete except for one page each; the Appendix; and three separate pages.[2] The Barrett Collection contains Chapter VII, complete except for three pages; 4/5 of chapter XXVIII; and thirteen separate pages. The Lilly Collection contains the complete Chapter XXXVI (II:V) plus one page from Chapter LVIII (II:XXVII).[3] The University of Pittsburgh Library contains Chapter IX complete. In the University of Wisconsin

Library are two of Clemens' and eleven of Warner's pages.[4] In the Mark Twain Papers are several discarded pages and unnumbered fragments by both Clemens and Warner and a two-page plot outline by Warner.[5] In the Mark Twain Library and Memorial (Clemens' Hartford residence) are seven Clemens and three Warner pages.[6] In the Berg Collection are three more Clemens pages and two of Warner's,[7] and at the Missouri Historical Society a page by each.[8]

Not only is the Morse Collection holding of *Gilded Age* manuscript the largest, but it also is the most revealing in its deletions, emendations, and alterations of diction. Its nucleus consists of four complete chapters (XXIV, XXVII, XXIX, XLIV [II:XIII]), two by Clemens and two by Warner, plus five separate pages.[9] It is a part of the large collection of Mark Twain works, manuscripts, letters, clippings, and criticism assembled by the late Willard Samuel Morse and presented to Yale University in 1942 by Walter Francis and Mary E. Dillingham Frear.[10] Since the Frear gift, accretions to the collection, chief of which (in *Gilded Age* material) is the Blum gift, have so far added 126 pages.[11]

Though only a little over 1/3 of the manuscript is contained in the combined holdings of the ten depositories—514 out of 1459 pages,[12] it is, fortunately, very representative of the total manuscript, extending from page 3 to page 1457. Besides the 12 complete chapters and the 3 nearly complete ones, there is 4/5 of Chapter XXVIII, over 2/3 of Chapter LIV (II:XXIII), nearly 1/2 of Chaper XXV, and about 2/5 of Chapter XLV (II:XIV). Of the 63 chapters of the novel, 48 are represented by from 1 to 32 pages, 31 of them by 4 or more pages. The 12 complete chapters constitute consecutive sequences of 61, 32, 23, 22, 20, 17, 15, and 7 pages, and there are besides consecutive sequences of 27 pages of Chapter XXVIII, 17 pages of Chapter VII, 15 pages of Chapter LX (II:XXIX) and 14 pages of Chapter LIV (II:XXIII); and 15 sequences of from 3 to 10 pages.[13]

Analyzed qualitatively the extant manuscript reveals three significant facts. The first fact that emerges is that Warner's later chapters (those after his initial twelve) were not assigned their "appropriate places" until the final collation; for Warner habitually numbered his pages afresh with each chapter, and his original folios remain on his pages, canceled, alongside the folios of the final collation. The second fact is that Clemens shifted portions of his own material once or twice in advance of the final collation, for the pages in some of his chapters carry an intermediate set of folios between the original set and the final sequence.[14] Clemens' episodic method lent itself to this kind of maneuvering, if indeed it did not actually contribute to it; Warner's greater sense of continuity kept him more steadily on a forward path of plot development. The third fact is that Clemens' claim that he wasted a far greater number of pages than Warner is completely borne out by the evidence.[15]

Both in a quantitative and in a qualitative analysis of the manuscript the sets of page folios are the magic key. Apparently the authors never sacrificed a scrap of written material that could in some way be salvaged. Many times, a half a leaf or less containing usable text is pasted onto a fresh sheet and the writing continued, the new, patched-up leaf being assigned a page number. Or conversely, the lower part of a leaf is pasted onto a fresh upper part when a revised opening of a passage or a new transition is called for. Consequently, the presence or absence of one folio in an otherwise unbroken sequence indicates the relative earliness or lateness of the material on a particular MS page.

Warner used violet ink, Clemens black. Warner's original folios (by chapter) are, therefore, also violet, and Clemens' original and intermediate folios (in sequences transcending chapter divisions) are black. But the folios of the final collation are violet and in Clemens' hand. Since Clemens' original and intermediate folios extended into three digits, he apparently borrowed Warner's ink for the ten-days' "revamping" in order to make the final collation perfectly clear by color contrast. The good sense of this is readily appreciated when one glances through the manuscript: at least two, often three, and sometimes even four folios appear on the same page.[16] Fortunately, the authors consistently added their new folios to the right of the canceled ones, so the sets of folios are in sequence according to their order from left to right.

Changes in chapter numbering reveal nothing conclusive regarding shifts of material. First pages are extant for only 23 out of the 63 chapters. The fact that all of these first pages show at least two sets of numbers becomes insignificant when it is realized that they represent only a consistent moving forward by one digit of all chapters from 5 to 50. (Apparently addition or division of material somewhere before the fifth chapter made this renumbering necessary.)

It is to be expected that further accretions of holograph manuscript subsequent to publication of the present volume will to some extent alter the foregoing statistical analysis.

Colonel Sellers' Railroad Map

THE IMPROVISED MAP of the railroad, which Colonel Sellers lays out on his dining table with eating utensils and toilet articles (Chap. XXVII), has to be visualized by today's reader of *The Gilded Age* from the details of the Colonel's monologue. In the original edition, however, an actual folding map was inserted at this point as an illustration. It is almost as funny as the Colonel's own description. The *Old and New* review considered it the "most ludicrous of all" the comical features of the book. "Who else [but Mark Twain] would have so contrived to mix up civil engineering and a schedule of the table and toilet furniture of a Western speculator, A.D. 1873? In a thousand years, this cut will have immense antiquarian value, like the paintings of utensils at Pompeii. . . ."[1]

Clemens had at first written only the briefest description for Sellers to speak, sketching in the map bit by bit between lines as he went along.[2] This interlinear map is drawn in pen and ink in Clemens' delightfully awkward, amateurish way. Then, evidently, the authors felt more should be done with the drawings and Clemens redrew them as one continuous illustration on a long sheet of paper.[3] But with the drawings eliminated from between the lines the text must have seemed somewhat bare and inadequate, for at this point in the manuscript occurs an insert in Warner's hand filling out the verbal description exactly as it is printed.[4] Considering that in later editions the tipped-in folding map (an expensive item to manufacture) was dropped, it is fortunate that Warner, probably in close consultation with Clemens, wrote out

Sellers' running commentary in full. It is so well done that the reader can relish the fun in the episode without benefit of illustration.

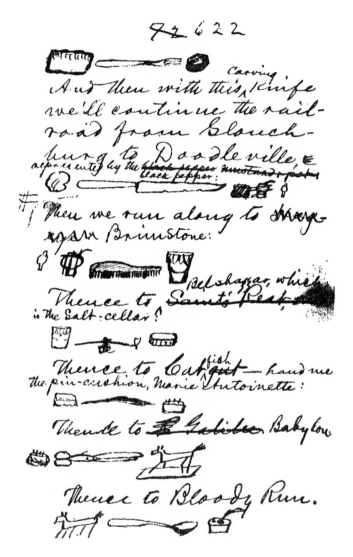

Clemens' Interlinear "Map"

The Chapter Mottoes

AS ONE LEAFS through *The Gilded Age,* the first thing that attracts attention, after the title page, is a two-line quotation in large Chinese characters prominently displayed on the next right-hand page, where normally the half-title would appear. Furthermore, at the head of each chapter, directly below the chapter number and title, appears a quotation, a different one for each of the sixty-three chapters, sometimes in English, Middle English, Old English, or one of the readily recognized languages, such as French, German, Spanish, Italian, Latin, and Greek, but more often than not in a language entirely unknown to most readers. This unusual feature of the book did not escape the notice of reviewers. In his *Old and New* review Fred Perkins, who may well have been in on the joke,[1] called special attention to the "grotesque parody on the motto business":

We strongly suspect that the writers may have purchased an assorted lot of spare mottoes from Mr. Trumbull, Prof. Whitney, or some of the other Connecticut linguists. There used to be, in "Horne's Introduction," or some such book, a set of specimens of the type used in the various translations of the Bible, which we thought at first had been transcribed; but we missed the Burmese passage. But Old French, Anglo-Saxon, Ethiopic, Erse, Syriac, ancient Mexican, Basque, Russian, Armenian, Chinese, Sanscrit, and in particular Chinook and Kanaka (which Mr. Clemens could furnish), Natick Indian, and other kindred language (which Mr. Trumbull could furnish), and even English, occur to us. Still, if Messrs. Clemens and Warner, or either of them, do habitually study in these and all the other languages of their mottoes, we beg to apologize, and wish them joy.[2]

According to Paine, the purpose of the quotations was "to excite interest and possibly to amuse the reader,"[3] but it seems obvious that the real intent was to add to the burlesque of contemporary literary fashion by a "parody on the motto business," then popular and overworked. There seems also to have been a secondary purpose, that of providing a lightly satiric running commentary on the plot. In any event, the purpose largely miscarried because the authors, evidently wanting to indulge in a private joke shared only among the initiated few or else hoping to elicit inquiries from readers, provided no translations. Not until the novel was republished in the 1899 "authorized Uniform Edition" of *The Writings of Mark Twain* was this oversight rectified, and by that time the trick had lost much of its original verve. At a later date, Clemens himself tacitly admitted, with characteristic chagrin, that the original idea had been a mistake. In *A Tramp Abroad*, as Hamlin Hill has pointed out, he writes, "A man who writes a book for the general public to read is not justified in disfiguring his pages with untranslated foreign expressions. It . . . is a very frank and impudent way of saying, 'Get the translation [*sic*] made yourself if you want them, this book is not written for the ignorant classes.' "[4]

The many-tongued quotations were "selected for their appropriateness"[5] by a Hartford neighbor, J. Hammond Trumbull, "a marvel of linguistic lore,"[6] who according to Paine was "the most learned man that ever lived in Hartford" and who according to Clemens could swear in twenty-seven languages.[7] Trumbull, one of the founders of the Monday Evening Club, which figures so frequently in Twain biography, was an eminent historian, bibliographer, philologist, and authority on Indian cultures,[8] and he prepared the texts in black ink for reproduction with painstaking care and impeccable accuracy.[9] He also provided the translations, mostly his own, which were not used until 1899.[10]

To guide Trumbull in his work, Warner furnished him with two pages of character descriptions and Clemens with a twenty-page synopsis of the novel.[11] These notes are presented for the first time in this appendix. A comparison of the contents of each chapter, as outlined by Clemens, with the resultant motto will go far toward explaining the apparent want of good judgment in the choice of material to be emblematized in certain chapters. Trumbull evidently followed Clemens' hasty outline, not the novel itself. Since Clemens frequently outlined surface plot rather than meaningful content, Trumbull can hardly be held entirely responsible for not always realizing the full possibilities of a given chapter. It must be conceded, however, that within the limitations of the outline his selection was very astute, particularly in view of the difficulty of finding adequate quotable lines from the less extensive esoteric literatures.

Character descriptions by Warner:

Col. Eschol Sellers is a gentleman of kindly nature, whose imagination runs away with him, and makes him a conspicuous example of an American visionary, who has the power of illuminating his present poverty with glorious expectations. His untruthfulness is that of the imagination and not of the heart.

Washington Hawkins is an inventive, inefficient, loose-jointed [?] fellow, who lives always in the expectation of a great fortune in the Tennessee Lands left by his father.

Abner Dillworthy [sic] is a smooth Senator, professing piety and all virtues, and deep in all subsidy and other schemes, whose final effort to buy his re-election is exposed.

Laura Hawkins. A lovely girl, beautiful woman somewhat accomplished by reading, betrayed by Col. Selby, becomes an experimenter on men's hearts, a lobbyist and finally kills Selby, and is tried for the murder and acquitted.

Harry Brierly is an accomplished young good-for-nothing, generous, insincere and full of large projects.

Philip Sterling. Fine young fellow, truthful, plucky—the average young American of good breeding and good habits.

Ruth Bolton. Quaker girl. Quiet, determined, spirited. A student of medicine. Finally marries Philip.

Synopsis outline by Clemens:

Chap. 1. Scene in Obedstown, East Tennessee. Squire Hawkins purchases 75,000 acres wild land as a future fortune for his children. Starts with his family for Missouri.

Chap. 2. Funeral of a poor woman. Adoption of her son Clay by the Hawkinses.

Chap. 3. Banks of the Mississippi. Night spectacle of first steamboat. Prayer of old negro, Uncle Dan'l, in behalf of the children.

Chap. 4. Journey on Mississippi boat. (Boreas.) Narrative of boat-race. Explosion of the Amaranth.

Chap. 5. Result of explosion, the adoption of Laura Van Brunt, a child found, by Hawkinses. Arrival at Murphysburg, Mo., & introduction of Col. Eschol Sellers & family. Ups & downs of Hawkins & Sellers.

Chap. 6. Skip 10 years. Laura pictured at 12. Poverty. Hawkins refuses large offer for Tenn. Land. Clay arrives with his earnings & helps them out.

Chap. 7. Washington Hawkins goes to Sellers at Hawkeye. Scene of candle-warmed stove & remarkable clock for continuous striking.
/8. Supper. Sellers unfolds Corn, Pork, Banking & Eye-water schemes. Gets Washington a situation as clerk in Gen. Boswell's real estate office.

Chap. 9. Washington H. meets & loves Louise Boswell. Called home— death of his father—who dies assuring his children they have a fortune in the Tennessee Land.

Chap. 10. Maj. Lackland dies. Laura finds letters among Judge Hawkins's papers which reveal that he was not her father.—Effect of gossip of the village upon her.

Chap. 11. Washington dines with Sellers on turnips & water. Plenty high talk, though. The plague preventive.

Chap. 12. Introduction of Philip Sterling & Harry Brierly, preparing to go to Missouri in a railroad operation.

Chap. 13. Arrival of S. & B. in St Louis & meeting with Sellers.

Chap. 14. Introduction of Ruth Bolton, Philip's sweetheart, & her family, in Philadelphia, & the firm of Pennibacker, Bigler & Small, railway specu- lators.

Chap. 15. Ruth attends medical college. Night scene in dissecting room.

Chap. 16. Philip & Harry go inland as engineers on the Salt Lick Pacific Extension, with Jeff Thompson. Goose Run (Columbus River), Stone's Landing (Napoleon). Scheme of Brierly & Sellers to improve the naviga- tion & build up the town.

Chap. 17. Continuation of railway. Arrival of Survey at Stone's Land- ing. Description of the town & river. Sellers & Harry plan the town on paper & propose appropriation from Congress to improve navigation.

Chap. 17½[12] 18. Interval of several years & mock marriage of Laura Hawkins with Col. Selby.

Chap. 18. 19. Brierly at Hawkeye. His flirtation with Laura. (Chap. 19[20].) Visit of Senator Dilworthy to Hawkeye. Takes an interest in the Hawkins family & the navigation scheme.—Reception & speech of Dil.

Chap. 21. Ruth attends school at Falkill. Introduction of Alice Montague.

Chap. 22. Visit of Philip & Harry to Fallkill.

Chap. 23. Philip goes to New York & Harry to Washington—the latter on Columbus River Slack-Water Navigation scheme.

Chap. 23. Arrival of Washington Hawkins in Washington. [24] Description of the city. Dilworthy. Progress of appropriation scheme.

Chap. 25. Appropriation succeeds. Sellers & Harry go to work at Napoleon. No funds. Break up in a riot. Sellers quells it.

Chap. 26. Ruth returns home. Increasing embarrassment of Mr. Bolton's business affairs. Ruth resumes medical studies.

Chap. 27. Sellers explains, maps out & illustrates his Salt Lick railway to his wife.

Chap. 28. Harry's interview with President of the Navigation Co in N.Y., & learns how Appropriation bills are got through & what becomes of the money. Stone's Landing "goes up."

Chap. 29. Philip goes to Ilium Pa., to examine Bolton's wild coal lands.— Thrashes a railway conductor.

Chap. 30. Laura & Sellers go to Washington upon Dilworthy's invitation.

Chap. 31. In Philadelphia Philip breaks his arm. Progress of his love affair. Harry goes to Washington.

Chap. 32. Laura's brilliant success in Washington Society.

Chap. 33. Laura visited by the 3 Aristocracies. Mrs. Gen. Fulke-Fulkerson & daughter. Hon. Mrs. Oliver Higgins; Hon. Mrs. Patrique Oreillé & Bridget; Mrs. Peter Gashly, Miss Gashly, Miss Emmeline Gashly. History of the Oreillé & the other families; Conversation on pet dogs.

Chap. 34. Increase of Laura's fashionable reputation. Whispers of Tenn. Land scheme & of her being a lobbyist. Washington's advent as a bright light in society.

Chap. 35. Laura reports progress to Dilworthy on Land Bill. Senator Balloon. Talk of Sellers & Hicks on politics.

Chap. 36. Laura's talk with bookstore clerk.

Chap. 37. Laura's interview with Congressman Buckstone. Love passage.

Chap. 38. Laura discovers Col. Selby at a reception.

Chap. 39. Her interview with Selby. Falls in love with him again. Wants him to divorce or desert his wife.

Chap. 40. Col. Sellers's expansion in the congenial air of Washington. Progress of the lobby schemes.

Chap. 41. Harry's jealousy of Laura. Wants Philip to come on. Phil's convalescence & progress in love affair. Goes to Washington.

Chap. 42. Buckstone & Laura conspire against Congressman Trollop. The interview. Laura produces the missing fragment of Trollop's speech in her own handwriting & he agrees to vote & work if she will be silent. She reports results to Dilworthy.

Chap. 43. Notice given of the Knobs Industrial University of East Tennessee bill. Excitement about it. All newspapers clamor against it.

Chap. 44. Philip interviews Laura. Tries to make her unfetter Harry.

Chap. 45. Exciting night session in the House. University Bill crowded through.

Chap. 46. Laura's flight with Brierly in pursuit of Col. Selby. Philip follows. Laura murders Selby. Arrest of Laura & Harry. Selby's dying deposition. Newspaper reports of the murder.

Chap. 47. Phil. gets Harry out of prison. Editorial comments on the murder. Sellers & Washington Hawkins visit Laura. Mrs. Nancy Hawkins comes also. Laura indicted. Phil goes to Ilium; takes Harry along.

Chap. 48. Bolton's increased embarrassment through Pennibacker, Bigler & Small. Love passage. Philip still working at the coal mine.

Chap. 49. Strikes coal! Informs the Boltons, who feel a temporary relief. Turns out to be no vein—only a worthless seam. Failure of Mr. Bolton. Philip buys the Ilium property at auction.

Chap. 50. Resumé of the bad fix into which everybody & everything connected with this history has got. Phil. visits Squire Montague, who helps him with a loan. Love passage with Ruth in Philadel—after which, Phil. returns to the mine.

Chap. 51. Sellers & Washington discuss Congressional "preliminaries." Sellers hurt by a political suggestion of Washington's.

Chap. 52. Washington develops as a Moral Ally of Dilworthy & forsakes the butterfly life of fashion.

Chap. 53. Dilworthy goes west to the Happy-Land-of-Canaan to look after re-election, at Saint's Rest. Makes Sunday School speech at Cattleville. Meets Noble.

Chap. 54. Laura's trial for murder. Leather-headed jury empaneled. Judge O'Shaunnessy.

Chap. 55. Examination of witnesses for prosecution. Speech of Dist. Atty. McFlynn. Opening speech of Mr. Braham for defence. Wrangle about Insanity plea.

Chap. 56. Mrs. Hawkins & Washington testify—also Sellers. While lawyers & Judge squabble over a technicality, Col. Sellers gets in a word to the jury. Closing speeches, charge, & jury retire.

Chap. 57. Sellers & Washington at the capital, awaiting news of the trial & Dilworthy's election. Telegrams arriving every moment. Noble betrays Dilworthy—election lost. The news reaches the Senate while 3d reading of University bill is up—& so *that* is killed. Laura acquitted. (Enough fun for *one* afternoon.)

Chap. 58. Bringing in of the verdict & kissing of Braham. Laura leaves court room but is *not* taken to the State Hospital for Criminal Lunatics. Interview of lecture agent with Laura. Philip sticks to his mine.—Parting of Laura & mother.

Chap. 59. U.S. Senate tries Noble for trying to take a bribe from Dilworthy. Scene & Evidence before Committee. Speeches on Committee's report. No action. Dilworthy approved by his own Conscience & constituents. Ovation tendered. Last vote is for salary steal.

Chap. 60. Laura attempts to lecture. Assailed by mob. Her death.

Chap. 61. Clay Hawkins returns. Washington tears up tax bill & refuses to chase the Tennessee Land longer. Will go home, marry Louise & start life anew. So will Sellers—he means to tackle the law & become Chief Justice U.S. Talk about the hair trunk. They leave for Hawkeye.

Chap. 62. Phil down to his last cent. The miners put in a parting blast for him. He finally mines alone. "If he could only strike that one infallible sign!" Puts in his last blast & resolves to quit mining forever. Don't even go into tunnel to see what the blast accomplished. Sits down outside. Throws coat on ground. By & bye picks it up—finds it wet! So he has struck the infallible sign—running water. Develops a great coal mine. Telegram stating Ruth's dangerous illness.

Chap. 63. Phil flies to Philadelphia, nurses Ruth back to life—the Bolton fortunes come up. General blissful ending.

Notes

Notes

THE FOLLOWING abbreviations of basic sources have been used throughout:

MANUSCRIPT COLLECTIONS

HEH: Henry E. Huntington Library, San Marino, California.
Lilly: Lilly Collection of Americana, Indiana University Library, Bloomington.
MTP: Mark Twain Papers, University of California Library, Berkeley.
Morse: Willard S. Morse Collection, Yale University Library, New Haven, Connecticut.

PUBLISHED WORKS

Autobiography: *Mark Twain's Autobiography*, ed. Albert Bigelow Paine (2 vols.; New York: Harper & Bros., 1925).

Autobiography (Neider ed.): *The Autobiography of Mark Twain*, ed. Charles Neider (New York: Harper & Bros., 1959).

Fairbanks Letters: *Mark Twain to Mrs. Fairbanks*, ed. Dixon Wecter (San Marino, Calif.: Huntington Library, 1949).

Letters: *Mark Twain's Letters*, ed. Albert Bigelow Paine (2 vols.; New York: Harper & Bros., 1917).

Love Letters: *The Love Letters of Mark Twain*, ed. Dixon Wecter (New York: Harper & Bros., 1949).

MT, Business Man: *Mark Twain, Business Man*, ed. Samuel Charles Webster (Boston: Little, Brown & Co., 1946).

Mr. Brown: *Mark Twain's Travels with Mr. Brown*, ed. Franklin Walker and G. Ezra Dane (New York: Alfred A. Knopf, 1940).

Muscatine Letters: *Mark Twain's Letters in the Muscatine Journal*, ed. Edgar M. Branch (Chicago: Mark Twain Association of America, 1942).

Speeches: *Mark Twain's Speeches*, ed. Albert Bigelow Paine (New York: Harper & Bros., 1923).

Twain-Howells: *Mark Twain-Howells Letters*, ed. Henry Nash Smith and William M. Gibson (Cambridge: Harvard University Press, 1960).

Writings: *The Writings of Mark Twain* (Author's National Edition; New York: Harper & Bros., 1907-1918).

CHAPTER I

1. Letter from Mark Twain to the editor of the *Daily Graphic*, in Merle Johnson, *A Bibliography of the Works of Mark Twain* (rev. ed.; New York: Harper & Bros., 1935), pp. 20-22; cf. *Letters*, I, 205.

2. DeLancey Ferguson, *Mark Twain: Man and Legend* (Indianapolis: Bobbs-Merrill, 1943), pp. 171-72. Clemens had registered *Roughing It* in the United Kingdom through the English publisher Routledge, a precaution that succeeded in discouraging the notorious London pirate John Camden Hotten from reprinting it as he had *The Innocents Abroad*, though the copyright did not meet the requirements of British law.

3. See letter from Mrs. Clemens from London [September or October] 1873, cited by Albert Bigelow Paine, *Mark Twain: A Biography* (4 vols.; New York: Harper & Bros., 1912), II, 489: "'. . . if he [Clemens] goes home before the book is published here he will lose his copyright.'" (For a discussion of the British copyright of *The Gilded Age* see Appendix A.)

4. Twain's letter to the *Daily Graphic* said, "It will be published early in the fall . . ." (Johnson, *op. cit.*, p. 22). In a letter to his friend Mrs. Fairbanks on April 16, Clemens said, "The book will issue in the end of summer" (*Fairbanks Letters*, p. 171). The *New-York Tribune* said "about the end of the Summer" (April 19, p. 6, col. 6).

Reporting cancellation of Mark Twain's scheduled Belfast lecture prior to his departure for the United States, the Belfast *Northern Whig*, January [8?, 1874], said: "His visit to England, we may mention, was not made with the object of giving lectures, but to secure, by personal residence, the copyright of a new novel, 'The Gilded Age,' which has just been issued in London" (clipping dated Thursday, January [missing] in MTP). Clemens sailed for home on January 13 (Paine, *op. cit.*, II, 500) (but cf. letter from Mrs. George ["Lilly"] Warner, Charles Dudley Warner's sister-in-law, to her husband, January 8, in MTP: "Mr. Clemens sails for home on the 17th").

5. Paine, *op. cit.*, II, 489. In a letter to the publisher from Edinburgh, July 27, Clemens asks: "Shall I look for Gilded Age sheets pretty soon?" (Yale University Library; typescript in MTP). The delay is confirmed in a letter from Clemens the same day to the Philadelphia lecture agent T. B. Pugh: "I have got to remain in London till the 25th of October to see my book through the English press. As this is business & can't be avoided, I thought I had . . . better let you know" (Morse; typescript in MTP); cf. *Chicago Tribune*, October 12, p. 10: "'The Gilded Age' . . . will probably be ready at the end of October or early in November." There is, besides, internal evidence that fall publication had originally been planned, for the first edition had two issues, the first with a publication date of 1873, the second with 1874, indicating a sudden postdating to accommodate delayed publication. (See Jacob Blanck, "The Gilded Age: A Collation," *Publisher's Weekly*, CXXXVIII (July 20, 1940), 187.

The contract with the publisher, the American Publishing Company, was flexible on this score: "The party of the second part agrees to publish said book as soon as practicable for them to do so, commencing upon the work with out [*sic*] unnecessary delay" (copy of contract in MTP, signed by Clemens, Warner, and Elisha Bliss, Jr. [for the Company], and dated May 8, 1873.)

6. Paine, *op. cit.*, II, 489, Mrs. Clemens' letter. The lectures had been promised the year before: "Mark Twain writes to a London paper as follows: 'Sir—With your kind permission, I desire to say to those societies in London and other cities of Great Britain under whose auspices I have partly promised to lecture, that I am called home by a cable telegram. I shall spend, with my family, the greatest part of next year here, and may be able to lecture a month during the autumn upon such scientific topics as I know least about, and may consequently feel less trammeled in dilating upon'" (undated clipping in Clemens' scrapbook for 1872-73 in MTP).

7. Paine, *op. cit.*, II, 490.

8. *Love Letters*, p. 364.

9. Paine, *op. cit.*, II, 500. Copyright deposit copies were received at the Library of Congress on January 6, 1874 (Blanck, *op. cit.*, p. 187).

10. In the clippings of headlines from the newspaper of April 16 which Mark Twain had incorporated into his *Daily Graphic* letter the next day the fifth and sixth

items are "WALL STREET PANICKY" and "TWO FAILURES, AND MONEY AT 150 PER CENT" (Johnson, *op. cit.*, p. 21).

11. For the financial crisis of 1873 see Clement Juglar, *A Brief History of Panics and Their Periodical Occurrence in the United States* (4th ed.; New York: G. P. Putnam's Sons, 1916), pp. 93-101; H. M. Hyndman, *Commercial Crises of the Nineteenth Century* (New York: Charles Scribner's Sons, 1902), pp. 99-127.

12. Paine, *op. cit.*, II, 500. The three printings, or impressions, of the first edition are not to be confused with the two, differently dated issues of this edition. It is possible that the second issue (1874) coincided with the second printing, Bliss having by then realized that distribution to western parts of the United States would extend well into the new year. Alma Borth Martin (*A Vocabulary Study of the "Gilded Age"* [Webster Groves, Mo.: Mark Twain Society, 1930], p. 15) is inaccurate in speaking of "the real first edition of 1873" and "the second edition of 1873" in referring to intermediate copies collated from different states of the same edition. See Blanck, *op. cit.*, p. 188.

13. The royalty to be divided as of March 1 was $12,833.95 on slightly over 35,000 copies ("Statement of Sales of Gilded Age . . ." from American Publishing Company to Chas. D. Warner, March 12, 1874, in Warner Papers [Watkinson Library, Trinity College, Hartford, Conn.]).

14. *Letters,* I, 215. "You are wonderful buyers, you Americans," Brown replied. "40,000 in two months & £13,000 of plunder" (letter dated Edinburgh, March 18, 1874, MTP).

15. Out of a total United States population of a little over 40,000,000 the unemployed were estimated at 3,000,000, and industrial and commercial stagnation prevailed in both the East and the West. (Hyndman, *op. cit.*, pp. 116-18.)

16. Hamlin Hill, "Mark Twain's Quarrels with Elisha Bliss," *American Literature,* XXXIII (January, 1962), 455; cf. Philip S. Foner, *Mark Twain: Social Critic* (New York: International Publishers, 1958), p. 80.

17. *Golden Multitudes: The Story of Best Sellers in the United States* (New York: Macmillan Co., 1947), p. 156.

18. Herbert Hungerford, *How Publishers Win* (Washington, D.C.: Ransdell, 1931), p. 281. Writing after the turn of the century, Robert Sterling Yard (*The Publisher* [Boston: Houghton Mifflin Co., 1913], p. 98) states: ". . . in these amazing days the familiar crudities of the old subscription business are to be witnessed only in the back waters of the swift current of universal cultivation."

"An advance salesman's dummy, or prospectus, consists of a selection of representative pages from the book offered for sale, bound in a sample binding. It usually contains frontispiece, title-page, a group of well-illustrated pages, and, on the inner back cover, specimen spines of the different bindings available. Also, blank pages were bound into the back of the prospectus for the agent's [canvasser's?] convenience in taking down the names, addresses, and specifications of copies ordered" (Denis Woodfield, "The 'Fake' Title-page of 'The Gilded Age': A Solution," *Papers of the Bibliographical Society of America,* L [3rd Quar., 1956], 295).

19. Hellmut Lehmann-Haupt, *The Book in America: A History of the Making, the Selling, and the Collecting of Books in the United States* (New York: R. R. Bowker Co., 1939), p. 202. According to Donald Sheehan (*This Was Publishing* [Bloomington: Indiana University Press, 1952], p. 152), Frank Compton's assertion that "probably ninety per cent of the book buyers of that time never entered a bookstore" cannot be proven statistically. (See F[rank] E. Compton, *Subscription Books* [New York: New York Public Library, 1939], p. 36.)

20. Lehmann-Haupt, *op. cit.*, p. 201.

21. Downing Palmer O'Harra, "Subscription Books and Their Publishers," *Publishers' Weekly,* CXV (May 18, 1929), 2346. "The publishers had no control over the sales methods after the books left the shop. If unfair methods were reported, the pub-

lisher would refer the complainant to the general-agent, who could do as he thought best" (*ibid.*, CXV [May 11, 1929], 2253). For an interesting firsthand account of such methods see *Facts* by a Woman (Oakland, Calif.: Pacific Press Publishing House, 1881), pp. 150-54 *et passim.* For their effect upon the problem of collating early editions of *The Gilded Age* see Woodfield, *op. cit.*, pp. 292-96; Frank C. Willson, "That *Gilded Age* Again: An Attempt to Unmuddle the Mystery of the Fifty-Seven Variants," *Papers of the Bibliographical Society of America*, XXXVII (2nd Quar. 1943), 141-56; and Blanck, *op. cit.*, p. 188. Cf. Johnson, *op. cit.*, p. 154. (For evidence of the bootlegging of *The Gilded Age* see Appendix B.)

22. O'Harra, *op. cit.*, p. 2346; Lehmann-Haupt, *op. cit.*, p. 202. According to Allan Nevins (*The Emergence of Modern America, 1866-1878* [New York: Macmillan Co., 1928], pp. 237-38), "even the old-established publishers, in order to reach the public in great areas bare of bookstores, used the subscription plan." Appleton, for example, had William Cullen Bryant edit *Picturesque America*, of which nearly a million sets were sold; Ford & Co. sold 80,000 copies of Horace Greeley's autobiography and Bryant's *Library of Poetry and Song*.

23. Lehmann-Haupt, *op. cit.*, p. 201.

24. O'Harra, *op. cit.*, p. 2346. Cf. Johnson, *op. cit.*, p. 154.

25. In writing of this publishing project Henry Seidel Canby characterizes its use of subscription bookselling as "audacious" (*Turn West, Turn East: Mark Twain and Henry James* [Boston: Houghton Mifflin Co., 1951], p. 188). The term seems unwarranted in view of the development of subscription publishing at the time.

Historians of bookselling and publishing almost invariably mention Mark Twain as one of the authors who themselves sold books in their youth. There is no evidence, however, that Clemens ever canvassed for subscription books as did some other authors. His single reference to his youthful job as a "bookseller's clerk" (in *Roughing It*) obviously denotes work in a bookstore, which may have been Jeff Jerman's bookshop, less than a block away from the Clemens home in Hannibal (*Roughing It*, II, 16, in *Writings*; Dixon Wecter, *Sam Clemens of Hannibal* [Boston: Houghton Mifflin Co., 1952], pp. 131, 208-9).

26. *Letters*, I, 402.

27. Mrs. J. W. Likins, *Six Years Experience as a Book Agent in California* (San Francisco: Women's Union Book and Job Printing Office, 1874), pp. 108, 128, 130. Subscription books often provoked indignant pronouncements such as the following: "The ordinary subscription book is manifestly made to catch the eye of the ignorant, who can be forced to buy it by means of the volubility, chicanery, and persistence of an agent interested, not in books in general, but in one book" (*Book News*, III [May, 1885], 209, quoted by Durant da Ponte, "American Periodical Criticism of Mark Twain, 1869-1917" [Ph.D. dissertation, University of Maryland, 1953], p. 15).

28. *Literature and Life* (New York: Harper & Bros., 1902), p. 15.

29. "The Gilded Age," *Old and New*, IX (March, 1874), 386.

30. Typescript in MTP.

31. Letter dated July 20, 1874, Warner Papers.

32. Letter dated July 31, 1874, MTP.

33. Edwin Valentine Mitchell, *Morocco Bound: Adrift Among Books* (New York: Farrar & Rinehart, 1929), p. 47; O'Harra, *op. cit.*, p. 2254.

34. O'Harra, *op. cit.*, p. 2254.

35. Kenneth R. Andrews, *Nook Farm, Mark Twain's Hartford Circle* (Cambridge: Harvard University Press, 1950), pp. 18-20.

36. O'Harra, *op. cit.*, p. 2345; *Encyclopedia of Connecticut Biography*, V (Boston, 1917), 71-72. See also Hamlin Hill, *Mark Twain and Elisha Bliss* (Columbia: University of Missouri Press, 1964), pp. 11-12.

37. Mott, *Golden Multitudes*, p. 156. Up to the year 1871, 100,000 copies of

Richardson's *The Secret Service—Field, Dungeon and Escape* had been sold, 60,000 copies of *The Innocents Abroad* (O'Harra, *op. cit.*, p. 2344).

38. Within five months after publication, 31,000 copies of *The Innocents Abroad* had been sold at prices of $3.50 and up, and at the end of a year sales had totaled 67,000. Nearly 40,000 copies of *Roughing It* were sold in the first three months (Paine, *op. cit.*, I, 382; II, 455; *American Annual Cyclopedia,* VIII [1868], 408 ff.).

When the stock of the company rose in value as a result of the publication of *The Innocents Abroad,* Clemens himself bought in and became a director (Andrews, *op. cit.*, p. 121).

39. Guy A. Cardwell, *Twins of Genius (Twain and Cable)* (Lansing: Michigan State College Press, 1953), p. 95. Andrews (*op. cit.*, p. 122) states that "Mark constantly recommended his friends to Bliss—Aldrich, Bret Harte, Joel Chandler Harris."

For an authoritative account of Clemens' grievances against the American Publishing Company see Hill *op. cit.*, pp. 153-57, *et passim*. See also *Autobiography,* I, 27; *Mark Twain in Eruption, Hitherto Unpublished Pages about Men and Events,* ed. Bernard DeVoto (New York: Harper & Bros., 1940), pp. 151-55; *Autobiography,* Neider ed., pp. 225-28.

40. Blanck, *op. cit.*, p. 187. The various states of collation in which the first edition appeared as a result of this practice, combined with the two separately dated issues and the several printings, present a difficult bibliographical problem—one not made easier by the insertion of "fake" title pages (see Appendix B).

41. From advertisement by American Publishing Company in first edition of *The Gilded Age.*

42. See, for example, the memoirs of two women canvassers who sold, among other titles, works by Twain: *Facts* (see above, n. 21), *passim,* and Likins (see above, n. 27), *passim.*

43. *Facts* and Likins, *op. cit., passim.* Mitchell, *op. cit.* (pp. 47-48) says, "I have read a little pamphlet on how to sell books put out by a Connecticut Yankee publisher many years ago for the instruction of his agents. It tells not only how to sell books, but also how agents can get free meals and a night's lodging from customers, especially when canvassing in country districts. This set of instructions probably kept many a poor bookman from sleeping under the stars in a haystack with an empty belly." This is apparently the pamphlet of instructions issued by Clemens' own Charles L. Webster & Co., described in *Twain-Howells,* II, 879.

44. Robert Ernest Cowan, *Booksellers of Early San Francisco* (Los Angeles: Ward Ritchie Press, 1953), pp. 11-13.

45. Likins, *op. cit.*, pp. 140, 145. "Copies were also issued with all edges gilt, this at the request of the purchaser who paid an additional fee for this feature" (Johnson, *op. cit.*, p. 18).

46. Likins, *op. cit.*, p. 140.

47. Da Ponte, *op. cit.*, p. 13.

48. May 1885, p. 209, as quoted by Da Ponte, *op. cit.*, p. 15.

49. *Galaxy,* X (November 1870), 734; reproduced in *Contributions to* The Galaxy, *1868-1871, by Mark Twain,* ed. Bruce R. McElderry, Jr. (Gainesville, Fla.: Scholars' Facsimiles & Reprints, 1961), p. 98. It should be pointed out that his sketch "The Canvasser's Tale" (*Writings,* XX, 363-70) was directed against door-to-door peddlers in general.

50. (Boston) *Literary World,* V (August, 1874), 40.

51. Quoted in *Literary World,* V (September, 1874), 63.

52. Johnson, *op. cit.*, p. 22; cf. *Letters,* I, 205. The statement that Warner had "dropped his 'Back-Log Studies'" apparently was merely for effect. The first seven studies had appeared in the July, 1871, and February-July, 1872, issues of *Scribner's Monthly,* after which they ceased. The entire series, totaling eleven, had already been published as a volume (see below, chap. ii, n. 64).

53. Quoted in Royal Cortissoz, *The Life of Whitelaw Reid* (New York: Charles Scribner's Sons, 1921), I, 273.

54. Letter dated April 10, 1873, Warner Papers.

55. Cortissoz, *op. cit.*, I, 273-74.

56. April 19, 1873, p. 6, col. 6. *My Summer in a Garden* (1870) was Warner's first book, a collection of informal essays he had published in the Hartford *Courant,* of which he was editor. *Minion* is 7-point type, used extensively in newspapers of the day.

57. Cortissoz, *op. cit.*, I, 274.

58. *Ibid.*, I, 275. My reconstruction of the episode, it should be said, is based strictly on internal evidence. Cortissoz states that Clemens' first impression of Hay's notice "appears to have been received from a bald, brief quotation in some exchange, and his expectations were cruelly disappointed." He claims that Clemens' second note was written after he had seen the actual notice in the *Tribune* of the 19th, which had been delayed through improper working of the mails. As none of Cortissoz' assumptions is documented and as he fails to mention the editorial of the 23rd, I believe my conjecture is the more probable one, for the later editorial appears to "say it *right*" and deceive "in the happy direction." (It is quite possible, however, that the paper of the 19th, a Saturday, was not delivered in Hartford until the 22nd, the following Tuesday.)

59. April 23, 1873, p. 4, col. 5.

60. Critics customarily referred to Warner's writings as "delicate," "graceful," or "quiet and genial" (Arthur L. Vogelback, "The Literary Reputation of Mark Twain in America, 1869-1885" [Ph.D. dissertation, University of Chicago, 1938], p. 78, n. 3).

61. The *New-York Tribune* items were quoted, respectively, in the issues of April 27 (p. 7), and May 4 (p. 10). In the latter the *Chicago Tribune* also quoted Twain's letter to the *Daily Graphic.* Other brief notices appeared October 12 (p. 10) (see above, n. 5) and November 16 (p. 9).

62. Undated reviews reprinted in large broadside, "Notices of the Press," in MTP. The first three phrases are quoted, respectively, from reviews by the Worcester *Daily Press,* Hartford *Daily Times,* and Springfield (Mass.) *Union.*

63. Letter dated "Xmas/1873," Warner Papers.

64. Letter from Stedman to Warner dated January 18, 1874, Warner Papers.

65. Index to Vol. XVIII, January to June, 1874, "Register of Books Received during the Half-year," "Miscellaneous." The publisher is given as "Hartford Publishing Co."

66. *Atlantic,* XXXIII (March, 1874), 374.

67. Letter dated December 28, 1873, Warner Papers.

68. "Concerning the scoundrel Edward H. House," unfinished MS dated March, 1890, DV 305, typescript p. 4, MTP. Cf. *Twain-Howells,* I, 374, n. 1.

69. Undated letter "Under Way, Sat. A.M."; typescript, MTP. "Eight or ten years later," Clemens heard a more plausible account of the incident from John Hay. "He said that the explanation . . . was, that Reid did not like House, and would not have entertained a proposition of any kind from him." Meanwhile, Clemens states, "I withdrew my smile from Reid, . . . and did not speak to him again for twelve or thirteen years" (DV 305, typescript pp. 4-5).

70. *Autobiography,* II, 69-70 (Neider ed., p. 274). In his letter of February 28, 1874, to his Edinburgh friend Dr. John Brown, he had written: "We are all delighted with your commendations of the Gilded Age—& the more so because some of our newspapers have set forth the opinion that *Warner* really wrote the book & I only added my name to the title-page in order to give it a large sale. It is a shameful charge to make" (original letter in Yale University Library; quoted, except for last sentence, in *Letters,* I, 214).

71. Vol. III, p. 351, col. 3.

72. See above, p. 4, and Appendix C.

73. See chap. i, n. 80; p. 20 and n. 88.

74. Over a decade later, Clemens, in instructions on sending out review copies of *Huckleberry Finn,* inserted parenthetically: "(*Never* send any to N. Y. Graphic.)" (*MT, Business Man,* p. 300).

75. See pp. 54 ff.

76. In March, 1880, Clemens wrote Howells: "I am justified in being afraid of the general press, because it killed the 'Gilded Age' before you had a chance to point out that there were merits in that book. The sale ceased almost *utterly* until the adverse criticisms were forgotten— . . ." (*Twain-Howells,* I, 294).

77. February 1, 1874, p. 9.

78. As quoted in the *Chicago Tribune,* April 5, 1874, p. 10.

79. IV (January, 1874), 126.

80. The restrained Boston *Transcript,* for example, said politely, "It were impossible, even for two pens, to fill to order so much space as these pages cover with real humor" (December 23, 1873, p. 6).

81. IX (March, 1874), 386-87. Fred Perkins, nephew of the women's suffrage leader Isabella Beecher Hooker and sometime member of the Nook Farm circle, was former editor of the *Galaxy* (Da Ponte, *op. cit.,* p. 36; Andrews, *op. cit.,* p. 56).

82. Vogelback, *op. cit.,* p. 110; Cortissoz, *op. cit.,* I, 104.

83. Cortissoz, *op. cit.,* I, 273.

84. IV, 126. (The *Chicago Tribune* called it a "pretended satire.")

85. XXVI (January 1, 1874), 1642. Nevins calls the *Independent* "best of the religious publications, because the broadest in interest" (*op. cit.,* p. 236).

86. IX, 388.

87. Quoted by Foner, *op. cit.,* p. 82.

88. December 22, 1873.

89. XI (January 10, 1874), 59. George T. Ferris, in his article, "Mark Twain," in the July 4 issue (XII, 15-18), remarks, "We have the word of the authors that there was no intention of making it humorous, the sole purpose being that of bitter satire, true and honest to the core."

Warner's own Hartford *Courant* said that "underneath all, and perceptible to everyone is a serious purpose, an evident desire to hold up the mirror of truth to the eyes of a nation . . ." (undated clipping, MTP). The Rochester (N.Y.) *Union Advertiser* called it "a powerful satire upon customs and events of the times" (undated review in "Notices of the Press," MTP).

90. VI (January 17, 1874), 38-39. In acknowledging his complimentary copy, the publisher James Osgood wrote Warner: ". . . I am sure the purpose with which the book was written was a serious one—or perhaps a serious *two,* to do good and to make money. The book will certainly do the first, and I hope for the authors' sakes it will the last" (letter dated January 28, 1874, Warner Papers).

91. Undated reviews in "Notices of the Press," MTP. Again using medical figure of speech, the Waterbury *Daily American* found there was "necessity for the use of the keen scalpel of satire that the vicious blood may be drawn from the body politic."

92. Da Ponte, *op. cit.,* p. 32.

93. The first sixty copies from the bindery were sent out, stitched without covers, as review copies (Johnson, *op. cit.,* p. 18). The following agreement is part of the contract made with Bliss: "A sheet of extracts to be sent with copy of the book to editors, said extracts to be selected by said Warner who shall also furnish a list of newspapers, from which he in connexion with the said E. Bliss, Jr. shall select such as they may deem proper, (say 500 more or less as they may agree,) to whom the said party of the second part [American Publishing Company] shall within 12 months from issue of the book send free copies at their own expense, with sheets of extracts. Copies of the book with extracts to be sent to the leading papers and periodicals of the great cities from first edition printed" (copy of contract, MTP).

94. Da Ponte, *op. cit.*, p. 32; Foner, *op. cit.*, p. 43.

95. For a discussion of the publication date of the British edition see Appendix C.

96. See above, n. 2.

97. In the case of *Routledge* v. *Low* (see Appendix A).

98. Following a list of Mark Twain's works available in Routledge's advertisement in the *Athenaeum* for December 20 is the statement, "Messrs. George Routledge & Sons are my only authorized London publishers. (Signed) Mark Twain" (p. 825). In the next issue (December 27, p. 880), however, appears an advertisement by Chatto & Windus for "Mark Twain's Choice Works. With extra passages to the 'Innocents Abroad,' now first reprinted, . . . 700 pages, cloth gilt, 7s. 6d." This volume, apparently pirated by the firm that eventually was to succeed Routledge as Twain's authorized British publisher, is advertised again, with no identification of publisher, in the *Times* of June 3, 1874, p. 12, col. 6, where it is described as "Revised and Corrected throughout by the Author."

99. *Letters*, I, 212.

100. Webster L. Smalley, "The Critical Reception of Mark Twain in England: 1870-1910" (Master's thesis, Columbia University, 1948), p. 13.

101. Letter dated January 18, 1874, Warner Papers.

102. December 29, 1873. Undated clipping in MTP; last sentence quoted and dated December 29 in the London *Times*, January 3, 1874, p. 6, col. 2, and June 9, p. 14, col. 4.

An undated, unidentified review quotes the *Standard* review with approval and adds: "We have no doubt the Americans will swallow the 'pill' with great avidity, and it will do them good" (clipping, MTP).

103. January 10, 1874, p. 53.

104. IX (February 28, 1874), 199.

105. XLVII (March 21, 1874), 371. Other London reviews I have found yield very little more. The *Queen* (January 17, 1874, p. 61), which devoted most of its review to quoted excerpts, commented: "The 'gilding' and the corruption which so greatly blur the noble qualities of the American nation were never more unsparingly exposed in a work of fiction, . . ." The *Pall Mall Budget* (January 17, p. 27) said: "The value of the book will be found to consist chiefly in touches of humour here and there, and in the ideas which we gain from it of American life and manners." And the *Saturday Review* (XXXVII [January 24, 1874], 128), with the succinctness it customarily accorded fiction, stated, "The name of Mark Twain will be a sufficient recommendation of the *Gilded Age*, a three-volume novel of the English form, purporting to be written jointly by him and Mr. C. D. Warner."

CHAPTER II

1. Albert Bigelow Paine, *Mark Twain: A Biography* (New York: Harper & Bros., 1912), II, 476-77; see also *Letters*, I, 12, 203-4. For restatement of Paine's version see Edward Wagenknecht, *Mark Twain, the Man and His Work* (New Haven: Yale University Press, 1935), p. 80; Edgar Lee Masters, *Mark Twain: A Portrait* (New York: Charles Scribner's Sons, 1938), p. 94; *Love Letters*, p. 182; and others.

2. Clemens made Stoddard his "secretary" during his 1873-74 London stay as an excuse to have his company.

3. *Exits and Entrances* (Boston: Lothrop Publishing Co., 1903), pp. 70-71.

4. *Five Famous Missourians* (Kansas City, Mo.: Hudson-Kimberly Publishing Co., 1900), p. 3. The preface adds that the data were also authenticated by references to families and friends "in order that apocryphal matter might not be used."

5. Thomas Bond Burnham ("Mark Twain and the Gilded Age" [Master's thesis, University of Idaho, 1937], p. 28) remarks: "What they said we do not know. Considering the eventual result of their labors, I think a logical guess would be that

they considered contemporary novels told too little; that they were too innocuous and soft-spoken, but of course it is no more than a guess. . . ."

A fourth and apparently apocryphal version is given by the newspaper columnist E. J. Edwards in 1910. This version, told to Edwards by Stephen A. Hubbard, managing editor and part owner of the Hartford *Courant* in the days when Warner was coeditor with his friend Joseph R. Hawley, claims that the challenge resulted from Mrs. Clemens' and Mrs. Warner's twitting of Clemens about the "accidental hit" made by *Innocents Abroad*. When they defied him to "write another work like it," he turned to Warner and suggested that they write a story together "chapter by chapter every morning," interweaving their work in such a way that their wives would not be able to tell who wrote what. About halfway through the writing of their practical joke, Clemens introduced Colonel Sellers and the authors then became seriously interested (New York *Evening Mail*, May 5, 1910; clipping in Yale University Library).

The account is so filled with other inaccuracies about the publication and sales of the book that the entire version should be considered worthless. One can only speculate how many other versions are buried in files of newspapers and magazines.

6. See Kenneth R. Andrews, *Nook Farm: Mark Twain's Hartford Circle* (Cambridge: Harvard University Press, 1950), p. 175.

7. *Scribner's Monthly*, IV (May, 1872), 47-48; *Backlog Studies* (Boston: James R. Osgood & Co., 1873), pp. 156-64. Though Warner (The Fire-Tender) makes little contribution to this colloquy, his views on the subject are effectively expressed in his essay on "Modern Fiction," published in the *Atlantic* ten years later: "This is preëminently the age of the novel. . . . everybody reads novels. Three quarters of the books taken from the circulating library are stories. . . . The result of this universal demand for fiction is necessarily an enormous supply, and as everybody writes, without reference to gifts, the product is mainly trash, and trash of a deleterious sort; for bad art in literature is bad morals. I am not sure but the so-called domestic, the diluted, the 'goody,' namby-pamby, un-robust stories, which are so largely read by school-girls, young ladies, and women, do more harm than the 'knowing,' audacious, wicked ones, also, it is reported, read by them, and written largely by their own sex" (LI [April, 1883], 464-74; reprinted in Warner, *The Relation of Literature to Life* [New York: Harper & Bros., 1897], pp. 135-67).

8. "When . . . Harper's wavered between 100,000 and 200,000, . . . the New York Ledger printed a steady 400,000." "Saturday Night's top boast was 250,000, the Weekly's 350,000" (Mary Noel, *Villains Galore: The Heyday of the Popular Story Weekly* [New York: Macmillan Co., 1954], pp. 5, 120).

9. *Nation*, XIV (May 23, 1872), 334.

10. See Noel, *op. cit.*; Helen Waite Papashvily, *All the Happy Endings* (New York: Harper & Bros., 1956); Fred Lewis Pattee, *The Feminine Fifties* (New York: D. Appleton-Century Co., 1940), *passim*.

11. "Bennett of the Herald and Jennings of the Times, unable to praise the publication of their friend Mr. Bonner on literary grounds, fell back upon its excellent moral tone" (Noel, *op. cit.*, p. 301).

12. Quoted in *ibid.*, p. 304.

13. Quoted in *ibid.*, p. 300.

14. "American Novels," *North American Review*, CXV (October, 1872), 366-78.

15. For authorship of *Miss Van Kortland* see *Nation*, XVII (December 4, 1873), 373.

16. *Fairbanks Letters*, pp. 134-37.

17. At the time Clemens formed a Browning group in the mid-eighties, Mrs. Clemens apparently formed a family Meredith group. Cyril Clemens describes it as follows: "Mrs. Clemens insisted upon reading aloud 'Diana of the Crossways' to the family. Clemens would remark from time to time that they heard so much about Diana whom the author is constantly praising to the skies, but 'she never seems to say a brilliant thing or do anything worth remembering.' And then the humorist would

challenge his wife to quote one really clever thing that Diana had ever said" ("Mark Twain's Reading," *Commonweal*, XXIV [August 7, 1937], 363-64).

For Clemens' dislike of Eliot and James see Harold Aspiz, "Mark Twain's Reading —A Critical Study" (Ph.D. dissertation, University of California at Los Angeles, 1949), pp. 203-4 ff.; also Clemens' letter to Howells, July 21, 1885, in *Twain-Howells*, II, 533-34. His opinions of Scott and Austen are well known.

18. *MT, Business Man*, p. 233. See also Paine, *op. cit.*, II, 765-66, who erroneously lists S. Watson Wolston.

19. "A Cure for the Blues" is reprinted together with the Royston romance as Mark Twain, *A Cure for the Blues* (Rutland, Vt.: Charles E. Tuttle Co., 1964); also in *Writings*, XXI, 388-460. For the passage on Scott see *Life on the Mississippi* (*Writings*, IX), 347-49; cf. 308-9, 341-42.

20. Mary Angela Bennett, *Elizabeth Stuart Phelps* (Philadelphia: University of Pennsylvania Press, 1939), p. 52. See Paine, *op. cit.*, IV, 1430. Clemens laboriously translated his travesty into German with the intention of publishing it surreptitiously, but thought better of the plan afterward. Harte's review appeared in the *Overland* in September, 1869 (III, 292-93); see Joseph B. Harrison, *Bret Harte* (New York: American Book Co., 1941), p. lxvi.

21. CXVI, 41-49, 266-76. Reprinted in *The Mysterious Stranger and Other Stories* (New York: Harper & Bros., 1922), pp. 223-78.

22. *Autobiography*, Neider ed., p. 277.

23. *The Gates Ajar* nourished in this country the wishful thinking of families of the Civil War dead and both here and elsewhere gave support to the orthodox in a period of active religious questioning brought about by the progress of science. It quickly reached nearly 100,000 circulation and was translated into French, German, Dutch, and Italian. It immediately inspired republication of an even more literal book entitled *The Gates Wide Open; or, Scenes in Another World* (Bennett, *op. cit.*, pp. 43-54). Shortly before publication of "Captain Stormfield" in *Harper's* Clemens had contemplated dumping it into his autobiography (to be posthumously published) along with other "old pigeonholed things of the years gone by which I or editors didn't das't to print" (in letter to Howells, *Twain-Howells*, II, 811; Paine, *op. cit.*, IV, 1312). By 1907, however, the clash between religious fundamentalism and science-oriented liberalism was largely a thing of the past.

24. Jacob Blanck, *Bibliography of American Literature* (New Haven: Yale University Press, 1957-   ), II, 173, 178. "Fitz Smythe's Horse," reprinted in the *Golden Era*, January 21, 1866, from the *Territorial Enterprise*, found its way "in some strange manner" into *Beadle's Dime Book of Fun, Number 3* (1866) (*The Washoe Giant in San Francisco: Being Heretofore Uncollected Sketches by Mark Twain Published in the Golden Era in the Sixties . . .*, ed. Franklin Walker [San Francisco: George Fields, 1938], pp. 99-101, 143). For the protest against the "yellowbacks" see Noel, *op. cit.*, pp. 301-2. According to Charles A. and Mary R. Beard (*The Rise of American Civilization* [New York: Macmillan Co., 1937], II, 445): "For every copy of Howells' Traveller from Altruria or Henry James' Portrait of a Lady that was sold in the marts of trade, doubtless a thousand copies of Buffalo Bill's desperate deeds, Diamond Dick's frantic exploits, and Beadle's blood-curdling jeopardies were consumed by the men who, with the consent of their wives, governed the country in the gilded age and by the boys who were to possess the future."

25. For the review of *Ingomar*, which appeared in the *Golden Era*, November 29, 1863, see *Washoe Giant*, pp. 58-60; for the co-operative novel, *Roughing It*, II (*Writings*, VIII), 96-105; for "The Loves of Alonzo . . . ," which was first published in *An Idle Excursion* (Blanck, *op. cit.*, II, 191), *Tom Sawyer Abroad . . . Etc.* (*Writings*, XX), 408-32. Similar "sensation novels" appeared in the *Golden Era* (Franklin Walker, *San Francisco's Literary Frontier* [New York: Alfred A. Knopf, 1939], p. 124).

An interesting study of Clemens' unpublished condensed-novel burlesques is found in Franklin R. Rogers, *Mark Twain's Burlesque Patterns: As Seen in the Novels and Narratives 1855-1885* (Dallas: Southern Methodist University Press, 1960), *passim.*

26. Aspiz, *op. cit.*, p. 224.

27. See *Life on the Mississippi* (*Writings*, IX), p. 295; Paine, *op. cit.*, I, 81-82; *Autobiography*, I, 143-47; *Autobiography*, Neider ed., pp. 95-97. For reference to *The Fortunes of Nigel* see [Mrs. James T. Fields], *Memories of a Hostess: A Chronicle of Eminent Friendships*, ed. M. A. De Wolfe Howe (Boston: Atlantic Monthly Press, 1922), p. 245.

Dixon Wecter (*Sam Clemens of Hannibal* [Boston: Houghton Mifflin Co., 1922], p. 209) remarks: "The real Hannibal was neither the total cultural desert imagined by Van Wyck Brooks in *The Ordeal of Mark Twain* nor the seat of the muses patriotically conceived by Minnie Brashear in *Mark Twain, Son of Missouri . . . .*"

28. *Memories of a Hostess*, p. 245.

29. Aspiz, *op. cit.*, p. 77.

30. Hellmut Lehmann-Haupt, *The Book in America* (New York: R. R. Bowker Co., 1939), p. 194; George Rothwell Brown, *Washington, a Not Too Serious History* (Baltimore: Norman Publishing Co., 1930), pp. 417-18. Brown says that Guild's hodge-podge shop, which overflowed onto the street, "had a fascination for Mark Twain," who ransacked the place each time "with the constantly invigorated zest of a confirmed bibliophile."

31. Aspiz, *op. cit.*, p. 232; Paine, *op. cit.*, I, 96.

32. X, 733; reproduced in *Contributions to* The Galaxy, *1868-1871, by Mark Twain*, ed. Bruce R. McElderry, Jr. (Gainesville, Fla.: Scholars' Facsimiles & Reprints, 1961), p. 97; reprinted in *Mark Twain: Life As I Find It*, ed. Charles Neider (Garden City, N.Y.: Hanover House, 1961), p. 72.

33. I (*Writings*, VII), 157.

34. Aspiz, *op. cit.*, p. 233.

35. II (*Writings*, XI), 61.

36. Pattee, *op. cit.*, pp. 77, 183; Noel, *op. cit.*, pp. 171, 225-26. So pervasive was the influence of these writers that Charles Warren Stoddard, poet, college professor, and close friend of Clemens, "looked back with unrepentant nostalgia upon his Ledger-reading days" and "spoke affectionately of Emerson Bennett and of Sylvanus Cobb, Jr." (Noel, *op. cit.*, p. 305).

An interesting sidelight is provided by Professor Joseph Jones of the University of Texas in a letter in *The Twainian* ("More Twain Found in New York *Weekly*," February, 1944, pp. 1-4). In the spring of 1867, apparently to build up the audience for his forthcoming *Jumping Frog* volume and his Cooper Union lecture, Clemens allowed the *New York Weekly* to reprint five of his Sandwich Islands letters written for the Sacramento *Union* in 1866. Commenting on the company among whom Mark Twain appeared, Jones says: "Serial fiction included such titles as *The Heir of Balfour Hall*, by Margaret Blount; *The Water-Wolf; or, The Demon of the Bermudas*, by Leon Lewis; *The Heiress of Egremont*, by Mrs. Leon Lewis; *Ethelbert the Wanderer; or, The Spirit Wife*, by Edward Minturn (likewise the author of *The Pearl of the Roof; or, The Diver's Daughter*, appearing during the same period); *Annie Graham's First Love*, by Mrs. Mary J. Holmes; *The Female Spy of Algiers*, by Harry Hazleton; with a great many moral tales for boys and girls, and short stories and sketches about desperadoes, drunkards, 'passion's proud slaves,' pursuits with bloodhounds, adventures with Indians, rescues at sea, disinherited daughters, slave girls, 'love at cross purposes', incidents of prison life, mother love, and runaway locomotives. . . ."

37. *Writings*, Vol. X.

38. See, for example, I, 80-81, 108-9; II, 324-25.

39. See above, notes 8 and 10.

40. Frank Luther Mott, *A History of American Magazines* (Cambridge: Harvard University Press, 1938), III, 224; II, 439.

41. S. M. Ellis, *Wilkie Collins, Le Fanu and Others* (London: Constable & Co., 1931), p. 182.

42. Walter C. Phillips, *Dickens, Reade, and Collins, Sensation Novelists* (New York: Columbia University Press, 1919), pp. 25-26.

43. Bernard DeVoto, *Mark Twain's America* (Boston: Little, Brown & Co., 1932), p. 285.

44. Carl Van Doren, *The American Novel* (New York: Macmillan Co., 1940), p. 145; Andrews, *op. cit.*, p. 184.

45. Paine, *op. cit.*, II, 477. As early as December 31, 1873, only a week after the novel had been issued, Warner wrote to the editor and literary critic Thomas Wentworth Higginson: "On second thought, it is not best to send you The Gilded Age. You would not care for it, and I have already found out that it is not much of a novel. It is rather of a raw satire on recent disagreeable things. You would only waste time on it" (Morse, file folder 112).

46. So dubbed by Arnold Bennett, whose epithet was quoted and given currency by Van Wyck Brooks (*The Ordeal of Mark Twain* [New York: E. P. Dutton & Co., 1920], p. 15). Let it be noted, however, that for Bennett the term "amateur" had no demeaning sense. "I begin to think that great writers of fiction are by the mysterious nature of their art ordained to be 'amateurs' " (*The Author's Craft* [London: Hodder & Stoughton, n.d.], p. 50). He accounted for "the amateur in all great artists" by the "exuberance of their sense of power" and their impatience with "the exactitudes of systematic study." "We can all point in excuse to Shakespere" (p. 51).

47. Holograph leaf in HEH, Container HM 1310. So integral did Clemens consider this little appendix that he noted at the top of the leaf: "This is to occupy the right hand side of the *leaf* which ends the story."

48. MS pp. 251-52, 257, in University of Pittsburgh Library.

49. This last phrase was substituted in the manuscript for the deleted one: "similar treasures which she hardly felt able to buy" (MS p. 844, Lilly).

50. See *Twain-Howells*, I, 13. The manuscript originally had "Mr. Howells' 'Venetian Life,' " but "Mr. Howells' " has been struck out, probably as too obvious, and the phrase "a copy of" substituted. A similarly deleted clause states that while Laura was perusing *Venetian Life* "economy and desire were struggling in her mind for the mastery" (MS page 845, Lilly). Clemens was obviously trying to keep his compliment to Howells within the bounds of what he considered good taste.

51. *Howells and the Age of Realism* (Philadelphia: J. B. Lippincott Co., 1954), p. 73. Carter finds significance in Clemens' singling out of Taine and Holmes, both of whom tried to be objective observers of society (p. 75).

52. IX (February 28, 1874), 199.

53. VI, 38. (See also above, pp. 20-21).

54. Undated clipping in MTP.

55. Mrs. James T. Fields, *Charles Dudley Warner* (New York: McClure, Phillips & Co., 1904), p. 38. Paine, *op. cit.* (II, 478) says that the book was begun in February; but cf. letter from Warner to Reid, April 7, 1873 (see above, p. 11).

56. *Old and New*, IX, 387.

57. February 1, 1874, p. 9. E. C. Stedman had written Warner: ". . . whether your genius for *humor*, & Twain's genius for *drollery*, are correlative, is a question which I am puzzled to pronounce upon" (letter, "Xmas, 1873" see above, chap. i, n. 63).

58. *Independent*, XXVI, 1642; *Budget*, XI, 623.

59. Undated review reprinted in large broadside, "Notices of the Press," in MTP.

It should be noted, in this connection, that a number of reviewers were satisfied with the stylistic result of the collaboration. The *New York Herald* said: "The temperaments of the two writers have admirably blended in the composition. There are no awkward creaks and crevices of style"; the Utica (N.Y.) *Morning Herald* called the novel "characteristic of both its authors." The *Golden Age* made the following analysis: "At first sight nothing seemed more incongruous than this union between two authors whose style and method were so absolutely dissimilar. To be sure both were popular writers; but Warner's quaint and delicate humor, and the rollicking wit of Mark Twain struck every one as elements as little likely to form a harmonious mixture as oil and water. But in this prediction everybody was mistaken. As in marriage, the shrewdest wiseacres are often proved to be wrong in their forecasts of happiness or unhappiness for the mated pair, so the critics were wrong in their notion that these two authors would find it impossible to write a book in which there should be any congruity" ("Notices of the Press," MTP).

60. W. D. Howells, "Mark Twain: an Inquiry," *North American Review*, CXCI (June, 1910), 841 (reprinted from the issue of February, 1901); Brander Matthews, *Playwrights on Playmaking and Other Studies of the Stage* (New York: Charles Scribner's Sons, 1923), p. 167.

61. Andrews, *op. cit.*, p. 84.

62. John Macy, *The Spirit of American Literature* (Garden City, N.Y.: Doubleday, Page & Co., 1913), p. 257.

63. Minnie M. Brashear, *Mark Twain, Son of Missouri* (Chapel Hill: University of North Carolina Press, 1934), pp. 8-9.

64. Thomas R. Lounsbury, "Biographical Sketch," in *The Complete Writings of Charles Dudley Warner* (Hartford: American Publishing Co., 1904), XV, vii, xiv-xv; Fred Lewis Pattee, *A History of American Literature Since 1870* (New York: Century Co., 1915), pp. 418-19.

Though there has been some bibliographical confusion in dating Warner's early writings, I believe the dates I have given are correct. My evidence follows: Warner's preface to *My Summer in a Garden* ("By Way of Dedication") is dated October, 1870, the copyright date of the book is 1870, and Mrs. James T. Fields states that the book was "published by Fields & Osgood in 1870" (*Charles Dudley Warner*, p. 28). While the title page of the first edition gives 1871, it also lists as publisher James R. Osgood & Co., "Late Ticknor & Fields, and Fields, Osgood, & Co.," a circumstance that seems to indicate that the date of publication corresponded roughly with that of Osgood's buying out of the older firm of Ticknor & Fields. Apparently there was a year-end publishing situation similar to that of *The Gilded Age*. The most reliable scholars have accepted 1870 as the correct date (see Lounsbury, Andrews, Pattee; also William B. Cairns, *A History of American Literature* [rev. ed.; New York: Oxford University Press, 1930], p. 337).

About *Saunterings* there is no disagreement (see Fields, *op. cit.*, p. 33; Andrews, *op. cit.*, pp. 152, 279; Robert E. Spiller *et al.*, *Literary History of the United States* [New York: Macmillan Co., 1948], II, 833 [Willard Thorp], III, 357).

Backlog Studies, copyrighted in 1872, is cited as having been published in that year by Mrs. Fields (*op. cit.*, p. 33) and by Thomas Wentworth Higginson ("Charles Dudley Warner," *Scribner's Monthly*, VII [January, 1874], 334). (See also Andrews, *op. cit.*, pp. 264, n. 56, and 279. Andrews contradicts himself, however, when he speaks of Howells' editing the volume for publication in 1873 [p. 91].) The first edition carries 1873 on the title page and refers to Warner as "Author of 'Saunterings,' 'My Summer in a Garden,' etc." Apparently this is another instance of year-end publishing.

Contemporaries, such as Clemens and Mrs. Fields, consistently spell the title *Back-Log Studies*, which is the spelling on the cover of the original edition. The same edition has *Back-log* on the spine and *Backlog* on the title page.

65. *Letters*, I, 180. So little was Warner recognized at the time he was writing *My Summer in a Garden* that he was mentioned neither in Hart's *Manual of American Literature* nor in Drake's *Dictionary of American Biography*, both published in 1872.

Publication of this first book did, however, gain for him recognition in Underwood's *Handbook of American Authors*, also published in 1872 (Higginson, *op. cit.*, p. 334).

66. Berg Collection, New York Public Library. Collaboration as such was not a new experience to Clemens. On two separate occasions as a young newspaper reporter he had written dispatches with a collaborator, the first time with Andrew J. Marsh of the Sacramento *Union* in covering the Nevada Constitutional Convention for the *Territorial Enterprise,* later with Clement T. Rice ("the Unreliable") in reporting the session of the third Territorial Legislature for both the *Enterprise* and Rice's paper, the Virginia City *Daily Union (Mark Twain of the* Enterprise, ed. Henry Nash Smith [Berkeley: University of California Press, 1957], p. 11).

67. Berg Collection. The "association" here referred to is the professional, literary one centered about *The Gilded Age.* It should not be confused with Clemens' personal association, or friendship, with Warner. Mrs. Fields quotes a letter from Clemens reply-ing to an appeal for Warner letters after the latter's death: "There were not many, of course, we being near neighbours, and communicating mainly by mouth. . . . I am of no use in reminiscing—my memory is worthless. Warner was always saying brilliant things, felicitous things, but one can't carry them in the mind in their exact language, and without that their glory is gone. But there is one remark—not made by Warner—which we do not forget. You will note in it the sunshine shed by his personality. One day a young friend of ours came in with a fine light in her eye, and said: 'I've just had a good-morning from Mr. Warner, and I'm a happy girl for the day!' " (*Charles Dudley Warner,* pp. 39-40).

68. Van Wyck Brooks, *New England: Indian Summer* (New York: E. P. Dutton & Co., 1940), pp. 210-11.

CHAPTER III

1. Charles Warren Stoddard, *Exits and Entrances* (Boston: Lothrop Pub. Co., 1903), p. 71.

2. Albert Bigelow Paine, *Mark Twain: A Biography:* (New York: Harper & Bros., 1912), II, 477.

Parts of the present chapter appeared originally in my article, "The *Gilded Age* Manuscript," *Yale University Library Gazette,* XXXV (July, 1960), 35-41.

3. See Clemens' letter to Howells, June 27, 1877 (*Twain-Howells,* I, 184; *Letters,* I, 297).

4. Holograph page in MTP, DeVoto (hereafter DV) No. 137; reproduced in Paine, *op. cit.,* II, 475.

5. Paine, *op. cit.,* II, 477.

6. *Fairbanks Letters,* p. 184; *Letters,* I, 214-15.

7. For the convenience of the reader the chapter numbers of Volume II of the two-volume edition of the novel in *Writings,* X and XI, have been added in parentheses after those of the first American (one-volume) edition. All chapter titles are from the Author's National Edition.

8. Ernest E. Leisy, "Mark Twain's Part in *The Gilded Age,*" *American Literature,* VIII (January, 1937), 445-47. See Warner's letter to Whitelaw Reid, April 7, 1873: "We have hatched the plot day by day, drawn out the characters, and written it so that we cannot exactly say which belongs to who; though the different styles will show in the chapters" (Royal Cortissoz, *The Life of Whitelaw Reid* [New York: Charles Scrib-ner's Sons, 1921], p. 273). Throughout the collaboration Warner appears to have been far more passive in his attitude than Clemens; certainly he did not show pride in tallying his contributions as his enthusiastic partner did.

9. The final holograph manuscript of Chapter XXIX is extant with the exception of pages 11¼ and 11½ (Morse, Container 11). On p. 11 occur the interlinear notes by Warner, *"(insert here page 11¼)"* and "[insert page 11½]." Significantly, the miss-ing page 11½ encompasses precisely the paragraph claimed by Clemens. It is possible

that the missing page 11¼, which presents the acid comment of a local justice of the peace on the practices of the railroad company, is also by Clemens, for Warner habitually wrote his own insertions on the reverse of the leaves on which he noted them.

Volume and page references enclosed between brackets in passages quoted from Leisy's article and between parentheses in my own text and footnotes are to the two-volume edition of *The Gilded Age* published as *Writings*, X and XI.

10. I have found no extant manuscript for Chapter LVI. The only corroborative evidence for Clemens' share in the chapter is to be found in his dramatization of the novel, *Colonel Sellers*, described in the Epilogue to this volume.

11. *Love Letters*, pp. 182-83.

Constance Fenimore Woolson, grandniece of James Fenimore Cooper, was a writer of local color fiction.

12. Morse, Container 8.

13. Cf. Chapter VI, sixth paragraph (II, 68-69). (Clemens was apparently off by one paragraph in his annotation; the first paragraph of the chapter is only one sentence.)

The "nip" of Miss Woolson's phrases, presumably imitated in the Warner passage (and, for that matter, in Clemens' rewrite), may be found in numerous, rather unoriginal descriptions of girls in her stories, replete with curls, braids, hats, scarves, and ribbons, such as that of the schoolgirls in "Round by Propeller" (*Harper's New Monthly Magazine*, XLV [September, 1872], 526), who appear "running down the street, curls flying and eyes dancing with merriment." When Clemens imputes detectable plagiarism to Warner, however, he may have in mind the description of Pearl in "Weighed in the Balance" (*Appleton's Journal*, VII [June 1, 1872], 591): "Pearl had thrown off her hat, and the moonlight lit up her golden curls like a halo; a white *shawl was draped gracefully about her shoulders,* her fair ungloved hands toyed with the black ribbons of her hat, . . ." [Italics mine—B.F.] (The similarity of phrasing in the latter example is the closest to be found in any of Constance Woolson's stories published before May, 1873; possible similarities to material in the missing leaf of deleted Warner MS must remain conjectural.) Clemens' characteristic scrupulosity in the matter is revealed in a letter to Howells, November 23, 1875 (*Twain-Howells*, I, 112): ". . . I have charged unconscious plagiarism upon Charley Warner: & *this* in turn reminds me that I have been delighting my soul . . . over a bran new . . . way of beginning a novel—& behold, all at once it flashes upon me that *Charley Warner* originated the idea 3 years ago & told me about it! Aha! So much for self-righteousness!"

Franklin Rogers (*Mark Twain's Burlesque Patterns: As Seen in the Novels and Narratives 1855-1885* [Dallas: Southern Methodist University Press, 1960], p. 97) is quite correct in saying that Clemens' letter to his wife "indicates that even in the process of revision the mingling of ideas and efforts continued." As the original folios of the MS pages involved are 1, 2, 3, and 4, corresponding to intermediate folios 163¼ 163½, 163¾, and the lower portion of 163 (after the "insert" instruction), and the entire sequence occurs in regular order preceding [164], 165, etc., it is obvious that the four-page "picture" of Laura was undertaken by the authors at some time after Clemens' Chapter VI was written but *before* the final collation of MS, in which the sequence has become 136-39. Evidently there was some dissatisfaction with the original passage; however, it was Warner's rewrite (apparently attempted on or before April 26, just as the ten-day period of revision began [see pp. 81-82] in which the alleged plagiarism occurred (cf. Rogers, *op. cit.*, p. 172, n. 5).

14. MS pp. 1137, 1141, and 1142 (Morse, 12b). As Warner's original folios were 2, 2¾, and 3 (the second, fifth, and sixth pages in what was largely his chapter) and as 1138, 1139, and 1140 (presumably his 2¼, 2½, and some other fractional folio [?]) are missing, it is possible that Clemens wrote only about half or less of the passage.

15. MS p. 1151, Warner's original 12 (Morse, 12b).

16. MS p. 1321, Warner's original 7 for this chapter (Morse, 12b). Cf. Leisy, *Amer. Lit.*, VIII, 447. (Warner's preceding MS page, 1320, contains a slight emendation by Clemens.)

17. MS pp. 1044, 1048, 1049, and 1050 (Morse, 12b), which occur within this passage, are by Warner and bear his original folios, 2, 6, 7, and 8. (The intervening leaves are missing.) The other extant leaves of manuscript for the portions of the chapter preceding and following this passage (p. 1042 and before and p. 1053 and beyond) are by Clemens and bear only the intermediate and final folios (see Appendix D) in the 400's and 1000's.

The only other unrecorded Warner interpolation in the extant portions of MS—one easily ignored by Clemens—is the verbal description of Colonel Sellers' dinner-table railroad map (MS p. 622½ [Morse, 2]) written when it was decided to incorporate Clemens' interlinear illustrations into a single fold-out map (Chapter XXVII [I, 296]). (See Appendix E.)

18. Pages originally numbered 305, 309, and 312 (MTP, DV 137). These folios correspond with Clemens' original numbering of his own chapters beginning with Chapter XXIV and ending with Chapter XLV. Discarded pages 305 and 309 also bear second folios by Warner (21 and 25 respectively), which correspond with the intermediate stage (Warner's rewrite) of Chapter XXXV. (See Appendix D.)

19. P. 312; sentence continued presumably on nonextant p. 313. The fragment as published reads: " 'It's a funny world. Good-bye, uncle. I'm going to see that chairman.'

"And humming a cheery opera air, she departed to her room to dress for going out. . . ."

20. P. 305; folio changed to 21.

21. P. 309; folio changed to 25.

22. Eight of the nine extant MS pages for Chapter XIII are entirely in Warner's hand. Only p. 348 is in Clemens', and it occurs at the end of a passage claimed as his own interpolation in his annotated copy. Its former folio 15¾ indicates the insertion of the passage between Warner's 15 and 16, and Clemens has added the note, "Run to 16" (Morse, 12b). The single extant MS page for Chapter XVIII (449 [Morse, 12b]) is entirely by Warner.

23. MS p. 1329 (top of leaf cropped off and folio added on left side-margin), Lilly.

24. Holograph fragment in MTP, DV 137.

25. Hamlin Hill's reading, "Bumeroy" (*Mark Twain and Elisha Bliss* [Columbia: University of Missouri Press, 1964], p. 75), is erroneous in having the medial *e*.

26. *Fairbanks Letters*, p. 171 (see above, p. 53).

27. *Ibid.* (see above, p. 53). Warner's outline ends: "The next summer Philip will strike coal, Ruth die, and close with Phil. successful, every body else played out, and conclude the works with idea that Phil is some time to marry Alice" (MTP, DV 137).

28. *Literary World*, IV (January, 1874), 126.

29. Undated review reprinted in large broadside "Notices of the Press," MTP. If Clemens was at all responsible for preparing this broadside of press notices, a number of which are reprinted only in part, he did not omit the paragraph of this review that contained the reference. The *Golden Age* review is placed first on the broadside.

30. In the original manuscript Clemens strengthened the description of the injury by changing the weaker "tore the skin from Laura's forehead" to the more suggestive "wounding Laura's forehead" (MS p. 1399, in HEH, container 1315).

31. Fred Lewis Pattee, *A History of American Literature Since 1870* (New York: Century Co., 1915), p. 420.

32. *Fairbanks Letters*, p. 170.

33. Warner wrote on the average 1.8 pages of manuscript per printed page (based on Author's National Edition), whereas Clemens wrote an average 2.6 MS pages per

printed page. They both used the same lined paper and wrote on one side only (except for occasional inserts added on the reverse).

34. Typical of Clemens' alterations is: "Laura's ~~anger grew again~~ morbid self-communing was renewed (MS p. 282 [Morse, 12b]; cf. I, 121). Other examples are: "an expression of contentment . . . ~~came~~ settled upon its face" (MS 105 [Morse, 12b]; I, 57); "inspect you with a ~~critical~~ severe eye" (MS 552 [Morse, 10]; I, 267); and "The Speaker of the House ~~said~~ rattled off" (MS 1013-14 [Morse 12b]; II, 134).

Typical of Warner's is: "Philip managed to complete his toilet by the ~~help~~ aid use of his pocket-handkerchief" (MS p. 686 [Morse, 11]; cf. I, 323). Other examples are: "run in a ~~horizontal shaft~~ tunnel" (MS 691 [Morse, 11]; I, 326); "every ~~firm~~ tradesman in the village" (MS 1026 [Morse, 2]; II, 140); and "Her ~~liaison~~ liaison intimacy with Selby" (MS 1031 [Morse, 2]; II, 142).

35. MS pp. 580-81 and 1245 (Morse, 12b); cf. I, 277; II, 246.

36. For example: "this tribute of respect which the nation has reared ~~in its over-flowing grati~~ as the symbol of its unappeasable gratitude" or "bad taste reduced to ~~scien~~ mathematical completeness" (MS pp. 548 and 550-51 [Morse, 10]; I, 265, 266).

37. "He was somewhat ~~bruised~~ bruised" (MS p. 680 [Morse, 11]; I, 319); "she has done ~~almost nearly~~ nearly as much" (MS p. 1029 [Morse, 2]; II, 141); etc.

38. MS p. 1056 (Morse, 12b); II, 154.

39. For example, on MS p. 1249 (Morse, 12b) occurs the following short paragraph concerning the impaneling of a prospective juror: "Patrick Coughlin. No particular business. Owned some terriers. Never fit 'em himself. Never heard of this case till this morning." All except the name has been crossed out and in an insertion written on the reverse of the leaf this terse information has been expanded into an amusing thirteen-line dialogue (II, 248-49).

40. MS pp. 284, 281, 1142, 1249 (Morse, 12b); I, 122, 121, and II, 196, 248.

41. MS p. 628 (Morse, 2); cf. I, 298. One is irresistibly reminded of Dickens' almost constant comment on tobacco chewing and expectoration in *American Notes*. Imagine the glee with which British reviewers would have pounced upon this sentence had it been retained!

42. Such as the spirit of George Washington "roosting" on the scaffolding of the uncompleted Monument (MS p. 548 [Morse, 10]; cf. I, 265).

43. Discarded p. 293 (MTP, DV 137).

44. MS p. 281 (Morse, 12b).

45. See *Traveling with the Innocents Abroad: Mark Twain's Original Reports from Europe and the Holy Land*, ed. Daniel Morley McKeithan (Norman: University of Oklahoma Press, 1958). In his annotations following each letter that was incorporated into *Innocents Abroad* McKeithan cites the alterations. Typical examples are: " 'the first pass we made' became 'the first adventure we had'; . . . 'when they run out they skirmish' became 'when the commissary department fails they "skirmish," as Jack terms it in his sinful, slangy way' " (p. 36). It should be noted that the deleted phrasings of *Gilded Age* MS seldom are quite as slangy as the published *Innocents Abroad*.

46. Invariably the lines immediately following a deletion in his text contain the substance of the omitted passage or a paraphrase, condensation, or expansion of it, often utilizing some of the same phrasings.

47. W. D. Howells, "Mark Twain: an Inquiry," *North American Review*, CXCI (June, 1910), 836-37; reprinted from *NAR*, February, 1901. In this connection Charles Warren Stoddard's comment is interesting. "As to the plot of the story," he writes, "it was never meant to have any; on the contrary, the story told itself" (*Exits and Entrances*, p. 71).

48. *Queen*, January 17, 1874, p. 61; Brander Matthews, *Playwrights on Playmaking and Other Studies of the Stage* (New York: Charles Scribner's Sons, 1923), p. 167.

49. *Love Letters*, p. 182.

50. Unpublished letter to "Sister & Bro," addressed to Orion and postmarked May 6; typescript in MTP.

51. Extant portions of holograph manuscript are analyzed in Appendix D.

CHAPTER IV

1. Merle Johnson, *A Bibliography of the Works of Mark Twain* (rev. ed.; New York: Harper & Bros., 1935), p. 22; *Letters*, I, 205.

2. Rudyard Kipling, *From Sea to Sea: Letters of Travel* (Garden City, N. Y.: Doubleday, Page & Co., 1913), Part II, p. 180.

3. See *Letters from Honolulu, Written for the Sacramento Union*, ed. Thomas Nickerson (Honolulu: Thomas Nickerson, 1939); *Letters from the Sandwich Islands, Written for the Sacramento Union*, ed. G. Ezra Dane (San Francisco: Grabhorn Press, 1937); and Walter Francis Frear, *Mark Twain and Hawaii* (Chicago: Lakeside Press, 1947), *passim*.

4. *The Tocsin of Revolt and Other Essays* (New York: Charles Scribner's Sons, 1922), p. 270.

5. Kipling, *op. cit.*, p. 180.

6. See Charles Duffy and Henry Pettit, *A Dictionary of Literary Terms* (rev. ed.; Denver: University of Denver Press, 1952), pp. 104-5; Heinrich Mahlberg, *Literarische Sachwörterbuch* (Bern: A. Francke Ag. Verlag, 1948), p. 194; Irving Wallace, *The Fabulous Originals* (New York: Alfred A. Knopf, 1955), p. 16.

7. Laurie Magnus, *A Dictionary of European Literature, Designed as a Companion to English Studies* (London: George Routledge & Sons, 1926), p. 441.

8. In the American edition. The British edition was subtitled merely *A Novel*.

9. The reviews identifying both Dilworthy and Laura were in *Old and New*, IX (March, 1874), 386-88, and in the Springfield (Mass.) *Union* (clipping in large broadside "Notices of the Press," in MTP). The others that identified Dilworthy were in the Boston *Transcript*, December 23, 1873, p. 6, Boston *Saturday Evening Gazette, Pomeroy's Democrat* (N.Y.) (clippings of last two in "Notices"), and, by implication, the *Independent*, XXVI (January 1, 1874), 1642. A British newspaper also named Laura (unidentified, undated clipping in MTP).

10. *Courant* (undated clipping, MTP); *Herald*, December 22, 1873; *Standard*, December 29 (see above, chap. i, n. 102).

11. "Notices of the Press," MTP.

12. Cf. Walter F. Taylor, "Mark Twain and the Machine Age," in *Fifty Years of the South Atlantic Quarterly*, ed. William Baskerville Hamilton (Durham: Duke University Press, 1952), p. 274 f.

13. *Mark Twain: A Biography* (New York: Harper & Bros., 1912), II, 478.

14. I have found only one historiographer who referred to Dilworthy as "imaginary." (See Frances Weston Carruth, "Washington in Fiction," *Bookman* [New York], XV [July, 1902], 454.)

15. Albert R. Kitzhaber, "Mark Twain's Use of the Pomeroy Case in *The Gilded Age*," *Modern Language Quarterly* (hereafter *MLQ*), XV (March, 1954), 42-56.

16. Chapters XXII, XXVI, and XXVIII of Volume II of the two-volume edition of the novel in *Writings*, X and XI.

17. Kitzhaber, *MLQ*, XV, 42.

18. "*Götterdämmerung* in Topeka: The Downfall of Senator Pomeroy," *Kansas Historical Quarterly* (hereafter *KHQ*), XVIII (August, 1950), 258. The press had become so formidable as a "purifying instrumentality" that Harlan joined the journalistic profession to get square with the correspondents. "His efforts in this direction were chiefly notable for their squeamishness and absurdity" (George Alfred Townsend, *Washington, Outside and Inside* [Hartford and Chicago: James Betts & Co., 1874], p. 136).

19. *Gilded Age,* I (*Writings,* X), 333.

20. Claude G. Bowers, *The Tragic Era: The Revolution after Lincoln* (Boston: Houghton Mifflin Co., 1929), p. 247.

21. *Iowa City Republican,* January 17, 1866, quoted in Johnson Brigham, *James Harlan* (Iowa City: State Historical Society of Iowa, 1913), p. 220.

22. Brigham, *op. cit.,* pp. 266, 239, 264.

23. Townsend, *op. cit.,* p. 536.

24. Kitzhaber, *KHQ,* XVIII, 254, n. 22. In a deleted passage in the original manuscript Senator Dilworthy is mentioned as the chairman of the "committee on kindred appropriations," to which he refers the Columbus River petition (MS p. 532, in HEH, container HM 1315).

25. Quoted by John B. Ellis, *The Sights and Secrets of the National Capital* (San Francisco: H. H. Bancroft & Co., 1869), p. 196.

26. "Each Congress brought forward a long appropriation bill with items for the benefit of this, that and the other tribe on account of some treaty" (Ellis Paxson Oberholtzer, *A History of the United States since the Civil War,* I [New York: Macmillan Co., 1917], 371).

27. George W. Julian, *Political Recollections, 1840 to 1872* (Chicago: Jansen, McClurg & Co., 1884), pp. 226-27.

28. Oberholtzer, *op. cit.,* I, 77. Oberholtzer claims that the project was abandoned because of remonstrances from adjoining states in Central America; Julian implies that it was because of the discovered fraud.

29. Editorial in *New-York Tribune,* January 30, 1873, p. 4, col. 3.

30. Numbers within parentheses refer to *Writings,* X and XI.

31. Townsend, *op. cit.,* p. 525.

32. *The Olivia Letters* (New York and Washington: Neale Publishing Co., 1906), p. 253.

33. *Ibid.,* pp. 134, 253.

34. Townsend, *op. cit.,* p. 525.

35. Editorial, "A Suspension of Judgment," *New-York Tribune,* February 7, 1873, p. 4, col. 2.

36. Kitzhaber, *KHQ,* XVIII, 249. See also Matthew Josephson, *The Politicos, 1865-1896* (New York: Harcourt, Brace & Co., 1938), p. 53; editorial, "The 'Christian Statesmen,'" *New-York Tribune,* March 1, 1873, p. 6, col. 2.

37. For years Clemens had castigated the hypocrisy of financially profitable religiosity, especially speculation by clergymen. (See, for example, *Sketches of the Sixties: by Bret Harte and Mark Twain,* ed. John Howell [San Francisco: John Howell, 1926], pp. 176-79; *Letters from Honolulu,* pp. 152-53 [Frear, *op. cit.,* p. 373].)

38. *Mark Twain of the* Enterprise, ed. Henry Nash Smith (Berkeley: University of California Press, 1957), p. 133.

39. Frear, *op. cit.,* pp. 452-53. Twain's published letters and newspaper correspondences are replete with deriding references to Nye, and a description of the relationship is given in Twain's autobiography (*Autobiography,* II, 305-7; *Autobiography,* Neider ed., pp. 103-4).

40. Townsend, *op. cit.,* p. 534.

41. In an article, "Doings in Nevada," published in the New York Sunday *Mercury,* February 7, 1864, Twain placed a facetious advertisement beginning: "FOR SALE OR RENT One Governor, entirely new. Attended Sunday-school in his youth, and still remembers it" (*Mark Twain of the* Enterprise, p. 125).

42. William R. Gillis (*Gold Rush Days with Mark Twain* [New York: Albert & Charles Boni, 1930], pp. 148-56) claimed that Clemens had also been Stewart's secretary for a month in Nevada. "Bill" Gillis, however, is an unreliable source. For amusing records of the Washington secretaryship see Twain's sketches, "My Late Senatorial

Secretaryship" and "The Facts Concerning the Recent Resignation," in *Sketches New and Old* (*Writings*, XIX, 190-96, 348-58) and *Reminiscences of Senator William M. Stewart of Nevada*, ed. George Rothwell Brown (New York and Washington: Neale Publishing Co., 1908) (hereafter *Stewart Reminiscences*), pp. 219-24. For serious accounts see Paine, *op. cit.*, I, 346-48; *Letters*, I, 151; Effie Mona Mack, *Mark Twain in Nevada* (New York: Charles Scribner's Sons, 1947), pp. 344-48.

43. George H. Haynes, *The Election of Senators* (New York: Henry Holt & Co., 1906), pp. 87, 88, 95.

44. "If the community had really become suspicious of my honesty, my lease on life would have been short" (*Stewart Reminiscences*, p. 159).

45. See *Stewart Reminiscences, passim,* particularly the passages quoted from Elliott Lord's *History of the Comstock*. The account of the court battle between the Chollar and Potosi companies (pp. 152-59) has many details suggestive of the Dilworthy case.

The French critic Léon Lemonnier (*Mark Twain* [Paris: Librairie Arthème Fayard, 1947], pp. 128-29) states that Dilworthy was Warner's original creation, a claim substantiated only to the extent that the character first appears in chapters written by Warner. Lemonnier admits, however, that "Mark Twain s'y est intéressé et l'a fait vivre dans des chapitres que nous savons être de lui et qui ne s'oublient pas." In this connection it is interesting to note that in his early manuscript Warner referred to "Bumroy" instead of "Dilworthy" (MS pp. 530-33, HEH, HM 1315; also holograph plot outline, MTP, DeVoto 137).

46. *Stewart Reminiscences*, p. 282.

47. It should be added that Clemens had some personal acquaintance with Pomeroy (see *Love Letters*, p. 154).

48. With the exception of a few well-selected references to the *New-York Tribune*, Kitzhaber relies largely upon the *Congressional Globe* and *Senate Reports* of the 42nd Congress, 3rd Session.

49. He had been a correspondent for both newspapers, and later appeared sporadically in their columns of letters to the editor.

50. In Clemens' scrapbooks in MTP are numerous clippings from the *Times*, many of them of a political nature.

51. Quoted by Kitzhaber, *KHQ*, XVIII, 272. Senator Thurman in his minority report for the committee, which declared Pomeroy to be guilty, stated that Pomeroy's allegations were "so opposed to the usual circumstances attending a business transaction . . . that reliance cannot be placed upon them" (*ibid.*, p. 276). The *New-York Tribune* commented: "The explanation of Senator Pomeroy is fantastic, . . . [a] structure of sophistries and shams" (March 4, 1873, p. 4, col. 5).

52. Quoted by Kitzhaber, *KHQ*, XVIII, 260.

53. February 22, 1873, p. 6. The editorial, which described how Nye stepped "briskly to the front" and "took his mother tongue by the hair," concluded, "He isn't nearly as funny as he used to be, but he 'bears aloft the dignity' of the Senate in a most touching and becoming manner."

54. In a speech before the Monday Evening Club in 1873 Clemens referred to "a United States Senate whose members are incapable of determining what crime against law and the dignity of their own body *is*" (*Speeches*, p. 46).

55. Quoted by Kitzhaber, *KHQ*, XVIII, 260.

56. *Mark Twain in Eruption: Hitherto Unpublished Pages about Men and Events,* ed. Bernard DeVoto (New York: Harper & Bros., 1940), p. 82 (dictation of January 30, 1907). Frequently Clemens made such utterances as "I am not a Congress, and I cannot distribute pensions, and I don't know any other legitimate way to buy a vote" (*Speeches*, p. 396).

57. In the vote on impeachment of Andrew Johnson, for example, Pomeroy was reported as having "tried to find out how much he could get for voting for acquittal,

and only became satisfied of Mr. Johnson's guilt when his enquiries proved unsatisfactory" (*Nation*, VI [May 28, 1868], 422).

58. The news broke on January 29.

CHAPTER V

1. The last mention of the use of the Fair case in *The Gilded Age* before 1936 appears to be in Walter M. Fisher, *The Californians* (San Francisco: A. L. Bancroft & Co., 1876), pp. 100-101.

2. "An Influence from San Francisco on Mark Twain's *The Gilded Age*," *American Literature*, VIII (March, 1936), 63-66.

Part of the present chapter appeared originally in my article, "Mark Twain, Laura D. Fair and the New York Criminal Courts," *American Quarterly*, XVI (Winter, 1964), 545-61, and is here republished with the kind permission of the editor.

3. Walker's propositions were based on (1) the fact that Laura was Clemens' heroine (see discussion of the "boss" chapter above, p. 53) and that it was he who was "responsible for the social history" of the novel and (2) the then-known division of labor given in Clemens' letter to Dr. Brown, corroborated by his letter to Mrs. Fairbanks, which was later published by Dixon Wecter (see above, p. 60, and chap. iii, n. 6). Leisy's study of Clemens' annotated copy of the novel, published ten months later, credited all of the pertinent chapters (XXXIX, XLVI, XLVII, LIV, LV, LVI, and LVIII) to Warner, with the exception of the final "boss" chapter, Colonel Sellers' testimony in Chapter LVI (II, 269-73), and the interview with the lecture agent in Chapter LVIII (II, 293-95), all of which were written by Clemens, and the paragraph containing Laura's hypothetical commitment to the Hospital for Lunatic Criminals in Chapter LVIII (II, 290-91), marked "W and C." Examination of extant portions of the manuscript reveals no serious deviation from Clemens' annotation.

4. There are certain discrepancies, however, between the real and the fictional incident that were not mentioned by Walker, as will appear later in this account.

5. Mrs. Fair "first met Crittenden [the victim of her later, fatal shooting] when he successfully defended her in her trial for the rash act. Mark Twain, as a local reporter, could hardly have failed to know both her and Crittenden" (Walker, *American Literature*, VIII, 66). For details of this earlier shooting, see George D. Lyman, *The Saga of the Comstock Lode* (New York: Charles Scribner's Sons, 1934), p. 170.

6. The murder was committed on November 3, 1870. The first trial, which began in April, 1871, ended on June 4 with a verdict of murder in the first degree and Mrs. Fair was sentenced to be hanged on July 28. On appeal, the Supreme Court stayed sentence until February, 1872, when a new trial was ordered on the grounds that the lower court had erred in allowing counsel for the defense to close the arguments and in having allowed evidence of "her former bad character for chastity." On June 9 a motion for a change of venue was overruled and a second trial set for the 24th. On the plea of inaccessibility of witnesses the defense got this trial postponed until the first Monday in September, then to September 9. On September 30, the jury, after being out nearly sixty hours, rendered a verdict of acquittal on the grounds of temporary insanity (*New York Times*, November 5, 1870; June 4, 1871; February 6, June 9 and 27, September 5, October 1, 1872).

7. Like Laura Hawkins, Mrs. Fair had been the mistress of a married man, Judge Alexander P. Crittenden, a leading San Francisco lawyer, though without the bigamous pretense of a false marriage.

In the manuscript the hotel was at one point called the Willard, then changed to the Southern (MS p. 1247, Morse, Container 12b). Did Warner at first intend to place the murder in Washington?

8. It having been announced that Mrs. Fair would deliver a lecture at Platt's Hall in San Francisco on November 21, 1872, a crowd of about two thousand people gathered

in front of the hall and another crowd outside her residence a few blocks away, both of them "boisterous and threatening" according to the *New York Times,* "anxious for a lark" but not noisy or demonstrative according to the San Francisco *Bulletin.* A carriage came for Mrs. Fair, but the Chief of Police warned her against venturing out. When a police posse took possession of the entrance to Mrs. Fair's lodging house, which men had attempted to force, and it was announced at the hall that the lecture had been canceled, the crowds dispersed, including "the man with the basket of spoiled eggs" (*Times,* November 22, 1872, p. 1, col. 6; *Bulletin,* November 22, p. 1, col. 1).

Laura Fair's pamphlet, published in San Francisco in 1873, carried the title originally intended for the lecture, *Wolves in the Fold.*

9. February 8, 1872, p. 4, col. 3. "The utter incompetency of some of the judges brought upon the bench by the system now prevailing in the city of New York, and the mediocre character, to say the least, of the majority of them, are too well known to be disputed for a moment" ("The Judiciary of New York," *North American Review,* CV [July, 1867], 154).

10. July 2, 1872, p. 4, col. 5.

11. Numbers in parentheses in the text refer to the two-volume edition of *The Gilded Age* in *Writings,* X and XI.

12. "The Judiciary of New York," CV (July, 1867), 166. See also "The Tammany Judges," *Harper's Weekly,* XV (December 2, 1871), 1122.

13. See *Nation,* XV (July 11, 1872), 18-19; *New York Times,* July 7, 1872, p. 1, col. 2; *New-York Tribune,* July 8, 1872, p. 8, col. 3; *North American Review,* CXIX (October, 1874), 396. I am indebted to Professor Hamlin Hill for the suggestion that John McCunn was O'Shaunnessy's original.

14. October 1, 1872, p. 4, col. 6. In its report of the acquittal, datelined San Francisco, September 30, the *Times* stated: "The verdict excites no surprise, on account of the inferior character of the jury" (p. 1, col. 7).

15. *Roughing It,* II (*Writings,* VIII), 76; *Speeches,* p. 35.

16. *New-York Tribune,* March 10, 1873, p. 5, as quoted by Arthur L. Vogelback, "Mark Twain, Newspaper Contributor," *Amer. Lit.,* XX (May, 1948), 113; reprinted in *Mark Twain: Life as I Find It,* ed. Charles Neider (Garden City, N.Y.: Hanover House, 1961), pp. 166-67. Cf. Twain's humorous letter to Josh Billings in the *New York Weekly,* July 14, 1873: "An ignorance so shining and conspicuous as yours— Now I have it—go on a jury" (*Twainian,* Vol. III, No. 5, p. 3, February, 1944).

17. G. Manigault, *The United States Unmasked* (London: Edward Stanford, 1879), p. 135.

18. MS p. 1248 (Morse 12b). A deleted sentence on MS p. 1254 states that some-one entering the courtroom "would have mistaken the jury box for the criminal dock, and the twelve good and true jurors for twelve criminals waiting trial" (Yale).

19. See Appendix D, "The *Gilded Age* Manuscript."

20. D. M. McKeithan, *Court Trials in Mark Twain and Other Essays* ([The Hague]: Martinus Nijhoff, 1958), p. 7.

21. William Dean Howells, *My Mark Twain* (New York: Harper & Bros., 1911), p. 15.

22. See McKeithan, *op. cit.,* p. 6. (There are murder trials in the later writings as well—*Tom Sawyer, Pudd'nhead Wilson,* and *Tom Sawyer, Detective.*)

23. See Thomas R. Lounsbury, "Biographical Sketch," in *The Complete Writings of Charles Dudley Warner* (Hartford: American Publishing Co., 1904), XV, ix-x.

24. The editorial (December 12, 1872, p. 4, col. 2) says in part: "When a woman shoots a man because she loves her, or because he does not, or because he says she loves him, or because he loves somebody else or because she does, or because he is sitting in the neighborhood of a person she wants to abolish, or for any other reason which seems good in her beautiful eyes, it is hard to say whether the majority of readers do not

at once jump to the conclusion that the gentle murderer must have suffered bitterly to have been driven to such extremity."

25. Scrapbook in MTP; "Killing No Murder," *Times*, November 25, 1872, p. 8, cols. 1-3.

26. "The defense was insanity; but, as her condition was certainly not insanity in the ordinary and usually accepted significance of that word, it was called 'emotional insanity'" (Theodore H. Hittell, *History of California* [San Francisco: N. J. Stone & Co., 1898], IV, 515).

Cf. *Official Report of the Trial of Laura D. Fair, for the Murder of Alex. P. Crittenden* (San Francisco: San Francisco Co-operative Printing Co., 1871), Preface: "The defense introduced medical testimony, to show that the defendant, at the time of the shooting, and long prior thereto, had been suffering from scanty and retarded menstruation, a chronic disease of the womb, an enemic condition of the blood, and great prostration of the nervous system; and that these organic diseases, together with the disappointment caused by the failure of the deceased to fulfill his promise to get a divorce from his wife and marry the accused, and also his permitting his wife and family to return to this State from the East, contrary to such promise, had affected her mind, and that hence, at times, before, after, and at the time of the shooting, she was crazed, and perfectly unconscious of everything that transpired."

27. The *Nation*, for example, in an editorial on "Jury Morality," had this to say: "The plea of insanity, too, by which murders are now so frequently excused, is receiving . . . dreadful amplification. . . . the symptoms of insanity have, in the hands of mad doctors, been worked up into a system of extreme delicacy and complexity, in which one of the obscurest of all fields of human investigation is elaborately mapped out and placed before ignorant jurymen with as much confidence as the plan of a house or a topographical survey.

". . . it would unquestionably not be a bad plan to follow the suggestion Governor Alcorn has made to the legislature of Mississippi, and deprive juries of all cognizance of the plea of insanity, and make it triable either by competent judges or by a medical tribunal, whose decision should on this point be final" (X [May 19, 1870], 315).

28. *Letters*, I, 188; cf. A. B. Paine, *Mark Twain: A Biography* (New York: Harper & Bros., 1912), II, 438-40.

29. The case of Bridget Dergan in section entitled "Blood" in Letter XXII, dated May 26, 1867, quoted in *Mr. Brown*, pp. 234-35; also in section entitled "Bridget Durgan [*sic*]" in Letter XXV, dated June 5 (*Mr. Brown*, p. 263).

30. *Sketches New and Old* (*Writings*, XIX), p. 250.

31. *Galaxy*, X (July, 1870), 136; reprinted in *The Curious Republic of Gondour and Other Whimsical Sketches* (New York: Boni & Liveright, 1919), p. 40, and *Mark Twain: Life as I Find It*, p. 125; reproduced in *Contributions to* The Galaxy, *1868-1871, by Mark Twain*, ed. Bruce R. McElderry, Jr. (Gainesville, Fla.: Scholars' Facsimiles & Reprints, 1961), p. 60.

32. *Express*, May 14, 1870; reprinted in *Curious Republic of Gondour*, pp. 110-18, and *Life as I Find It*, pp. 109-12. Twain commented again on the McFarland case in the *Galaxy* in July (X, 137-38) under the general heading, interestingly, of "Unburlesquable Things" (see *Life as I Find It*, pp. 126-29; *Contributions to* The Galaxy, pp. 61-62).

33. McKeithan's criticism (p. 20) that the temporary deception of the reader in *The Gilded Age* is not a successful method of satire because it causes irritation is a subjective judgment that completely overlooks the burlesque intent.

34. Hittell, *op. cit.*, p. 516.

35. *The Californians*, p. 100.

36. October 1, 1872, p. 4, col. 5.

37. September 30, 1872, p. 2, col. 1.

38. Ernest E. Leisy, "Mark Twain's Part in *The Gilded Age*," *American Literature*, VIII (January, 1937), 447; *Fairbanks Letters*, p. 171.

39. The *Times* commented editorially: "With such a shepherdess to preside over the innocent lambs of the Pacific coast, and to warn them against the wolves that are always prowling about seeking an entrance into the fold, we see no reason why California should not speedily become a second Garden of Eden, . . ." (November 20, 1872, p. 4, col. 2).

40. *New-York Tribune*, June 5, 1871, p. 1, col. 4.

41. *Times*, July 2, 1872, p. 4, col. 5.

42. This fact goes far toward explaining why the authors did not make more of Colonel Selby's dying deposition in the trial, a seeming oversight pointed out by McKeithan (*op. cit.*, p. 14).

As a lad of seventeen Clemens had accepted unquestioningly the prejudices of his period, casting occasional jibes at women in his brother Orion's *Journal* (Dixon Wecter, *Sam Clemens of Hannibal* [Boston: Houghton Mifflin Co., 1952], pp. 179-80, 258); and fifteen years later, at the age of thirty-two, his attitude was much the same (see Edgar Marquess Branch, *The Literary Apprenticeship of Mark Twain* [Urbana: University of Illinois Press, 1950], p. 192; Frear, *op. cit.*, p. 144). He was favorably impressed, however, with the views of the women's rights leader Anna Dickinson when he heard her lecture in 1867 (*Mr. Brown*, pp. 105-6), and after his marriage his attitude began to change noticeably.

43. Quoted in *Official Report*, p. 2.

44. *Official Report*, p. 1.

45. New Orleans *Times*, n.d., quoted in *New York Times*, July 18, 1871, p. 3, col. 1. See also *Official Report*, Preface.

46. *New York Times*, January 23, 1872, p. 2, col. 6.

47. *Ibid.*, November 23, 1872, p. 8, col. 2.

48. See p. 244.

49. *Colonel Sellers* (Elmira, N.Y., 1874), MS in MTP (Paine 163), Act V, pp. 27-28. This is a stage director's or prompter's copy (see Epilogue, n. 47).

Sellers in his testimony has prepared the audience for Laura's sudden death by mentioning her heart disease.

50. DeLancey Ferguson, "Mark Twain's Lost Curtain Speeches," *South Atlantic Quarterly*, XLII, 262-63; *Chicago Tribune*, September 27, 1874.

51. *Colonel Sellers* (Paine 163), Act IV, pp. 14-15.

52. *Ibid.*, Act V, pp. 22-23.

53. *Ibid.*, Act V, pp. 23-24. A variant MS (Paine 163a, MTP [see Epilogue p. 250 and n. 64; p. 254, n. 76]), a somewhat shortened version, contains a different summation by the prosecution, placing more stress on the ignorant jury theme: "You know it is also said that no Man can take his place here as a Juror untill [*sic*] he has proved to Court & Counsel that he reads neither books nor papers, that he has formed no opinion upon any subject, that he is totally incapable of forming an opinion, that his mind is filled with maudlin sentimentality, & his simpathy's [*sic*] frame his verdict & not his intellect. . . ."

Similarly, Duffer in this version speaks of the emotional insanity plea directly: ". . . this poor injured girl . . . in a fit of emotional insanity killed her destroyer. The law has no *right* & no *desire* to punish her *for* it. For the Law punishes only criminals of sound mind."

54. George Alfred Townsend, *Washington, Outside and Inside* (Hartford and Chicago: James Betts & Co., 1874), pp. 455-57. The "celebrated Mrs. C—," indeed, was not unlike Laura in appearance: "a pretty, dark-eyed, dark-ringleted, girlish person" (Grace Greenwood, "Women at the Capital," *Every Saturday*, III [August 12, 1871], 167).

55. Albert R. Kitzhaber, *"Götterdämmerung* in Topeka: The Downfall of Senator Pomeroy," *Kansas Historical Quarterly*, XVIII (August, 1950), 249.

56. Townsend, *op. cit.*, p. 456. Like Laura, "Mrs. Straitor was a dark eyed lady, . . . very elegant in figure and dress."

57. Emily Edson Briggs, *The Olivia Letters* (New York and Washington: Neale Publishing Co., 1906), p. 92.

58. Mary Clemmer Ames *(Ten Years in Washington: Life and Scenes in the National Capital, as a Woman Sees Them* [Hartford: A. D. Worthington & Co., 1874], p. 128) tells of "a lady in private life in Washington,—a scholar and caustic writer,— [who] used to earn all her pin money . . . by writing, in the solitude of her room, the learned, witty and sarcastic speeches which were thundered in Congress the next day, by some Congressional Jupiter, who could not have launched such a thunder-bolt to have saved his soul had it not been first forged and electrified by a woman. . . ." See also Mrs. John A. Logan, *Thirty Years in Washington* (Hartford: Worthington & Co., 1901), p. 482.

59. *The Emergence of Modern America, 1865-1878* (New York: Macmillan Co., 1928), p. 96.

60. Communication from "Indignant Bachelor" in his brother's Hannibal *Journal*, June 3, 1852, as quoted in Wecter, *op. cit.*, p. 179.

61. Twain, "Female Suffrage. The Iniquitous Crusade . . . ," St. Louis *Daily Missouri Democrat*, March 15, 1867, quoted in Branch, *op. cit.*, p. 192.

62. "The Temperance Crusade and Woman's Rights" (1873), in *Europe and Elsewhere* (New York: Harper & Bros., 1923), pp. 29-30.

63. Ames, *op. cit.* pp. 124-25. Mary Clemmer Ames wrote for the New York *Independent* a penetrating column entitled "A Woman's Letter from Washington" (see George Rothwell Brown, *Washington, a Not Too Serious History* [Baltimore: Norman Publishing Co., 1930], p. 114). See also Logan, *op. cit.*, p. 119.

64. Ben: Perley Poore, *Perley's Reminiscences of Sixty Years in the National Metropolis* (Philadelphia: Hubbard Bros., 1886), p. 48.

65. Townsend, *op. cit.*, p. 456.

66. John B. Ellis, *The Sights and Secrets of the National Capital* (San Francisco: H. H. Bancroft & Co., 1869) p. 428.

67. MTP, DeVoto 137. The leaf is numbered 376 and is apparently from Clemens' original draft of Chapter XLII (II:XI).

68. Claude G. Bowers, *The Tragic Era: The Revolution after Lincoln* (Boston: Houghton Mifflin Co., 1929), pp. 283-84. An interesting contemporary description of the various types of women lobbyists is given in Edward Winslow Martin, *Behind the Scenes in Washington* (Philadelphia: National Publishing Co., 1873), pp. 224-33.

69. *The Ordeal of Mark Twain*, (rev. ed.; New York: E. P. Dutton & Co., 1933), p. 203. Writing before Franklin Walker's article had appeared, Brooks apparently did not know of the Fair case, nor did he recognize the type of the woman lobbyist; hence, his interpretation dwells upon the inhibiting "surveillance" of the authors' wives with their "refined sensibilities," a facet of his general thesis of Twain the thwarted genius. A more accurate interpretation is Minnie M. Brashear's, that Laura "did not properly 'belong,' was not typical of the women whom the men there delighted to honor" (*Mark Twain, Son of Missouri* [Chapel Hill: University of North Carolina Press, 1934], p. 258).

70. Bernard DeVoto, *Mark Twain at Work* (Cambridge: Harvard University Press, 1942), p. 95. "Laura Hawkins of *The Gilded Age,* for instance, is just bisque and Joan of Arc is no more than tears."

71. The thesis of Clemens' sexual squeamishness so popular in the psychoanalytical criticism of the twenties and thirties is hardly borne out by his published writings. Consider, for example, this description of two "regulars" in a San Francisco jail: "The

two women were nearly middle-aged, and they had only had enough liquor to stimulate instead of stupefy them. Consequently they would fondle and kiss each other for some minutes, and then fall to fighting . . ." ("Goldsmith's Friend Abroad Again," Letter V, *Galaxy*, X [November, 1870], 728; reprinted in *Curious Republic of Gondour*, p. 90, and *Life As I Find It*, p. 81; reproduced in *Contributions to* The Galaxy, p. 92).

CHAPTER VI

1. VI (January 17, 1874), 38. See also *Independent*, XXVI (January 1, 1874), 1642.

2. In MTP.

3. M. R. Werner, *Tammany Hall* (New York: Doubleday Doran & Co., 1928), p. 240.

4. Numbers within parentheses refer to the two-volume edition of the novel in *Writings*, X and XI.

5. Charles F. Wingate, "An Episode in Municipal Government," II, *North American Review*, CXX (January, 1875), 139.

6. May 11, 1870, p. 12, col. 1; May 13, p. 4, col. 4. Clemens had previously called this incident "eminently unburlesquable" (in "Unburlesquable Things," *Galaxy*, X [July, 1870], 137-38; reproduced in *Contributions to* The Galaxy, *1868-1871, by Mark Twain*, ed. Bruce R. McElderry, Jr. [Gainesville, Fla.: Scholars' Facsimiles & Reprints, 1961], pp. 61-62; reprinted in *Mark Twain: Life as I Find It*, ed. Charles Neider [Garden City, N.Y.: Hanover House, 1961], pp. 126-29).

7. Matthew Josephson, *The Politicos, 1865-1896* (New York: Harcourt, Brace & Co., 1938), p. 95. The hypothesis that Murphy was O'Riley's original is strengthened by two facts: (1) Laura speaks to Mrs. Oreillé of "a dear old friend of our family named Murphy," whom she proceeds to ridicule with little subtlety and with pointed *double-entendre;* (2) the real Thomas Murphy was Collector of the Port of New York under Grant, and Twain goes out of his way to make a jibe or two at the New York Customs House (see, for example, II, 90).

8. Charles A. and Mary R. Beard, *The Rise of American Civilization* (New York: Macmillan Co., 1937), II, 310; Werner, *op. cit.*, p. 166.

9. See James Ford Rhodes, *History of the United States from the Compromise of 1850 to the Final Restoration of Home Rule at the South in 1877* (New York: Macmillan Co., 1920), VI, 396.

10. Regarding Tweed at Albany see Allan Nevins, *The Emergence of Modern America, 1865-1878* (New York: Macmillan Co., 1928), p. 183; Ellis Paxson Oberholtzer, *A History of the United States Since the Civil War*, II (New York: Macmillan Co., 1922), 583.

11. CV (July, 1867), 148.

12. For Jennings' campaign see Oberholtzer, *op. cit.*, II, 586, 588; Samuel P. Orth, *The Boss and the Machine* (New Haven: Yale University Press, 1919), p. 75.

Clemens wanted Nast as illustrator: "I want him, solitary & alone, to illustrate this next book, it being an essentially *American* book, & he will enjoy doing it. Nast only has just one *first-class* talent (caricature,) & no more—but this book will exercise that talent, I think" (letter to Elisha Bliss, March 4, 1873, in C. Waller Barrett Collection, University of Virginia Library, Charlottesville, quoted in Hamlin Hill, *Mark Twain and Elisha Bliss* [Columbia: University of Missouri Press, 1964], pp. 76-77).

13. P. 6, col. 1. See Arthur L. Vogelback, "Mark Twain and the Tammany Ring," *PMLA*, LXX (March, 1955), 69-77.

14. *The Curious Republic of Gondour and Other Whimsical Sketches* (New York: Boni & Liveright, 1919), pp. 9-10; reprinted from *Atlantic Monthly*, XXXVI (October 1875), 463.

15. G. Manigault, *The United States Unmasked* (London: Edward Stanford, 1879), pp. 129-30.

16. ". . . even those publishers whose political and social convictions carry them a long way with him in the views herein expressed shrank from becoming god-fathers to his bantling. To do so would jeopardize their business interests, . . ." ("Preface").

17. Edgar Lee Masters, *Mark Twain: A Portrait* (New York: Charles Scribner's Sons, 1938), p. 137. See Kenneth S. Lynn, *Mark Twain and Southwestern Humor* (Boston: Little, Brown & Co., 1959), pp. 201-2: "Twain's new enthusiasm for the Republican party was destined to be short-lived."

18. So named after a similar financing organization in France which precipitated a period of wild stock gambling during the Second Empire. *Mobilier* means "movable" in the sense of property securing a loan. (See *New-York Tribune*, February 6, 1873, p. 2, col. 5.)

19. See Louis M. Hacker and Benjamin B. Kendrick, *The United States Since 1865* (New York: F. S. Crofts & Co., 1932), pp. 34-35; Charles F., Jr., and Henry Adams, *Chapters of Erie, and Other Essays* (Boston: James R. Osgood & Co., 1871), p. 146.

20. Ames letter of January 25, 1868, quoted in *New York Times*, January 7, 1873, p. 5, col. 3. "We want more friends in this Congress, and if a man will look into the law, . . . it is difficult to get them to do it unless they have an interest to do so."

21. Hacker and Kendrick, *op. cit.*, p. 35.

22. Testimony of Henry S. McComb, reported in *New York Times*, January 7, 1873, p. 5, col. 2.

23. Oberholtzer, *op. cit.*, II, 607-8.

24. Before being elected to Congress, Patterson had been professor of astronomy and meteorology at Dartmouth College (William H. Barnes, *History of the Thirty-Ninth Congress of the United States* [New York: Harper & Bros., 1868], p. 609).

25. Possibly, Benjamin Ham, treasurer of the Crédit Mobilier.

26. Unused Clemens holograph MS pages, numbered 3, 4, and 5, MTP, DeVoto 137.

27. In Clemens' 1872-73 scrapbook (MTP) is an undated, unidentified clipping (probably from the Hartford *Courant*) giving quotations from the Boston *Advertiser* and New York *World* on Ames's testimony.

It is interesting, in this connection, that Senator Harlan, Twain's Brother Balaam, was accused of accepting $10,000 from the Union Pacific ring to help purchase his re-election in 1866 (Johnson Brigham, *James Harlan* [Iowa City: State Historical Society of Iowa, 1913], p. 280).

28. The Boston *Saturday Evening Gazette*, for example, stated that the Crédit Mobilier scheme was "depicted with photographic accuracy" (undated review reprinted in large broadside, "Notices of the Press," in MTP).

29. XV (April, 1873), 560-61.

30. "The effect of the Crédit Mobilier revelations on popular feeling was far-reaching. They were regarded as confirming the worst suspicions current in reference both to the methods of railway corporations and to the influences pervading official life at Washington" (William Archibald Dunning, *Reconstruction, Political and Economic, 1865-1877* [New York: Harper & Bros., 1907], p. 233).

A group becoming as notorious as the "Christian Statesmen" were the "Railway Congressmen" (see Josephson, *op. cit.*, p. 53). "McCulloch says the ring of railroad men . . . is controlling Congress" (Gideon Welles, *Diary of Gideon Welles* [Boston: Houghton Mifflin Co., 1911], III, 425; see also pp. 460, 474, 576).

31. Oberholtzer, *op. cit.*, I (1917), 328.

32. *Report of the Secretary of the Interior*, U.S. 39th Cong., 1st sess., H. Ex. Doc. 1 (Washington, D.C., 1865), pp. 980-81.

33. Article in the Cincinnati *Gazette*, probably by H. V. Boynton, quoted in John B. Ellis, *The Sights and Secrets of the National Capital* (San Francisco: H. H. Bancroft & Co., 1869), p. 192.

34. Ellis, *op. cit.*, pp. 191-92, 199. See also E. H. Grant, *Twelve Years in the*

United States Senate: A Brief Sketch of the Senatorial Record of Hon. S. C. Pomeroy of Kansas, Compiled from the Congressional Globe (Washington, D.C.: Privately printed, 1872), pp. 13-14.

35. In 1868, for example, Harlan was exposed as having withdrawn from sale along the extension of the Burlington and Missouri River Railroad "a tract large enough for a very respectable State" for the benefit of himself and "the honorable Senator from Kansas" and their personal friends (article by H. V. Boynton in Cincinnati *Gazette,* quoted in Brigham, *op. cit.,* pp. 238-40).

36. Article in Leavenworth (Kansas) *Times,* datelined Washington, June 23, 1866 (clipping in album, Political Record of S. C. Pomeroy, in library of Kansas State Historical Society).

37. "Salt Lick," in fact, becomes "Salt Lake" in the play *Colonel Sellers* (Act III) (MTP, Paine 163).

38. In an unsigned article written when he was in Missouri as a railroad surveyor ("Salt Lake and the New Saratoga," *Putnam's Monthly,* II [September, 1853], 260-64), Charles Dudley Warner confesses "with all modesty" to a partiality for the very route he was surveying, "westward to St. Joseph, up the south bank of the North Ford of the Platte to Fort Laramie, and so through South Pass to Salt Lake."

39. Ellis Paxson Oberholtzer, *Jay Cooke, Financier of the Civil War* (Philadelphia: George W. Jacobs & Co., 1907), II, 165.

40. *Ibid., loc. cit.*

An editorial entitled "The Railroad Fraternity," in the *Nation,* May 21, 1868 (VI, 406-8), outlines the corruption that tainted "the very birth of nine-tenths of the roads." Showing how a company would start with a portion of its stock given away before it had "really come into existence," the article relates in sober exposition the subject presented in the dialogue of Harry Brierly and the company president.

41. Quoted in Oberholtzer, *Jay Cooke,* II, 190.

42. *Ibid.,* II, 179-80.

43. For example, in 1871 he published his *Burlesque Autobiography,* which had running through it a series of cartoons of the Erie Railroad Ring presented as a modified version of "The House That Jack Built" to illustrate the Ring's swindling methods and caricaturing Jay Gould, "Jim" Fiske, and others (Albert Bigelow Paine, *Mark Twain: A Biography: The Personal and Literary Life of Samuel Langhorne Clemens* [New York: Harper & Bros., 1912], I, 433). And in his Sandwich Island lecture in Brooklyn on February 7, 1873, he gave as an example of the probability of the Kanakas' doing "everything wrong end first" if the Islands were annexed: "Instead of fostering and encouraging a judicious system of railway speculations, . . . they will elect the most incorruptible men to Congress" (Walter Francis Frear, *Mark Twain and Hawaii* [Chicago: p. p., 1947], p. 435).

44. Clemens made a brief trip to Washington in July, 1870, to lobby for a bill of interest to "our Tennesseans." The bill, which failed to pass, was for division of Tennessee into two judicial districts and had no known connection with the family Tennessee Land (see *Love Letters,* p. 153).

45. "The scheme was worthy of such a Christian Statesman as Senator Dillworthy [*sic*]" (deleted sentence from MS p. 1044, by Warner [Morse, Container 12b]).

46. MS p. 1003 (Morse, 12b).

47. See Nevins, *op. cit.,* p. 16.

48. William M. Stewart, *Reminiscences of Senator William M. Stewart of Nevada* (New York and Washington, Neale Publishing Co., 1908), p. 198.

49. Grant, *op. cit.,* p. 10.

50. Quoted by Kenneth R. Andrews (*Nook Farm, Mark Twain's Hartford Circle* [Cambridge: Harvard University Press, 1950], pp. 181 and 264, n. 73).

51. *New-York Tribune,* March 4, 1873, p. 1, col. 2.

52. Pomeroy had introduced bills for steamship lines with Europe, China, Japan, and Australia (Grant, *op. cit.*, p. 10).

53. Oberholtzer, *History*, II, 516-18; III (1926), 131-32.

54. Mark Twain had already taken a dig at earlier, unsuccessful attempts of the steamship lobby in the October, 1870, issue of the *Galaxy*, saying that the American consul at San Francisco would have to continue charging the extortionate immigration fee "dishonestly until next Congress makes it legitimate" ("Goldsmith's Friend Abroad Again," Letter II [X, 569-70]; reprinted in *Curious Republic of Gondour*, p. 78, and *Mark Twain: Life As I Find It*, p. 76; reproduced in *Contributions to* The Galaxy, pp. 79-80).

55. James Truslow Adams, *The March of Democracy* (New York: Charles Scribner's Sons, 1933), II, 146-47; Josephson, *op. cit.*, p. 186.

56. Dunning, *op. cit.*, p. 234.

57. *Mark Twain's Notebook* (New York: Harper & Bros., 1935), p. 130.

58. Benjamin F. Butler, former Union general and congressman from Massachusetts, spearheaded the Salary Grab action "with an insolence that could only have come from a sense of supreme command of the situation" (Josephson, *op. cit.*, p. 186).

59. J. T. Adams, *op. cit.*, p. 147.

60. Unused Clemens MS leaf, MTP, DV 137. In the top margin are two notes, one "Foot-note. small," the other "Perhaps this better go on a fly-leaf *after* last chapter." In a letter to the *New-York Tribune* (April 11, 1873, p. 5), he mentions "the project of paying Congressmen over again for work which they had already been paid to do, that is to say, the labor of receiving Credit Mobilier donations and forgetting the circumstance" (Vogelback, "Mark Twain Newspaper Contributor," *American Literature*, XX [May, 1948], 117).

61. Josephson, *op. cit.*, pp. 143-46.

62. Nevins, *op. cit.*, pp. 166-67; Dunning, *op. cit.*, pp. 140-41.

63. Anthony Bimba, *The History of the American Working Class* (London: Martin Lawrence, Ltd., 1927), p. 162, quoting Perlman, *History of Trade Unionism in the United States*, p. 51.

64. Oberholtzer, *History*, III, 87. Senator Pomeroy, it might be noted, had recommended increasing the national currency by twenty million (Grant, *op. cit.*, p. 10).

65. Oberholtzer, *Jay Cooke*, II, 288; *History*, III, 87-88. When brought to book, Boutwell tried to turn the blame onto his assistant, William A. Richardson.

66. Mark Twain's own opinion of greenbacks is given in "A Royal Compliment," *Galaxy*, X, 429-30, where he speaks of being offered the Spanish throne: "My salary must be paid in gold; when greenbacks are fresh in a country, they are too fluctuating" (*Gondour*, pp. 61-62; *Contributions*, pp. 73-74; *Life As I Find It*, pp. 120-22).

67. Mrs. John A. Logan, *Thirty Years in Washington* (Hartford: A. D. Worthington & Co., 1901), p. 512.

68. See account of this experience in Chapter VII.

69. The "Alabama claims" were made against Great Britain for damages inflicted upon Northern shipping by the famous Confederate armed raider the *Alabama*, which had been built in England and outfitted with guns made there. British law had been technically evaded by the transparent device of outfitting the British-made vessel with its British-made armor on the high seas (Oberholtzer, *History*, II, 391 ff).

70. See sarcastic editorial in the *Nation*, XII (May 18, 1871), 329-30; also pp. 349, 373, 393.

71. Logan, *op. cit.*, p. 127.

72. Ellis, *op. cit.*, p. 150.

73. Mark Twain apparently found the franking abuse so symptomatic of Congressional morality that he referred to it no less than three times in the novel: II, 50, 52-53, 301.

74. II Pet. 2:15; Num. 22:5-24:25.

75. See above, p. 92. In the original manuscript he is, in fact, called "Senator Bly"; then *Bly* has been deleted and replaced with *Balloon*.

76. Emily Edson Briggs, *The Olivia Letters* (New York and Washington: Neale Publishing Co., 1906), p. 51; George Alfred Townsend, *Washington, Outside and Inside* (Hartford and Chicago: James Betts & Co., 1874), p. 372. Clemens himself described him as "looking around to each speaker with the air of a man who has half a mind to crush them [*sic*]" (*Notebook*, p. 116).

77. Briggs, *op. cit.*, p. 32. One of the few national legislators accorded more than a line or two in Clemens' notebook is "Alison [*sic*] of Iowa," who "plays for handsome looks" and "stands around where women can see him" (*Notebook*, p. 114).

78. See Edward McPherson, *The Political History of the United States of America During the Period of Reconstruction* (Washington, D.C.: Philp & Solomons, 1871), pp. 182, 183, 347, 348, 508. (Clemens gives a "John Buckland (O.)" in his notebook list [*Notebook*, p. 114].) For the last-mentioned I am indebted to Hamlin Hill, whose suggestion it is.

79. It should be added, however, that Twain's description of Trollop's appearance as a "grave, carefully dressed and very respectable-looking man, with a bald head, standing collar, and old-fashioned watch seals" indicates that he may have had a real person in mind.

80. Briggs, *op. cit.*, pp. 229-35; see also Andrews, *op. cit.*, p. 36.

81. VI (January 17, 1874), 38.

82. Letter dated Rodney, Mississippi, February 20, 1874, in MTP.

83. See [Warner,] *Putnam's Monthly*, II, 260; James G. Blaine, *Twenty Years of Congress* (Norwich, Conn.: Henry Bill Publishing Co., 1886), I, 558.

84. March 16, 1872, p. 203, col. 3. "JEFF haunts the saloons," the report continues, "and takes the oath of allegiance (with a little sugar) as often as his fellow-citizens invite him." (In *The Gilded Age,* Jeff boasts of his ability "to drink from a jug with one hand. It's as easy as lying" [I, 188].)

85. See above, p. 137.

86. Edwin L. Sabin, *Building of the Pacific Railway* (Philadelphia: J. B. Lippincott Co., 1919), pp. 74-75, 215.

87. Duff Green had engineered through the Pennsylvania legislature a bill authorizing the Pennsylvania Fiscal Agency, which later was renamed Crédit Mobilier of America (see George Francis Train, *My Life in Many States and in Foreign Lands* [New York: D. Appleton & Co., 1902], p. 285).

88. Sabin, *op. cit.*, pp. 75, 215; Julius Grodinsky, *Jay Gould: His Business Career, 1867-1892* (Philadelphia: University of Pennsylvania Press, 1957), p. 122; "Sidney Dillon," *Dictionary of American Biography.*

In the manuscript, Schaick at first is called "Gold," a circumstance that suggests that Warner originally had in mind Jay Gould, the power behind Dillon. The description, however, which has not been altered, does not touch on Gould's most salient characteristics, and "Gold" may be no more than a symbolic cognomen for a person of great wealth. It is, incidentally, suggestive that the first syllables of *Dill*on and *Dill*worthy (as it was originally spelled in early Warner manuscript) are identical.

89. Thompson's letter states that "Ben Grayson lives at Fort Dodge, Iowa." Thompson writes: ". . . John Duff, Senator Pomeroy—Grayson, and others, *I knew at first sight,* . . . ."

Thompson also appears to have known the original of Harry Brierly, a young man named Henry Dakin. Thompson writes Warner: "Your description of him is true to life, and I hope some rich widow has adopted him, and provided for him." I have been unable to trace Dakin further.

90. This delightfully satirical name combines real and imaginatively suggestive names. Tunkhannock is on the Lehigh Valley Railroad; and Youngwomanstown echoes

Youngwood (Pa.), Elizabethtown (Pa.), and Youngstown (O.), all on the Pennsylvania Railroad.

91. Blaine, *op cit.*, I, 524, 526; II, 221, 397.

92. See J. Thomas Scharf and Thompson Westcott, *History of Philadelphia, 1609-1884* (Philadelphia: L. H. Everts & Co., 1884), I, 680. Interestingly, the merchants of Philadelphia were afraid of losing trade to another city, as, about the same time, those of Hannibal, Missouri, were when the planning of the Hannibal and St. Jo began (see pp. 162-63).

93. See Henry Kirke White, *History of the Union Pacific Railway* (Chicago: University of Chicago Press, 1895), p. 23; Train, *op. cit.*, pp. 285-86; n. 87 above.

The satirical name Pennybacker is of course a parody of the Philadelphia name Pennypacker (see Scharf and Westcott, *op. cit.*, II, 1168).

94. In Warner's manuscript for this passage, a later reference to Simon as "Cameron" has been deleted and the pronoun "he" substituted (MS p. 1116, in HEH, Container HM 470).

95. MS p. 840, in Lilly; photostat in MTP.

96. George Rothwell Brown, *Washington, a Not Too Serious History* (Baltimore: Norman Publishing Co., 1930), p. 322.

97. George C. D. Odell, *Annals of the New York Stage* (New York: Columbia University Press, 1927-1949), I, 337-61.

98. Frank Luther Mott, *A History of American Magazines* (Cambridge: Harvard University Press, 1938), II, 37-38 and n. 50.

99. Mott, *op. cit.*, I, 442.

100. Begun in 1848, this monthly was published in Philadelphia by J. S. Skinner & Son.

101. The date of the first number is January 1, 1873.

102. Hamlin Hill has pointed out to me, for example, that a reference to "Japs" in Chapter XXXVIII (II, 73) reflects a precedent-breaking arrival of a Japanese delegation at Washington in 1871, and that the sale of West Point cadetships in Chapter LI (II, 220) refers to a minor political scandal of 1870.

CHAPTER VII

1. *Autobiography*, I, 3-4, 88, 93-94; Neider ed., pp. 22, 18, 24-25.

2. Dixon Wecter, *Sam Clemens of Hannibal* (Boston: Houghton Mifflin Co., 1952), p. 278, n. 9; *Mark Twain in Eruption: Hitherto Unpublished Pages about Men and Events*, ed. Bernard DeVoto (New York: Harper & Bros., 1940), p. xviii.

3. DeLancey Ferguson, *Mark Twain: Man and Legend* (Indianapolis: Bobbs-Merrill Co., 1943), p. 50.

4. Letter from St. Louis dated March 9, 1858, in *Letters*, I, 38.

5. *Ibid.*, I, 50.

6. Letter from Honolulu dated May 22, 1866, in *MT, Business Man*, p. 87. See also notebook entry, "At sea, Mar. 9 [1866] Just read letters from home . . . Accounts of oil on the Tenn. land" (*Mark Twain's Notebook* [New York: Harper & Bros., 1935], p. 9).

7. Letter from Buffalo dated September 9, 1870 (*Letters*, I, 176); cf. Albert Bigelow Paine, *Mark Twain: A Biography: The Personal and Literary Life of Samuel Langhorne Clemens* (New York: Harper & Bros., 1912), II, 478. Also see letter of November 9, 1869, to his sister, Pamela, in St. Louis: "Ma thinks it is hard that Orion's share of the land should be swept away just as it is right on the point (as it always *has* been) of becoming valuable. . . . This letter is his ample authority to sell *my* share of the land *immediately* and appropriate the proceeds . . ." (*Letters*, I, 167).

In April, 1906, Clemens discovered that "a correction of the ancient surveys" showed that John Clemens' heirs, now only Pamela's son and daughter and himself, still owned a thousand acres. "This time I hope we shall get rid of the Tennessee land for good and all and never hear of it again. It was created under a misapprehension; my father loaded himself up with it under a misapprehension; he unloaded it on to us under a misapprehension, and I should like to get rid of the accumulated misapprehensions and what is left of the land as soon as possible" (*Autobiography*, II, 321-22; Neider ed., p. 219).

8. *Autobiography*, I, 94; cf. Neider ed., p. 24.

9. Numbers within parentheses refer to the two-volume edition of the novel in *Writings*, X and XI.

10. Ferguson, *op. cit.*, p. 17.

11. *Autobiography*, I, 88, 4; Neider ed., pp. 18, 22. See also Paine, *op. cit.*, I, 6.

12. *Autobiography*, I, 5; Neider ed., p. 23.

13. "Correction (1906)—it was above 100,000 it appears" (Mark Twain's footnote, *Autobiography*, I, 88). Cf. Neider ed.: "around 100,000 acres" (p. 22).

14. Paine, *op. cit.*, I, 6; also Ferguson, *op. cit.*, p. 17. Cf. *Autobiography*, I, 3 (Neider ed., p. 22), quoted above p. 146.

15. *Autobiography*, I, 4-5; Neider ed., pp. 22-23. The latter edition has "around 1860" in place of "eight years ago."

16. In 1897-98, Clemens, apparently forgetful of his earlier statement, has his father saying "that in the course of time railways would pierce to that region and then the property would be property in fact as well as in name" (*Autobiography*, I, 88; Neider ed., p. 18).

17. *Autobiography*, I, 89 (Neider ed., p. 19). See also I, 6 (Neider ed., p. 24): ". . . my father would brighten up and gather heart, even upon his death-bed, when he thought of the Tennessee land. He said that it would soon make us all rich and happy. And so believing, he died."

18. Paine, *op. cit.*, I, 23.

19. *MT, Business Man*, p. 11.

20. *Ibid.*, pp. 16-17. As early as 1841 or 1842 John Clemens was trying to raise money on the land (Paine, *op. cit.*, I, 43).

21. *The Gilded Age*, I, 69-76. The many abortive ventures to sell the Tennessee land, both by John Clemens and, after his father's death, by Orion seem to have been epitomized in this episode, which distils the essential psychological components of such ventures into a single scene. Mark Twain writes: "After my father's death we reorganized the domestic establishment, but on a temporary basis, . . . believing, as we all did, that it was not worth while to go at anything in serious earnest until the land was disposed of and we could embark intelligently in something" (*Autobiography*, I, 6-7; Neider ed., p. 24). See also Ferguson, *op. cit.*, p. 54.

22. *Autobiography*, I, 93-94; Neider ed., p. 24. Cf. Webster, in *MT, Business Man*, p. 88: "The Tennessee land finally drifted away somehow. Perhaps there was a flood. My mother has a vague memory of getting two hundred and fifty dollars from it for a quitclaim deed. I think I remember signing some papers about it myself, . . ."

23. As already noted (see above, n. 7), there was in real life an anticlimactic discovery of a contested one thousand acres. (See Paine, *op. cit.*, I, 6 [written shortly afterward]: "The land is priceless now, . . ."; cf. Philip S. Foner, *Mark Twain: Social Critic* [New York: International Publishers, 1958], p. 10: ". . . the land proved to be so poor that it yielded nothing but potatoes and wild grass . . . .")

24. Paine, *op. cit.*, II, 478.

25. *Ibid.*, I, 2, 5.

26. *Ibid.*, I, 14; Wecter, *op. cit.*, p. 50.

27. MS p. 4, in Morse, Container 12b. The facts stated, so typical of John Clemens, were deleted by Mark Twain, undoubtedly as being irrelevant at this point in the story and possibly as seeming to present a side of Squire Hawkins that he did not plan to emphasize.

In the *Autobiography*, Neider ed., pp. 23-24 (I, 6), Clemens writes that his father "did the friendly office of 'going security' for Ira Stout, and Ira walked off and deliberately took the benefit of the new bankrupt law—a deed which enabled him to live easily and comfortably along till death called for him, but a deed which ruined my father, sent him poor to his grave and condemned his heirs to a long and discouraging struggle with the world for a livelihood. . . ."

28. Wecter, *op. cit.*, p. 30.

29. *Autobiography*, I, 87-88 (Neider ed., p. 18); Paine, *op. cit.*, I, 5; Wecter, *op. cit.*, p. 30.

30. Paine, *op. cit.*, I, 2, 5; Minnie M. Brashear, *Mark Twain, Son of Missouri* (Chapel Hill: University of North Carolina Press, 1934), pp. 87-88; *Gilded Age*, I, 14.

31. Paine, *op. cit.*, I, 7-8; cf. Wecter, *op. cit.*, pp. 33-34.

It is an interesting side note that one of the subscription canvassers for *The Gilded Age* had the authenticity of the novel brought home to her when she delivered three books at a stage stop in Concord, California, receiving the money from her seat on the stage: "I could not help laughing—as I filled those orders—which reminded me of 'Hawkin's' [*sic*] post-office in the 'Gilded Age,' where there were from two to three letters received in about so many months. My book business in Costa Contra [*sic*] County gave me plenty of time to rest between deliveries, as that post-office did the 'Squire' " (*Facts* by a woman [Oakland, Calif.: Privately printed, 1881], p. 107).

32. Wecter (*op. cit.*, pp. 30-31) quotes a manuscript in MTP entitled "The Tennessee Land," which Clemens evidently used as the basis for this passage. As later incorporated into the Neider edition of the *Autobiography* (p. 23) it reads: " 'Jim's come back from Kaintuck and fotch a stuck-up gal with him from up thar; and bless you they've got more new-fangled notions, massy *on* us! Common log house ain't good enough for *them*—no indeedy!—but they've tuck 'n' gaumed the inside of theirn all over with some kind of nasty disgustin' truck which they say is all the go in Kaintuck amongst the upper hunky and which they calls it plarsterin'!' "

33. *Autobiography*, I, 5; cf. Neider ed., p. 23.

34. *Ibid.*, I, 5, 7; Neider ed., pp. 1, 23.

35. Paine, *op. cit.*, I, 10-11.

36. In the manuscript is added Twain's crossed-out note: "That is to say, they started to Missouri" (MS p. 33 [Morse, 12b]).

37. See above, p. 45 and Chapter II, n. 38.

38. Léon Lemonnier, *Mark Twain* (Paris: Librairie Arthème Fayard, 1946), p. 77: ". . . il semble que Mark Twain a l'intention, comme dans *Tom Sawyer*, d'affaiblir le lien de parenté afin de se sentir plus libre et de ne pas manquer de respect à son père."

It is noteworthy in this connection that both Nancy Hawkins and Aunt Polly are sympathetic characters evoking respect.

39. Letter to Warner from Jeff Thompson, February 20, 1874, in MTP.

40. *Autobiography*, I, 100; Neider ed., p. 6. See also Walter Blair, *Mark Twain & Huck Finn* (Berkeley: University of California Press, 1960), p. 107; Wecter, *op. cit.*, p. 100.

41. The episode to a certain extent stems out of the tradition of the southwestern humorists and in its underlying tone (though not style) is anticipated in one of Twain's Snodgrass letters. Upon seeing his first locomotive Snodgrass has "three chills and a stroke of palsy in less than five minutes" (Samuel Langhorne Clemens, *The Adventures of Thomas Jefferson Snodgrass* [Chicago: Pascal Covici, 1928], pp. 19-33). Cf. *Gilded Age*, I, 36: "The awful thunder of a mud-valve suddenly burst forth, . . . and as suddenly Uncle Dan'l snatched a child under each arm and scoured into the woods . . . ."

42. Fred Lewis Pattee (*A History of American Literature Since 1870* [New York: Century Co., 1915], p. 61) states: "The steamboat race and the explosion in chapter four of *The Gilded Age* have few equals in any language for mere picturing power."

43. Commentators have generally assumed that the wreck of the steamboat *Amaranth* in *The Gilded Age* is based simply on that of the ill-fated *Pennsylvania*, which

killed Henry Clemens (see, for example, Edgar Lee Masters, *Mark Twain: A Portrait* [New York: Charles Scribner's Sons, 1938], p. 31; Laurens D. Mason, "Real People in Mark Twain's Stories," *Overland Monthly*, LXXXIX [January, 1931], 13). This is to a large extent true. The "little wee French midshipman of fourteen" in the novel, who when he is told that he cannot survive his injuries replies, "Then do not waste your time with me—help those that can get well" (I, 53), is obviously the "young French naval cadet of fourteen" described in *Life on the Mississippi,* who was "fearfully scalded" in the *Pennsylvania* explosion "but bore his tortures manfully" (*Writings,* IX, 173). After the fictional *Amaranth's* boilers explode, the "whole forward half of the boat" is left "a shapeless ruin, with the great chimneys lying crossed on top of it" (I, 51); when the *Pennsylvania's* boilers exploded, "the whole forward third of the boat was hoisted toward the sky" and then the "main part of the mass, with the chimneys, dropped upon the boat again" (*Writings,* IX, 172).

The little Frenchman is the unmistakable link; the location of the explosion and its effect upon the chimneys can be taken as typical of such disasters, as can many of the lesser details of the two accounts, such as the entrapment of passengers under the debris, the outbreak of fire, the forcing back of the fire-fighters by the heat, and the cries of the still-conscious abandoned victims. The similarity of some of the wording is possibly significant, though it may mean nothing more than identical authorship. In any case, Clemens is writing about the *Amaranth* out of firsthand experience with river disasters, and the authenticity of description is as convincing as anything in the later, autobiographical *Life on the Mississippi.* The compelling motivation for his using elements of the *Pennsylvania* disaster was his deep feeling of personal guilt for his brother's presence on this boat at the time of its wreck and for his own absence (Paine, *op. cit.,* I, 140 ff.).

Bernard DeVoto (*Mark Twain's America* [Boston: Little, Brown & Co., 1932], pp. 253-54) has pointed out a remarkable similarity between the *Gilded Age* episode and the description of a steamboat race in the sketch "Stopping to Wood," which first appeared in the St. Louis *Reveille,* September 22, 1845, and was reprinted in the *Spirit of the Times,* October 11, 1845, in J. M. Field's *The Drama in Pokerville* (1847), and in *Major Thorpe's Scenes in Arkansaw* (1858). Mark Twain may well have borrowed from this widely circulated sketch as part of the effort for topicality.

44. Paine, *op. cit.,* I, 68, n. 1; 80.

45. Wecter, *op. cit.,* p. 183.

46. See *MT, Business Man,* pp. 51-58.

47. *Letters,* II, 787.

48. *Autobiography,* Neider ed., pp. 79-80.

49. *MT, Business Man,* pp. 55, 57.

50. "Dear Master Wattie: The Mark Twain—David Watt Bowser Letters," ed. Pascal Covici, Jr., *Southwest Review,* XLV (Spring, 1960), 106, 108.

51. *Notebook,* p. 183.

52. *Autobiography,* Neider ed., p. 81.

53. *MT, Business Man,* p. 55; *Autobiography,* Neider ed., p. 81.

54. See above, pp. 65-66.

55. *Autobiography,* Neider ed., pp. 81-82.

56. According to Webster (*MT, Business Man,* pp. 4-5), Jane Clemens, Sam's mother, once said that they had intended to settle in St. Louis but had decided to go on to Florida when they heard that a Negro boy had been lynched and that there was cholera in the city. If Jane Clemens' memory was reliable, her account, so at variance with Paine's account of the Quarles letter, probably indicates at most a quite typical indecisiveness on the part of her husband.

57. *Autobiography,* I, 7. In a facetious passage written twenty years later Twain says: "The village contained a hundred people and I increased the population by 1 per

cent. It is more than many of the best men in history could have done for a town" (I, 95). The later passage is substituted for the earlier statement, without comment, in the Neider edition (p. 1).

58. Cf. Brashear, *op. cit.*, p. 51.

59. In the manuscript, Hawkeye is at first introduced as Hawkeye Forks, then Forks is immediately dropped (MS p. 178 [Morse, 12b]).

60. Advertisement, "Lots for Sale in the Town of Florida," Columbia *Missouri Intelligencer*, April 16, 1831, reproduced in Brashear, *op. cit.*, opp. p. 30; *ibid.*, p. 49; Wecter, *op. cit.*, p. 36.

61. See Brashear, *op. cit.*, plate opp. p. 30, p. 49; *The Twainian*, Vol. I, No. 2, p. 3.

62. Brashear, *op. cit.*, pp. 49, 50; "Salt River Navigation," Hannibal *Commercial Advertiser*, January 4, 1838, reproduced in *ibid.*, opp. p. 50; Wecter, *op. cit.*, p. 47.

63. Wecter, *op. cit.*, p. 41. Wecter notes that "from an early day the Missouri phrase to 'go up Salt River' or be 'rowed up Salt River' signified defeat and banishment into the ultimate backwater" (p. 47); see also Paine, *op. cit.*, I, 20, and Brashear, *op. cit.*, p. 44, n. 34.

64. See "The Private History of a Campaign That Failed," *Century*, XXXI (n.s. IX) (December, 1885), 203 (reprinted in *Merry Tales* [New York, 1892], p. 47, and *Writings*, XXI, 256); *Notebook*, p. 183; Paine, *op. cit.*, II, 811.

65. Note the similarity of the names "Salt Lick" and "Salt River." *Lick* means a surface outcropping of salt deposit, and the river apparently derived its name from the salt springs reportedly "about one day's sail" up the river (Lieutenant Pike's *Journal* [1810], quoted in Brashear, *op. cit.*, p. 40). The name, therefore, has *double-entendre* (see above, p. 126).

66. Brashear, *op. cit.*, pp. 50, 89; Wecter, *op. cit.*, pp. 47, 49-50.

67. "I knew he interested himself in Salt River navigation" (letter from SLC to J. W. Atterbury, January 20, 1886, quoted in Wecter, *op. cit.*, p. 110).

68. Colonel Sellers' map is a temporary one extemporized on the dining table out of various household objects. See Appendix E.

69. See above, pp. 125-26.

70. See Henry Kirke White, *History of the Union Pacific Railway* (Chicago: University of Chicago Press, 1895), p. 48.

71. *Letters*, I, 2; Ferguson, *op. cit.*, p. 20; Brashear, *op cit.*, pp. 60, 90.

72. Brashear, *op. cit.*, pp. 90-91; Wecter, *op. cit.*, p. 110.

73. Brashear, *op. cit.*, pp. 135-36. See also p. 146.

74. "I never knew before that my father was a pioneer railroad man; . . . this railroad matter is entirely new to me" (letter to Atterbury, Wecter, *op. cit.*, p. 110).

75. See "My First Literary Venture," *Writings*, XIX, 111.

76. "Letter from 'Mark Twain,'" May 26, 1867, reprinted in *Mr. Brown*, pp. 141-48; cf. Edgar Marquess Branch, *The Literary Apprenticeship of Mark Twain* (Urbana: University of Illinois Press, 1950), pp. 266-68. "The ups and downs I have exaggerated a little in Hannibal's case will fit a good many towns in the Mississippi Valley, and Marysville and one or two others on the Pacific Coast. Keokuk, Iowa, was one of the most stirring and enterprising young cities in America seven years ago, but railroads and land speculations killed it in a single night, almost, . . ."

An anecdote recounts Mark Twain's getting out of a private railroad car, when the train was stopped at a water tank, and pretending to be president of the Virginia Railway. He tells a boy that he intends to build another railroad along the opposite bank of the adjoining river. "I want fine railroads to be built everywhere, up and down both sides of all such fine streams as this." (*Mark Twain Anecdotes*, ed. Cyril Clemens [Webster Groves, Mo.: Mark Twain Society, 1929], pp. 27-28).

77. See *Autobiography*, I, 102 (Neider ed. p. 7).

78. *Autobiography*, I, 89 (Neider ed., p. 19); Cf. I, 121 (Neider ed., p. 29): "'Colonel Sellers' was a Lampton, and a tolerably near relative of my mother's; . . ."

79. Letter to Howells, May 7, 1875, in *Twain-Howells,* I, 82.

80. See p. 236.

81. "Many persons regarded Colonel Sellers as a fiction, an invention, an extravagant impossibility, and did me the honor to call him a 'creation'; but they were mistaken" (*Autobiography,* I, 89 [Neider ed., p. 19]); cf. letter to Howells, May 7, 1875 (*Twain-Howells,* I, 81-82): "The actual truth is, that *nobody* created Sellers—I simply put him on paper as I found him in life . . . ."

82. F. H. Sosey, quoted in Brashear, *op. cit.,* pp. 66-67.

83. See Brashear, *op. cit.,* pp. 66-67.

84. As Webster writes (*MT, Business Man,* p. 31), "Probably all the enraged citizens along the Mississippi had read *Martin Chuzzlewit.*" For Clemens' reading of Dickens before 1873 see Wecter, *op. cit.,* p. 240; Foner, *op. cit.,* p. 16; Branch, *op. cit.,* p. 282, n. 59; Brashear, *op. cit.,* p. 212; Henry August Pochmann, "The Mind of Mark Twain" (Master's thesis, University of Texas, 1924); Harold Aspiz, "Mark Twain's Reading— A Critical Study" (Ph.D. dissertation, University of California at Los Angeles, 1949). Also see discussion of literary influences above, pp. 236ff.

For Dickens' use of Marion City, see Brashear, *op. cit.,* pp. 68-70.

85. *Writings,* IX, 421: "Marion City has gone backward in a most unaccountable way. This metropolis promised so well that the projectors tacked 'city' to its name in the very beginning, with full confidence; but it was bad prophecy. When I first saw Marion City, thirty-five years ago, it contained one street, and nearly or quite six houses. It contains but one house now, and this one, in a state of ruin, is getting ready to follow the former five into the river.

"Doubtless Marion City was too near to Quincy. . . ."

86. *Mr. Brown,* p. 154.

87. Wilfred R. Hollister and Harry Norman, *Five Famous Missourians* (Kansas City, Mo.: Hudson-Kimberly Publishing Co., 1900), pp. 56 f.: "Mr. Clemens has frequently stated that if Mulberry Sellers is drawn from any man in particular, that man was William M. Muldrow . . . ." If Clemens did make such a statement, it was probably to protect James Lampton from unflattering notoriety among his fellow Missourians. It must be remembered that the *Autobiography,* in which Sellers is identified as Lampton, was written "from the grave." (Also see above, chap. ii, n. 4.) See also F. H. Sosey, *Missouri Historical Review,* XXIII, 361, quoted by Brashear (*op. cit.,* p. 71, n. 80), who states that Clemens "secured his famous pen character, Colonel Sellers," from Marion City.

88. Brashear, *op. cit.,* p. 71.

89. Letter dated Wednesday [November, 1872?], *MT, Business Man,* pp. 120-21.

90. Paine, *op. cit.,* II, 477; *Letters,* I, 12, 203-4. See also above, p. 25.

91. See above, n. 87. See also Henry Watterson, "Mark Twain—An Intimate Memory," *American Magazine,* LXX (July, 1910), 372: ". . . I received a letter from him in which he told me he had made in Col. Mulberry Sellers a close study of a certain mutual kinsman and thought he had drawn him to the life, 'but for the love of Heaven,' he said, 'don't whisper it, for he would never understand, or forgive me, if he did not thrash me on sight' "; cf. Henry Watterson, *Marse Henry—An Autobiography* (New York: George H. Doran Co., 1919), I, 121.

92. Paine, *op. cit.,* I, 23; *MT, Business Man,* pp. 17-18, 121; *Autobiography,* I, 91 (Neider ed., p. 20).

93. Paine, *op. cit.,* I, 23. The expression "There's millions in it" epitomized frontier promoters of the time. In John W. De Forest's story "The Colored Member" in the *Galaxy* for March, 1872, Daddy Abel says to carpetbagger Jack Hunt: "They's heaps o' money in this railroading business o' yourn. Some folks tells me they's as much as a million in it."

94. Letter dated October 25, 1861 (*Letters,* I, 60-62; Paine, *op. cit.,* I, 180).

95. See *Autobiography*, I, 91-93 (Neider ed., pp. 20-21); also Paine, *op. cit.*, II, 792.

96. The Cable version, the MS of which is in the Cable Collection at Tulane University, is given verbatim in Arlin Turner, "James Lampton, Mark Twain's Model for Colonel Sellers," *Modern Language Notes*, LXX (December, 1955), 592-94.

97. *Gilded Age*, I (*Writings*, X), 154.

98. Webster writes (*MT, Business Man*, p. 60) that Lampton "was always going to make a million, never less, but he was always temporarily hard-up."

99. See, for example, pp. 26, 57, 66, above.

100. *Gilded Age*, I (*Writings*, X), 125-31.

101. See above, pp. 107-8, and Epilogue.

102. *Autobiography*, I, 89 (Neider ed., p. 19). Annie Moffet Webster, Clemens' niece, in commenting skeptically on "Uncle Sam's" claim that the incident was true, said, "but I always found that Cousin James set a very good table" (*MT, Business Man*, p. 60), which was undoubtedly true when he could afford to.

103. MS p. 306 (Morse, 12b; originally in Owen F. Aldis Collection, Yale University Library).

104. Clemens may also have remembered the huge Ormsby County turnip which he had sent to a certain Col. Williams in Carson City, Nevada, requesting that he extract blood from it, whereupon Col. Williams had eaten it raw, with a smile on his face, during the chaplain's prayer in the legislative sessions (letter to the *Territorial Enterprise*, December 12 [1862], in *Mark Twain of the* Enterprise, ed. Henry Nash Smith [Berkeley: University of California Press, 1957], p. 39).

105. *Autobiography*, I, 89-90 (Neider ed., p. 19). In Mark Twain's curtain speech the opening night of the play *Colonel Sellers* he said, with thinly veiled criticism of Raymond's rendition, "I meant that turnip dinner to be pathetic, for how more forcibly can you represent poverty and misery and suffering than by such a dinner, and of course if anything would bring tears to people's eyes, *that* would; but this man eats those turnips as if they were the bread of lfe, and so of course the pathos is knocked clean out of the thing. But I think he will learn" (DeLancey Ferguson, "Mark Twain's Lost Curtain Speeches," *South Atlantic Quarterly*, XLII [July, 1943], 263).

For further discussion of Raymond's interpretation of Sellers see the Epilogue.

106. See Isaac F. Marcosson, *"Marse Henry," A Biography of Henry Watterson* (New York: Dodd, Mead & Co., 1951), p. 207 f.; Joseph Frazier Wall, *Henry Watterson: Reconstructed Rebel* (New York: Oxford University Press, 1956), p. 117.

107. Watterson, *American Magazine*, LXX, 372-73; cf. *Marse Henry*, I, 121-24.

108. Henry W. Fisher, *Abroad with Mark Twain and Eugene Field* (New York: Nicholas L. Brown, 1922), p. 99. According to Watterson, "When Mark Twain had worked himself into a state of mind talking to one of us about 'Old Jim,' his eyes would flood with tears" (*American Magazine*, LXX, 373).

Clemens' affection for "Old Jim" did not, however, extend to his wife, Ella, or to other members of the Lampton clan (see *MT, Business Man*, pp. 136, 213-14, 288, 316, 321, 366).

109. *American Magazine*, LXX, 372; *Marse Henry*, I, 123.

110. Wecter, *op. cit.*, p. 27.

111. "Certes, avec une pudeur que l'on comprendra, Mark Twain a prétendu que le Colonel Sellers avait eu pour modèle un cousin de sa mère; ce n'est pas impossible, mais il est surtout l'image de ce que le père de Mark Twain fut jadis . . ." (Lemmonier, *op. cit.*, p. 77).

112. Paine, *op. cit.*, II, 478. Orion's name was accented on the first syllable (*ibid.*, I, 5; Wecter, *op. cit.*, p. 29).

113. Paine, *op cit.*, II, 495; Kenneth R. Andrews, *Nook Farm, Mark Twain's Hartford Circle* (Cambridge: Harvard University Press, 1950), pp. 23-24.

114. *Writings*, X, 77-78.

115. *Letters*, I, 12.

116. William Dean Howells, *My Mark Twain: Reminiscences and Criticisms* (New York: Harper & Bros., 1911), p. 80.

117. See, for example, Vernon L. Parrington, *Main Currents in American Thought* (New York: Harcourt, Brace & Co., 1927-1930), III, 88; Stephen Leacock, *Mark Twain* (New York: D. Appleton & Co., 1933), p. 89; Brashear, *op. cit.*, p. 229; Edward Wagenknecht, *Mark Twain, the Man and His Work* (New Haven: Yale University Press, 1935), pp. 3, 128, 164; Walter Fuller Taylor, "Mark Twain and the Machine Age," *South Atlantic Quarterly*, XXXVII (October, 1938), 387, and *The Economic Novel in America* (Chapel Hill: University of North Carolina Press, 1942), p. 130; Bernard DeVoto, *Mark Twain at Work* (Cambridge: Harvard University Press, 1942), p. 107; Ferguson, *op. cit.*, pp. 134, 156; Guy A. Cardwell, *Twins of Genius (Twain and Cable)* (Lansing: Michigan State College Press, 1953), p. 10.

118. "De sa ressemblance avec son héros, il aura d'ailleurs parfaitement conscience et au début d'une lettre pleine de grands projets, il écrira: 'Je me sens comme le Colonel Sellers'" (Lemmonier, *op. cit.*, pp. 77-78).

Significant in this connection is the following remark ascribed to Clemens by Paine (*op. cit.*, III, 1540): "If Byron—if any man—draws 50 characters, they are all himself—50 shades, 50 moods, of his own character."

119. See George Hiram Brownell, "Mark Twain's Inventions," *Twainian*, III (n.s. IV) (January, 1944), 1-5; also Will Clemens, *Mark Twain: His Life and Work* (San Francisco: Clemens Publishing Co., 1892), p. 193, and Van Wyck Brooks, *The Ordeal of Mark Twain* (rev. ed.; New York: E. P. Dutton & Co., 1933), p. 168.

120. An exception, however, was a history game played with stakes outdoors, which Clemens designed to teach his children the chronology of historical events and which he feverishly developed in an indoor cribbage-board form as a memory builder in various fields until its very unwieldiness made it unplayable. (Paine, *op. cit.*, II, 752-53).

121. According to the rather unreliable Will Clemens, it made a fortune for its publishers; but Clemens claimed the firm failed before he personally was able to profit from it (*Autobiography*, Neider ed., p. 230).

122. *American Magazine*, LXX, 374; *Marse Henry*, I, 127.

123. *Turn West, Turn East: Mark Twain and Henry James* (Boston: Houghton Mifflin Co., 1951), p. 187.

124. *MT, Business Man*, p. 309.

125. Bill Stewart (William Morris Stewart, *Reminiscences of Senator William M. Stewart of Nevada*, ed. George Rothwell Brown [New York and Washington: Neale Publishing Co., 1908], p. 222), relates how Clemens approached him to subsidize the writing of *Innocents Abroad*: "'I have a proposition,' said Clemens, . . . 'There's millions in it. All I need is a little cash stake.'" Though the entire passage is written in imitation of the Mark Twain manner, the spirit of the episode is typical.

126. *Letters*, I, 20.

127. Paine, *op. cit.*, I, 109.

128. See letter to Jane Clemens and Pamela Moffett, February 8, 1862 (*Letters*, I, 64); also Effie Mona Mack, *Mark Twain in Nevada* (New York: Charles Scribner's Sons, 1947), p. 125.

129. *Letters*, I, 73; also see Paine, *op. cit.*, I, 197-98.

130. Clara Clemens, *My Father Mark Twain* (New York: Harper & Bros., 1931), p. 34.

131. *Autobiography*, Neider ed., p. 232. Also see pp. 229-33; Paine, *op. cit.*, II, 725-27. At the very time *The Gilded Age* was being written, Clemens was endorsing "White's Portable Folding Fly and Musketo Net Frame" (see Gilbert McCoy Troxell, "Samuel Langhorne Clemens, 1835-1910," *Yale University Library Gazette*, XVIII (July, 1943), 1-5.

132. See *Autobiography*, I, 70-78; Paine, *op. cit.*, III, 906 ff.

133. Paine, *op. cit.*, III, 978. During such times, as Paine has written, Clemens would be "eagerly excited, worried, impatient, alternately suspicious and overtrusting, rash, frenzied, and altogether upset" (II, 728).

Within a month after his bankruptcy debts were paid off, Clemens was ready to invest fifteen hundred thousand dollars in a carpet-pattern machine and was restrained from doing so only by the strong admonition of his friend and financial adviser H. H. Rogers (Paine, *op. cit.*, III, 1056-57; *Letters*, II, 660-62).

134. Clemens never adopted the pseudonym "Colonel Sellers," as stated by Edgar Lee Masters (*Mark Twain*, p. 46), thereby having it at hand for use in *The Gilded Age*. Masters is thinking of Clemens' claim that he adopted his pen name, "Mark Twain," from the scribbling pilot Isaiah Sellers, who wrote river news for the New Orleans *Picayune* (see letter in *Daily Alta California*, June 9, 1877, quoted in Mack, *op. cit.*, p. 228). For evidence controverting this widely accepted claim see Ferguson, *op. cit.*, pp. 56, 85; Ernest E. Leisy, "Mark Twain and Isaiah Sellers," *American Literature*, XIII (January, 1942), 398-405; George Hiram Brownell, "A Question as to the Origin of the Name, 'Mark Twain,'" *Twainian*, n.s. Vol. I, No. 2 (February, 1942), pp. 4-7.

135. Arthur Hobson Quinn, *American Fiction: An Historical and Critical Survey* (New York: D. Appleton-Century Co., 1936), pp. 246-47. Quinn was supplied information by Charles C. Sellers (p. ix).

136. Undated clipping of unsigned interview with Sellers in Chattanooga *Republican*, MTP. (Sellers, then eighty-two, had settled in the Mission Ridge section of Chattanooga.)

137. See p. 193.

138. See Hamlin Hill, "Escol Sellers from Uncharted Space: A Footnote to *The Gilded Age*," *American Literature*, XXXIV (March, 1962), 107-13. ". . . Warner is my most intimate friend, & as such we have been in the habit . . . of discussing our respective affairs very thoroughly . . . ; so that it is quite probable that I have spoken to him of you as associated with our business affairs in a very important way" (Barton to Sellers, December 26, 1873, quoted by Hill, *op. cit.*, p. 109).

139. *Autobiography*, I, 90 (Neider ed., p. 20).

140. See J. Thomas Scharf and Thompson Westcott, *History of Philadelphia, 1609-1884* (Philadelphia: L. H. Everts & Co., 1884), III, 2263-65; Henry Graham Ashmead, *History of Delaware County, Pennsylvania* (Philadelphia: L. H. Everts & Co., 1884), pp. 545-47; *History of Gallatin, Saline, Hamilton, Franklin and Williamson Counties* (Chicago: Goodspeed Publishing Co., 1887), p. 576; Gilbert Cope and Henry Graham Ashmead (eds.), *Genealogical and Personal Memoirs of Chester and Delaware Counties, Pennsylvania* (New York and Chicago: Lewis Publishing Co., 1904), pp. 197-99; Horace Wells Sellers, "Engravings by Charles Willson Peale, Limner," *Pennsylvania Magazine of History and Biography*, LVII (1933), 155-56; Harold Sellers Colton, "Mark Twain's Literary Dilemma and Its Sequel," *Arizona Quarterly*, XVII (Autumn, 1961), 229-32.

Also see Evansville (Ind.) *Courier*, March 7, 1875, quoted in Hartford *Courant* (of which Warner was associate editor), [March ?, 1875] (clipping in Yale University Library); Chattanooga *Republican* (see above, n. 136). According to Hamlin Hill, "subsequent investigation revealed that the [Evansville *Courier*] story was a practical joke played by a friend of the Sellers family" (*op. cit.*, p. 111), yet in its main facts the story appears to be correct.

141. Paine, *op. cit.*, II, 501; cf. *Autobiography*, I, 91 (Neider ed., p. 20): ". . . we changed the name back to Colonel Mulberry Sellers in the plates"—another instance of Clemens' faulty memory. Also see Hill, *op. cit.*, pp. 109-11. "Months later Sellers still could not buy a copy of the corrected version" (Hill, *Mark Twain and Elisha Bliss* [Columbia: University of Missouri Press, 1964], p. 78). "Ultimately, Escol Sellers was mollified, but the facts suggest that he actually caused not a minute's delay because of the changing of the plates—which Bliss took his own good time to accomplish" (*ibid.*).

Clemens' *second*, "unrelated" Eschol Sellers, "a college-bred gentleman of courtly manners and ducal upholstery" who threatened libel, was actually the same man (cf. Paine, *op. cit.*, II, 501-2). George Escol Sellers' grandnephew, Harold Colton (see above, n. 140), states that Sellers, though a cultured gentleman, was not a college graduate. According to this relative, when reports of Sellers' reputation as the prototype of the fictional colonel reached the financial circles in Philadelphia, the further development of the industries at Sellers' landing became impossible. "His career was greatly injured."

142. See the second foreword to *The American Claimant*, entitled "Explanatory," in which Clemens has his facts correct (cf. above, n. 141); also Jacob Blanck, "The Gilded Age: A Collation," *Publishers' Weekly*, CXXXVIII (July 20, 1940), 188.

143. See James Bruce Anderson, "Mark Twain in Shawneetown, Illinois, Home of Tom Sawyer and Colonel Sellers," *Charlatan*, No. 2 (1964), especially the quotations from the *History of Southern Illinois* (1912) and L. O. Trigg, *Along Trigg's Trails and Tours*, cited by him.

144. According to Quinn, *op. cit.*, p. 247. Escol's father, Coleman (the elder), had a residence at 10 North Sixth Street (Cope and Ashmead, *op. cit.*, I, 197), and his uncle, Rembrandt Peale, lived at the "head of Mulberry Court, leading from Sixth, three doors above Market Street" (Scharf and Westcott, *op. cit.*, II, 1037). Was Escol born in the Peale mansion? and had *Mulberry* been Warner's alternative proposal? Is there here an anticipation of the name *Huckleberry?*

145. Yet on March 29, 1896, Warner, still protesting his innocence, was writing a Mr. Ridgway, "I never saw Col Escoll [*sic*] Sellers of Illinois nor did Mr. Clemens, nor did we ever hear of him till the book was published—at least not in any such connection. . . . The name was an accident" (letter in Warner Papers, Watkinson Library, Trinity College, Hartford).

In this connection, the interesting testimony of Hardin County residents, presented by James Anderson (see above, n. 143), as to Clemens' possible knowledge of George Escol Sellers during his steamboating days in the late 1850's is not to be overlooked. It is a noteworthy coincidence, for instance, that Sellers lived in the Saline (Salt) River country, famous for its salt springs and licks.

146. Colton, *op. cit.*, p. 230.

147. So translated by James Moffatt (*A New Translation of the Bible* [rev. ed.; New York: Harper & Bros., 1935], p. 166).

148. Robert Young, *Analytical Concordance to the Bible* (22nd Amer. ed. rev.; New York: Funk & Wagnalls, 1955), p. 307.

149. *Ibid.*, p. 89.

150. James Hastings (ed.), *Dictionary of the Bible*, I (New York: Charles Scribner's Sons, 1901), 274.

151. *Ibid.*, single-volume ed. (New York: Charles Scribner's Sons, 1925), p. 56.

152. Matthew Josephson, *The Politicos, 1865-1896* (New York: Harcourt, Brace & Co., 1938), p. 105.

153. Robert Shackleton, *The Book of Washington* (Philadelphia: Penn Publishing Co., 1922), p. 227.

154. For this early visit see *Autobiography*, II, 287 (Neider ed., p. 95); Paine, *op. cit.*, I, 101; DeVoto, *Mark Twain's America*, p. 87; *Muscatine Letters*, p. 5.

155. The letter, "Washington Correspondence," dated February 18, 1854, is given in full in Branch, *Literary Apprenticeship*, pp. 219-21, and *Muscatine Letters*, pp. 18-21.

156. From "The Externals of Washington," *Atlantic*, XXXII (December, 1873), 701-16. See Ben: Perley Poor, *Perley's Reminiscences of Sixty Years in the National Metropolis* (Philadelphia: Hubbard Bros., 1886), p. 261: "The streets [on Grant's ascendancy] generally were wagon tracks, muddy in the winter and dusty in the summer"; also Claude G. Bowers, *The Tragic Era: The Revolution after Lincoln* (Boston: Houghton Mifflin Co., 1929), p. 242.

157. Chapter XXIV (*Writings*, X, 261-72).

158. MS p. 548 (Morse, 10). The wording of this passage was anticipated in Clemens' letter to the *Alta California* published February 14, 1868: "That ungainly old chimney . . . is just the general size and shape, and possesses about the dignity, of a sugar-mill chimney. It may suit the departed George Washington. . . . It may be a comfort to him to look at it out of the clouds. He may enjoy perching on it to look around upon the scene of his earthly greatness, but it is not likely. It is not likely that any spirit would be so taken with that lumbering thing as to want to roost there." (I am indebted to Hamlin Hill for this comparison.)

159. See George Fort Milton, *The Age of Hate: Andrew Johnson and the Radicals* (New York: Coward-McCann, 1930), p. 7: "The unfinished Washington Monument, which had climbed to only a third of its projected height, stood forth in bold relief against the distant green of the Virginia hills, a pathetic reminder of the nation's forgetfulness and neglect. . . ."

160. ". . . cows, pigs, and chickens wandered as freely as the inhabitants" (Peirce, *Atlantic*, XXXII, 711).

161. MS p. 549 (Morse, 10).

162. See *Mark Twain*, pp. 22-23.

163. Frances Weston Carruth, "Washington in Fiction," *Bookman* (New York), XV (July, 1902), 452-53. Carruth also contrasts Twain's definition of the White House as "a fine large white barn, with wide unhandsome grounds about it" with Dickens' as "like an English club-house" (p. 455).

164. ". . . un parti pris de dénigrement, une exécration naïve et sincère de tout ce que les hommes peuvent construire" (p. 35).

165. Letter dated February 21, [1868], in *MT, Business Man*, pp. 98-99.

166. Letter to Orion, February 21, [1868] (*Letters*, I, 150-51).

167. "Washington Society," *Atlantic*, XL (December, 1877), 657.

168. See C. H. Forbes-Lindsay, *Washington, the City and the Seat of Government* (Philadelphia: John C. Winston Co., 1908), p. 291; Josephson, *op. cit.*, p. 88; Bowers, *op. cit.*, p. 246; Charles A. and Mary R. Beard, *The Rise of American Civilization* (rev. ed.; New York: Macmillan Co., 1937), II, 384-85, 394.

169. The one general social custom among the men that he singles out for comment is that of conferring gratuitous titles. Colonel Sellers says (II, 280): " '. . . Look at me. When we first came here, I was *Mr.* Sellers, and *Major* Sellers, and *Captain* Sellers, but nobody could ever get it right, somehow; but the minute our bill went through the House, I was *Colonel* Sellers every time. . . .' " The contemporary social chronicler John B. Ellis writes: "Every body in Washington has a title. If it does not legally belong to him, he appropriates it, and that answers the same purpose. . . . on all occasions, the ear is wearied with the incessant repetitions of 'Senator,' 'Judge,' 'Secretary,' 'Mr. Speaker,' 'Governor,' 'Marshal,' 'General,' 'Captain,' 'Colonel,' 'Major,' . . ." (*The Sights and Secrets of the National Capital* [San Francisco: H. H. Bancroft & Co., 1869], pp. 423-24).

170. Chapter XXXII, "Laura's Success in Washington Society," and Chapter XXXIII, "Laura Receives Calls from the Aristocracies" (*Writings*, XI, 5-13, 14-37).

171. Letter in *Golden Era*, published September 27, 1863, reprinted in *The Washoe Giant in San Francisco*, ed. Franklin Walker (San Francisco: George Fields, 1938), pp. 33-38.

172. Letter dated February 23, printed in *Mr. Brown*, pp. 101-10.

173. *Ten Years in Washington: Life and Scenes in the National Capital, As a Woman Sees Them* (Hartford: A. D. Worthington & Co., 1874), p. 261. See also Beard and Beard, *op. cit.*, II, 386.

174. Milton, *op. cit.*, p. 8; Bowers, *op. cit.*, p. 250; Shackleton, *op. cit.*, pp. 202-3.

175. Shackleton, *op. cit.*, p. 203: ". . . a sort of social alluvial soil, . . ."

176. Ellis, *op. cit.*, pp. 416-17. The "social atmosphere" of this set was "heavy with the taint of Southern institutions."

177. Is not Clemens revealing here his own ambivalent feelings about the respectability of New England and Nook Farm?

178. For Peaseley see Gladys Carmen Bellamy, *Mark Twain as a Literary Artist* (Norman: University of Oklahoma Press, 1950), p. 293; Mack, *op. cit.*, pp. 194-97. For Henry Gaither ("Harry") Worthington, see Mark Twain's letter from Washington in the *Territorial Enterprise*, December 22, 1867, which says of Worthington, "his main business here is to get one more tribe, because, the way he is averaging the rations now, the tribe he has got won't be likely to hold out long, and of course he wants something to fall back on." Cf. *The Gilded Age*, II, 22: "The Hon. Higgins had not come to serve his country in Washington for nothing. The appropriation which he had engineered through Congress for the maintenance of the Indians in his Territory would have made all those savages rich if it had ever got to them." I am indebted to Hamlin Hill for the suggestion and for the *Enterprise* citation.

179. See above, pp. 118-19.

180. *Writings*, I, 300.

181. *Mark Twain's America*, p. 287.

182. See, for example, the comic description by George Alfred Townsend (*Washington, Outside and Inside* [Hartford and Chicago: James Betts & Co., 1874], p. 695) of the behavior of congressmen William D. Kelly and Dionysius Dennis O'McCarthy.

183. Beard and Beard, *op. cit.*, II, 399.

184. In Chapter XXXVIII (*Writings*, XI, 70 ff.).

185. John G. Schumaker was in the forty-first Congress (1869-70), a year after Clemens' Washington sojourn (see Edward McPherson, *The Political History of the United States of America During the Period of Reconstruction* [Washington, D.C.: Philp & Solomons, 1871], p. 508). Clemens' acquaintance with the Schumakers is entirely conjectural.

186. Quoted by Ellis, *op. cit.*, p. 431.

187. Quoted at length in Emily Edson Briggs, *The Olivia Letters* (New York and Washington: Neale Publishing Co., 1906), pp. 173-80.

188. Paine, *op. cit.*, I, 346.

189. *Ibid.* It must be kept in mind that although Mark Twain had not yet achieved the national recognition that came to him at the publication of *Innocents*, his reputation was high in the section of the country from which Stewart hailed.

190. See *Fairbanks Letters*, p. 1; *MT, Business Man*, p. 95; *Traveling with the Innocents Abroad*, ed. Daniel Morley McKeithan (Norman: University of Oklahoma Press, 1958), p. 313.

191. Paine, *op. cit.*, I, 347. Much has been written about this short-lived arrangement and the alleged rift it caused between Stewart and Clemens. Whatever rift there was was apparently caused by the appearance in *Roughing It* of a picture of Stewart with a patch over his eye. In repayment Stewart in his *Reminiscences* devoted a chapter to the Clemens secretaryship, burlesquing the episode unmercifully à la Twain. As Clemens had been publicly needling Stewart from the time he first knew him in Nevada, the duel appears to have been much more good-natured than literal-minded biographers have admitted. (See Paine, *op. cit.*, I, 347, n. 1; Stewart, *Reminiscences*, pp. 219-24.) For biographers who, taking their cue from Paine, in varying degree accept the hostility at face value see Wagenknecht, *op. cit.*, p. 70; *MT, Business Man*, p. 99; Ferguson, *op. cit.*, p. 128; DeVoto, *Mark Twain's America*, p. 131; Masters, *op. cit.*, p. 65; Bellamy, *op. cit.*, p. 20.

For Clemens' relations with Stewart in the Nevada days see Mack, *op. cit.*, pp. 233-34, 238-39, 240, *et passim*; *Mark Twain of the* Enterprise, pp. 63, 97, 142, 162; and, with reservations, Cyril Clemens, *Young Sam Clemens* (Portland, Me.: Leon Tebbetts Editions, 1942), pp. 151-52, 165.

192. See *Sketches New and Old* (*Writings*, XIX, 190-96 and 348-58). The best account of the episode is presented by Mack (*op. cit.*, pp. 344-48).

193. Among the satirical sketches are several that bear on topics given emphasis in *The Gilded Age*: "The Facts in the Case of the Great Beef Contract" (*Writings*, XIX, 121-31), on red tape; "The Facts in the Case of George Fisher, Deceased" (*ibid.*, pp. 132-42), on profiteering; "A New Crime: Legislation Needed" (*ibid.*, pp. 244-50), on the insanity plea (see above, pp. 102-3), to name a few. See Bellamy, *op. cit.*, pp. 101-2, and, for "The Great Beef Contract," the *Galaxy*, X (September, 1870), 431-32, and *Autobiography*, I, 324-26.

194. *Letters*, I, 148-49; *MT, Business Man*, pp. 96-99; *Love Letters*, pp. 60-62.

195. Paine, *op. cit.*, I, 348.

196. In the *Olivia Letters* for March 2, 1868 (Briggs, *op. cit.*, p. 47); quoted at second hand by Clemens in *Autobiography*, II, 72 (Neider ed., p. 275).

197. Paine, *op. cit.*, I, 348, 351, 357, 358; *Letters*, I, 142, 145, 146. See also *Fairbanks Letters*, pp. 6, 14-15, 31, 36; *Mark Twain's Letters to Will Bowen*, ed. Theodore Hornberger (Austin: University of Texas Press, 1941), pp. 16-17; *Love Letters*, p. 358; Mark Twain, *Republican Letters*, ed. Cyril Clemens (Webster Groves, Mo.: International Mark Twain Society, 1941), and *Washington in 1868*, ed. Cyril Clemens (Webster Groves, Mo.: International Mark Twain Society, 1943).

198. Paine, *op. cit.*, I, 358-59; *Autobiography*, I, 323-24; *Mark Twain in Eruption*, pp. 351-54; (*Autobiography*, Neider ed., pp. 154-55).

199. *Who's Who in America*, 1899-1900 ed., p. 710; Foner, *op. cit.*, p. 168.

200. *New York Times*, October 26, 1892, p. 5, col. 3; *Dictionary of American Biography*, XVIII, 252-53.

201. William Carey Jones, *Illustrated History of The University of California* (San Francisco: Frank H. Dukesmith, 1895), pp. 110-11; William Warren Ferrier, *Origin and Development of the University of California* (Berkeley: Sather Gate Book Shop, 1930), pp. 355, 361.

202. *Mark Twain in Eruption*, p. 353 (*Autobiography*, Neider ed., p. 154); *Autobiography*, I, 324.

203. Johnson Brigham, *James Harlan* (Iowa City: State Historical Society of Iowa, 1913), p. 242.

204. See George Rothwell Brown, *Washington, a Not Too Serious History* (Baltimore: Norman Publishing Co., 1930), pp. 334-36. Clemens also knew George Alfred Townsend of the *Chicago Tribune*, the "Yankee Dickens with the head of a prize-fighter and the manners of a Philadelphia *Bourgeoise*" (Henry Watterson in *Views and Interviews on Journalism*, ed. Charles F. Wingate [New York: F. B. Patterson, 1875], p. 20), from whom I have quoted throughout this volume (see *Love Letters*, pp. 153-54).

205. Brown, *op. cit.*, pp. 334-35; see also Forbes-Lindsay, *op. cit.*, p. 261.

206. See Chapter XL, "How Washington News Leaks Out" (*Writings*, XI, 88-96). See also above, p. 133, regarding Sellers' "leak" of the Alabama Treaty.

207. See *Gilded Age*, II (*Writings*, XI), 130, 134-36. Other instances are found on pp. 93, 284, and 300.

208. "The Pressure upon Congress," *Atlantic*, XXV (February, 1870), 157. Distinction should be made between unscrupulousness, which Mark Twain makes the exception, and sensationalizing the news, a practice which he lampoons, especially in connection with Laura's murder trial (see *Gilded Age*, II, 167-69, 178, 282-83).

209. *Letters*, II, 542; Paine, *op. cit.*, III, 916.

210. From aphorism of "Pudd'nhead Wilson's New Calendar," head of Chapter VIII, *Following the Equator*, I (*Writings*, V), 98.

211. It is often implied that his impressions of Washington date from no time earlier than 1867-68. See, for example, Wecter in *Fairbanks Letters* (p. 237): "this experience left him with those sardonic impressions recorded in *The Gilded Age*, . . ."

212. Letter of July 8, [1870], *Love Letters*, pp. 154-55.

213. *Muscatine Letters*, pp. 19-20.

214. Brashear, *op. cit.,* pp. 117-19.

215. See, for example, Letter X in New Orleans *Daily Crescent,* March 30, 1861 (*The Letters of Quintus Curtius Snodgrass,* ed. Ernest E. Leisy [Dallas: Southern Methodist University Press, 1946], pp. 65-66); "The Christmas Fireside," in *Californian,* December 23, 1865 (*Sketches of the Sixties: by Bret Harte and Mark Twain,* ed. John Howell [San Francisco: John Howell, 1926], p. 205); "On Linden, Etc.," in *Californian,* April 7, 1866 (*ibid.,* p. 208); "Hawaiian Legislature" and "Solons at Work," in Sacramento *Weekly Union,* June 23, 1866 (*Letters from the Sandwich Islands, Written for the Sacramento Union,* ed. G. Ezra Dane [San Francisco: Grabhorn Press, 1937], pp. 80-95).

216. See *Mark Twain of the* Enterprise, pp. 130-78, *et passim;* also Effie Mona Mack, "Life and Letters of William Morris Stewart, 1827-1909" (Ph.D. dissertation, University of California, 1930), pp. 31-33; Foner, *op. cit.,* pp. 65-66.

217. *Notebook,* p. 114; cf. Paine, *op. cit.,* I, 361.

218. Archibald Henderson, *Mark Twain* (London: Duckworth & Co., 1911), p. 114; see also Paine, *op. cit.,* IV, 1472-73. For other allusions to congressmen as thieves see *Mark Twain in Eruption,* pp. 71-72; *Speeches,* p. 55; Andrews, *op. cit.,* p. 175; Arthur L. Vogelback, "Mark Twain Newspaper Contributor," *American Literature,* XX (May, 1948), 117.

A canceled sentence of Colonel Sellers in the original manuscript of *The Gilded Age* reads: "God bless me, sometimes I feel like a Congressman, & then I can't keep my hands off of things" (MS p. 1205 [Morse, 12b]).

219. *Mr. Brown,* p. 157.

220. *Autobiography,* Neider ed., p. 281. See also Paine, *op. cit.,* II, 724; *Letters,* I, 161; *Mr. Brown,* p. 254.

221. *Notebook,* pp. 131-32.

222. *The Education of Henry Adams* (New York: Modern Library, 1931), p. 261.

223. Rudyard Kipling, *From Sea to Sea: Letters of Travel* (Garden City, N.Y.: Doubleday, Page & Co., 1913), Part II, p. 174.

It is interesting to note in connection with Clemens' attitude toward congressmen Champ Clark's claim that it was said Clemens for years "nursed an ambition to be a member of the House" (*My Quarter Century of American Politics* [New York: Harper & Bros., 1920], II, 24).

224. Thomas R. Lounsbury, "Biographical Sketch," in *The Complete Writings of Charles Dudley Warner* (Hartford: American Publishing Co., 1904), XV, i-xxxviii; Pattee, *op. cit.,* pp. 418-19; William H. Rideing, *The Boyhood of Famous Authors* (New York: T. Y. Crowell & Co., 1908), pp. 178-86.

225. *Gilded Age,* I (*Writings,* X), 132-42, 178-99, 257-60.

226. Chapters LIV, LV, LVI (CDW and SLC), and LVIII (CDW and SLC) (*Writings,* XI, 242-93).

227. The description of the seminary (I, 236-37) is typical of a small New England (or upstate New York) academy, and the town of Fallkill boasts an inn named in good Indian fashion the Sassacus Hotel.

228. Mrs. James T. Fields, *Charles Dudley Warner* (New York: McClure, Phillips & Co., 1904), p. 21.

229. Letter to CDW, dated Rodney, Mississippi, February 20, 1874, in MTP. (See above, p. 137.)

230. See above, p. 56.

231. [Thomas Wentworth Higginson], "Charles Dudley Warner," *Scribner's Monthly,* VII (January, 1874), 332. (For Higginson's authorship of the article see review of *The Gilded Age, Cincinnati Daily Times,* in large broadside "Notices of the Press," MTP.) His work at the Astor Library apparently also preceded his surveying trip to Missouri, another parallel with Philip's career (see letter of introduction from Lewis Gaylord Clark, dated March 31, 1853, Warner Papers).

Do we hear an echo of Warner's self-admonition in Harry Brierly's comment: "Well, why don't you go into something? You'll never dig it out of the Astor Library" (I, 132).

232. See above, pp. 162-63, n. 74.

233. Two railroad passes are made out to Charles D. Warner, Esq., Engineer H & St Jo RR, one, dated January 1, 1854, on the New York & Erie Railroad, the other, dated March 12, 1854, on the Chicago & Rock Island Rail-Road (Warner Papers).

234. Jeff Thompson mentions a "Henry Dakin" whom he recognized "*at first sight*" (letter to CDW, February 20, 1874, MTP). He tells Warner, "Your description of him is true to life, and I hope some rich widow has adopted him, and provided for him." I have been unable to discover anything about this person. The Chief Engineer of the *Montana,* the ship on which Clemens returned to New York from San Francisco in 1868, was apparently named Brierly (SLC Notebook No. 10—1868 [typescript in MTP], p. 10).

235. Letter in Warner Papers. Duff is probably the son of John Duff, the Union Pacific Director. (". . . [John Duff] sent his son as a guest with Chief Engineer Dodge upon an advance survey expedition" [Edwin L. Sabin, *Building the Pacific Railway* (Philadelphia: J. B. Lippincott Co., 1919), p. 74].) I have been unable to discover anything about his partner, George Y. Learned.

236. The letters, which are copies in Warner's hand, are attested by him as having been delivered as described.

It is uncertain whether Warner was an employee of the Hannibal & St. Jo Company or of their agents Duff & Learned.

237. Both note and release are in the Warner Papers.

238. Quinn, *op. cit.,* pp. 246-47.

239. [Eli K. Price], *Centennial Meeting of the Descendants of Philip and Rachel Price* (Philadelphia: Caxton Press of C. Sherman, Son & Co., 1864), pp. 41-42.

240. *Ibid.,* p. 42. See above, p. 139.

241. Scharf and Westcott, *op. cit.,* II, 1536-37; J. Smith Futhey and Gilbert Cope, *History of Chester County, Pennsylvania, with Genealogical and Biographical Sketches* (Philadelphia: Louis H. Everts, 1881), p. 694. Eli was well known for his "Price Act," enacted April 18, 1853, governing conveyancing.

242. Price, *op. cit.,* p. 83. Could it be that Warner's friend Dr. J. H. Barton was Philip Price's nephew? Warner's use of the Price family was borne out by George Escol Sellers (see Hill, *American Literature,* XXXIV, 113). And according to Hamlin Hill (in a letter to me, January 5, 1965) Eli Price had a daughter who died in 1862 (Warner had intended to have Ruth Bolton die [see above, p. 75]).

243. MS pp. 1141, 1142, 1143, 1144, 1145, 1147, 1149, 1150, and 1151 (Morse, 12b), from Chapter XLIX (II, 196-201); of these, pp. 1141-42 and 1151 overlap material claimed by Clemens in his annotated copy of *The Gilded Age* (see Appendix D). P. 1431 (Berg Collection, New York Public Library), from Chapter LXII (by Clemens) is the only page of the ten that is in Clemens' hand.

244. In a letter to Livy [April, 1873] he wrote: "I want you to ask the boys to find out from Fulton one thing—to-wit:—when one is after a coal vein in a tunnel, and that vein is well canted up, or stands perpendicular, does water always burst out when they strike into the vein (if below the water level, of course,) and *is the bursting out of the water a sign* that they've struck the main lead?

"It is always the case in silver mining" (typescript in MTP).

245. *Autobiography,* II, 135.

246. *Ibid.,* II, 130.

247. From letter dated Lockport, February 27 [1869] (*Love Letters,* p. 68).

248. As a matter of fact, Clemens became rather closely identified with Langdon's coal interests and, through that contradiction in his nature that forced him to side with his personal allegiances when they conflicted with his social convictions, defended his wife's father against the "anti-monopoly thieves" who attacked J. Langdon & Com-

pany and its regional cartel, the Anthracite Coal Association, for price fixing (see *Love Letters*, pp. 108-9). And he sought the older man's advice on the coal tract in the Tennessee Land, hoping that he might sell or lease it to the Langdon company (see *Letters*, I, 167-68; *Love Letters*, pp. 119, 152).

249. *Autobiography*, II, 135; MS p. 1119, in HEH container 470.

250. Ernest E. Leisy, "Mark Twain's Part in *The Gilded Age*," *American Literature*, VIII (January, 1937), 447.

251. Letter dated February 7(?), 1873, in 1873 correspondence file, MTP. Pugh was manager of The Star Course of Lectures in Philadelphia.

252. The only other allusion from Clemens' background that I am aware of is Colonel Sellers' reference to "old Dr. McDowells" (I, 128). Dr. John McDowell was a friend of the Lamptons and it is his cave ("McDougal's Cave") that figures in *Tom Sawyer*. (See Wecter, *op. cit.*, pp. 160 ff.)

CHAPTER VIII

1. Mrs. James T. Fields, *Charles Dudley Warner* (New York: McClure, Phillips & Co., 1904), pp. 38-39.

2. By Clemens' own estimate *The Gilded Age* sold approximately 60,000 copies in the United States in nine years compared with 75,000 of *Roughing It* for the same period (*MT, Business Man*, p. 190). Although least popular of Twain's works in England, it ran into ten British editions in seventy years (Robert M. Rodney, "Mark Twain in England: A Study of the English Criticism of and Attitude toward Mark Twain: 1867-1940" [Ph.D. dissertation, University of Wisconsin, 1945], p. 63). (This compares with thirty-five for *Innocents* and thirty each for *Tom Sawyer* and *Huck Finn*.)

Such figures must be weighted, of course, by the fact that the later editions were published as volumes included in Twain's collected works and do not therefore reflect demand accurately.

3. See above, p. 81.

4. *Mark Twain* (New York: D. Appleton & Co., 1933), p. 141.

5. *The Great Tradition* (New York: Macmillan Co., 1933), p. 72.

6. *American Fiction: An Historical and Critical Survey* (New York: Hubbard Bros., 1936), pp. 246, 247.

7. *Mark Twain's America* (Boston: Little, Brown & Co., 1932), pp. 287-88.

8. *Turn West, Turn East: Mark Twain and Henry James* (Boston: Houghton Mifflin Co., 1951), pp. 97 ff.

9. *A History of American Literature Since 1870* (New York: Century Co., 1915), p. 59.

10. *The Economic Novel in America* (Chapel Hill: University of North Carolina Press, 1942), pp. 116-47. "To a degree that is astonishing . . . the actual persons and doings of the early Gilded Age pass in review in the novel . . . ." Cf. Taylor, *A History of American Letters* (New York: American Book Co., 1936), pp. 262-74. For a few other hints see also Claude Reherd Flory, *Economic Criticism in American Fiction, 1792 to 1900* (Philadelphia: n. p., 1936) (a published Ph.D. dissertation, University of Pennsylvania), p. 72.

11. See, for example, Gladys Carmen Bellamy, *Mark Twain as a Literary Artist* (Norman: University of Oklahoma Press, 1950), Ch. XVII, "Revolt from the Village," pp. 287 ff.; Ima Honaker Herron, *The Small Town in American Literature* (Durham: Duke University Press, 1939), pp. 237 ff.; DeVoto, *Mark Twain's America*, pp. 285 ff.

12. One cannot help wondering if the title *The Gilded Age* suggested itself to Clemens as a parody of *The Golden Era*, a San Francisco journal to which he had frequently contributed.

13. *Mark Twain: Social Critic* (New York: International Publishers, 1958), pp. 69-86 *et passim*.

14. See Charles F. Richardson, *American Literature, 1607-1885* (one-volume ed.; New York: G. P. Putnam's Sons, 1893 [copyright, 1886]), p. 521; George Edward Woodberry, *America in Literature* (New York: Harper & Bros., 1903), pp. 159-61. Writing to Howells in 1875, Clemens says that it "gravels" his wife that he is "so persistently glorified as a mere buffoon" (*Twain-Howells*, I, 107; *Letters*, I, 264). See Paine's comment in *Mark Twain's Notebook* (New York: Harper & Bros., 1935), p. 400: "He saw life at a quizzical slant, but he was not, first of all, a humorist"; also letter from Charles Dudley Warner to a Mr. Simons, dated Hartford, February 9, 1873 (in Morse, file 114): "I know him [Clemens] very well (since a year) and think very highly of his ability other than as a mere humorist."

15. *Autobiography*, Neider ed., p. 273.

16. *Expression in America* (New York: Harper & Bros., 1932), p. 231.

17. From "A Couple of Sad Experiences," *Galaxy*, IX (June, 1870), 858; reprinted in *The Curious Republic of Gondour and Other Whimsical Sketches* (New York: Boni & Liveright, 1919), p. 33, and *Mark Twain: Life As I Find It*, ed. Charles Neider (Garden City, N.Y.: Hanover House, 1961), p. 55; reproduced in *Contributions to The Galaxy, 1868-1871, by Mark Twain*, ed. Bruce R. McElderry, Jr. (Gainesville, Fla.: Scholars' Facsimiles & Reprints, 1961), p. 47.

18. ". . . Mark Twains früher Humor war wild und angriffslustig, voll Empörung und Bitterkeit, voller Protest und Satire" (*Mark Twain als literarische Persönlichkeit* [Jena: Verlag der Frommannschen Buchhandlung, 1925], p. 18).

19. Quoted from *Aus dem amerikanischen Dichterwald* (Leipsic, 1881) in Edgar H. Hemminghaus, *Mark Twain in Germany* (New York: Columbia University Press, 1939), p. 25 (Translation by Hemminghaus.)

20. "Mark Twains Humor ist also sozial-politisch. Das ist jedenfalls sein Hauptvorzug" (*Die Amerikanische Literatur, Vorlesung, gehalten an der Königlichen Friedrich-Wilhelms-Universität zu Berlin* [Berlin: Weidmannsche Buchhandlung, 1912], p. 335).

21. "Malheureusement nous sommes trop disposés en France à prendre pour une continuation de cet âge d'or l'âge plus ou moins *doré* que MM. Mark Twain et Dudley Warner nous présentent enfin sous son vrai jour avec ses plaies et ses souillures" (L'Age Doré en Amerique," *Revue des Deux-Mondes*, VIII [March 15, 1875], 320).

22. ". . . les Américains ont reproché à MM. Mark Twain et Warner de ne montrer qu'une seule face des faits . . ."; ". . . tout en constatant que le peinture était grossière et outrée, personne n'a nié qu'elle ne fût vraie par le fond" (*ibid.*, p. 342).

23. ". . . espérons que les personnages de Mark Twain, grands seigneurs du pétrole, courtiers d'intrigue à gages, représentans qui vendent leur votes et juges qui vendent leur arrêts, passeront très prochainement aussi à l'état de mythes ou de souvenirs" (*ibid.*, p. 343).

Bentzon does not, of course, disregard literary criticism. "Au point de vue de l'ordonnance et de la composition, l'énergique satire qu'ils ont intitulée *the Gilded Age* laisse beaucoup à désirer; il y règne un désordre, une exubérante confusion" (*ibid.*, p. 320).

24. *Les Contemporains étrangers*, n.s. (Lausanne: Librairie Payot et Cie, 1914), II, 183-84.

25. "American Literature," *Harper's New Monthly Magazine*, LII (March, 1876), 526.

26. See DeVoto's essay, "The Symbols of Despair" (*Mark Twain at Work* [Cambridge: Harvard University Press, 1942], pp. 105-30), in which it is maintained that Clemens had a guilt complex and that he blamed himself for his own failure, for his wife's illness, and for his daughter's illness and death. The "symbols," born of a guilt fantasy, are revealed in the stories of the uncompleted manuscripts; they are (1) a great person cast down from a high position, (2) a beloved wife maddened by despair, and (3) a beloved daughter dying in agony.

27. "Salutation Speech," *New York Herald*, December 30, 1900, and photographic

reproduction of original MS (San Francisco, 1929); "Stupendous Procession," MTP, and in part in Paine, *op. cit.*, III, 1149-50; "Person Sitting in Darkness," *North American Review*, CLXXII (February, 1901), 161-76; "Defense of General Funston," *ibid.*, CLXXIV (May, 1902), 613-24; "Czar's Soliloquy," *ibid.*, CLXXX (March, 1905), 321-26 (the last two items are reprinted in *Life As I Find It*, pp. 241-52, 267-72). Similar pieces are "To My Missionary Critics," *North American Review*, CLXXII (April, 1901), 520-34; "The War Prayer," MTP, Paine 118; and *King Leopold's Soliloquy* (Boston: P. R. Warren Co., 1905) (last item reprinted in *Life As I Find It*, pp. 275-95). For an extended treatment of these writings see Foner, *op. cit.*, pp. 269-303.

28. *New York Herald*, December 30, 1900, quoted in Foner, *op. cit.*, p. 266.

29. *North American Review*, CLXXII (February, 1901), 165.

30. See, for example, M[aurice] Mendelson, "Mark Twain Accuses," *Soviet Literature*, 1948, No. 7, pp. 151-61; R. Samarin, "The True Mark Twain," *ibid.*, 1950, No. 6, pp. 179-86.

31. *Old and New*, IX (March, 1874), 387. The Boston *Literary World* said: "We have no doubt that the descriptions here given . . . are measurably accurate" (see above, p. 19).

According to one British working-class observer, "exaggeration of either the people or the country, even by a professional romanticist, would be next to an impossibility" (James Dawson Burn, *Three Years Among the Working-Classes in the United States During the War* [London: Smith, Elder & Co., 1865], p. ix).

32. Letter dated February 20, [1868], quoted in *Fairbanks Letters*, p. 19.

33. *Mark Twain's America*, p. 286; see also pp. 288-89, 291, and Herron, *op. cit.*, pp. 237 ff.

34. "Mark Twain: an Inquiry," *North American Review*, CXCI (June, 1910), 841 (reprinted from issue of February, 1901).

35. See Archibald Henderson, *Mark Twain* (London: Duckworth & Co., 1911), p. 62; Vernon L. Parrington, *Main Currents in American Thought* (New York: Harcourt, Brace & Co., 1927-1930), III, 23; C. Hartley Grattan, in *American Writers on American Literature*, ed. John Macy (New York: Tudor Publishing Co., 1931), p. 278; Matthew Josephson, *The Politicos, 1865-1896* (New York: Harcourt, Brace & Co., 1938), p. 175; Carl Van Doren, *The American Novel, 1789-1939* (rev. ed.; New York: Macmillan Co., 1940), p. 145.

36. Parrington, *op. cit.*, III, 23.

37. November 19, 1874, p. 4, cols. 5-6.

38. Wilfred R. Hollister and Harry Norman, *Five Famous Missourians* (Kansas City, Mo.: Hudson-Kimberly Publishing Co., 1900), pp. 55-56.

39. "The American on the Stage," *Scribner's Monthly*, XVIII (July, 1879), 328.

40. John Macy, *The Spirit of American Literature* (Garden City, N.Y.: Doubleday, Page & Co., 1913), p. 257.

41. Brander Matthews, *Playwrights on Playmaking and Other Studies of the Stage* (New York: Charles Scribner's Sons, 1923), p. 170; cf. his *Inquiries and Opinions* (New York: Charles Scribner's Sons, 1907), p. 146.

42. See, for example, *Facts*, by a woman (Oakland, Calif.: Pacific Press Publishing House, 1881), p. 119: "I became quite enthused, a la 'Sellers,' . . ."; or Parrington, *op. cit.*, III, 37: "Jay Cooke was chief amongst the Beriah Sellerses of the day."

43. Charles A. and Mary R. Beard, *The Rise of American Civilization* (rev. ed.; New York: Macmillan Co., 1937), II, 395.

44. Van Wyck Brooks, *New England: Indian Summer* (New York: E. P. Dutton & Co., 1940), p. 209. See also Taylor, *Economic Novel*, pp. 126-27.

45. *American Literature as an Expression of the National Mind* (rev. ed.; New York: Henry Holt & Co., 1949), pp. 466 f.

46. Canby, *op. cit.*, p. 130.

47. *Mark Twain: A Portrait* (New York: Charles Scribner's Sons, 1938), pp. 113 ff.

48. *Nook Farm, Mark Twain's Hartford Circle* (Cambridge: Harvard University Press, 1950), pp. 117, 126, 236.

49. *American Quarterly,* V (Winter, 1953), 344-56. ". . . the usual satire on flatulence is concerned with its hypocrisy in glossing over actual problems, and there is no concern for these problems in Clemens' burlesque" (p. 349).

50. *The Ordeal of Mark Twain* (New York: E. P. Dutton & Co., 1920; rev. ed., 1933).

51. In 1932 Bernard DeVoto, in *Mark Twain's America,* effectively exploded Brooks's psychoanalysis, showing its eclectic use of bits of Freudian, Adlerian, and Jungian psychology inconsistently and to fit the occasion (pp. 228-29). Thirty-seven years later, Mr. Brooks, having himself undergone psychotherapy, writes that the psychoanalytic approach to literary criticism "reduces a person to a type, a congerie of inhibitions, complexes and what not" and that in *The Ordeal of Mark Twain* his "over-concern with psychology left no room for literary appreciation" (*Days of the Phoenix: The Nineteen-Twenties I Remember* [New York: E. P. Dutton & Co., 1957], p. 173). He also admits that during the years he was writing *Ordeal* he was "possessed by the notion that American writers were, for whatever reason, foredoomed to fail" (p. 170).

In opposition to Brooks's completely nihilistic treatment DeVoto put forth his own hypothesis that Twain fulfilled himself abundantly as a writer and that it was the frontier that "completed" him as a writer. Unquestionably a contribution to Twain study and a badly needed realist corrective to Brooks's metaphysics, DeVoto's frontier theory was in its own way as one-dimensional as the psychoanalytical approach. It made the unacceptable assumption that Twain's growth as a writer stopped prior to or at the writing of *Innocents Abroad.* And it provided ostensible historical support for the long-standing popular estimate of Twain as merely a humorist (see also "Mark Twain: The Ink of History," in *Forays and Rebuttals* [Boston: Little, Brown & Co., 1936], pp. 351-55). Its net gain, therefore, was almost negligible, especially in view of DeVoto's own subsequent capitulation to the psychological fad.

DeVoto was not alone in his criticism of Brooks's thesis. See, for example, Schöne-mann, *op. cit.,* p. 18, n. 3; Lucy Lockwood Hazard, *The Frontier in American Literature* (New York: Thomas Y. Crowell Co., 1927), p. 221.

52. Edgar Marquess Branch, *The Literary Apprenticeship of Mark Twain, with Selections from His Apprentice Writing* (Urbana: University of Illinois Press, 1950), p. 182.

53. Parrington, *op. cit.,* III, 94, 169 f. DeVoto accuses Parrington of trying to make Mark Twain conform to his preconceived system, in this case Jeffersonian liber-tarianism (*Forays and Rebuttals,* pp. 396-97).

54. "Mark Twain and the Machine Age," reprinted from *South Atlantic Quarterly,* October, 1938, in *Fifty Years of the South Atlantic Quarterly,* ed. William Baskerville Hamilton (Durham: Duke University Press, 1952) pp. 277 ff.

55. *History,* p. 269.

56. *Fifty Years,* p. 274; *Economic Novel,* pp. 125 ff.

57. *Economic Novel,* p. 126.

58. See above, p. 138.

59. *Economic Novel,* p. 126.

60. Hazard, *op. cit.,* p. 226.

61. *Economic Novel,* p. 124.

62. Parrington, *op. cit.,* III, 20-22. "Whiggery," it should be noted, has for Par-rington a quasi-Marxian meaning: "For a capitalistic society Whiggery is the only rational politics, for it exalts the profit-motive as the sole object of parliamentary concern."

63. *Mark Twain and Southwestern Humor* (Boston: Little, Brown & Co., 1959), p. 177.

64. Andrews, *op. cit.,* p. 184; cf. p. 183: "The abuses are traced to the occupancy of positions of power by individuals who are not among the best people."

65. See Lynn, *op. cit.,* p. 176.

66. Parrington, *op. cit.,* III, 94.

67. *Fifty Years,* p. 280. Cf. *Economic Novel,* p. 127.

68. *American Political and Social History* (6th ed.; New York: Appleton-Century-Crofts, 1952), p. 516.

69. "Mark Twain and the Gilded Age" (Master's thesis, University of Idaho, 1937), pp. 30-31.

70. *The Liberation of American Literature* (New York: Charles Scribner's Sons, 1932), pp. 326-27.

71. *Ibid.,* pp. 230 ff. Calverton's thesis is well represented in the following statement: "The frontier background, because of rather than despite its hardships, provided an ideal environment for the realization of petty bourgeois ideals. The individual freedom from molestation on the top by the big bourgeoisie, gave the frontiersman that sense of personal security and self-reliance which endowed individualism with a meaning in America that it never acquired in any other country" (p. 227).

72. Foner, *op. cit.,* pp. 84-85.

73. *Ibid.,* p. 84; cf. p. 310: "He was sharply concerned with the corruption of the processes of representative government by the business elements who were, as he showed in *The Gilded Age,* the real but hidden rulers of the nation; . . ." As Burnham says (*op. cit.,* p. 34), "it depends on whether or not you agree with the authors as to the identity of the 'real leaders.'"

74. See Bernard DeVoto (ed.), "Passages from 'Outlines of History,'" *Saturday Review of Literature,* XIX (December 10, 1938), 4; also Twain, *Letters from the Earth,* ed. Bernard DeVoto (New York: Harper & Row, 1962), pp. 107-11.

75. Untitled sheet of notes, passage beginning "The Start," DV 127, MTP. This sheet is apparently what is referred to by Foner (*op. cit.,* pp. 161-62) as "Notes for a Social History of the United States from 1850 to 1900" (cf. Andrews, *op. cit.,* p. 238). Since there appears to have been no project so entitled, it may be that the supposed title is derived from a notation accompanying the MS in DV 127, evidently written by Rosamund Chapman, DeVoto's assistant: "Notes for Social History of recent past & the future."

76. *The Politicos,* pp. 101-3.

77. Hazard states: "The significant addition which Mark Twain makes to the interpretation of the business man in American literature is the relation of Big Business to the government. The Triumphant Democracy of Andrew Carnegie's effusive eulogy is here shown for the first time as the soiled plaything of a little group of greedy men" (p. 228).

78. "He had never risen to the conception of literature as a great impersonal social instrument. An irresponsible child himself, he could not even feel that he had a right to exercise a will-to-satire that violated the wishes of those to whom he had subjected himself. Consequently, instead of satirizing the spirit of his age, he outwardly acquiesced in it and even flattered it" (*Ordeal,* p. 271).

79. *Ordeal,* p. 77. Taylor has pointed out that as early as *America's Coming-of-Age* (1915) Brooks had formulated the premise "that business interests are necessarily hostile to the creative life" (*Economic Novel,* pp. 3-4). See Brooks, *America's Coming-of-Age* (New York: B. W. Heubsch, 1924 [copyright, 1915]), p. 109.

With some observers this tenet of liberalism might have led to critical bohemianism as an escape, the illusory comfort of the imagined alienation of the spirit. With Brooks, however, it led inward to a probing of Clemens' psyche, the equally illusory satisfaction of attaining a consistent, pseudoscientific frame of reference.

80. Lewisohn, *op. cit.,* p. 223.

81. Van Doren, *op. cit.*, p. 144.

82. Matthew Josephson, *Portrait of the Artist as American* (New York: Harcourt, Brace & Co., 1930), pp. 158-59.

83. Hazard, *op. cit.*, p. 223.

84. *Economic Novel*, p. 129.

85. Calverton, *op. cit.*, p. 327.

86. [Mrs. James T. Fields], *Memories of a Hostess: A Chronicle of Eminent Friendships*, ed. M. A. De Wolfe Howe (Boston: Atlantic Monthly Press, 1922), pp. 252-53.

87. See Taylor, *Economic Novel*, pp. 131-32: ". . . if one part of his nature tugged against another part, he was, even in this, almost perfectly a type of his age, reflecting within himself its waverings between plunging and prudence, between speculative adventure and security."

88. It is to be noted that the secondary conflict between Laura and a male-dominated society is skilfully woven into the larger one.

89. See, for example, DeLancey Ferguson, *Mark Twain: Man and Legend* (Indianapolis: Bobbs-Merrill Co., 1943), p. 170, or Masters, *op. cit.*, pp. 109-13.

90. Such a conclusion has been commonly used as evidence of the authors' noviceship and inexperience.

91. His only venture into the theoretical realm was his suggestion that the suffrage be enlarged in such a way as to weight it in favor of persons of "position" and those having higher education (see "The Curious Republic of Gondour," *Atlantic*, XXXVI (October, 1875), 461-63 [particularly p. 463]; reprinted in *The Curious Republic of Gondour and Other Whimsical Sketches* [New York: Boni & Liveright, 1919], pp. 1-11), an unconsciously antidemocratic proposal prompted by his discouragement at the low political understanding of the American electorate.

In this proposal, so at variance with his usual democracy, he clearly showed the effects of environmental influences. To it should be compared his ideas for a balance-of-power "Casting Vote Party" (MTP, quoted in Foner, *op. cit.*, pp. 91-92) and on woman suffrage (see above, p. 111). With it, also, should be contrasted his tribute to universal suffrage in *Connecticut Yankee* (*Writings*, XVI, 219).

92. ". . . the consequences of the crisis endured up to the autumn of 1879" (H. M. Hyndman, *Commercial Crises of the Nineteenth Century* [2d ed.; London: Swan Sonnenschein & Co., and New York: Charles Scribner's Sons, 1902], p. 100; see also William Archibald Dunning, *Reconstruction, Political and Economic, 1865-1877* [New York: Harper & Bros., 1907], p. 237).

93. See above, pp. 4 ff.

94. Hyndman, *op. cit.*, pp. 100-101, 112. ". . . the crisis of 1873 may be called 'The Crisis' " (Theodore E. Burton, *Financial Crises and Periods of Industrial and Commercial Depression* [New York: D. Appleton & Co., 1916], p. 287).

95. Hyndman, *op. cit.*, pp. 105 ff.

96. "The depression was the natural effect of overproduction of agricultural and manufactured goods, overexpansion of the railroad net and excessive speculation—all so characteristic of the periods of the Civil War and reconstruction. . . . [etc.]" (Louis M. Hacker and Benjamin B. Kendrick, *The United States Since 1865* [New York: F. S. Crofts & Co., 1932], pp. 54-55).

97. Hyndman, *op. cit.*, pp. 115-16.

98. *Ibid.*, pp. 107-8; Burton, *op. cit.*, pp. 287-88.

99. James Ford Rhodes, *History of the United States from the Compromise of 1850 to the Final Restoration of Home Rule at the South in 1877* (New York: Macmillan Co., 1920), VII, 37; Clement Juglar, *A Brief History of Panics and Their Periodical Occurrence in the United States*, 4th ed. trans. and ed. De Courcy W. Thom (New York: G. P. Putnam's Sons, 1916), p. 94.

100. See Calverton, *op. cit.*, pp. 334 ff.

101. Hyndman, *op. cit.*, pp. 108-9.

102. *Politicos*, p. 101.

103. *Ibid.*, p. 104; see also Hacker and Kendrick, *op. cit.*, pp. 132-33.

104. Claude G. Bowers, *The Tragic Era: The Revolution after Lincoln* (Boston: Houghton Mifflin Co., 1929), pp. 116, 117.

105. *Diary of Gideon Welles* (Boston: Houghton Mifflin Co., 1911), III, 65.

106. *Writings*, X, v-vi.

107. *The Gilded Age* (London, 1873), I, v-vi.

108. *Fifty Years*, p. 275. See also Burnham, *op. cit.*, p. 33.

109. Foner, *op. cit.*, p. 85.

110. *Mark Twain's America*, pp. 286-87.

111. See Flory, *op. cit.*, pp. 65-70.

112. Taylor, *Economic Novel*, p. 67.

113. *Atlantic*, XXX (December, 1872), 676-84; reprinted in *Stories by American Authors* (New York: Charles Scribner's Sons, 1900), IV, 137-61.

114. *Stories by American Authors*, IV, 154.

115. Ananias, instead of laying the full proceeds of the sale of his possession at the feet of the apostles Peter and John, "kept back *part* of the price" (Acts 5:1-2).

116. New York: G. P. Putnam & Sons, 1872.

117. A variant subtitle, *The Days of Tammany*, is listed on the Library of Congress catalogue card and in George Arthur Dunlap, *The City in the American Novel, 1789-1900* (Philadelphia, Privately printed, 1934) (a published dissertation, University of Pennsylvania), pp. 154, 157.

118. Barton Seacrist is described as having a head "skillfully cut from the finest and purest Italian marble, . . . a face . . . exquisitely chiselled; . . . a tall and elegantly moulded person of rather delicate structure" (Niles, *op. cit.*, p. 29). Like Hall, his ambition is to be Mayor of New York.

119. Dunlap, *op. cit.*, p. 154. The novels are *John Andross* (1874), by Rebecca Harding Davis; *An Average Man* (1884), by Robert Grant; *An American Politician* (1884), by F. Marion Crawford; *The Bostonians* (1886), by Henry James; *A New York Family* (1891), by Edgar Fawcett; and *The Honorable Peter Sterling* (1894), by Paul Leicester Ford.

120. *Five Hundred Majority*, p. 92. Other *Gilded Age* topics touched on by this novel are "a mad and bewildering spirit of speculation" (p. 90), ignorant trial juries (p. 188) and their manipulation (p. 191), and current sensation fiction (p. 60).

121. See Herron, *op. cit.*, p. 204. The novel was published as a volume by Orange Judd & Co. (New York, 1873); all references are to this edition.

122. *Mystery of Metropolisville*, p. 11.

123. *Ibid.*, p. 97; see also pp. 152-53. The original of Metropolisville was Cannon City, Minnesota (William Randel, *Edward Eggleston* [New York: Twayne Publishers, 1963], p. 100).

124. *Ibid.*, pp. 214-15.

125. *Ibid.*, p. 320.

126. *Ibid.*, p. 296. A slightly later novel with a similar theme was *A Paper City* (Boston, 1879), by David Locke Ross ("Petroleum V. Nasby").

127. Henry Watterson, in Charles F. Wingate (ed.), *Views and Interviews on Journalism* (New York: F. B. Patterson, 1875), p. 20.

128. John W. Forney, *Anecdotes of Public Men* (New York: Harper & Bros., 1873), II, 244.

129. See *The National Cyclopedia of American Biography*, XIII, 157.

130. See *Contributions to* The Galaxy, pp. xiv, 134, 140.

131. *National Cyclopedia of American Biography*, XIII, 157.

132. Piatt, *Life in the Lobby*, p. 55.

133. *Ibid.*, p. 38.

134. *Ibid.*, p. 47.

135. *Ibid.*, pp. 20-21.

136. *Ibid.*, pp. 21, 14-15, 19. Reference is also made to the Freedman's Bank (p. 10) (not in *The Gilded Age*) and to current "dime novels" (p. 2).

137. *Ibid.*, p. 44; (Excavation Company) p. 38.

138. New Haven: Richmond & Patten, 1875; serialized in the *Atlantic Monthly*, July-November, 1873.

139. New York, 1875.

140. *Honest John Vane*, ed. Joseph Jay Rubin (State College, Pa.: Bald Eagle Press, 1960), p. 163. According to Rubin, "the Great Subfluvial and the Sub-Tunnel, corporate names De Forest used for legal and artistic reasons rather than their archetypes, the Union Pacific and the Credit Mobilier, are both composites of two actual wildcat schemes of the day: a drainage tunnel under the Comstock Lode and a plan to save 'the alluvial' running into the Gulf of Mexico" (pp. 49-50).

141. Taylor, *Economic Novel*, p. 63.

142. ". . . these early writers usually explored some specific economic or political problem, such as fraudulent land speculation, illicit mining schemes, bad labor conditions, the threat of monopoly, or corruption in government. Some of them perceived a unifying principle underlying the various problems; others considered the problems as isolated phenomena. All were outspoken in their dissatisfaction with affairs of the status quo" (Edward E. Cassady, "Muckraking in the Gilded Age," *American Literature*, XIII [May 1941], 135).

143. See Parrington, *op. cit.*, pp. 144-45.

144. ". . . we may conclude that the problems involved either did not seem to our novelists particularly acute, or that the writers of fiction felt the novel form inadequate to a developed analysis and criticism of the problems" (Flory, *op. cit.*, p. 64).

145. Wagenknecht, *op. cit.*, p. 124.

146. *Economic Novel*, p. 61.

147. See Dunlap, *op. cit.*, pp. 157, 163, 178; Flory, *op. cit.*, pp. 76, 78, 79, 246, 247. The reformist novels were numerous; many of the most prominent of these "novels of exposure" are listed in the bibliography of Robert E. Spiller *et al.*, *Literary History of the United States* (New York: Macmillan Co., 1948), III, 330-31.

148. Published respectively in 1901, 1906, and 1914.

149. January 17, 1874, p. 61.

150. *The Cambridge History of American Literature* (New York), III (1921), 6, 14.

151. "Die meisten der Charaktere sind intim geschilderte Persönlichkeiten aus Clemens' frühem Leben, insbesondere *Colonel* Sellers, . . . [etc.] Immerhin könnte der Verfasser in der Art der Behandlung der Charaktere von Vorgängern, hier von Dickens gelernt haben.

. . . .

"Das kleinbürgerliche Milieu des „*Gilded Age*" mag an die vielen Kleinbürger in Dickens' Welt erinnern, Laura an Emily im „*Copperfield*", doch nur sehr wenig, . . ." (pp. 44-45). See also Walther Fischer [rev. of Schönemann], *Englische Studien*, LXI (1926-27), 137.

152. Schönemann, *op. cit.*, p. 46. See also Hemminghaus, pp. 103-4.

153. Dating at least from 1851 (see Dixon Wecter, *Sam Clemens of Hannibal* [Boston: Houghton Mifflin Co., 1952], p. 240; also Foner, *op. cit.*, p. 16; Branch, *op. cit.*, p. 282; *Mark Twain of the* Enterprise, ed. Henry Nash Smith [Berkeley: University of California Press, 1957], p. 92; *Autobiography*, Neider ed., pp. 174-75, 176).

154. *American Notes and Pictures from Italy* (London: Macmillan & Co., 1903), pp. 104-5.

155. See Edward H. Weatherly, "Beau Tibbs and Colonel Sellers," *Modern Language Notes*, LIX (May, 1944), 310-13.

156. DeVoto, *Mark Twain's America*, p. 257.

157. Parrington, *op. cit.*, III, 92.

158. Lynn, *op. cit.*, pp. 178-79.

159. *The Flush Times of Alabama and Mississippi*, in "American Century Series" (New York: Sagamore Press, 1957), pp. 2-3, 5, 6.

160. *Forays and Rebuttals*, p. 388.

161. *Love Letters*, p. 76. (See also Clemens' letter of February 18, 1854, from Washington, printed in Orion's Muscatine *Journal* [*Muscatine Letters*, p. 19].)

162. In letter dated January 9, [1872] (*Love Letters*, p. 172).

163. " 'Pozolochennyi vek' predstavliaet soboi vazhneishii etap v stanovlenii Tvena-satirika" (*Mark Tven* [rev. ed.]; Moscow: "Molodaia Gvardiia" ("Young Guard") Publishing House, 1958], p. 188).

164. See *Traveling with the Innocents Abroad*, ed. Daniel Morley McKeithan (Norman: University of Oklahoma Press, 1958); see also above, Ch. III, n. 45.

165. *Writings*, I, 368-71.

EPILOGUE

1. See George C. D. Odell, *Annals of the New York Stage* (New York), IX (1937), 556 f.; also Clemens' letter to Howells, September 20, 1874, in *Twain-Howells*, I, 26 and n. 2. Smith and Gibson have presented a useful outline of the main circumstances of the play's launching in their appendix (see "The Dramatic Version of *The Gilded Age*," *Twain-Howells*, II, 861-63).

2. "The stage name is 'Col. Sellers,' and, inasmuch as that purely American creation is the conspicuous figure in the piece, it is correctly named after him" (review, "Mark Twain, the Playwright," *Chicago Tribune*, September 27, 1874, p. 7). The *New York Times* (review, September 17, 1874, p. 6) said that the play "pleased chiefly on account of a character not at all essential to the main story."

3. Arthur Hobson Quinn, *A History of the American Drama from the Civil War to the Present Day* (rev. ed.; New York: F. S. Crofts & Co., 1936), p. 114; Odell, *op. cit.*, IX, 557.

4. Odell, *op. cit.*, IX, 556.

5. According to the known records, *Colonel Sellers* was performed at least at the following times and places: January 11-?, 1875, Opera House, Hartford; April 19-?, Globe Theatre, Boston; August 16-October 2, Union Square Theatre, New York; November 22-?, Brooklyn Theatre, Brooklyn; January 31-February 5, 1876, Varieties Theatre, New Orleans; February ?-March 4, McVicker's Theatre, Chicago; November 13-18, Boston Theatre, Boston; November 20-25, Brooklyn Theatre, Brooklyn; April 30-May 19, 1877, Park Theatre, New York; May 28-June 2, Park Theatre, Brooklyn; June 4-16, Grand Opera House, New York; April 15-17, 1880, Park Theatre, Brooklyn; April 26-May 1, Grand Opera House, New York; May 3-8, Novelty Theatre, Williamsburgh; September 6-11, Grand Opera House, New York; October 16-23, 1882, Park Theatre, New York; December 22-27, 1883, Grand Opera House, New York (week shared with alternate play, *In Paradise*) (cf. *Twain-Howells*, I, 448); November 7-8, 1884, Park Theatre, Brooklyn; October 22-24, 1885, Park Theatre, Brooklyn; and October 22-24, 1888, H. R. Jacobs' New Lyceum Theatre, Brooklyn (see Odell, *op. cit.*, X [1938], 20, 121, 210-11, 215, 314, 322, 398, 595; XI [1939], 56, 172, 203, 273-74; XII [1940], 462, 561; XIII [1942], 144; XIV [1945], 194; T. Allston Brown, *A History of the New York Stage* [New York: Dodd, Mead & Co., 1903], II, 621; III, 195, 197, 207; John S. Kendall, *The Golden Age of the New Orleans Theater* [Baton Rouge: Louisiana State University Press, 1952], pp. 456, 462, 482; Eugene Tompkins, *The History of the Boston Theater, 1854-1901* [Boston: Houghton Mifflin Co., 1908], pp. 234, 247; also

Boston *Evening Transcript,* April 20, 1875, p. 1; *Chicago Tribune,* February 27, 1876, p. 8; Hartford *Courant,* January 12, 1875).

6. In a letter to Frank Finlay dated Hartford, November 10, [1874] (*The Twainian,* Vol. IV, No. 1, p. 2, October, 1944).

7. See, for example, Will M. Clemens, *Mark Twain: His Life and Work* (San Francisco: Clemens Publishing Co., 1892), p. 125; John Curtis Underwood, *Literature and Insurgency* (New York: Mitchell Kennerley, 1914), p. 12; Minnie M. Brashear, *Mark Twain, Son of Missouri* (Chapel Hill: University of North Carolina Press, 1934), p. 10; Edward Wagenknecht, *Mark Twain, the Man and His Work* (New Haven: Yale University Press, 1935), p. 76; Kenneth R. Andrews, *Nook Farm, Mark Twain's Hartford Circle* (Cambridge: Harvard University Press, 1950), p. 158. Cf. Albert Bigelow Paine, *Mark Twain: A Biography: The Personal and Literary Life of Samuel Langhorne Clemens* (New York: Harper & Bros., 1912), II, 517-18; *Letters,* I, 223 ff.; *Mark Twain's Notebook,* ed. Albert Bigelow Paine (New York: Harper & Bros., 1935), p. 123. The summary in *Twain-Howells* is of course the one exception (see above, n. 1).

8. San Francisco *Bulletin,* April 22, 1874, p. 4, col. 3; also p. 3, col. 5. Quinn (*op. cit.,* p. 114) is off by one day when he gives April 23 as the date of production, for the April 23 *Bulletin* reviews the performance of the evening before.

9. *Twain-Howells,* II, 861.

10. The copyright of the title of the "Dramatic Composition" "The Gilded Age: A Drama" is dated May 19, 1873. It is accompanied by a printed title page, which gives a brief synopsis of the plot. (In the Clemens Papers, Watkinson Library, Trinity College, Hartford, Conn.)

11. Quoted in William Winter, *The Life of David Belasco* (New York: Moffat, Yard & Co., 1918), I, 64.

12. Unpublished letter in MTP.

13. Paine, *op. cit.,* II, 517.

14. *Idem.* On "May 10 or 11" he wrote his brother, Orion, regarding "a fraud in San Francisco" who had made a "great hit" with the dramatization: "But I've got *him* foul, because I copyrighted the thing as a drama a year ago. He will have to lay down his stolen goods" (unpublished letter in MTP). Clemens was ever alert for piracy.

15. Typescript of unpublished letter, MTP.

16. Apparently Clemens believed that Densmore had written the unauthorized extension of Harte's story "M'liss" for the *Golden Era* the year before. Harte had written James R. Osgood on April 2, 1873, "I find now that the 'Golden Era' is reprinting the second story [Harte's own attempt at a lengthened version, partially written and abandoned in 1863—B.F.] in three columns with an advertisement saying that it will be completed in 'sixty-two' chapters. Of course this means a swindle on the public, or a *forgery*" (*The Letters of Bret Harte,* ed. Geoffrey Bret Harte [Boston: Houghton Mifflin Co., 1926], p. 23). If Densmore authored one of the numerous pirated stage versions of "M'liss," I have found no evidence. (See T. Edgar Pemberton, *The Life of Bret Harte* [New York: Dodd, Mead & Co., 1903], pp. 263-64; cited by Henry Childs Merwin, *The Life of Bret Harte* [Boston: Houghton Mifflin Co., 1911], p. 234; cf. George R. Stewart, Jr., *Bret Harte, Argonaut and Exile* [Boston: Houghton Mifflin Co., 1931], p. 229.)

17. The synopsis of the "drama" given on this title page (see above, n. 10) contains all the essential material of the novel, both Clemens' and Warner's, indicating that at that early date no serious consideration had been given to the probable exigencies of dramatic adaptation.

18. Paine, *op. cit.,* II, 518; also *Letters,* I, 227.

19. Paine, *op. cit.,* II, 517.

20. *Twain-Howells,* pp. 862 f.

21. The article appeared on the front page.

22. See above, pp. 119-20.

23. Quoted in full in Winter, *op. cit.*, 66-67. See also Paine, *op. cit.*, II, 517; *Letters,* I, 228; *Twain-Howells,* II, 862.

24. *Twain-Howells,* II, 862; Paine, *op. cit.*, II, 517-18.

25. William Dean Howells, *My Mark Twain: Reminiscences and Criticisms* (New York: Harper & Bros., 1911), p. 22. Howells apparently had in mind another unauthorized dramatization of *The Gilded Age,* which was to be presented by the comedian Willie Gill in Salt Lake City beginning February 8, 1875, but which was stopped by an injunction from Clemens served by his legal agents on the evening it was to open (Salt Lake City *Daily Herald,* February 7 and 9, 1875).

26. *Twain-Howells,* II, 862; Paine, *op. cit.*, II, 518.

27. *Twain-Howells,* II, 861.

28. Paine, *op. cit.*, II, 518; *Twain-Howells,* II, 862.

29. Unpublished letter, MTP. Clemens, forgetting that the *Sun* article did not appear until November 2, has noted on the envelope of this letter, postmarked August 28: "Densmore in answer to my charge that he inspired the 'Sun' article."

30. *Twain-Howells,* II, 862; Paine, *op. cit.*, II, 518. Cf. Raymond's statement (in letter to *Sun,* Winter, *op. cit.*, p. 67): "I sent the manuscript to Mr. Clemens, but not until after he had finished his play and read it to me, . . ."

31. Laurence Hutton, referring to the play some seventeen years later, stated, "Mr. Warner and Mr. Clemens, jointly with John T. Raymond, are responsible for the character of Colonel Mulberry Sellers" (*Curiosities of the American Stage* [New York: Harper & Bros., 1891], p. 43), an imputation that has been paraphrased and published as late as 1940 (see Mary Caroline Crawford, *The Romance of the American Theatre* [New York: Halcyon House, 1940; original copyright 1913], p. 483).

32. Letter dated Elmira, July 15 [25?], [1874] (*Twain-Howells,* I, 20 f.).

33. "Mark Twain—An Intimate Memory," *American Magazine,* LXX (July, 1910), 372-73; see also *Marse Henry—An Autobiography* (New York: George H. Doran Co., 1919), I, 121. See Henry W. Fisher, *Abroad with Mark Twain and Eugene Field* (New York: Nicholas L. Brown, 1922), p. 99: " 'I wrote it for Edwin Booth. That is, I had Edwin Booth in mind when I did the play. But Raymond was the superior money-maker. He had the masses with him—and I was pressed for funds.' " Whether Booth ever saw the script is uncertain. Daniel Frohman says that "the tragedian . . . failed to see himself in the part" (*Memories of a Manager* [Garden City, N.Y.: Doubleday Page & Co., 1911], p. 50). William Winter, in his biography of Booth, states merely that the actor "read many manuscripts of new plays that were offered to him, but he seldom or never found a piece that he could practically adopt" (*Life and Art of Edwin Booth* [New York: Macmillan Co., 1906], p. 166).

Before leaving for England in May, 1873, Clemens had gone to see the actor-dramatist Dion Boucicault with a view to the latter's dramatizing the novel. Clemens, who considered Boucicault "in some minor respects . . . an ass," would "not consent to his having more than one-third" for the dramatization (unpublished letter to Warner, dated "Under Way, Sat. A.M.," typescript in MTP).

34. Letter from Lawrence Barrett, May 25, 1874, MTP.

35. "The first real success of Mr. Raymond's engagement [at the California Theatre] was achieved last night, in the character 'Colonel Sellers,' which most happily suits his peculiar style, and enables him to display those qualities which in old times endeared him to us, . . ." (review in San Francisco *Evening Bulletin,* April 23, 1874). See also David Belasco (quoted in Winter, *Life of Belasco,* I, 64-65): "It was . . . another instance of the personality of the player being fitted to the part, and in the *rôle* [*sic*— W.W.] of *Colonel Mulberry Sellers* John T. Raymond found himself and, incidentally, fame and fortune."

36. According to Raymond, when he heard that Clemens had enjoined Densmore's play he immediately communicated with him, even before he had heard from Densmore,

"with a view of having him write a play with *Colonel Sellers* as the chief character" (letter to *Sun*, quoted in Winter, *Life of Belasco*, I, 66).

37. *Twain-Howells*, I, 27, n. 2; cf. *Fairbanks Letters*, pp. 188-89.

38. Letter dated Elmira, September 4, 1874 (*Letters*, I, 224-25).

39. Odell, *op. cit.*, IX, 428, 556; see also Brown, *op. cit.*, III, 191.

40. Odell, *op. cit.*, IX, 557 *et passim*.

41. *Ibid.*, 12-13, 485.

42. *New-York Tribune*, September 18, 1874, p. 4, col. 5. The *New York Times* also praised her (September 17, p. 6).

43. *New York Times*, September 17, p. 6.

44. *New-York Tribune*, September 18, p. 4, col. 5.

45. See Howells, *op. cit.*, p. 16: " . . . he would as lief do a sum as follow a plot on the stage." Clemens himself attributed his prejudice to his required theater beat as a young reporter on the San Francisco *Morning Call* (*Mark Twain in Eruption: Hitherto Unpublished Pages about Men and Events*, ed. Bernard DeVoto [New York: Harper & Bros., 1940], p. 255; also *Autobiography*, Neider ed., p. 119).

In the last days of Clemens' life he had a recurrent dream about "a play in which the title-rôle of the general manager was always unfilled" (Paine, *op. cit.*, IV, 1572), and in 1907 he confessed to Paine, "There was never any question with the managers about my plays. They always said they wouldn't *act*" (IV, 1414).

46. Letter dated Hartford, September 20 [1874] (*Twain-Howells*, I, 26; *Letters*, I, 227).

47. A complete amanuensis manuscript of the play is in MTP (Paine 163). It contains cue marks for Raymond's entrances, and Paine has noted on the cover: "The Sellers play as performed by Mr. Raymond [.]"

48. XXXV, 749-51; reprinted in *My Mark Twain*, pp. 115-19.

49. See above, p. 14.

50. Howells, *My Mark Twain*, p. 116. *Appleton's Journal* [XIII (January 2, 1875), 23], said, ". . . it is something for a dramatist to give a glimpse of possibilities in the direction of national characterizations;" and *Harper's Monthly* (L [April, 1875], 698), ". . . [Colonel Sellers] rallies to the theatre thousands nightly to roar in laughter over the exaggeration of an extravagant feature in our American society."

51. *My Mark Twain*, p. 115.

52. Charles F. Wingate (ed.), *Views and Interviews on Journalism* (New York: F. B. Patterson, 1875), p. 190.

53. *The Wallet of Time* (New York: Moffat, Yard & Co., 1913), p. 297.

54. *Scribner's Monthly*, XVIII (July, 1879), 328. See also the *Arcadian* review, quoted in the Hartford *Courant*, September 26, 1874: "It would have been easy for Mr. Raymond to have taken the one single step from the sublime to the ridiculous, and made a burlesque of his part. . . . It speaks therefore all the more highly of his talent and power that he should have achieved a triumph without in one single instance departing from the principles of true art"; the New York *World* (quoted in Hartford *Courant*, September 26), expressed a similar view.

55. Kendall, *op. cit.*, p. 482.

56. T. Allston Brown, *History of the American Stage* (New York: Dick & Fitzgerald, 1870), pp. 304-5; Odell, *op. cit.*, IX, 141.

57. *American Magazine*, LXX, 372; *Marse Henry*, I, 121.

58. [Mrs. James T. Fields], *Memories of a Hostess: A Chronicle of Eminent Friendships*, ed. M. A. De Wolfe Howe (Boston: Atlantic Monthly Press, 1922), p. 253.

59. Quoted in DeLancey Ferguson, "Mark Twain's Lost Curtain Speeches," *South Atlantic Quarterly*, XLII (July, 1943), 265. The one hundredth performance took place December 23, 1874 (Brown, *A History of the New York Stage*, III, 191).

60. Clemens believed that Raymond had taken advantage of him. See letter to

Charles Webster, November 30, 1883 (*MT, Business Man*, p. 228): "He knows that *I* know, that as a liar he has not his equal, either in hell or out of it."

61. *Autobiography*, Neider ed., p. 19. In this passage written some twenty years later, Clemens, with Frank Mayo's successful dramatization of *Pudd'nhead Wilson* still fresh in mind, adds: "There was only one man who could have played the whole of Colonel Sellers, and that was Frank Mayo" (*Autobiography*, I, 90 [omitted in Neider ed.]).

62. *My Mark Twain*, pp. 117, 119. Cf. "G. L. S." in the *Argonaut*, October 13, 1906: "He did not present the genial yet dignified, unsophisticated yet refined, day-dreaming gentleman of the old school that Mark Twain tells us Colonel Sellers was in real life; but he did act the busy-brained, enthusiastic and impractical, over-sanguine and impecunious American that more than half of the millions who saw him on the stage knew personally under some other name."

63. *My Mark Twain*, p. 118.

64. Besides Paine 163 (see above, n. 47) there is in MTP a second amanuensis copy (Paine 163a), which is described below (n. 76).

65. *Twain-Howells*, I, 83.

66. Paine 163, MTP, Act V, pp. 7-8.

67. *Ibid.*, Act IV, pp. 3, 5.

68. *American Magazine*, LXX, 372-73; cf. *Marse Henry*, I, 123-24.

69. *My Mark Twain*, pp. 22-23; see also Paine, *op. cit.*, II, 518-19.

70. Letter to Howells, September 5, 1881, *Twain-Howells*, I, 372; see also Rodman Gilder, "Mark Twain Detested the Theatre," *Theatre Arts*, XXVIII (February, 1944), 111.

71. See above, pp. 107 ff., 168, 170-71, 210 ff.

72. Paine 163, MTP, Act III, pp. 1-4.

73. *Ibid.*, Act V, pp. 16-17.

74. See above, p. 109.

75. *The Gilded Age*, I (*Writings*, X), 125. Washington Hawkins' name had apparently already changed to Lafayette in Clemens' mind as he set to work on his dramatization (see above, n. 19), for on May 10, in a letter to Howells, Clemens refers to young Hawkins by the latter designation: "(see opening chapters of Gilded Age—my brother is 'Lafayette Hawkins.')" (*Twain-Howells*, I, 17).

In this connection, it is interesting to note that in the original manuscript Washington, who as late as Chapter IX appears as Frank [short for Franklin?] (University of Pittsburgh Library; also chapters VI [p. 160, Jacob Zeitlin, rare book dealer, Los Angeles] and VII [C. Waller Barrett Collection, Alderman Library, University of Virginia, Charlottesville; incomplete]), for several chapters becomes Marmion Hawkins (chs. XI, XXIV-XXV [Morse, containers 10, 12b]), in obvious ridicule of Sir Walter Scott's influence (see above, p. 34 and chap. ii, n. 19). He later becomes Washington; but another hit at Scott is retained in the name of a second Sellers child, Roderick Dhu (*Writings*, X, 126). "In those old days . . . there was hardly a family, at least in the West, but had a Washington in it—and also a Lafayette, a Franklin, and six or eight sounding names from Byron, Scott, and the Bible" (footnote to p. 125, *Writings*, X).

In the same spirit Clay, who originally appears as Dan (chapters III [p. 59, Barrett Collection], V [p. 110, Henry W. and Albert A. Berg Collection, New York Public Library], and IX [Pittsburgh]), receives as his full name Henry Clay Hawkins (*Writings*, I, 58-59).

76. Paine 163, MTP, Act IV, p. 4. Uncle Daniel is listed in the "Cast of Characters" as *"An old Stammering Negro. (He Stammers if anecdote used. not otherwise.)"*

The variant manuscript, Paine 163a, which is evidently a later version and which Paine labeled as "script copies apparently of two plays" (meaning that it was assembled from two separate scripts), differs largely in its strengthening of Laura's story. For instance, lines are added in Act II to reveal Laura's desire to be somebody and not vegetate in a frontier village; better motivation for the shooting (in Act IV) is provided by open insults from Selby; and minor changes in Act V dialogue underline the emotional insanity plea more strongly.

77. Much of the background of this prolonged interest is to be found in the recently published correspondence between Clemens and Howells and the excellent footnotes thereto (see *Twain-Howells, passim*). See also Paine, *op. cit.*, II, 706-7, 757 ff., III, 918; *Letters*, I, 347, 352 ff., 424 ff., 437-38, II, 441, 529-30; Howells, *My Mark Twain*, pp. 22 ff.; Mildred Howells (ed.), *Life in Letters of William Dean Howells* (Garden City, N.Y.: Doubleday Doran & Co., 1928), I, 246, 276-77, 306 ff., 312 f., 324, 339, 354 ff., 382-83; *MT, Business Man*, pp. 204, 227 ff., 253-54, 264, 273 ff., 356-57; Brander Matthews, *Playwrights on Playmaking and Other Studies of the Stage* (New York: Charles Scribner's Sons, 1923), pp. 174 ff.; Phillip Walker, "Mark Twain, Playwright," *Educational Theater Journal*, VIII (October, 1956), 185-93.

78. Clemens had always been interested in the theme that humble folk might be lawful heirs to an earldom, for his mother's kin were proud of their descent from the family of the Earl of Durham (see *Autobiography*, I, 87, 120 ff., Neider ed., pp. 18, 28-29; *Notebook*, p. 158; *MT, Business Man*, p. 321; Watterson, *American Magazine*, LXX, 373, *Marse Henry*, I, 120 ff.; unpublished memorandum, MTP, DV 206), and one relative insisted he was the rightful heir (see Watterson, *American Magazine*, LXX, 373, *Marse Henry*, I, 124-25; John W. Chapman, "The Germ of a Book—A Footnote on Mark Twain," *Atlantic*, CL, 720-21). Clemens also knew of an American claimant who was a friend of his father's family (*Autobiography*, I, 81-82). The winter he was in London reading proofs of *The Gilded Age*, he had his "secretary," Charles Warren Stoddard, collecting newspaper clippings about the current Tichborne claimant case (see Paine, *op. cit.*, II, 496-97, III, 1086; *Autobiography* I, 139; *Notebook*, p. 242; *MT, Business Man*, pp. 380-81; Watterson, *American Magazine*, LXX, 373, *Marse Henry*, I, 125).

The play as written in collaboration with Howells, *Colonel Sellers as a Scientist*, has been published in *The Complete Plays of W. D. Howells*, ed. Walter J. Meserve (New York: New York University Press, 1960), pp. 209-41.

79. Paine, *op. cit.*, II, 761; Howells, *My Mark Twain*, p. 26.

80. See letter to Howells, May 20, 1891 (*Twain-Howells*, II, 645-46; *Letters*, II, 548).

81. See *Letters*, II, 562-63; Joseph Francis Daly, *The Life of Augustin Daly* (New York: Macmillan Co., 1917), p. 551.

APPENDIX A

1. The case is cited in Copinger both as 1865 and as 1868 ([W. A.] Copinger and [F. E. and E. P.] Skone James, *Law of Copyright* [9th ed.; London: Sweet & Maxwell, 1958], pp. xxxii; 325, nn. *s, t*; 332, n. *b*; 367 n. *c*).

2. Augustine Birrell, M.P., *The Law and History of Copyright in Books* (London: Cassell & Co.; New York: G. P. Putnam's Sons, 1899), pp. 149-52.

3. Kenneth R. Andrews, *Nook Farm: Mark Twain's Hartford Circle* (Cambridge: Harvard University Press, 1950), p. 263, n. 34.

4. In the Warner Papers, Watkins Library, Trinity College, Hartford, Connecticut. This document reads in part:

We Samuel Langhorne Clemens late of Hartford Connecticut in the United States of America but now of   in the Dominion of of [sic] Canada Author and Charles Dudley Warner also late of Hartford aforesaid but now of   aforesaid Author do solemnly and sincerely declare as follows:

1. That from the   day of   one thousand eight hundred and seventy   up to the present time we have been continually and still are residing at   in the Dominion of Canada.

5. Warner Papers.

6. As the authoritative Copinger states, there was a "complicated state of circumstances . . . for the rights of an author in foreign countries varied according to the particular treaty or Order in Council, . . ." (Copinger and Skone James, *op. cit.*, p. 333).

7. See below, Appendix C.

APPENDIX B

1. "The 'Fake' Title-page of 'The Gilded Age': A Solution," *Papers of the Bibliographical Society of America,* L (3rd Quar. 1956), 292-96.

2. Jacob Blanck, "The Gilded Age: A Collation," *Publishers' Weekly,* CXXXVIII (July 20, 1940), 186-88.

3. Woodfield, *op. cit.,* p. 293.

4. Much uninvited bootlegging of the American Publishing Company's books was carried on, and *The Gilded Age* was no exception. According to Blanck (*op. cit.,* p. 188), "certain agents sold copies to shops (at a cut rate profitable to both agent and shop) but in order to avoid detection in one case the original title-page was deleted and another printed from types similar to, but not the same as, that of the publisher [apparently Woodfield's "fake"—B.M.F.]. In these cancel-titles the name of one of the illustrators, *White,* is omitted. In other instances renegade agents merely cut their name from the title-page, thus leaving a rectangular hole concealing the source of the book. . . ."

5. *Bibliography of American Literature* (New Haven: Yale University Press, 1957-), II, 184, item 3357.

APPENDIX C

1. See Appendix A.

2. Unpublished letters in Morse. It will be remembered that Clemens intended to do all of his proofreading in England.

3. P. 12, col. 4.

4. P. 12, col. 3.

5. P. 8, col. 2.

6. P. 825.

7. P. 871.

8. Pp. 1092, 1099.

9. *The Gilded Age* was published in the United States "a day or two before Christmas" (Albert Bigelow Paine: *Mark Twain: A Biography: The Personal and Literary Life of Samuel Langhorne Clemens* [New York: Harper & Bros., 1912], II, 500). See above, p. 4.

The statement in Jacob Blanck, *Bibliography of American Literature* (New Haven: Yale University Press, 1957-   ), II, 185, item 3359, that "According to PC June 17, 1873, the London and the Hartford editions were to be issued simultaneously" appears faulty. I have been unable to find any such announcement in that or any other issue of the *Publishers' Circular.*

10. *A Bibliography of the Works of Mark Twain* (rev. ed.; New York: Harper & Bros., 1935), p. 20. Several years before publication of the revised edition of Johnson's *Bibliography,* Walter Bliss had discovered Johnson's error and corrected it in his notes (*Twainiana Notes from the Annotations of Walter Bliss,* ed. Frances M. Edwards [Hartford: The Hobby Shop, 1930], p. 17).

11. "Mark Twain in England; A Study of the English Criticism of and Attitude toward Mark Twain: 1867-1940" (Ph.D. dissertation, University of Wisconsin, 1945), p. 290.

12. *Publishers' Circular,* XXXVII (June 16, 1874), 39. Also see the *English Catalogue of Books* (1872-1880, p. 468).

13. II, 236, item 3606. The "shelfback" is that part of a book completely exposed to view on a shelf between other books; synonymous with *spine, backbone.*

APPENDIX D

1. The actual number of leaves is slightly greater than the number of MS pages, for there are several fractionally numbered leaves, containing later additions, interspersed among the collection.

2. Containers HM 1315, HM 1312, HM 1309, HM 1318, HM 470, HM 1317, HM 1311, HM 1315, HM 1310, and HM 453 respectively. The single pages are Clemens (hereafter SLC) MS p. 29 and Warner (hereafter CDW) MS pp. 1449 and 1450. (Figures between parentheses in the text refer to the chapter numbers of Vol. II of the two-volume edition of the novel in *Writings*, X and XI.)

3. See above, pp. 68-69. MS page 1329 is pasted on the inside front cover of a Merle Johnson copy of the first American edition. On the flyleaf opposite is penciled the following note: "Page of mss in Warners hand—corrected in Mark Twain's hand—the only page known in which is shown Mark's supervision of Warner's mss. Appears pp. 527-528 of the book as corrected. [Signed] Merle Johnson" (David A. Randall, Rare Book Librarian, Indiana University, in a letter to me, January 13, 1960).

4. SLC pages 146 and 1199; CDW pages 330-35, 414-17, and 1454.

5. Discarded SLC pages 293, 305, 309, and 312 (see above, pp. 78, 67-68); discarded CDW page numbered 25 (see above, p. 71); an unnumbered SLC fragment and two unnumbered CDW fragments (see above, pp. 69, 71); and CDW two-page outline (see above, pp. 70-71). All of these items are in DeVoto file 137.

6. SLC pages 143 and 742 (in file folders M-CL-6 and M-CL-5/M-WA-2 respectively); CDW pages 316 and 317 (in M-CL-5/M-WA-2) and 714 (in D-Wa 3). At date of writing, the library was purchasing five more SLC pages, 670-72 and 1337-38. This collection also contains two CDW pages of character descriptions and a twenty-page SLC chapter outline prepared for J. Hammond Trumbull (see Appendix F).

7. SLC pages 110, 1070, and 1431; CDW pages 350 and 390. Pages 350 and 1070 are inserted in the Berg Collection copy of *The Gilded Age* (John D. Gordan, Curator, in a letter to me, February 3, 1960).

8. SLC page 47; CDW page 608.
At date of writing, one other CDW page (320) was owned by Claude Simpson, at Stanford University; one SLC page (160) was in the possession of Jacob Zeitlin, rare book dealer, Los Angeles; and another SLC page (55) was at the Seven Gables Bookshop (for first and last items: Hamlin Hill, in a letter to me, November 6, 1964).

9. Morse, containers 10, 2, 11, 2, and 8 respectively. Container 10 includes the following holograph affidavit: "This manuscript is the original autograph printers copy of chapter 24th 'The Gilded Age', published Dec. 1873 [Signed] Walter Bliss Dec 3/1912." Container 2 also has Clemens' original drawing of the fold-out railroad map inserted in Chapter XXVII of the first edition (see above, chap. iii, n. 17, and Appendix E). Containers 2, 10, and 11 are bound volumes in which the corresponding printed chapters from the first American edition have been bound in following the MS chapters. Container 8 is also a bound volume containing SLC MS pages 137 and 139 and CDW MS pages 136 and 138 followed by the printed pages of Chapter VI of the first American edition, the corresponding SLC lines underlined in black ink and the CDW lines in red ink.

10. For a description of the entire Morse Collection (Frear gift) see Gilbert McCoy Troxell, "Samuel Langhorne Clemens, 1835-1910," *Yale University Library Gazette*, XVIII (July, 1943), 1-5.

11. The gift of Mr. and Mrs. W. Robert Blum in memory of W. Robert Blum, Jr., is referred to throughout this volume as Morse, 12b. This boxed container holds only loose MS leaves, arranged in numerical order, and includes, in addition to the large Blum gift, a leaf from the George Buell Alvord Memorial Collection (SLC page 4) and one

(SLC page 306) removed from the Aldis copy of the first edition (gift of Owen Franklin Aldis). (See also Bryant Morey French, "The *Gilded Age* Manuscript," *Yale University Library Gazette,* XXXV [July, 1960], 35-41.)

12. This total appears to be certain, for CDW page 1457 is within two pages of the end of the book, measured by Warner's overall average of 1.8 MS pages per printed page of Author's National Edition (see above, chap. iii, n. 30).

13. The research value of these holdings is enhanced by the fact that a large portion of *Gilded Age* manuscript was bound into the first volume of a limited "edition de luxe" of *The Writings of Mark Twain,* published by the American Publishing Company, Hartford, 1899, in 1,000 numbered sets, No. 513 of which is with the Mark Twain Papers.

14. There are six sets of original SLC folios: 1-399 (for Chapters I-XI); [1-7?] 8-478 (for Chapters XXIV-XXV, XXVII- XXVIII, [XXX], XXXII-XXXVII, [XLII]- XLIII, XLV); 1-28 [29-53?] 54-75 (for Chapters LI-LII- [LIII], LVI); [1?] 2-8 [?] 9-23 (for Chapter LX); [1-18?] 19 (for Chapter LXI); and [1-8?] 9 [10-19?] (for Chapter LXII). (Numerals in brackets indicate missing chapters and pages.) Clemens began numbering afresh when he resumed his part of the novel after (Warner's) Chapter XXIII and continued this second sequence of folios for his own chapters through Chapter XLV. After (Warner's) Chapter L, he began a third sequence of folios, which lasted apparently until (Warner's) Chapter LVIII. Chapters LX, LXI, and LXII he numbered individually, in Warner's fashion. There is at present no information on Chapters LIII and LVI.

Intermediate SLC folio sequences occur between the end of Chapter V and the beginning of Chapter XI (139-340), in Chapter XXXVI (132-49), and in Chapter LI (25-26). They reveal a discarding of over 60 pages of the original MS. The original folios of Chapter XXXVI indicate that it at first apparently came before Chapter XXXII.

Between the intermediate sets of folios and the final sequence there is a further discarding of pages which, when added to the discarding that appears between the original and final folios in sections of MS that lack an intermediate stage, amounts to more that 135 discarded pages. (This total has been weighted by the very low number of pages added.)

15. In a sampling of 284 SLC pages the loss amounts to 48 per cent. Clemens' attested loss of 300 pages out of a theoretical total of approximately 1030—300 plus his half of the MS (*ca.* 730)—amounts to 41 per cent.

Not enough evidence exists regarding Warner's wastage to be significant. In four representative instances of his discarding or adding, the gain and loss about cancel one another, and only two or three pages are involved in any one instance.

16. The only apparent exception to this state is the sequence of pages for Clemens' first five chapters, which carries only one set of folios until next to the last page of Chapter V.

Of some interest in this connection is Walter Blair's evidence of Clemens' consistent use of violet ink in Hartford between 1876 and 1880 (*Mark Twain & Huck Finn* [Berkeley: University of California Press, 1960], p. 201).

APPENDIX E

1. *Old and New,* IX (March, 1874), 387.

2. MS pp. 621-23, in Morse, Container 2.

3. This sheet, made by pasting two or three smaller sheets together, was folded and inserted in the MS after p. 624 to indicate how it should occur in the finished book. P. 624 ends: ". . . Now here you are with your railroad complete, and showing its continuation to Hallelujah, and thence to Corruptionville:" At the bottom of the page is the note: "(Insert Map.)" (Morse, 2).

4. MS p. 622½ (Morse, 2), written on reverse of p. 622. A number of place names have undergone change in manuscript, the most notable being "Hogeye" to "Brimstone,"

"Galilee" to "Babylon," and "Catgut" to "Catfish," all of which may have been partly dictated by a desire to avoid offense, and, most interesting of all, "Saint's Rest" to "Belshazzar." "Saint's Rest," a name used previously by Petroleum V. Nasby (Walter Fuller Taylor, *The Economic Novel in America* [Chapel Hill: University of North Carolina Press, 1942], p. 127, n. 33), was to be saved for the capital (Topeka) of the Happy-Land-of-Canaan (Kansas), home base of Senator Dilworthy (see above, p. 88).

APPENDIX F

1. Perkins was well acquainted with the Nook Farm circle (see above, chap. i, n. 67).

2. IX (March, 1874), 387.

3. Albert Bigelow Paine, *Mark Twain: A Biography: The Personal and Literary Life of Samuel Langhorne Clemens* (New York: Harper & Bros., 1912), II, 478, n.

4. Quoted by Hill in *Mark Twain and Elisha Bliss* (Columbia: University of Missouri Press, 1964), p. 83.

5. "Publisher's Note," *The Gilded Age*, I (*Writings*, X), ix.

6. Charles Warren Stoddard, *Exits and Entrances* (Boston: Lothrop Publishing Co., 1903), p. 71.

7. Paine, *op. cit.*, II, 478, n.

8. *Twain-Howells*, I, 120, n. 2; Kenneth Andrews, *Nook Farm, Mark Twain's Hartford Circle* (Cambridge: Harvard University Press, 1950), p. 256, n. 11.

9. The original holograph copy for the mottoes is in a notebook in the Mark Twain Library and Memorial, Hartford, Connecticut, folder SM-TR-1.

10. In Morse (Clemens 21) are the thirty-seven sheets of complete copy for the translations as they are published in the 1899 edition. They were prepared by pasting on the chapter number, writing the chapter title underneath, pasting the printed motto (cut apparently from corrected proofs) below this, and finally writing the translation.

11. In Mark Twain Library and Memorial, folders M-CL-4 and M-WA-1. At the top of Warner's first page is the following note by Trumbull: "Outline of 'The Gilded Age'—the first two pages in Warner's writing, the others (1-20) by Clemens. Sent to me as a guide to the mottoes."

12. This and similar half-chapters occurring in the original manuscript indicate an uncertainty on Clemens' part about chapter arrangement and probably should be taken as evidence that the synopsis was outlined before the final collation was finished. Clemens has gone over the synopsis, correcting the chapter numbering. His corrected numbers only are used in the present version.

Bibliography

Bibliography

IN PREPARATION of this volume I have examined manuscripts, newspapers, magazines, and books at the following libraries: Bancroft Library, University of California, Berkeley; Bibliothèque Nationale, Paris; Hartford Public Library; Henry E. Huntington Library; Kansas State Historical Society, Topeka; Los Angeles Public Library; Mark Twain Library and Memorial, Hartford; San Francisco Public Library; University of California Library, Berkeley; University of Pittsburgh Library; University of Southern California Library; Watkinson Library, Trinity College, Hartford; Yale University Library.

PRIMARY SOURCES

MANUSCRIPT COLLECTIONS

C. Waller Barrett Collection, Alderman Library, University of Virginia.
Henry W. and Albert A. Berg Collection, New York Public Library.
Henry E. Huntington Library.
Lilly Collection of Americana, Indiana University Library.
Mark Twain Library and Memorial, Hartford.
Mark Twain Papers, University of California Library, Berkeley.
Willard S. Morse Collection, Yale University Library.
Warner Papers, Watkinson Library, Trinity College, Hartford.

PUBLISHED WORKS
By Samuel L. Clemens

I. ITEMS FIRST PUBLISHED IN BOOKS

The Autobiography of Mark Twain, ed. Charles Neider. New York: Harper & Bros., 1959.
King Leopold's Soliloquy. Boston: P. R. Warren Co., 1905.

Letters from the Earth, ed. Bernard DeVoto. New York: Harper & Row, 1962.

The Love Letters of Mark Twain, ed. Dixon Wecter. New York: Harper & Bros., 1949.

Mark Twain, Business Man, ed. Samuel Charles Webster. Boston: Little, Brown & Co., 1946.

Mark Twain-Howells Letters, ed. Henry Nash Smith and William M. Gibson. 2 vols. Cambridge: Harvard University Press, 1960.

Mark Twain in Eruption: Hitherto Unpublished Pages about Men and Events, ed. Bernard DeVoto. New York: Harper & Bros., 1940.

Mark Twain's Autobiography, ed. Albert Bigelow Paine. 2 vols. New York: Harper & Bros., 1924.

Mark Twain's Letters, ed. Albert Bigelow Paine. 2 vols. New York: Harper & Bros., 1917.

Mark Twain's Notebook, ed. Albert Bigelow Paine. New York: Harper & Bros., 1935.

Mark Twain's Speeches, ed. Albert Bigelow Paine, with an Appreciation by William Dean Howells. New York: Harper & Bros., 1923.

Mark Twain to Mrs. Fairbanks, ed. Dixon Wecter. San Marino: Huntington Library, 1949.

The Mysterious Stranger and Other Stories. New York: Harper & Bros., 1922.

The Writings of Mark Twain, Author's National Edition. 25 vols. New York: Harper & Bros., 1907-1918.

II. ITEMS FIRST PUBLISHED IN PERIODICALS AND REPRINTED IN BOOKS

The Adventures of Thomas Jefferson Snodgrass, ed. Charles Honce. Chicago: Pascal Covici, Inc., 1928.

Contributions to The Galaxy, 1868-1871, by Mark Twain, ed. Bruce R. McElderry, Jr. Gainesville, Fla.: Scholars' Facsimiles & Reprints, 1961.

The Curious Republic of Gondour and Other Whimsical Sketches. New York: Boni & Liveright, 1919.

Europe and Elsewhere. New York: Harper & Bros., 1923.

Letters from Honolulu, Written for the Sacramento Union, ed. Thomas Nickerson. Honolulu: Thomas Nickerson, 1939.

Letters from the Sandwich Islands, Written for the Sacramento Union, ed. G. Ezra Dane. San Francisco: Grabhorn Press, 1937.

The Letters of Quintus Curtius Snodgrass, ed. Ernest E. Leisy. Dallas: Southern Methodist University Press, 1946.

Mark Twain: Life as I Find It, ed. Charles Neider. Garden City, N.Y.: Hanover House, 1961.

Mark Twain of the Enterprise, ed. Henry Nash Smith. Berkeley: University of California Press, 1957.

Mark Twain's Letters in the Muscatine Journal, ed. Edgar M. Branch. Chicago: Mark Twain Association of America, 1942.

Mark Twain's Travels with Mr. Brown, Being Heretofore Uncollected Sketches Written by Mark Twain for the San Francisco Alta California *in 1866 and 1867 . . . ,* ed. Franklin Walker and G. Ezra Dane. New York: Alfred A. Knopf, 1940.

A Salutation Speech from the Nineteenth Century to the Twentieth Taken Down in Shorthand by Mark Twain. Photo repro. of original manuscript issued for members of Roxburghe Club, San Francisco, 1929.

Sketches of the Sixties: by Bret Harte and Mark Twain, ed. John Howell. San Francisco: John Howell, 1926.

Traveling with the Innocents Abroad: Mark Twain's Original Reports from Europe and the Holy Land, ed. Daniel Morley McKeithan. Norman: University of Oklahoma Press, 1958.

The Washoe Giant in San Francisco, Being Heretofore Uncollected Sketches by Mark Twain Published in the Golden Era *in the Sixties, . . . ,* ed. Franklin Walker. San Francisco: George Fields, 1938.

III. ITEMS PUBLISHED IN PERIODICALS ONLY

"Dear Master Wattie: The Mark Twain–David Watt Bowser Letters," ed. Pascal Covici, Jr., *Southwest Review,* XLV (Spring, 1960), 105-21.

"Memoranda," *Galaxy,* IX (May 1870), 717 to XI (April, 1871), 618, *passim.*

"Passages from 'Outlines of History,' " ed. Bernard DeVoto, *Saturday Review of Literature,* XIX (December 10, 1938), 4.

SUPPLEMENTARY SOURCES

BIBLIOGRAPHIES

ASSELINEAU, ROGER. *The Literary Reputation of Mark Twain from 1910 to 1950.* Paris: Librairie Marcel Didier, 1954.

BLANCK, JACOB. *Bibliography of American Literature.* New Haven: Yale University Press, II (1957), 173-254.

JOHNSON, MERLE. *A Bibliography of the Works of Mark Twain,* rev. ed. New York: Harper & Bros., 1935.

SPILLER, ROBERT E. *et al. Literary History of the United States.* 3 vols. New York: Macmillan Co., 1948. III, 442-50.

BIOGRAPHICAL, CRITICAL, AND HISTORICAL REFERENCES

I. BOOKS

ADAMS, CHARLES F., JR., and ADAMS, HENRY. *Chapters of Erie, and Other Essays.* Boston: James R. Osgood & Co., 1871.

ADAMS, HENRY. *The Education of Henry Adams,* Modern Library ed. New York, 1931.

ADAMS, JAMES TRUSLOW. *The March of Democracy.* 2 vols. New York: Charles Scribner's Sons, 1933.

AMES, MARY CLEMMER. *Ten Years in Washington: Life and Scenes in the National Capital, As a Woman Sees Them.* Hartford: A. D. Worthington & Co., 1874.

ANDREWS, KENNETH R. *Nook Farm, Mark Twain's Hartford Circle.* Cambridge: Harvard University Press, 1950.

ASPIZ, HAROLD. "Mark Twain's Reading—A Critical Study." Unpublished Ph.D. dissertation, University of California at Los Angeles, 1949.

BALDWIN, JOSEPH G. *The Flush Times of Alabama and Mississippi* ("American Century Series.") New York: Sagamore Press, 1957.

BARNES, WILLIAM H. *History of the Thirty-Ninth Congress of the United States.* New York: Harper & Bros., 1868.

BEARD, CHARLES A. and MARY R. *The Rise of American Civilization,* rev. ed. New York: Macmillan Co., 1937.

BELLAMY, GLADYS CARMEN. *Mark Twain as a Literary Artist.* Norman: University of Oklahoma Press, 1950.

BENNETT, ARNOLD. *The Author's Craft.* London: Hodder & Stoughton, n.d.

BENNETT, MARY ANGELA. *Elizabeth Stuart Phelps.* Philadelphia: University of Pennsylvania Press, 1939.

BIMBA, ANTHONY. *The History of the American Working Class.* London: Martin Lawrence, Ltd., 1927.

BIRRELL, AUGUSTINE, M.P. *The Law and History of Copyright in Books.* London, Paris, and Melbourne: Cassell & Co.; New York: G. P. Putnam's Sons, 1899.

BLAINE, JAMES G. *Twenty Years of Congress.* 2 vols. Norwich, Conn.: Henry Bill Publishing Co., 1886.

BLAIR, WALTER. *Mark Twain & Huck Finn.* Berkeley: University of California Press, 1960.

BLANKENSHIP, RUSSELL. *American Literature as an Expression of the National Mind,* rev. ed. New York: Henry Holt & Co., 1949.

[BLISS, WALTER]. *Twainiana Notes from the Annotations of Walter Bliss,* ed. Frances M. Edwards. Hartford: The Hobby Shop, 1930.

BOWERS, CLAUDE G. *The Tragic Era: The Revolution after Lincoln.* Boston: Houghton Mifflin Co., 1929.

BRANCH, EDGAR MARQUESS. *The Literary Apprenticeship of Mark Twain, With Selections from His Apprentice Writing.* Urbana: University of Illinois Press, 1950.

BRASHEAR, MINNIE M. *Mark Twain, Son of Missouri.* Chapel Hill: University of North Carolina Press, 1934.

BRIGGS, EMILY EDSON. *The Olivia Letters.* New York and Washington: Neale Publishing Co., 1906.

BRIGHAM, JOHNSON. *James Harlan.* Iowa City: State Historical Society of Iowa, 1913.

BROOKS, VAN WYCK. *America's Coming-of-Age.* New York: B. W. Huebsch, 1924.

―――. *Days of the Phoenix: The Nineteen-Twenties I Remember.* New York: E. P. Dutton & Co., 1957.

―――. *New England: Indian Summer.* New York: E. P. Dutton & Co., 1940.

―――. *The Ordeal of Mark Twain.* New York: E. P. Dutton & Co., 1920; rev. ed., 1933.

BROWN, GEORGE ROTHWELL, *Washington, a Not Too Serious History.* Baltimore: Norman Publishing Co., 1930.

BROWN, T. ALLSTON. *History of the American Stage.* New York: Dick & Fitzgerald, 1870.

―――. *A History of the New York Stage.* 3 vols. New York: Dodd, Mead & Co., 1903.

BURN, JAMES DAWSON. *Three Years Among the Working-Classes in the United States During the War.* London: Smith, Elder & Co., 1865.

BURNHAM, THOMAS BOND. "Mark Twain and the Gilded Age." Unpublished Master's thesis, University of Idaho, 1937.

BURTON, THEODORE E. *Financial Crises and Periods of Industrial and Commercial Depression.* New York: D. Appleton & Co., 1916.

CAIRNS, WILLIAM B. *A History of American Literature,* rev. ed. New York: Oxford University Press, 1930.

CALVERTON, V. F. *The Liberation of American Literature.* New York: Charles Scribner's Sons, 1932.

CANBY, HENRY SEIDEL. *Turn West, Turn East: Mark Twain and Henry James.* Boston: Houghton Mifflin Co., 1951.

CARDWELL, GUY A. *Twins of Genius (Twain and Cable).* Lansing: Michigan State College Press, 1953.

CARTER, EVERETT. *Howells and the Age of Realism.* Philadelphia: J. B. Lippincott Co., 1954.

CLARK, CHAMP. *My Quarter Century of American Politics.* 2 vols. New York: Harper & Bros., 1920.

CLEMENS, CLARA. *My Father Mark Twain.* New York: Harper & Bros., 1931.

CLEMENS, CYRIL. *Young Sam Clemens.* Portland, Me.: Leon Tebbetts Editions, 1942.

CLEMENS, WILL M. *Mark Twain: His Life and Work.* San Francisco: Clemens Publishing Co., 1892.

The Complete Plays of W. D. Howells, ed. Walter J. Meserve. New York: New York University Press, 1960.

COMPTON, F[RANK] E. *Subscription Books.* New York: New York Public Library, 1939. (Fourth of the R. R. Bowker Memorial Lectures, First Series.)

COPINGER, [W. A.], and SKONE JAMES, [F. E. and E. P.]. *Law of Copyright,* 9th ed. London: Sweet & Maxwell, 1958.

CORTISSOZ, ROYAL. *The Life of Whitelaw Reid.* 2 vols. New York: Charles Scribner's Sons, 1921.

COWAN, ROBERT ERNEST. *Booksellers of Early San Francisco.* Los Angeles: Ward Ritchie Press, 1953.

CRAWFORD, MARY CAROLINE. *The Romance of the American Theatre.* New York: Halcyon House, 1940.

DALY, JOSEPH FRANCIS. *The Life of Augustin Daly.* New York: Macmillan Co., 1917.

DE FOREST, J[OHN] W. *Honest John Vane,* ed. JOSEPH JAY RUBIN. State College, Pa.: Bald Eagle Press, 1960.

DEVOTO, BERNARD. *Mark Twain at Work.* Cambridge: Harvard University Press, 1942.

————. *Mark Twain's America.* Boston: Little, Brown & Co., 1932.

DICKENS, CHARLES. *American Notes and Pictures from Italy.* London: Macmillan & Co., 1903.

DUFFY, CHARLES, and PETTIT, HENRY. *A Dictionary of Literary Terms,* rev. ed. Denver: University of Denver Press, 1952.

DUNLAP, GEORGE ARTHUR. *The City in the American Novel, 1789-1900.* Philadelphia: Privately printed, 1934.

DUNNING, WILLIAM ARCHIBALD. *Reconstruction, Political and Economic, 1865-1877.* (*The American Nation: A History,* ed. A. B. HART, Vol. XXII.) New York: Harper & Bros., 1907.

EGGLESTON, EDWARD. *The Mystery of Metropolisville.* New York: Orange Judd & Co., 1873.

ELLIS, JOHN B. *The Sights and Secrets of the National Capital.* San Francisco: H. H. Bancroft & Co., 1869.

ELLIS, S. M. *Wilkie Collins, Le Fanu and Others.* London: Constable & Co., 1931.

English Catalogue of Books. 1872-1880.

Facts by a woman. Oakland, Calif.: Pacific Press Publishing House, 1881.

FAULKNER, HAROLD UNDERWOOD. *American Political and Social History.* 5th ed. New York: Appleton-Century-Crofts, 1948.

FERGUSON, DELANCEY. *Mark Twain: Man and Legend.* Indianapolis: Bobbs-Merrill Co., 1943.

FERRIER, WILLIAM WARREN. *Origin and Development of the University of California.* Berkeley: Sather Gate Book Shop, 1930.

FIELDS, MRS. JAMES T. *Charles Dudley Warner.* ("Contemporary Men of Letters Series.") New York: McClure, Phillips & Co., 1904.

[——]. *Memories of a Hostess: A Chronicle of Eminent Friendships,* ed. M. A. DEWOLFE HOWE. Boston: Atlantic Monthly Press, 1922.

FISHER, HENRY W. *Abroad with Mark Twain and Eugene Field.* New York: Nicholas L. Brown, 1922.

FISHER, WALTER M. *The Californians.* San Francisco: A. L. Bancroft & Co., 1876.

FLORY, CLAUDE REHERD. *Economic Criticism in American Fiction, 1792 to 1900.* Philadelphia, 1936.

FONER, PHILIP S. *Mark Twain: Social Critic.* New York: International Publishers, 1958.

FORBES-LINDSAY, C. H. *Washington, the City and the Seat of Government.* Philadelphia: John C. Winston Co., 1908.

FORNEY, JOHN W. *Anecdotes of Public Men.* 2 vols. New York: Harper & Bros., 1873.

FREAR, WALTER FRANCIS. *Mark Twain and Hawaii.* Chicago: Privately printed, 1947.

FROHMAN, DANIEL. *Memories of a Manager.* Garden City, N.Y.: Doubleday Page & Co., 1911.

GILLIS, WILLIAM R. *Gold Rush Days with Mark Twain.* New York: Albert & Charles Boni, 1930.

GRANT, E. H. *Twelve Years in the United States Senate: A Brief Sketch of the Senatorial Record of Hon. S. C. Pomeroy of Kansas, Compiled from the Congressional Globe.* Washington, D.C.: Privately printed, 1872.

GRODINSKY, JULIUS. *Jay Gould: His Business Career, 1867-1892.* Philadelphia: University of Pennsylvania Press, 1957.

HACKER, LOUIS M., and KENDRICK, BENJAMIN B. *The United States Since 1865.* New York: F. S. Crofts & Co., 1932.

HARRISON, JOSEPH B. *Bret Harte.* New York: American Book Co., 1941.

HASTINGS, JAMES (ed.). *Dictionary of the Bible.* 5 vols. New York: Charles Scribner's Sons, 1901-1905. Single-vol. ed., 1925 [c. 1909].

HAYNES, GEORGE H. *The Election of Senators.* New York: Henry Holt & Co., 1906.

HAZARD, LUCY LOCKWOOD. *The Frontier in American Literature.* New York: Thomas Y. Crowell Co., 1927.

HEMMINGHAUS, EDGAR H. *Mark Twain in Germany.* New York: Columbia University Press, 1939.

HENDERSON, ARCHIBALD. *Mark Twain.* London: Duckworth & Co., 1911.

HERRON, IMA HONAKER. *The Small Town in American Literature.* Durham, N.C.: Duke University Press, 1939.

HICKS, GRANVILLE. *The Great Tradition.* New York: Macmillan Co., 1933.

HILL, HAMLIN. *Mark Twain and Elisha Bliss.* Columbia: University of Missouri Press, 1964.

HITTELL, THEODORE H. *History of California.* 4 vols. San Francisco: N. J. Stone & Co., 1898.

HOWELLS, WILLIAM DEAN. *Life in Letters of William Dean Howells,* ed. Mildred Howells. 2 vols. Garden City, N.Y.: Doubleday Doran & Co., 1928.

——. *Literature and Life.* New York: Harper & Bros., 1902.

——. *My Mark Twain: Reminiscences and Criticisms.* New York: Harper & Bros., 1911.

HUNGERFORD, HERBERT. *How Publishers Win.* Washington, D.C.: Ransdell, Inc., 1931.

HUTTON, LAURENCE. *Curiosities of the American Stage.* New York: Harper & Bros., 1891.

HYNDMAN, H. M. *Commercial Crises of the Nineteenth Century,* 2nd ed. London: Swan Sonnenschein & Co., and New York: Charles Scribner's Sons, 1902.

JONES, WILLIAM CAREY. *Illustrated History of The University of California.* San Francisco: Frank H. Dukesmith, 1895.

JOSEPHSON, MATTHEW. *The Politicos, 1865-1896.* New York: Harcourt, Brace & Co., 1938.

———. *Portrait of the Artist as American.* New York: Harcourt, Brace & Co., 1930.

JUGLAR, CLEMENT. *A Brief History of Panics and Their Periodical Occurrence in the United States,* 4th ed. Translated and edited by DE COURCY W. THOM. New York: G. P. Putnam's Sons, 1916.

JULIAN, GEORGE W. *Political Recollections, 1840 to 1872.* Chicago: Jansen, McClurg & Co., 1884.

KENDALL, JOHN S. *The Golden Age of the New Orleans Theater.* Baton Rouge: Louisiana State University Press, 1952.

KIPLING, RUDYARD. *From Sea to Sea: Letters of Travel.* Garden City, N.Y.: Doubleday, Page & Co., 1913.

LEACOCK, STEPHEN. *Mark Twain.* New York: D. Appleton & Co., 1933.

LEHMANN-HAUPT, HELLMUT. *The Book in America: A History of the Making, the Selling, and the Collecting of Books in the United States.* New York: R. R. Bowker Co., 1939.

LEMONNIER, LÉON. *Mark Twain.* Paris: Librairie Arthème Fayard, 1946.

The Letters of Bret Harte, ed. GEOFFREY BRET HARTE. Boston: Houghton Mifflin Co., 1926.

LEWISOHN, LUDWIG. *Expression in America.* New York: Harper & Bros., 1932.

LIKINS, MRS. J. W. *Six Years Experience as a Book Agent in California, including My Trip from New York to San Francisco via Nicaragua.* San Francisco: Women's Union Book and Job Printing Office, 1874.

LOGAN, MRS. JOHN A. *Thirty Years in Washington.* Hartford: Worthington & Co., 1901.

LYMAN, GEORGE D. *The Saga of the Comstock Lode: Boom Days in Virginia City.* New York: Charles Scribner's Sons, 1934.

LYNN, KENNETH S. *Mark Twain and Southwestern Humor.* Boston: Little, Brown & Co., 1959.

MACK, EFFIE MONA. "Life and Letters of William Morris Stewart." Unpublished Ph.D. dissertation, University of California, 1930.

———. *Mark Twain in Nevada.* New York: Charles Scribner's Sons, 1947.

McKEITHAN, D[ANIEL] M[ORLEY]. *Court Trials in Mark Twain and Other Essays.* 'S-Gravenhage (The Hague): Martinus Nijhoff, 1958.

McPHERSON, EDWARD. *The Political History of the United States of America During the Period of Reconstruction.* Washington, D.C.: Philp & Solomons, 1871.

MACY, JOHN. *The Spirit of American Literature.* Garden City, N.Y.: Doubleday, Page & Co., 1913.

MAGNUS, LAURIE. *A Dictionary of European Literature, Designed as a Companion to English Studies.* London: George Routledge & Sons, 1926.

MAHLBERG, HEINRICH. *Literarisches Sachwörterbuch.* Bern: A. Francke Ag. Verlag, 1948.

MANIGAULT, G. *The United States Unmasked.* London: Edward Stanford, 1879.

MARCOSSON, ISAAC F. *"Marse Henry," A Biography of Henry Watterson.* New York: Dodd, Mead & Co., 1951.

Mark Twain Anecdotes, ed. Cyril Clemens. Webster Groves, Mo.: Mark Twain Society, 1929.

MARTIN, ALMA BORTH. *A Vocabulary Study of the "Gilded Age."* Webster Groves, Mo.: Mark Twain Society, [1930].

MARTIN, EDWARD WINSLOW. *Behind the Scenes in Washington.* Philadelphia: National Publishing Co., 1873.

MASTERS, EDGAR LEE. *Mark Twain: A Portrait.* New York: Charles Scribner's Sons, 1938.

MATTHEWS, BRANDER. *Inquiries and Opinions.* New York: Charles Scribner's Sons, 1907.

———. *Playwrights on Playmaking and Other Studies of the Stage.* New York: Charles Scribner's Sons, 1923.

———. *The Tocsin of Revolt and Other Essays.* New York: Charles Scribner's Sons, 1922.

MENDELSON, M. *Mark Tven,* rev. ed. Moscow: "Molodaia Gvardiia" ("Young Guard") Publishing House, 1958.

MERWIN, HENRY CHILDS. *The Life of Bret Harte.* Boston: Houghton Mifflin Co., 1911.

MILTON, GEORGE FORT. *The Age of Hate: Andrew Johnson and the Radicals.* New York: Coward-McCann, 1930.

MITCHELL, EDWIN VALENTINE. *Morocco Bound: Adrift Among Books.* New York: Farrar & Rinehart, 1929.

MOFFATT, JAMES. *A New Translation of the Bible,* rev. ed. New York: Harper & Bros., 1935.

MOTT, FRANK LUTHER. *Golden Multitudes: The Story of Best Sellers in the United States.* New York: Macmillan Co., 1947.

———. *A History of American Magazines.* 3 vols. Cambridge: Harvard University Press, 1938.

MURET, MAURICE. *Les Contemporains étrangers,* n.s. 2 vols. Lausanne: Librarie Payot et Cie, 1914.

NEVINS, ALLAN. *The Emergence of Modern America, 1865-1878.* (A *History of American Life,* Vol. VIII.) New York: Macmillan Co., 1928.

NILES, WILLYS (J. F. HUME). *Five Hundred Majority: A Tale for the Times.* New York: G. P. Putnam & Sons, 1872.

NOEL, MARY. *Villains Galore: The Heyday of the Popular Story Weekly.* New York: Macmillan Co., 1954.

OBERHOLTZER, ELLIS PAXSON. *A History of the United States since the Civil War.* 5 vols. New York: Macmillan Co., 1917-1937.

———. *Jay Cooke, Financier of the Civil War.* 2 vols. Philadelphia: George W. Jacobs & Co., 1907.

ODELL, GEORGE C. D. *Annals of the New York Stage.* 15 vols. New York: Columbia University Press, 1927-49.

Official Report of the Trial of Laura D. Fair for the Murder of Alex P. Crittenden. San Francisco: San Francisco Co-operative Printing Co., 1871.

ORTH, SAMUEL P. *The Boss and the Machine.* ("Chronicles of America Series," Vol. XLIII.) New Haven: Yale University Press, 1919.

PAINE, ALBERT BIGELOW. *Mark Twain: A Biography. The Personal and Literary Life of Samuel Langhorne Clemens.* 4 vols. New York: Harper & Bros., 1912.

PAPASHVILY, HELEN WAITE. *All the Happy Endings.* New York: Harper & Bros., 1956.

PARRINGTON, VERNON LOUIS. *Main Currents in American Thought.* 3 vols. in one. New York: Harcourt, Brace & Co., 1927-1930.

PATTEE, FRED LEWIS. *The Feminine Fifties.* New York: D. Appleton-Century Co., 1940.

———. *A History of American Literature Since 1870.* New York: Century Co., 1915.

PEMBERTON, T. EDGAR. *The Life of Bret Harte.* New York: Dodd, Mead & Co., 1903.

PHILLIPS, WALTER C. *Dickens, Reade, and Collins, Sensation Novelists.* New York: Columbia University Press, 1919.

PIATT, DONN. *Life in the Lobby: A Comedy in Five Acts.* Washington: Judd & Detweiler, 1875.

POCHMANN, HENRY AUGUST. "The Mind of Mark Twain." Unpublished Master's thesis, University of Texas, 1924.

DA PONTE, DURANT. "American Periodical Criticism of Mark Twain,

1869-1917." Unpublished Ph.D. dissertation, University of Maryland, 1953.

POOR, BEN: PERLEY. *Perley's Reminiscences of Sixty Years in the National Metropolis.* Philadelphia: Hubbard Bros., 1886.

QUINN, ARTHUR HOBSON, *American Fiction: An Historical and Critical Survey.* New York: D. Appleton-Century Co., 1936.

———. *A History of the American Drama from the Civil War to the Present Day,* rev. ed. New York: F. S. Crofts & Co., 1936.

RANDEL, WILLIAM. *Edward Eggleston.* New York: Twayne Publishers, 1963.

Report of the Secretary of the Interior. U.S. 39th Cong., 1st sess., H. Exec. Doc. 1. Washington, D.C.: Government Printing Office, 1865.

RHODES, JAMES FORD. *History of the United States from the Compromise of 1850 to the Final Restoration of Home Rule at the South in 1877.* 7 vols. New York: Macmillan Co., 1920.

RICHARDSON, CHARLES F. *American Literature, 1607-1885,* 1-vol. ed. New York: G. P. Putnam's Sons, 1893. [c. 1886.]

RODNEY, ROBERT M. "Mark Twain in England; A Study of the English Criticism of and Attitude toward Mark Twain: 1867-1940." Unpublished Ph.D. dissertation, University of Wisconsin, 1945.

ROGERS, FRANKLIN R. *Mark Twain's Burlesque Patterns: As Seen in the Novels and Narratives, 1855-1885.* Dallas: Southern Methodist University Press, 1960.

SABIN, EDWIN L. *Building the Pacific Railway.* Philadelphia: J. B. Lippincott Co., 1919.

SCHARF, J. THOMAS, and WESTCOTT, THOMPSON. *History of Philadelphia: 1609-1884.* 3 vols. Philadelphia: L. H. Everts & Co., 1884.

SCHÖNEMANN, FRIEDRICH. *Mark Twain als literarische Persönlichkeit.* ("Jenaer Germanistische Forschungen," VIII.) Jena: Verlag der Frommannschen Buchhandlung, 1925.

SHACKLETON, ROBERT. *The Book of Washington.* Philadelphia: Penn Publishing Co., 1922.

SHEEHAN, DONALD. *This Was Publishing.* Bloomington: Indiana University Press, 1952.

SMALLEY, WEBSTER L. "The Critical Reception of Mark Twain in England: 1870-1910." Unpublished Master's thesis, Columbia University, 1948.

SMITH, CHARLES ALPHONSO. *Die Amerikanische Literatur.* ("Bibliothek der Amerikanischen Kulturgeschichte," II.) Berlin: Weidmannsche Buchhandlung, 1912.

STEWART, GEORGE R., JR. *Bret Harte, Argonaut and Exile.* Boston: Houghton Mifflin Co., 1931.

[STEWART, WILLIAM MORRIS.] *Reminiscences of Senator William M. Stewart of Nevada,* ed. GEORGE ROTHWELL BROWN. New York and Washington: Neale Publishing Co., 1908.

STODDARD, CHARLES WARREN. *Exits and Entrances.* Boston: Lothrop Publishing Co., 1903.

TAYLOR, WALTER FULLER. *The Economic Novel in America.* Chapel Hill: University of North Carolina Press, [1942].

————. *A History of American Letters.* New York: American Book Co., 1936.

TOMPKINS, EUGENE. *The History of the Boston Theater, 1854-1901.* Boston: Houghton Mifflin Co., 1908.

TOWNSEND, GEORGE ALFRED. *Washington, Outside and Inside.* Hartford and Chicago: James Betts & Co., 1874.

TRAIN, GEORGE FRANCIS. *My Life in Many States and in Foreign Lands.* New York: D. Appleton & Co., 1902.

UNDERWOOD, JOHN CURTIS. *Literature and Insurgency.* New York: Mitchell Kennerley, 1914.

VAN DOREN, CARL. *The American Novel, 1789-1939,* rev. ed. New York: Macmillan Co., 1940.

VOGELBACK, ARTHUR LAWRENCE. "The Literary Reputation of Mark Twain in America, 1869-85." Unpublished Ph.D. dissertation, University of Chicago, 1939.

WAGENKNECHT, EDWARD. *Mark Twain, the Man and His Work.* New Haven: Yale University Press, 1935.

WALKER, FRANKLIN. *San Francisco's Literary Frontier.* New York: Alfred A. Knopf, 1939.

WALL, JOSEPH FRAZIER. *Henry Watterson: Reconstructed Rebel.* New York: Oxford University Press, 1956.

WALLACE, IRVING. *The Fabulous Originals.* New York: Alfred A. Knopf, 1955.

WARNER, CHARLES DUDLEY. *Backlog Studies.* Boston: James R. Osgood & Co., 1873.

————. *My Summer in a Garden.* Boston: Fields, Osgood, & Co., 1870.

————. *The Relation of Literature to Life.* New York: Harper & Bros., 1897.

WATTERSON, HENRY. *Marse Henry—An Autobiography.* 2 vols. New York: George H. Doran Co., 1919.

WECTER, DIXON. *Sam Clemens of Hannibal.* Boston: Houghton Mifflin Co., 1952.

WELLES, GIDEON. *Diary of Gideon Welles.* 3 vols. Boston: Houghton Mifflin Co., 1911.

WERNER, M. R. *Tammany Hall.* New York: Doubleday Doran & Co., 1928.

WHITE, HENRY KIRKE. *History of the Union Pacific Railway.* Chicago: University of Chicago Press, 1895.

WINGATE, CHARLES F. (ed.). *Views and Interviews on Journalism.* New York: F. B. Patterson, 1875.

WINTER, WILLIAM. *Life and Art of Edwin Booth.* New York: Macmillan Co., 1906.

————. *The Life of David Belasco.* 2 vols. New York: Moffat, Yard & Co., 1918.

————. *The Wallet of Time.* 2 vols. New York: Moffat, Yard & Co., 1913.

WOODBERRY, GEORGE E. *America in Literature.* New York: Harper & Bros., 1903.

WOOLSON, CONSTANCE FENIMORE. *Castle Nowhere: Lake-Country Sketches.* Boston: James R. Osgood & Co., 1875.

YARD, ROBERT STERLING. *The Publisher.* Boston: Houghton Mifflin Co., 1913.

YOUNG, ROBERT. *Analytical Concordance to the Bible,* 22nd Amer. ed. rev. New York: Funk & Wagnalls Co., 1955.

II. ARTICLES

BLANCK, JACOB. "The Gilded Age: A Collation," *Publishers Weekly,* CXXXVIII (July 20, 1940), 186-88.

"Elisha Bliss," *Encyclopedia of Connecticut Biography,* V, 71-72.

BROWNELL, GEORGE HIRAM. "Mark Twain's Inventions," *Twainian,* n.s., Vol. III, No. 4 (January, 1944), pp. 1-5.

————. "A Question as to the Origin of the Name 'Mark Twain,'" *Twainian,* n.s., Vol. I, No. 2 (February, 1942), pp. 4-7.

CARRUTH, FRANCES WESTON. "Washington in Fiction," *Bookman* (New York), XV (July, 1902), 451-63.

CASSADY, EDWARD E. "Muckraking in the Gilded Age," *American Literature,* XIII (May, 1941), 134-41.

CHAPMAN, JOHN W. "The Germ of a Book — A Footnote on Mark Twain," *Atlantic,* CL (December, 1932), 720-21.

CLEMENS, CYRIL. "Mark Twain's Reading," *Commonweal*, XXIV (August 7, 1937), 363-64.

COLTON, HAROLD SELLERS. "Mark Twain's Literary Dilemma and Its Sequel," *Arizona Quarterly*, XVII (Autumn, 1961), 229-32.

DE FOREST, J[OHN] W. "An Inspired Lobbyist." In *Stories by American Authors*. 10 vols. New York: Charles Scribner's Sons, 1900. IV, 137-61. (Reprinted from *Atlantic*, XXX [December, 1872], 676-84).

DEVOTO, BERNARD. "Mark Twain: The Ink of History." In *Forays and Rebuttals*. Boston: Little, Brown & Co., 1936.

FERGUSON, DELANCEY. "Mark Twain's Lost Curtain Speeches," *South Atlantic Quarterly*, XLII (July, 1943), 262-69.

FISCHER, WALTHER. Review of *Mark Twain als literarische Persönlichkeit*, *Englische Studien*, LXI (1926-27), 135-39.

FRENCH, BRYANT MOREY. "The *Gilded Age* Manuscript," *Yale University Library Gazette*, XXXV (July, 1960), 35-41.

———. "Mark Twain, Laura D. Fair and the New York Criminal Courts," *American Quarterly*, XVI (Winter, 1964), 545-61.

GILDER, RODMAN. "Mark Twain Detested the Theatre," *Theatre Arts*, XXVIII (February, 1944), 109-16.

GRATTAN, C. HARTLEY. "*Mark Twain.*" In JOHN MACEY, ed., *American Writers on American Literature*. New York: Tudor Publishing Co., 1931, pp. 274-84.

GREENWOOD, GRACE. "Women at the Capital," *Every Saturday*, III (August 12, 1871), 167.

[HIGGINSON, THOMAS WENTWORTH]. "Charles Dudley Warner," *Scribner's*, VII (January, 1874), 332, 334.

HILL, HAMLIN. "Eschol Sellers from Uncharted Space: A Footnote to *The Gilded Age*," *American Literature*, XXXIV (March, 1962), 107-13.

———. "Mark Twain's Quarrels with Elisha Bliss," *ibid.*, XXXIII (January, 1962), 442-56.

HOLLISTER, WILFRED R., and NORMAN, HARRY. "Samuel L. Clemens. 'Mark Twain.' *Litterateur*," In *Five Famous Missourians*. Kansas City, Mo.: Hudson-Kimberly Publishing Co., 1900.

HOWELLS, W[ILLIAM] D[EAN]. "Mark Twain: An Inquiry," *North American Review*, CXCI (June, 1910), 836-50. (Reprinted from *ibid.*, February, 1901.)

"The Judiciary of New York," *North American Review*, CV (July, 1867), 148-76.

"Kansas." *American Annual Cyclopaedia*, XIII, 394-98.

KITZHABER, ALBERT R. *"Götterdämmerung* in Topeka: The Downfall of Senator Pomeroy," *Kansas Historical Quarterly,* XVIII (August, 1950), 243-78.

──────. "Mark Twain's Use of the Pomeroy Case in *The Gilded Age,*" *Modern Language Quarterly,* XV (March, 1954), 42-56.

LEISY, ERNEST E. "Mark Twain and Isaiah Sellers," *American Literature,* XIII (January, 1942), 398-405.

──────. "Mark Twain's Part in *The Gilded Age,*" *ibid.,* VIII (January, 1937), 445-47.

LOUNSBURY, THOMAS R. "Biographical Sketch." In *The Complete Writings of Charles Dudley Warner.* 15 vols. Hartford: American Publishing Co., 1904. XV, i-xxxviii.

MABIE, HAMILTON W. "Charles Dudley Warner," *Critic,* XXXVII (December, 1900), 547-49.

MASON, LAURENS D. "Real People in Mark Twain's Stories," *Overland,* LXXXIX (January, 1931), 12-13, 27.

MATTHEWS, J. BRANDER. "The American on the Stage," *Scribner's,* XVIII (July, 1879), 321-33.

MENDELSON, M[AURICE]. "Mark Twain Accuses," *Soviet Literature,* 1948, No. 7, pp. 151-61.

O'HARRA, DOWNING PALMER. "Subscription Books and Their Publishers," *Publishers' Weekly,* CXV (May 11 and 18, 1929), 2252-54, 2344-46.

PEIRCE, ZINA FAY. "The Externals of Washington," *Atlantic,* XXXII (December, 1873), 701-16.

PERRY, T[HOMAS] S[ERGEANT]. "American Novels," *North American Review,* CXV (October, 1872), 366-78.

RIDEING, WILLIAM H. "Charles Dudley Warner." In *The Boyhood of Famous Authors.* New York: Thomas Y. Crowell & Co., 1908. Pp. 178-86.

SAMARIN, R. "The True Mark Twain," *Soviet Literature,* 1950, No. 6, pp. 179-86.

SCHMIDT, PAUL. "Mark Twain's Satire on Republicanism," *American Quarterly,* V (Winter, 1953), 344-56.

SHERMAN, STUART P. "Mark Twain." *Cambridge History of American Literature,* III, 1-20.

"John Swinton." *Who's Who in America, 1899-1900,* p. 710.

"William Swinton." *Dictionary of American Biography,* XVIII, 252-53.

TAYLOR, WALTER F. "Mark Twain and the Machine Age," *South Atlantic Quarterly,* XXXVII (October, 1938), 384-96. (Reprinted in *Fifty Years of the South Atlantic Quarterly,* ed. William Baskerville Hamilton. Durham, N.C.: Duke University Press, 1952, pp. 272-84).

TROXELL, GILBERT McCOY. "Samuel Langhorne Clemens, 1835-1910," *Yale University Library Gazette*, XVIII (July, 1943), 1-5.

TURNER, ARLIN. "James Lampton, Mark Twain's Model for Colonel Sellers," *Modern Language Notes*, LXX (December, 1955), 592-94.

VOGELBACK, ARTHUR L. "Mark Twain and the Tammany Ring," *Publications of the Modern Language Association*, LXX (March, 1955), 69-77.

————. "Mark Twain Newspaper Contributor," *American Literature*, XX (May, 1948), 111-28.

WALKER, FRANKLIN. "An Influence from San Francisco on Mark Twain's *The Gilded Age*," *American Literature*, VIII (March, 1936), 63-66.

WALKER, PHILLIP. "Mark Twain, Playwright," *Educational Theater Journal*, VIII (October, 1956), 185-93.

[WARNER, CHARLES DUDLEY.] "Salt Lake and the New Saratoga," *Putnam's Monthly*, II (September, 1853), 260-64.

"Washington Society," *Atlantic*, XL (December, 1877), 652-58.

WATTERSON, HENRY. "Mark Twain—An Intimate Memory," *American Magazine*, LXX (July, 1910), 372-75.

WEATHERLY, EDWARD H. "Beau Tibbs and Colonel Sellers," *Modern Language Notes*, LIX (May, 1944), 310-13.

WHIPPLE, EDWIN P. "American Literature," *Harper's Monthly*, LII (March, 1876), 514-33.

WILLSON, FRANK C. "That Gilded Age Again: An Attempt to Unmuddle the Fifty-Seven Variants," *Papers of the Bibliographical Society of America*, XXXVII (1943), 141-56.

WOODFIELD, DENIS. "The 'Fake' Title-page of 'The Gilded Age': A Solution," *Papers of the Bibliographical Society of America*, L (1956), 292-96.

REVIEWS OF *The Gilded Age*

I. IN NEWSPAPERS

Boston *Saturday Evening Gazette*. In large broadside "Notices of the Press," MTP.

Boston *Transcript*, December 23, 1873, p. 6.

Boston *Traveler*. In "Notices of the Press," MTP.

Bridgeport (Conn.) *Standard*. In "Notices of the Press," MTP.

Chicago Tribune, February 1, 1874, p. 9.

Cincinnati Daily Times. In "Notices of the Press," MTP.

Hartford *Courant*. Clipping in MTP.

Hartford *Daily Times*. In "Notices of the Press," MTP.

London *Evening Standard*, December 29, 1873.

New York *Evening Mail*. In "Notices of the Press," MTP.

New York Herald, December 22, 1873.

New York *World*. In "Notices of the Press," MTP.

Philadelphia *Sunday Press*. In "Notices of the Press," MTP.

Pomeroy's Democrat. In "Notices of the Press," MTP.

Rochester (N.Y.) *Union Advertiser*. In "Notices of the Press," MTP.

Springfield (Mass.) *Republican*. In "Notices of the Press," MTP.

Springfield (Mass.) *Union*. In "Notices of the Press," MTP.

St. Louis Democrat. Quoted in *Chicago Tribune*, April 5, 1874, p. 10.

Syracuse (N.Y.) *Standard*. In "Notices of the Press," MTP.

Utica (N.Y.) *Morning Herald*. In "Notices of the Press," MTP.

Waterbury (Conn.) *Daily American*. In "Notices of the Press," MTP.

Worcester (Mass.) *Daily Press*. In "Notices of the Press," MTP.

II. IN MAGAZINES

Appleton's Journal, XI (January 10, 1874), 59.

Athenaeum, January 10, 1874, p. 53.

BENTZON, THÉRÈSE. "L'Age Doré en Amérique," *Revue des Deux-Mondes*, VIII (March 15, 1875), 319-43.

(Boston) *Congregationalist*. In "Notices of the Press," MTP.

(Boston) *Literary World*, IV (January, 1874), 126.

Galaxy, XVII (March, 1874), 428.

Golden Era. In "Notices of the Press," MTP.

Graphic (London), IX (February 28, 1874), 199.

Hearth and Home, VI (January 17, 1874), 38-39.

Independent, XXVI (January 1, 1874), 1642.

New York *Home Journal*. In "Notices of the Press," MTP.

Pall Mall Budget, January 17, 1874, p. 27.

[PERKINS, FRED]. *Old and New*, IX (March, 1874), 386-88.

Queen, January 17, 1874, p. 61.

Saturday Review (London), XXXVII (January 24, 1874), 125-28.

Spectator, XLVII (March 21, 1874), 371-72.

REVIEWS OF *Colonel Sellers* (OR *The Gilded Age*, DRAMA)

Appleton's Journal, XII (October 3, 1874), 446.

Arcadian, quoted in Hartford *Courant*, September 26, 1874.

Boston *Transcript*, April 20, 1875, p. 1.

Chicago Tribune, September 27, 1874, p. 7; February 27, 1876, p. 8.

Harper's Monthly Magazine, L (April, 1875), 698.

HOWELLS, W. D. *Atlantic*, XXXV (June, 1875), 749-51.

New York Herald, quoted in Hartford *Courant*, September 18, 1874.

New York Times, September 17, 1874, p. 6; August 17, 1875, p. 4; October 3, 1875, p. 7; May 1, 1877, p. 5; January 12, 1878, p. 5.

New-York Tribune, September 18, 1874, p. 4; November 19, 1874, p. 4; December 30, 1874, p. 5; August 17, 1875, p. 5; May 1, 1877, p. 5; August 1, 1877, p. 5.

New York *World*, quoted in Hartford *Courant*, September 18, 1874.

Index

Index